Tattoo

From Idea to Ink

Joy Surles

Published by:
Wolfgang Publications Inc.
PO Box 223
Stillwater, MN 55082
www.wolfpub.com

Legals

First published in 2008 by Wolfgang Publications Inc.,
PO Box 223, Stillwater MN 55082

The information in this book is true and complete to the best of our knowledge. All recommendations are made without any guarantee on the part of the author or publisher, who also disclaim any liability incurred in connection with the use of this data or specific details.

We recognize that some words, model names and designations, for example, mentioned herein are the property of the trademark holder. We use them for identification purposes only. This is not an official publication.

ISBN number: 1-929133-52-9

Printed and bound in China

Tattoo From Idea to Ink

Acknowledgements

I would like to thank each of the artists who contributed artwork to this book and especially the artists who agreed to sit down with me for an interview. Their insight into what makes the styles in which they specialize powerful enough to stand the test of time was an education for me, and they made producing this work fun!

Additionally, this book would not be possible without the cooperation of all the clients who sacrificed a section of their skin on the altar of tattoo art. Thanks to each of you whose tattoos appear in this work.

I would also like to thank Johnny and Estelle Surles and Deanna, Billy, and Sara MacIntosh for being the best family a girl could ask for. And finally, I wouldn't have the knowledge to write a tattoo book at all without Jean-Chris Miller, Jeffrey "Sugar" James, Yolanda D'Amico, Mike Hendrix, Casey Exton, and the rest of the Art And Ink Publications team. Thanks for making it fun to go to work!

Introduction

This book is dedicated to introducing you to the possibilities available in tattoo art today. Whether you are getting your first tattoo or your fiftieth, I hope you'll find the history and descriptions of the various styles of tattoo and the artwork in these pages to be inspirational in your search for the subject matter for your next tattoo.

The information here is intended both for artists and collectors. I expect that the images and descriptions of the various styles of tattoo will be useful for artists when talking with clients about the kind of artwork they are looking for, especially with "newbies" who are less familiar with what is possible in tattoo art, and the photo-heavy nature of the book will make it an excellent addition to an art-reference library. I also hope that both novice collectors and tattoo aficionados will find this work to be a useful resource when looking for art or artists.

Chapter One

Introduction

Finding Your Artist And Your Art

Welcome to Tattoo: From Art To Ink. By choosing to use this book as a resource in planning your tattoo, you have made a smart decision. Many of us get tattoos impetuously; however, taking time to educate yourself about the indelible art, the industry, and the tradition behind the imagery will increase your enjoyment of both the process of getting the tattoo and the finished product.

From deciding on your artist and your artwork to finalizing the image, we will guide you in these first chapters through the process of finding

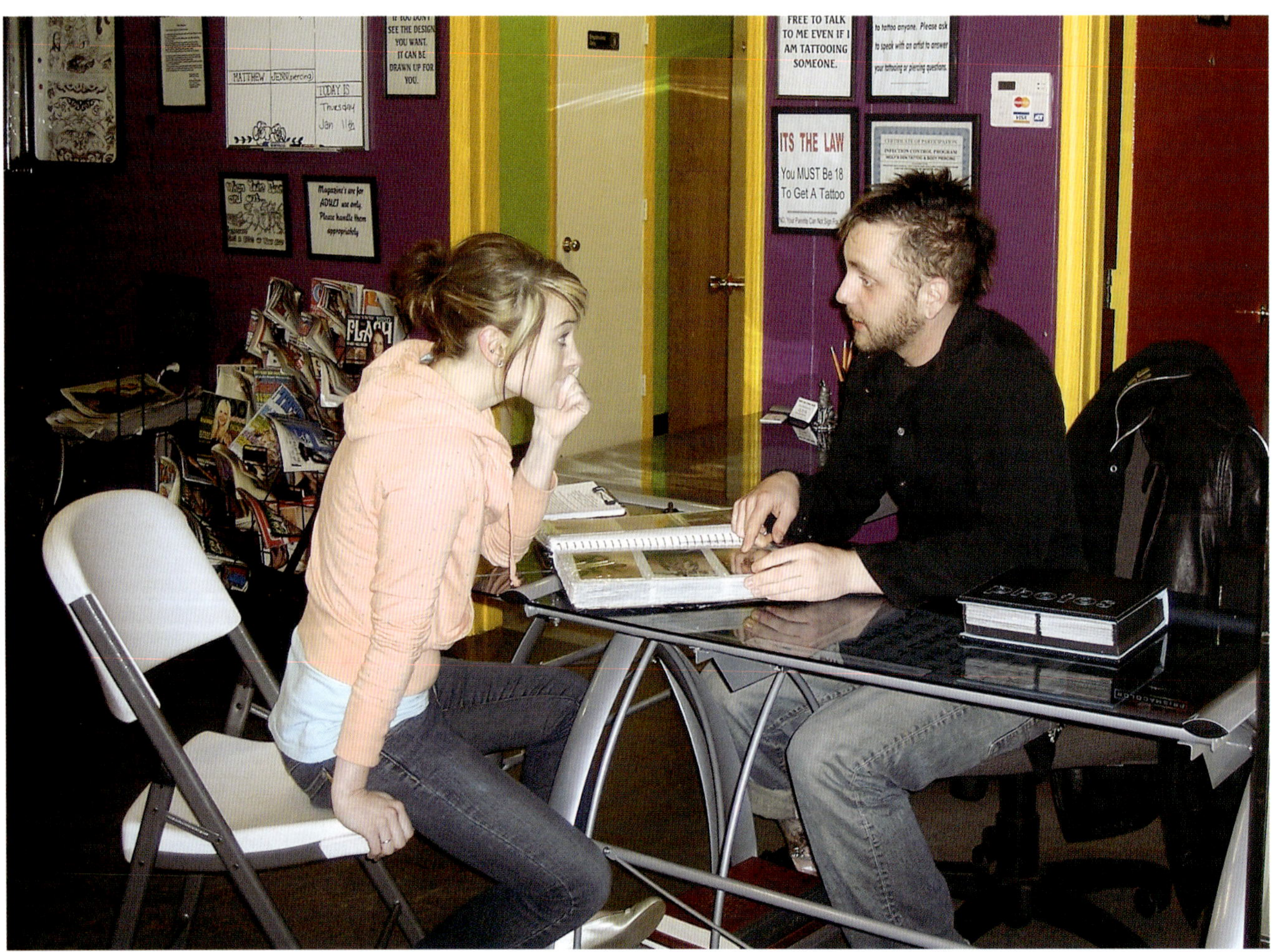

Client Jennifer Small, talking with Matty Evans, www.myspace.com/mattyevanstattoo.

the right artist and art for you. In the later chapters, we will give you a historical overview of the various styles of tattoo that are most popular today, which we hope will give you a great starting place in deciding not only on the subject matter of the tattoo you want, but the style. Becoming more familiar with various styles will also help you to find an artist who works in a style that you find appealing, which will help you greatly in your search for an artist to complete your work. We have also included an art gallery from some of the finest artists working in the industry today and whose work covers a variety of styles for you to use as reference material in planning your piece, as well as an appendix from tattooist and graphic designer David Allen of Bluebird Tattoo in Portage, Indiana describing how to use Photoshop to tweak your artwork to ensure you get the highest quality reference image.

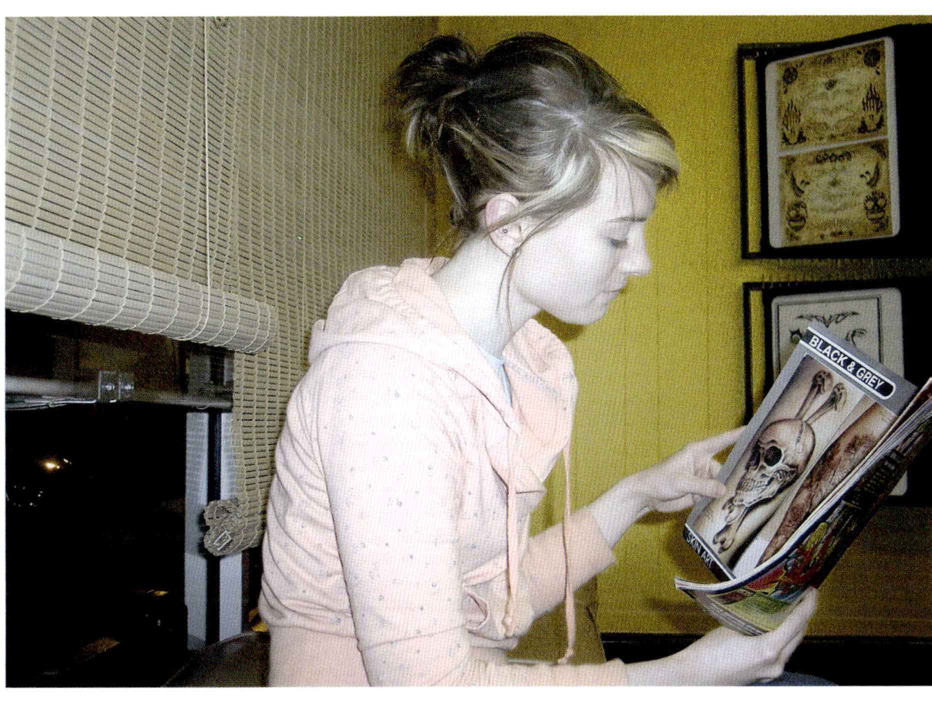

Jennifer Small reviews a tattoo magazine while deciding on her artwork.

Whether you are doing research for your first tattoo or you are a tattoo aficionado, we hope you will find this book to be an excellent guide for helping you get the tattoo you've always wanted.

What Kind Of Tattoo Is Right For You?

There are many reasons why we decide to get tattooed. Sometimes we want to mark a memorable moment in our lives with a

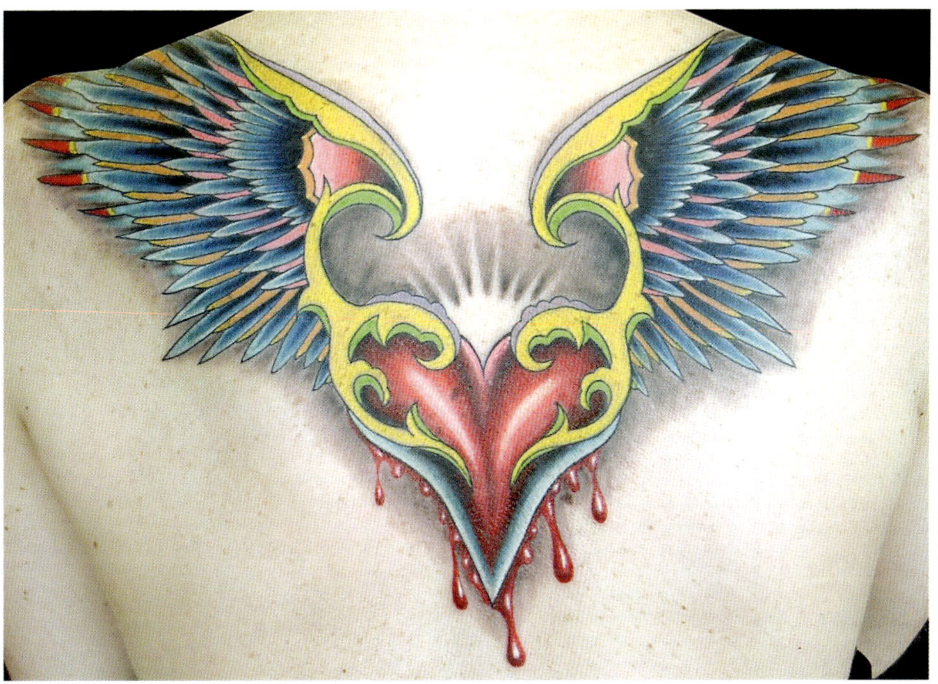

Clean line work from All Or Nothing's Brandon Bond

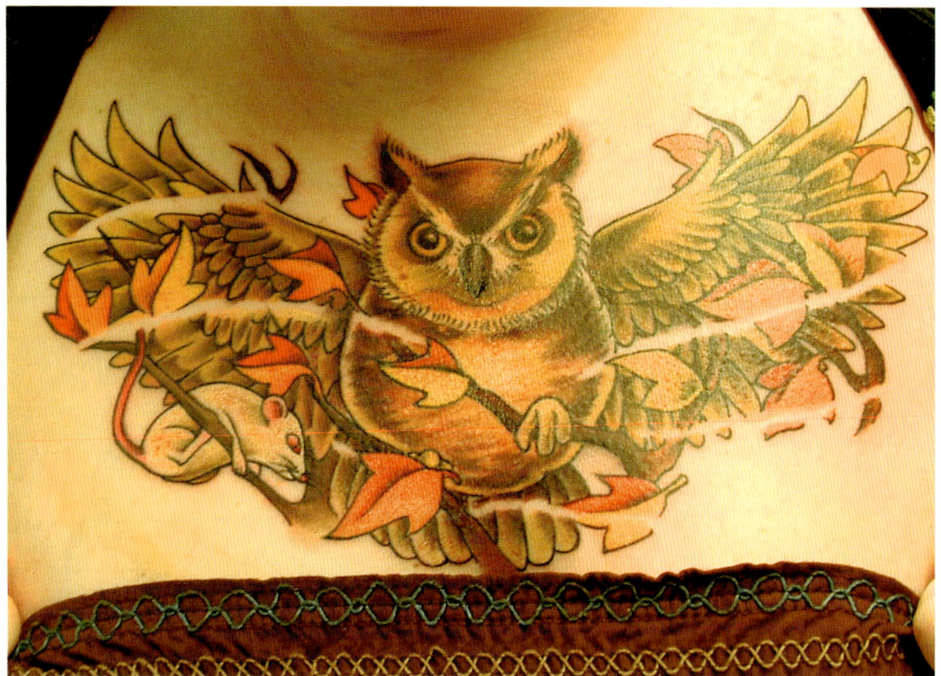

Chest piece by Sarah Peacock.

work of art that can always bring us back to that special memory. Other times, we want to commemorate a lost loved one, a newborn baby, or an experience that we hope never to forget. Sometimes we are just drawn to a particular image for its aesthetics or its symbolism, or we might find ourselves attracted to a particular artist's style and want to give that artist a canvas to create his or her unique work. Other times, we want to accentuate or express our sexuality or simply to beautify our bodies with an image that will reflect to the outside world something about the way we feel on the inside. Some of us want to stand out from the crowd, to mark ourselves as indelibly different from the rest, and we hope to tap into tattoo art's long history of representing society's outsiders. Whatever the reasons behind your decision, choosing to get tattooed is a deeply personal, unique experience, and the individual character of this experience can be enhanced even further if you choose to get custom art.

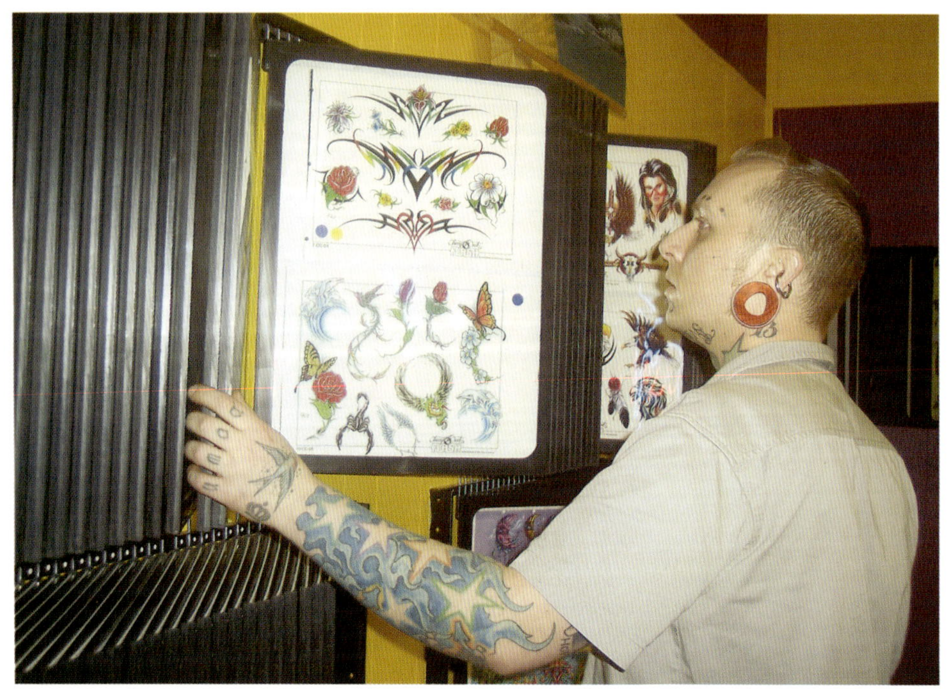

John Boyd takes a look at some flash artwork.

In addition to the many different styles of tattoo artwork that we will discuss in the later chapters of this book, tattoo art can be divided into two sub-types: custom art and flash. The images you see in the racks covering the walls when you walk into almost every tattoo shop are what we call "flash art." Tattooists and other artists draw and mass-produce these images and sell them to other shops, often making a secure second living selling their most popular designs. While many of these images are interesting and beautiful, they are mass-produced and generally planned for rapid-fire tattooing. Traditionally, flash art is displayed on the walls or in binders in shops, and artists might trade them or purchase them from one another as a trade courtesy; however, modern tattoo flash is often purchased from websites that specialize in mass-market production of popular images that tattooists can bang out quickly, thereby maximizing the number of clients they can see in one day to increase their profits. Additionally, the flash designs sold on the internet and in catalogs often come with a set of line drawings, which further saves time for the artist, who otherwise would have to produce the line drawing by him or herself.

Often, discerning members of the tattoo industry refer to this type of artwork as "pork chop" art, derisively referencing the industry that has grown up around this style of art for its consumer-driven, cookie-cutter approach. Critics also suggest that flash designs are detracting from much of the hands-on, artistic aspects of the trade of tattoo-making by requiring a tattooist to be less of an artist and more of a technician proficient in copying designs that are already produced. It also takes away from the uniqueness many of us are searching for when we decide to get tattooed. If you select a piece of flash art from the wall of your tattoo shop, there is no guarantee that you won't see that same image on someone else. To avoid this situation, tattoo aficionados often choose to get custom artwork.

Custom artwork is generally both more time-consuming and more expensive for the artist to produce and for the eager client waiting to get a new tattoo. It takes considerably more work for your artist to design something especially for you as opposed to pulling a stock image from a pre-designed flash set. Most tattooists will require an art deposit to begin working on the design for your piece, and after consulting with you about

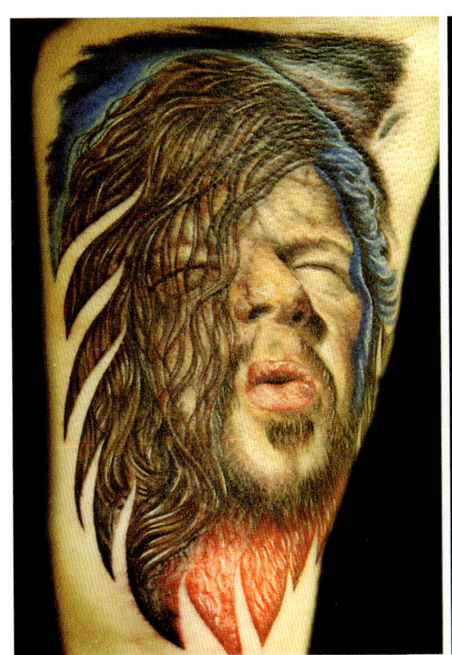

Dimebag Darrel Portrait By Nate Beavers.

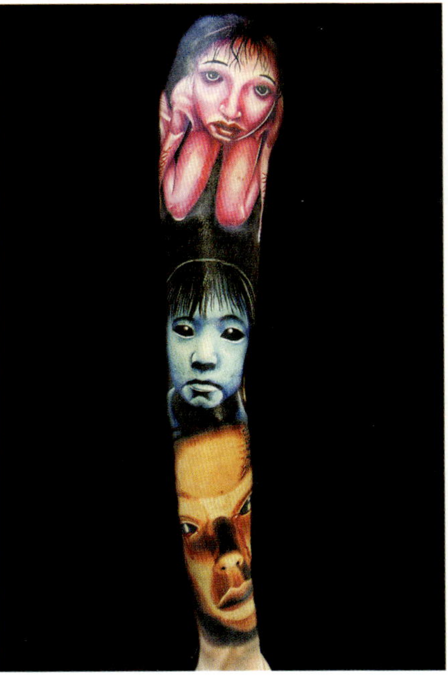

Horror Sleeve By Brandon Bond.

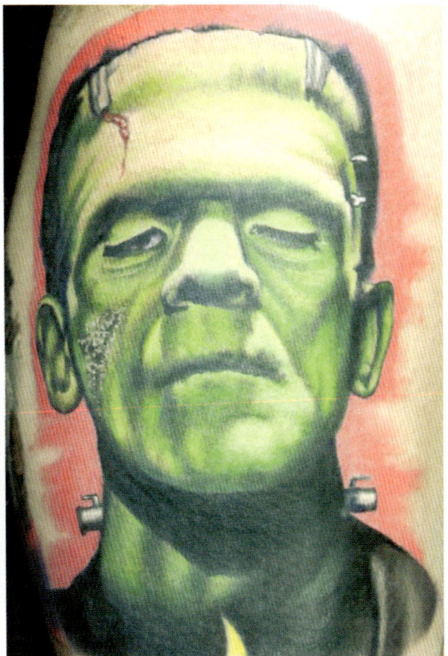

Nate Beavers.

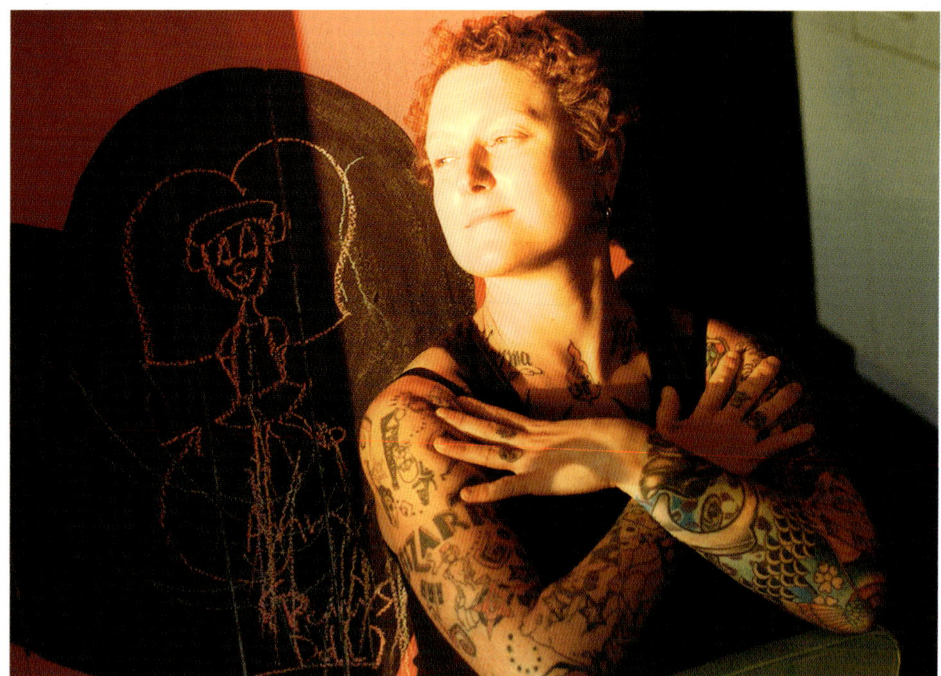

Custom Tattoo Artist Sarah Peacock of Artfuel in Wilmington, NC.

what you want, discussing placement and taking measurements, and perhaps beginning some preliminary sketches or discussing possible reference material, the artist will begin his or her own process of designing an image especially for you. This process generally takes anywhere from a few days to a few weeks to complete, which eliminates the impetuosity that makes many of us get our first tattoos.

And while this process takes much longer and is generally more expensive, most people who are fans of custom artwork agree that the experience is much more satisfying. You will never bump into someone with the same design as you, and the design will be something that you and your artist have worked on together to make sure that you both are happy with the final outcome. Tattoo collectors who have many custom pieces often become great friends with their tattooists after spending so much time together planning and executing their work, and the development of the relationship can be another rewarding aspect of the process.

The best artists are also often partial to tattooing their own designs as opposed to executing the stock images common in flash collections. There are some exceptions to these rules, such as Mario Desa from Chicago Tattoo, who prefers to divide his time

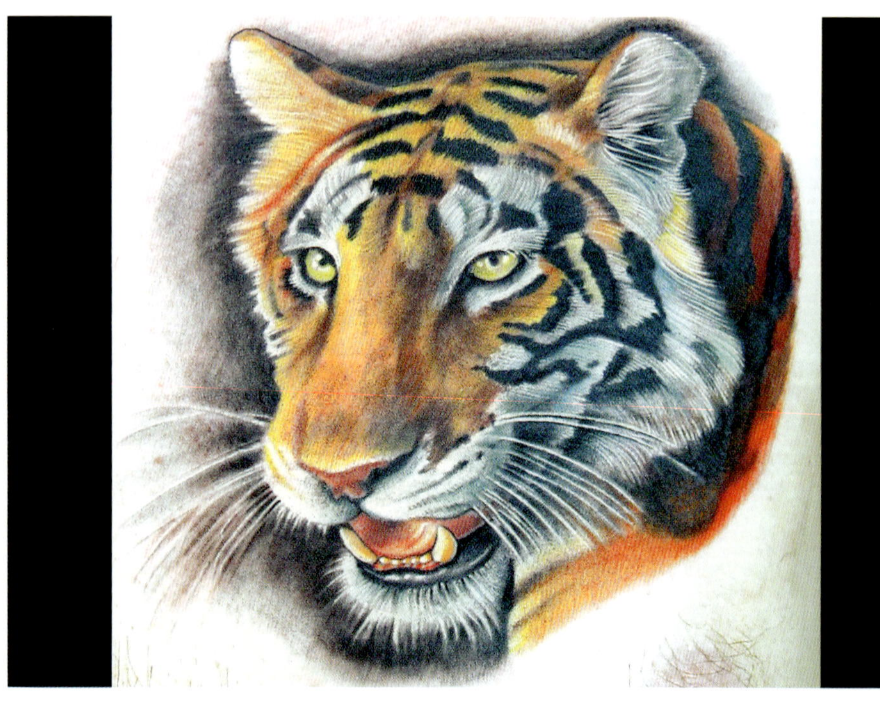

Beautiful Color Work From Nate Beavers.

equally between flash and custom work; however, many tattooists who have been in the industry long enough to have a following of their own will avoid doing flash work as much as possible, and some refuse to tattoo images derived from flash collections at all. The advantages of getting one of these more experienced artists to do your work are innumerable. From generally having a lighter touch with their machines, saving their clients a significant amount of pain, to having reliable color resilience, solid linework, and predictability in the way their tattoos will withstand the test of time, taking the time to find an artist with experience will pay off, and if your artist is hesitant about doing a flash tattoo, it might be in your best interest to cooperate with the artist on designing a unique, custom piece just for you.

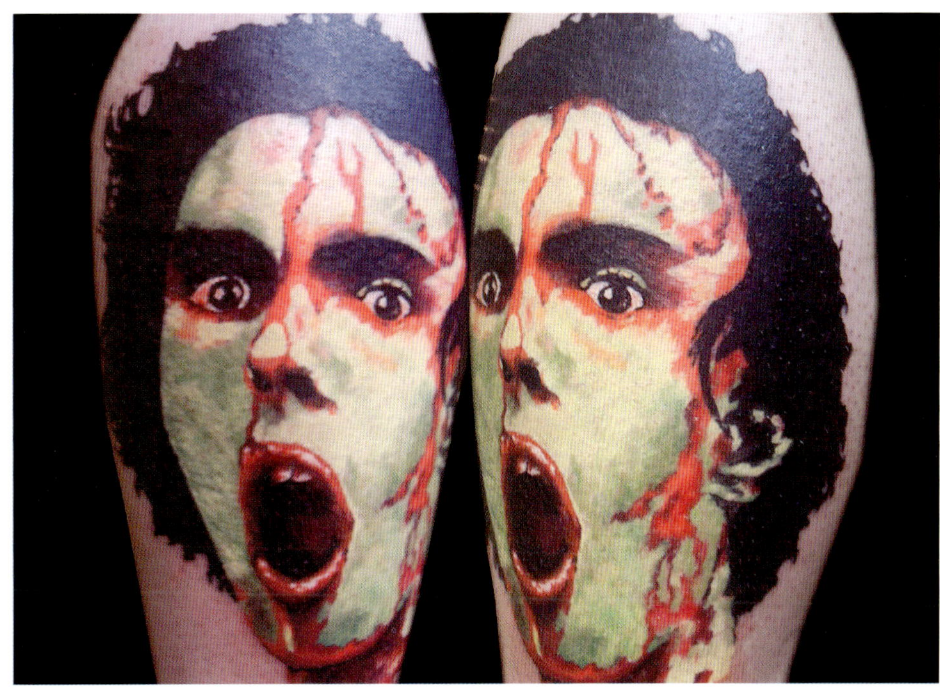

Gerald Gaddy, Charlotte, NC.

After considering the advantages and disadvantages of custom art vs. flash art, it is always possible to find ways to incorporate the elements you like best in a flash image into a piece that would be uniquely your own. You can also consider using your chosen flash design as reference work for your artist. By asking him or her to modify that design to make it original, capturing the essence of the image that caught your eye, you can make it uniquely yours. Background images can be added or manipulated, shapes can be modified, col-

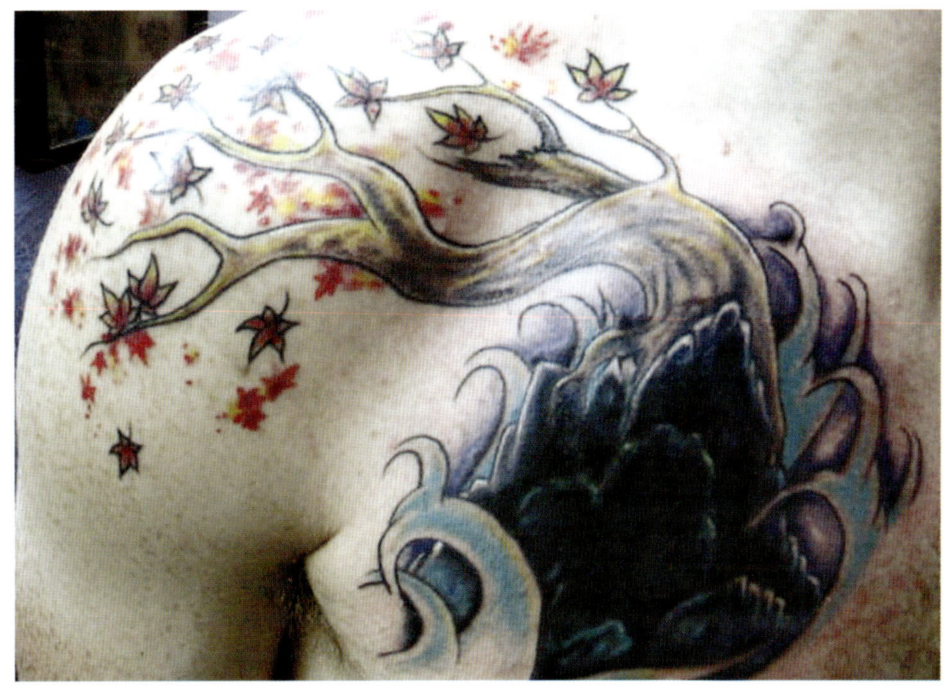

Vitality Tattoo's Shannon Schober is known for his effective use of the body's natural shape in his tattoo placement.

ors can be changed…there are limitless ways that your artist can alter a design to make it one of a kind.

Reference Material

Tattooists refer to the artwork and other items that they use in designing your tattoo as their "reference material." Different artists rely on different kinds of reference, and when looking for your artist, you might ask them about the process they use in designing custom art. Finding an artist whose work you respect and whose process of designing and implementing their tattoos intrigues you can make the experience of getting your ink much more enjoyable and interesting.

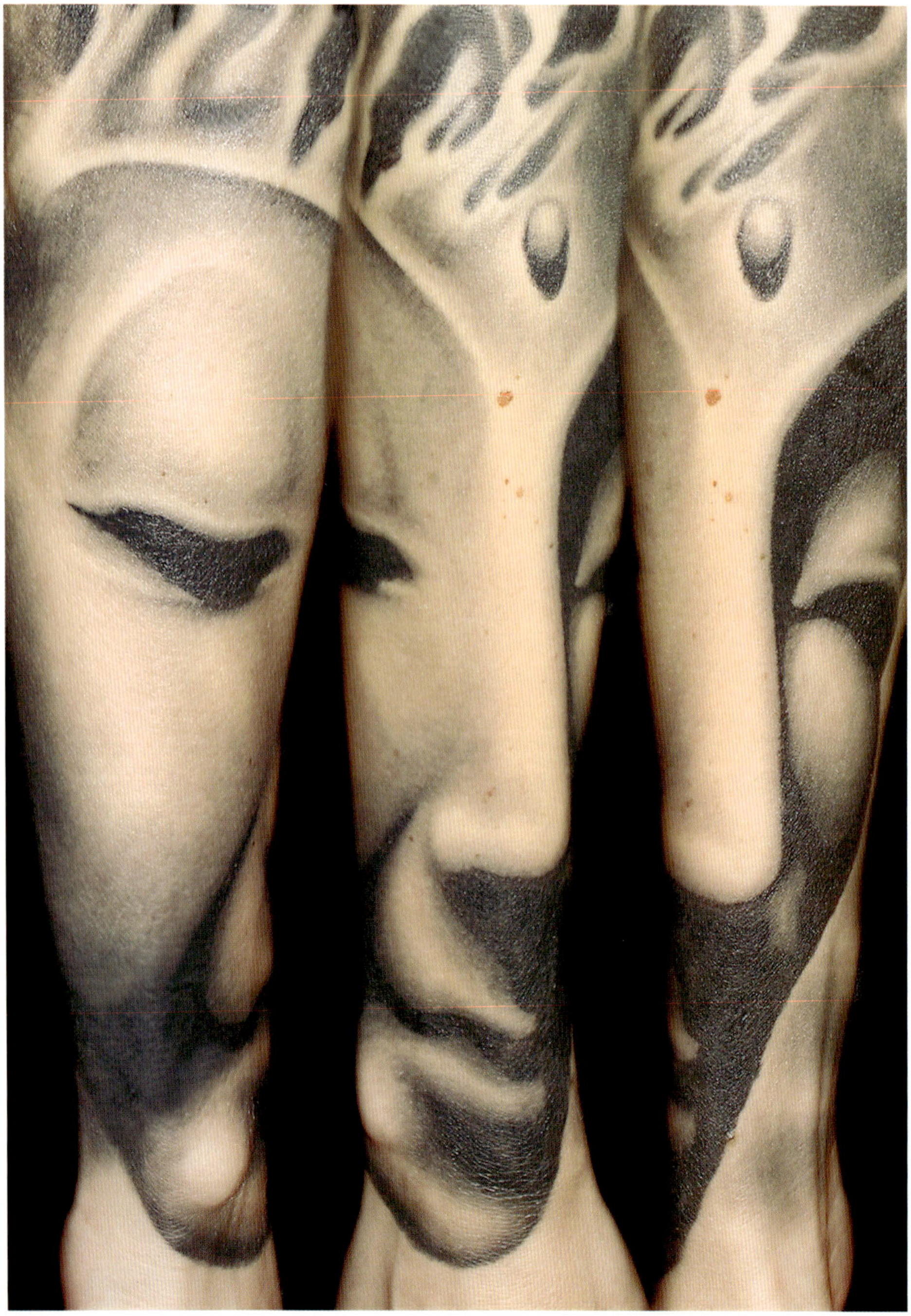

The world is full of sources for reference material, and the more ideas you can give to your artist, the more success you'll have in finding a satisfying image. Several decades ago, much of tattoo art was simple, clean images (the kinds of images that we discuss in the "Traditional" section of this book). While these classic, bold tattoo designs will never go out of style, in recent decades, the possibilities for images for tattoos have become practically limitless. From full color, realistic portraits to abstract, three dimensional designs, the world is rife with material that you can use in planning your artwork, so keep an open mind - and open eyes - while you are planning your tattoo.

Some of the most interesting tattoos come from surprising or strange reference sources. A current trend in tattooing includes photorealistic images, often featuring faces from horror movies. We will cover the trend in photorealism more thoroughly in a later chapter, where we will talk about this new style with Nate

Delicate shading from Brandon Bond.

Beavers of I45 Ink in Houston, Texas, who is one of the forefathers of this exciting new style. Perhaps because of its association in the first half of the twentieth century with the seamy underworld of bikers, sailors, and Coney Island style freakshows, tattoo art often tends toward the macabre. The twenty first century trend of photorealistic images from horror movies and other sources pays homage to the tattoo art's dark heritage, and at the same time allows artists to use Photoshop and other design tools to manipulate images to enable the artist to showcase the most modern color techniques. Other sources for photorealistic reference include photographs of family members, which can be manipulated using Photoshop and other techniques to heighten particular colors, wildlife photography, celebrity images, or album covers. The possibilities are limitless, and in the search for the right material to bring to your artist, it is wise to collect anything that catches your eye.

In the next chapter, we will further explore the many resources you can explore to find your perfect reference material. For now, we will move on to another of the preliminary steps to getting great custom work: choosing the right artist.

Finding The Right Artist

Once you have an idea of the kind of image you'd like to have tattooed, it is crucial for you to find the right artist to execute your plan. While you might have very strong ideas about the image that you want, we hope that you will keep an open mind when you present these ideas to your artist. Once you find an artist you trust, it would be wise to give some of the control over the design and placement of the

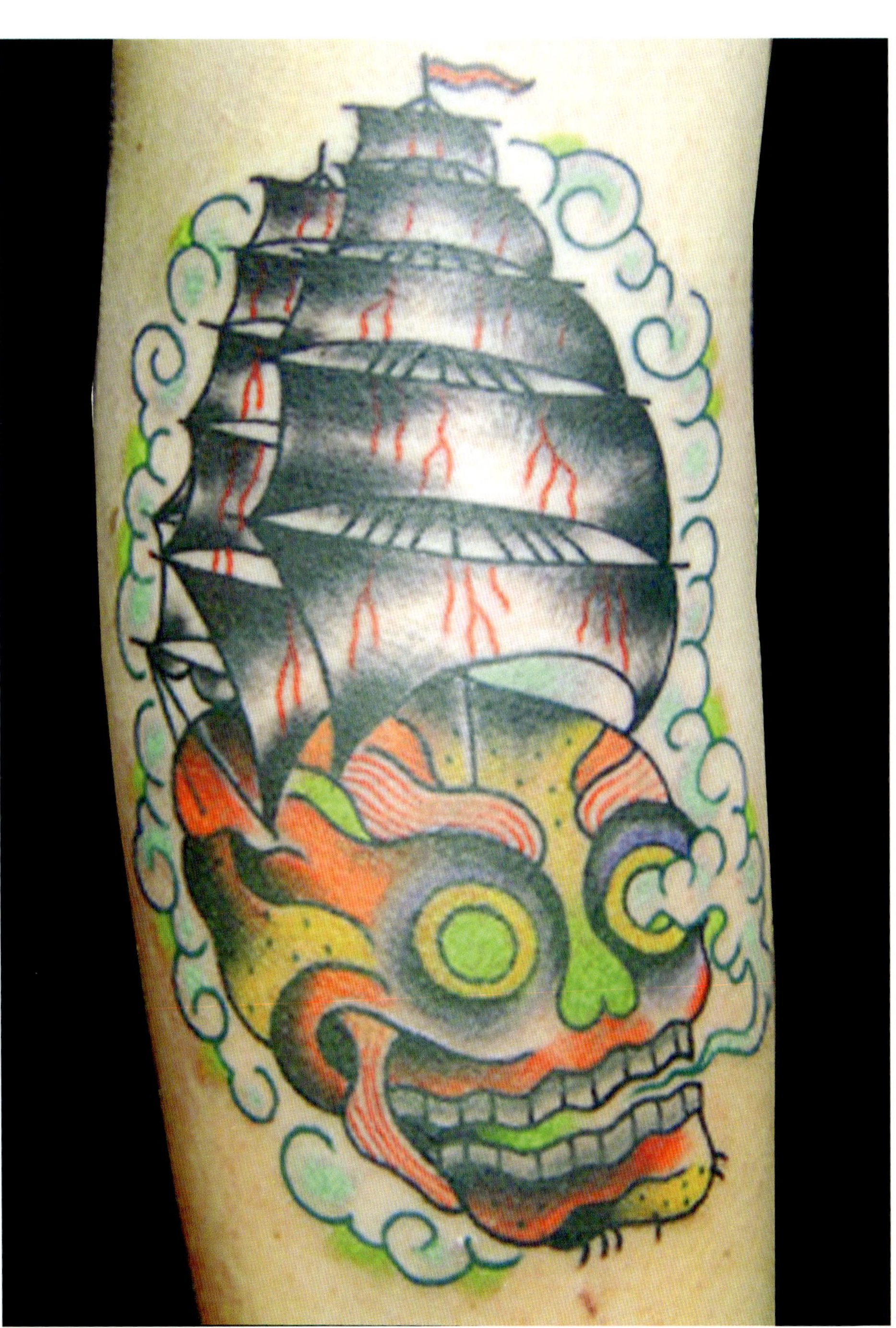

Mario Desa's funky hybrid style. Chicago Tattoo, Chicago, IL.

image to him or her. Ideally, your artist will understand both what is most important to you about the image you have selected and how to carry out the tattoo in the manner that will make it the most beautiful and meaningful. Tattooists have devoted their lives to understanding which images will look best in which locations on the body, and they may have a better insight into the size, shape, color, or other elements of the design of your tattoo than is possible for those of us who are not tattooists ourselves. Working with your artist and keeping an open mind to his or her suggestions about these aspects of the design process will likely result in a more satisfactory experience for both of you.

Another important consideration when you are searching for your artist is his or her friendliness, openness, and customer service skills. Particularly if you are getting larger work that may take several sessions, you and your artist will be spending quite a lot of time together. You'll enjoy the experience much more if you find an artist whose company you enjoy and who makes you feel comfortable. Tattoo artists should be open to discussing your ideas with you and should present a competent, professional demeanor when discussing your art. Artists are generally open to discussing their process, their vision for the final product of the tattoo, and any questions you might have regarding the cost of the tattoo, the sanitation practices of the shop, or anything else that comes up. If you find yourself in an environment where you feel like your artist is withholding information or covering something up, it might be in your best interest to find someone else to execute your piece.

Before you go to find your artist, it will also be helpful for you to take some time to familiarize

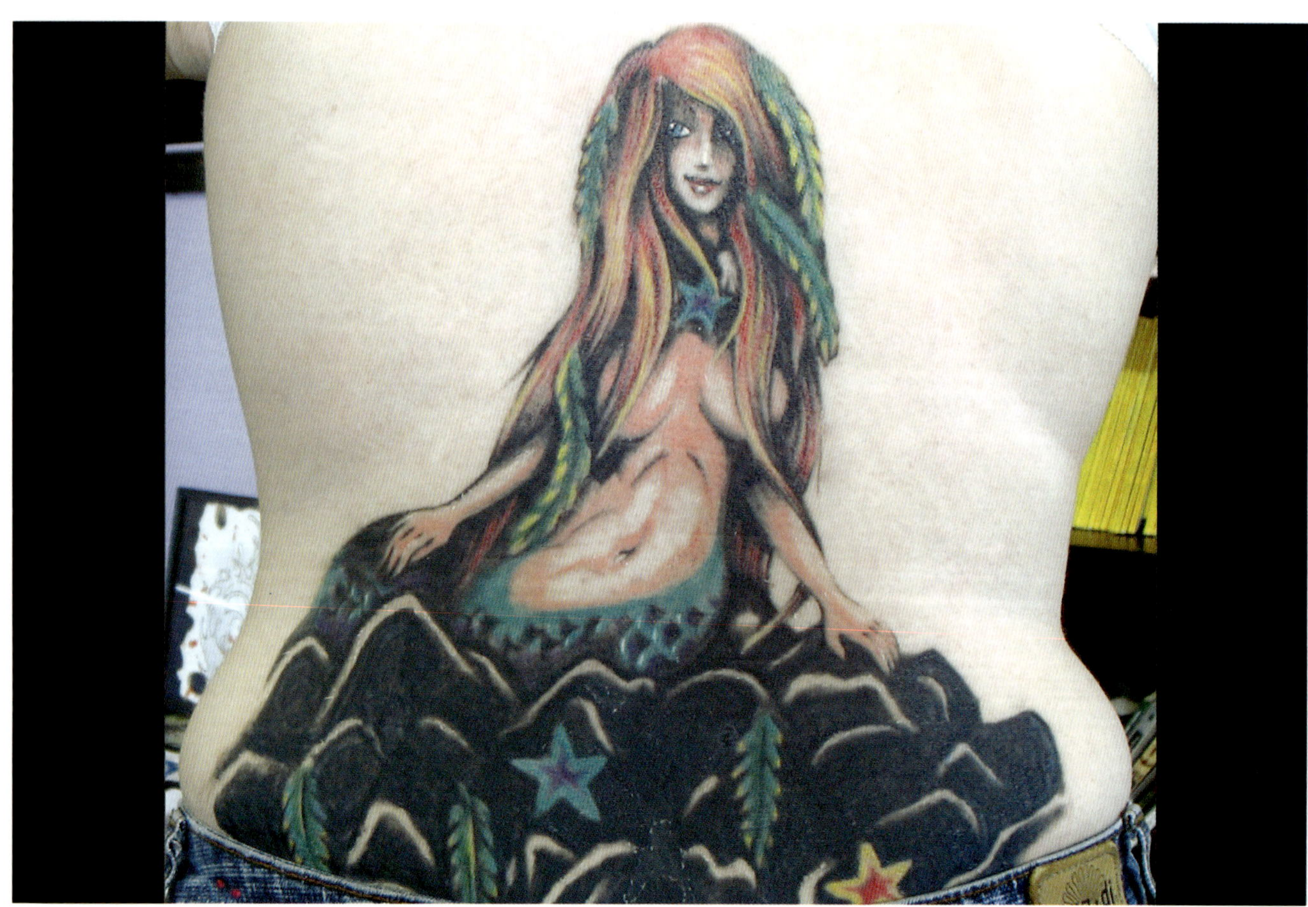

Vitality Tattoo's Shannon Schober is known for his effective use of the body's natural shape in his tattoo placement.

yourself with the variety of artists available. One great place to begin is in the middle chapters of this book, where we describe the most common styles of tattoo artwork that are popular in the industry today. You can use these sections to help you select an artist who specializes in these styles...either by finding an artist in these pages whose work appeals to you and seeking him or her out to execute your piece, or by using their images and names in your conversations with your local artists to give them ideas about the kind of work you are hoping to achieve. By educating yourself on the different kinds of artwork available, you will be building a vocabulary that can help you better convey your ideas to the artists you eventually meet.

You might also look to the tattoo media. There are a variety of tattoo magazines and websites available, many of which cater to specific interests or styles of tattoo. Your tattoo artist will appreciate your doing a little research and knowing about the different kinds of art available, and it will help you in evaluating candidate artists' portfolios if you know what to look for. You might also find an artist whose work appeals to you consistently through exploring the different tattoo media. If the artist is local, then that's great; however, even if the artist isn't local, being familiar with well known artists' work can serve you well in a few ways. First, being familiar with tattooists that your own artist might know can help you communicate the style of tattoo that appeals most to you, as it is likely that your artist will also be familiar with these tattooists. Secondly, you might decide to make an appointment with an artist you find in a magazine, online, or in the pages of this book. Even if he or she is not local, it might be worth the time and money it will take

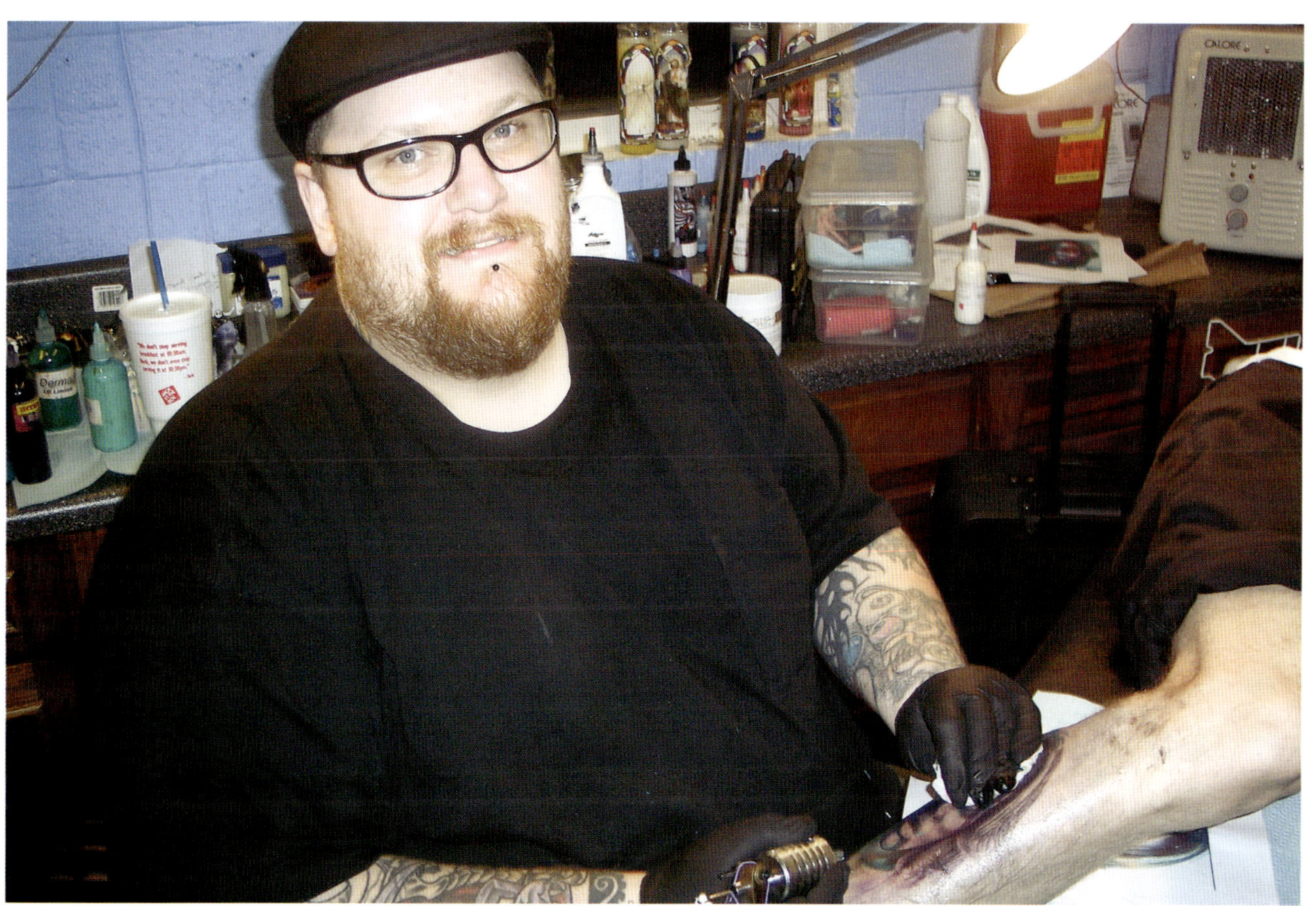

Custom Artist Nate Beavers from I45 Tattoo in Houston, TX.

to procure the body art you want from your ideal tattooist. After all, you'll be looking at your tattoo for the rest of your life! You might as well invest the time and money it takes to get the right work for you. Some artists who have achieved a level of notoriety in the industry cater to clients who will be traveling to get work done from out of town. Brandon Bond of All Or Nothing in Atlanta, Georgia has even set up a separate, private studio for these special clients. His A.N.T.I. Art Elite atelier, offers pickup service from airports and helps set up accommodations for people who take the time to travel to his studio to get work done. It is also possible to find some of the artists whose work you admire on the road, as many tattooists hit up the convention circuit or do guest spots at shops far away from their home bases. You could get lucky and be able to get an appointment with your ideal tattooist if you follow his or her touring schedule.

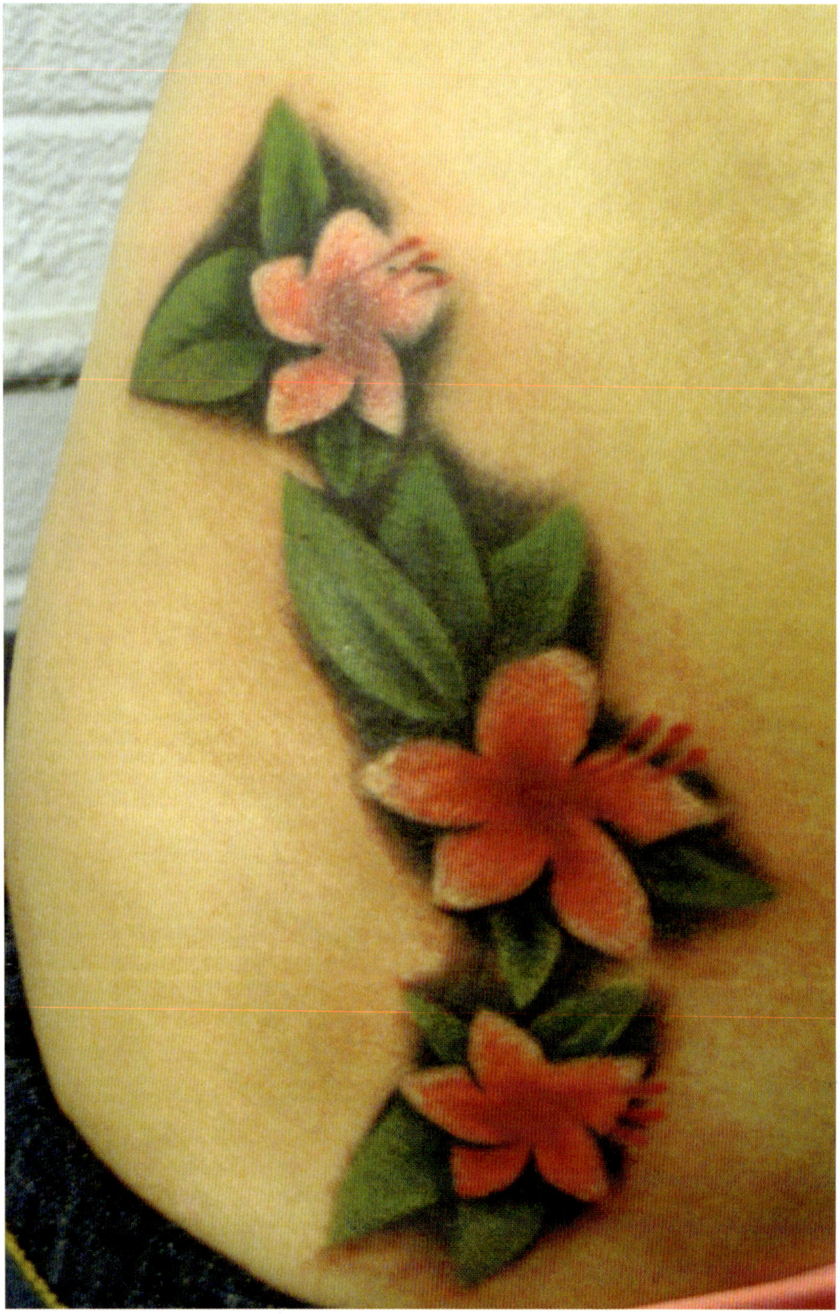

Vitality Tattoo's Shannon Schober.

Once you've decided what style of tattoo you're interested in, look for an artist who's proficient in that style. Some artists specialize in a particular style of tattoo. Joe Capobianco, for instance, is famous for his voluptuous, boldly colored pin-ups. Mario Desa has an unusual, hybrid style, mixing traditional tattoo imagery in new and interesting ways. Nate Beavers specializes in Photorealism, and Derek Dufresne works largely in Asian style work. Finding an artist who specializes in the style of art you want can make the process a bit easier and might make your outcome more beautiful.

Other artists, however, are known for being skilled in a variety of styles. If you are drawn to a particular kind of tattoo or the style of a particular artist, then it would be wise to find an artist proficient in that style. If you are more concerned with your subject matter and less attracted to a particular style or tattoo technique, then you might work better with an artist who is adept at many styles and who can adapt the subject matter to a style that fits it best.

Portfolio Evaluation

Another important step in deciding on your artist is digging into his or her portfolio. Particularly if you are attempting to find your artist by shopping around at the various tattoo studios available in your area, it is important to take the time to look at the work that each artist you are considering has done in the past. By comparing several artists' portfolios, you will go a long way towards making sure that the artist you finally settle on for your work is the right artist for you. If you start looking at an artist's portfolio and you do not like much of what you see, then you probably have not found the right artist for you. If the artist has not done much work in the style that you have in mind for your tattoo design, then he or she is, again, probably not the right artist. The portfolio is the key to this information, and taking the time to review it thoroughly will help you make sure you get the right art from the right artist.

There are many issues to consider when you begin to evaluate an artist's portfolio. Before beginning your artist search and the portfolio review process, you'd be wise to thumb through the later chapters of this book to get a feel for the various styles of tattoos available as well as to become more familiar with what a great tattoo looks like. In the same way that an art connoisseur can pick out fine flaws in a work of art that might look great to the everyday viewer, a knowledgeable tattoo collector will have a similarly solid understanding of what elements make up a good tattoo. By reviewing artwork that demonstrates competency at crucial tattooing skills, you will be better prepared to determine whether or not the artists you are encountering are the right artists for you.

We have complied the following lists to help you in your portfolio evaluation. We hope that you will find the questions in the following checklist to be helpful in determining the quality of each artist's portfolio.

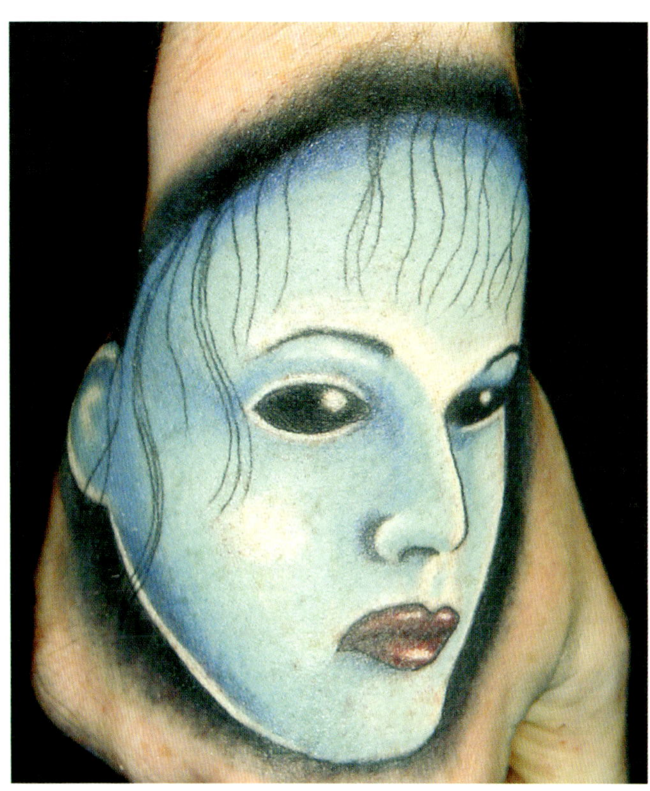

Hand by Brandon Bond from All Or Nothing, Atlanta, GA

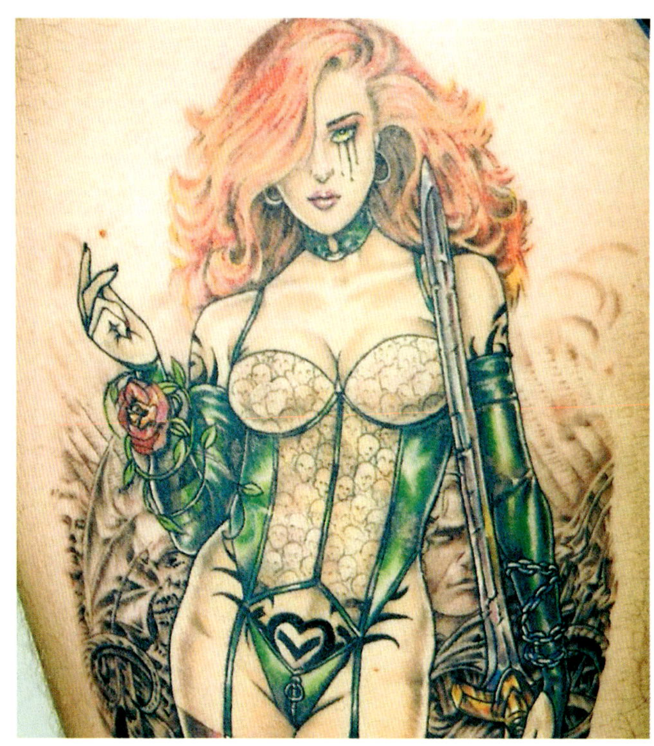

Sarah Peacock, Artfuel, Wilmington, NC

Portfolio Evaluation Checklist

Lines

Are the artist's lines clean, straight, and regular?

Can you find places where there are breaks in the lines?

Are there signs of the artist not having a steady hand, such as wavering lines?

Are circles shaped like circles? Are angles sharp and crisp?

Are there lines in places where there shouldn't be? Does the artist use a line to achieve an effect that would have better been achieved through shading or other techniques?

Color blending

Are colors bold? Are they muddy?

Do the colors that the artist uses appeal to you?

If there is negative space in the tattoo, is it used effectively?

Does the artist thoroughly saturate the tattoo with color, working from line to line to fill the entire area being tattooed?

Does the artist offer evidence of how his or her work withstands the test of time?

Body placement

Does the artist advise you about what would be the most effective placement for your body type or how best to fill an area of the body?

In the artist's portfolio, can you determine that he or she considers the placement on the body for each tattoo (especially large tattoos)?

Does the placement on the body enhance the natural shapes and lines of the body? Does the tattoo flow with the body's musculature and seem placed in a manner that makes sense with the body's natural movement?

Does the placement on the body enhance the tattoo through the natural shape and movement of the body?

Shading

Is the shading convincing? If the artist is attempting to achieve realistic effects through shading, does he or she accomplish this goal?

Does the artist shade from the line, or is there an apparent difference between the shaded area and the line?

Does the artist's style of shading appeal to you?

Skin Color Experience

What kinds of skin does the artist have the most experience tattooing?

If you are a person of color, does the artist demonstrate proficiency tattooing skin tones similar to your own in his or her portfolio?

Sanitation

Another very important issue for you to consider in your selection of an artist is sanitation. Because it is possible for people to carry blood borne diseases without outward physical manifestations, an unclean tattoo shop can pose a serious potential health risk for artists and clients alike. Hepatitis viruses, in particular, have been associated with unsanitary tattoo conditions because these viruses can continue living on a surface for several days after a tattoo if the environment and the instruments used in the tattoo are not properly cleaned or discarded. Other infectious diseases of concern include HIV infection and dangerous skin infections such as *Staphylococcus aureus*, which are commonly known as Staph. In recent years in particular, an antibiotic resistant strain of Staph has been plaguing visitors of unclean tattoo shops. Known as *Methicillin-resistant Staphylococcus aureus* (or MRSA for short), this bacteria can cause such unsavory skin conditions as boils and rashes. It can become more dangerous, however, if it spreads to other systems, where it can cause a deadly pneumonia.

While the issue of proper sanitation and the prevention of the transmission of infections disease is important for you to consider, a responsible tattooist will be educated on how to control the spread of infection and will follow proper procedures for cleaning, disinfection, and sterilization, which will keep the risks of cross-contamination at a minimum.

In many states, tattooists have a legal obligation to protect their clients against exposure to health risks, and the procedures that they must follow are

Sanitation Checklist

mandated by the government; even in areas where tattooing is relatively unregulated, however, an artist has an ethical responsibility to ensure that you will not be exposed to harm. When you are selecting your artist, you should feel comfortable asking the artists that you meet about their sanitation policies and procedures. A responsible artist will respect your concern for your own health and will be willing to answer your questions and demonstrate that he or she is using proper sanitation procedures to keep you safe.

Sanitation Checklist

We have prepared the checklist below for you to use as you are meeting artists and to give you some issues to keep in mind as you are learning more about tattoo sanitation procedures. You can use the checklist below to evaluate for yourself whether or not your tattooist is practicing his or her art safely.

Is there a separate area where artists clean their instruments?

Are the surfaces in the tattooing areas easily cleanable?

Are there waste receptacles that can be opened without using a lid?

Do the artists set out materials that they will need during the tattoo for each session?

Does the artist use disposable versions of the following items:

Ink caps?

Razors?

Are non-disposable items, such as tubes and needle bars, made of stainless steel and sterilized after each use?

Some items are not disposable and cannot be sterilized. Does your artist cover these items with a plastic barrier to prevent contamination? These items include:

Spray bottles, Clip cords, Tattoo machines.

Does your artist create a barrier using plastic or material such as a dental bib to create a disposable work surface for the area where he or she will be tattooing?

Does the tattoo shop have an autoclave?

Does your artist present an instrument that will be reused to you in a sealed, dated autoclave bag? A responsible tattooist will be able to explain the autoclaving procedure to you, so you should feel comfortable asking questions.

Are needles disposed of directly into a sharps container?

Finally

We hope that now you have a thorough understanding of many aspects of getting a new tattoo for you to consider in planning your artwork and finding your artist. While there are lots of things to think about when you are getting ready for your new tattoo, the more educated you become about the art, the process, and its rich traditions, the more we believe you will enjoy your new body art. Now we have given you an overview of the primary considerations of the process, it is time to turn to the art and its meaning in the following chapters. First, we will give you a more in-depth review of the process an artist might use in developing your artwork, and then we proceed to demonstrate the many different styles of tattoo you have to choose from.

You are now well on your way to your beautiful new body art!

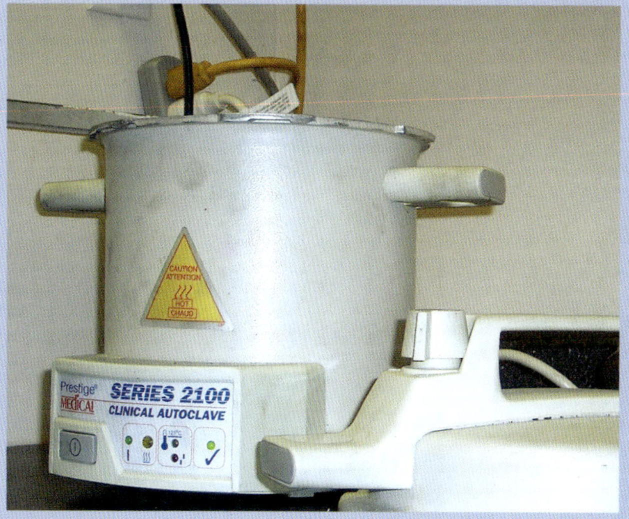

Autoclave

Chapter Two

From Concept to Sketch

Understanding The Process

One of the most rewarding aspects of getting a custom tattoo is the relationship that often emerges between an artist and his or her client. It's an aspect of the process of getting a tattoo that many of us forget to explore when we decide it's time for some new ink, but the interaction between the artist and the client is a multi-faceted affair, and finding an artist who can meet your needs on many levels will enhance your experience of getting the right art.

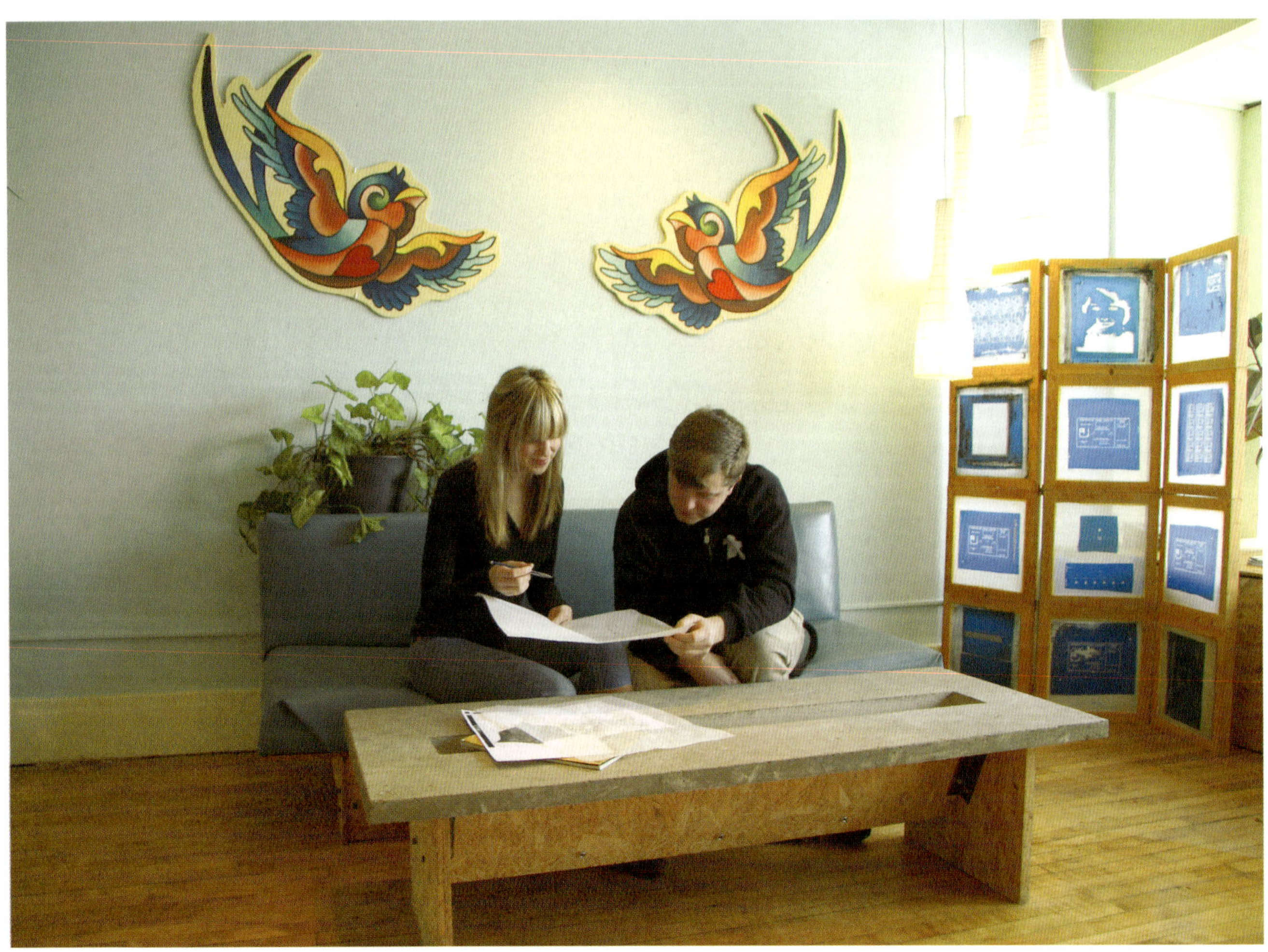

An artist and client review the possibilities for new art.

From the earliest inkling of an idea for a tattoo, the best images often come from some serious thought, consultation, and research on the part of both the artist and the client.

Even in smaller, more spontaneous pieces, it is possible to allow room for artistic freedom for your artist. Most tattooists worth privileging with your skin will be excited to do a custom piece and eager to take the time necessary to plan and execute a sketch for your artwork that will be pleasing for both of you. Artists who are most excited about the process of design often will introduce the idea of getting a custom tattoo to a client who has been lured in by the art on the wall, either suggesting ideas for modifications to make a piece of flash art unique or showing the client some designs for artwork that the artist would like to do. Some artists even insist on modifying an image to make it unique, arguing that there's nothing lamer than walking down the street and bumping into someone who has the same tattoo as you. While many of us decide to get tattooed impetuously, we promise that taking the time to do a little research and allowing your artist to modify

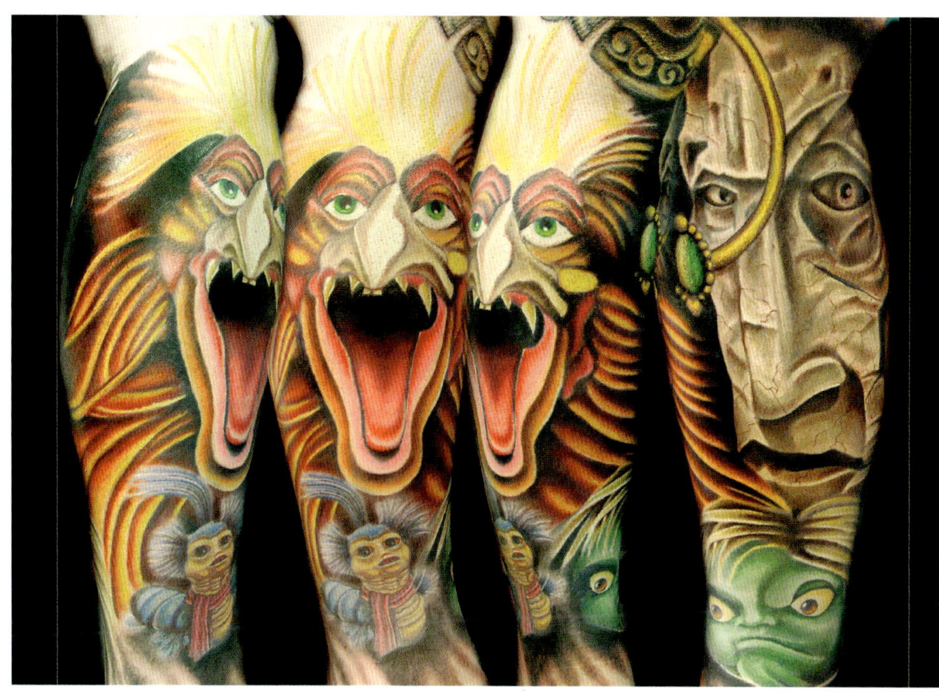

A beautiful example of custom art by Brandon Bond, All Or Nothing, Atlanta, GA.

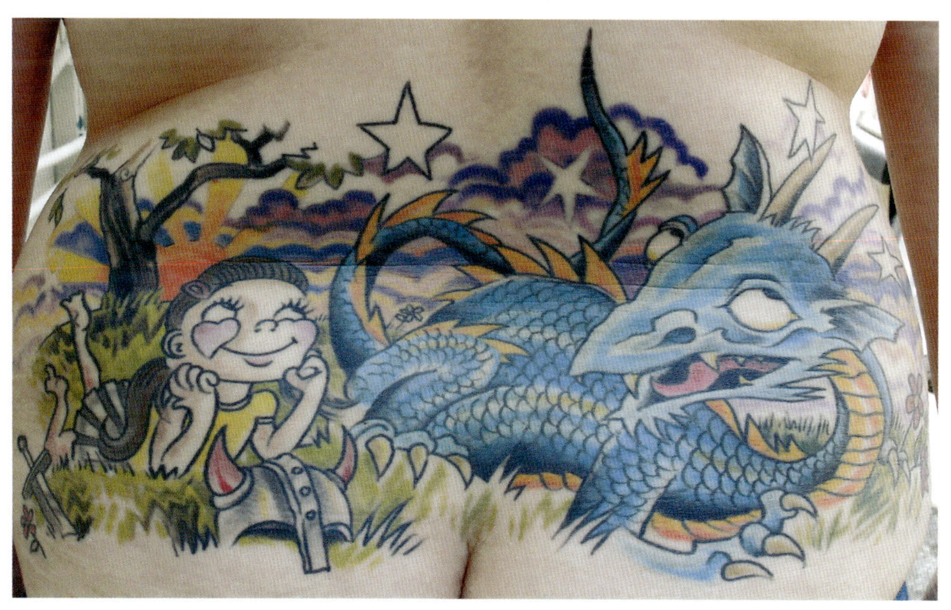

Mark Heggie, Big Top, Utica, MI.

the design will give you a piece you enjoy much more.

In addition to looking to tattoo flash for your ideas, consider consulting any of the resources we have suggested in the following list of suggestions for places where you might find other sources of inspiration for the images in your design. The most well informed clients approach an artist with lots of patience, time, ideas, and an open mind, particularly for larger scale work.

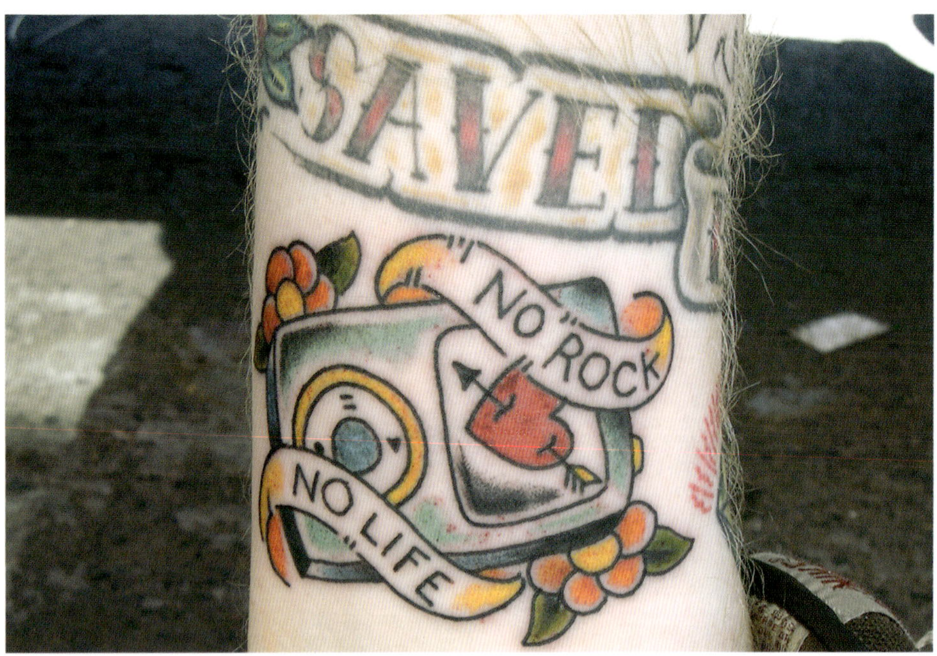

A tribute to the Ipod in traditional style by Adam Patterson, Body And Soul, Jersey City, NJ.

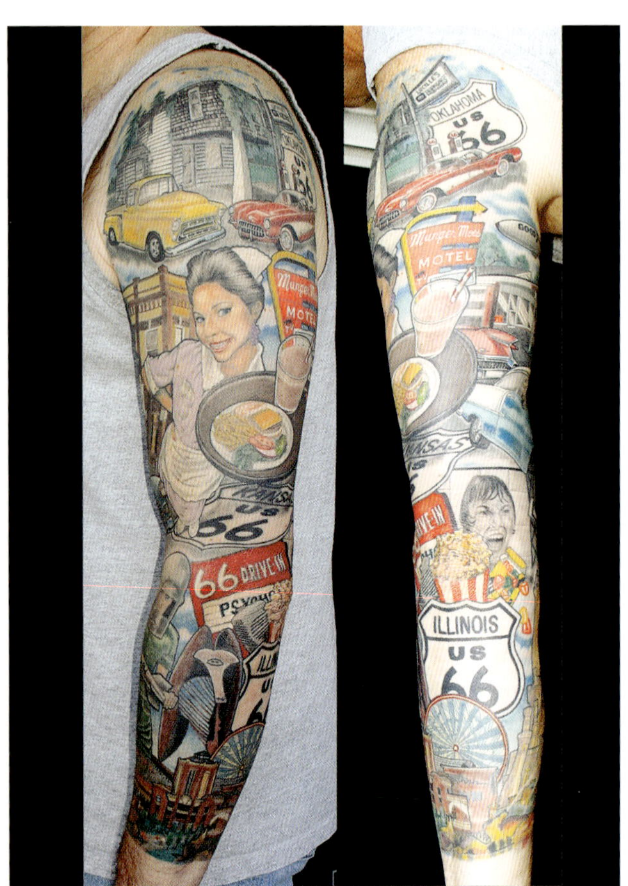

If you'd like to get a sleeve tattoo, finding an artist like Larry Brogan who has some experience with composing large scale pieces will be worth your while.

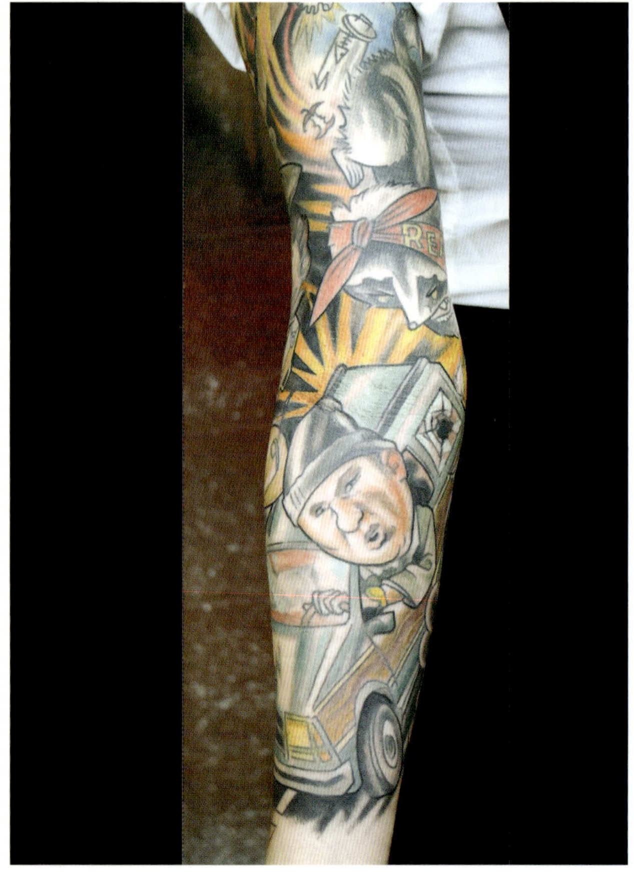

Mark Heggie.

Before you go to meet with your artist, you might consider consulting some of the following sources to get some more ideas:

Internet sources

One great place to begin a search for reference material is on the internet. If, for instance, you know you are interested in getting a demon tattooed on your arm, you could begin with a Google Image search (www.images.google.com). Try several keywords, like

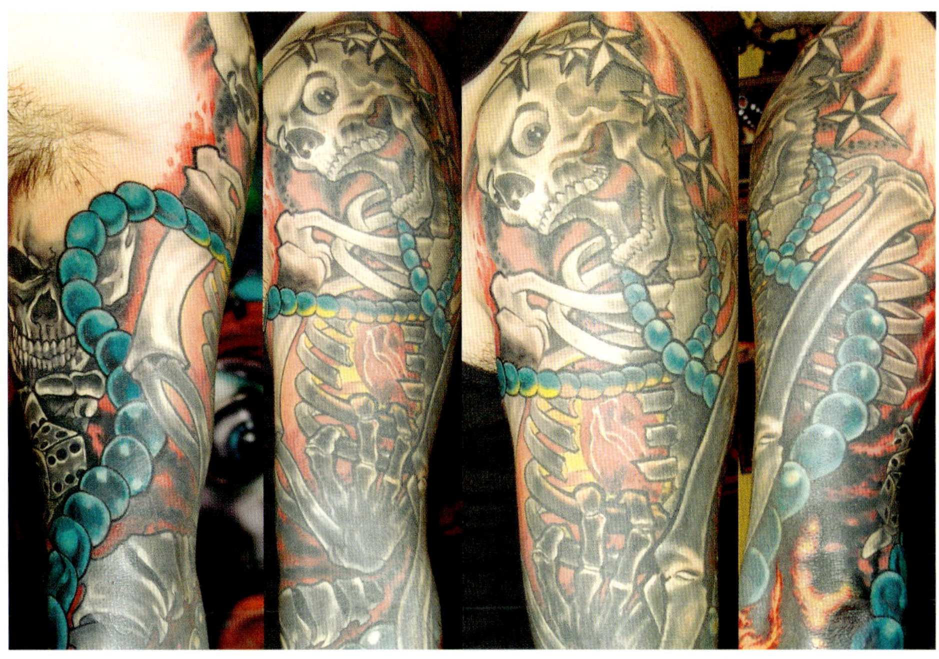

Many of these images are tattoo classics, from the nautical stars to the skull, from the gambling theme to the heart. In spite of referencing many tattoo classics, this piece from Zsolt Sarkozi of Dark Arts in Budapest, Hungary, is still one of a kind.

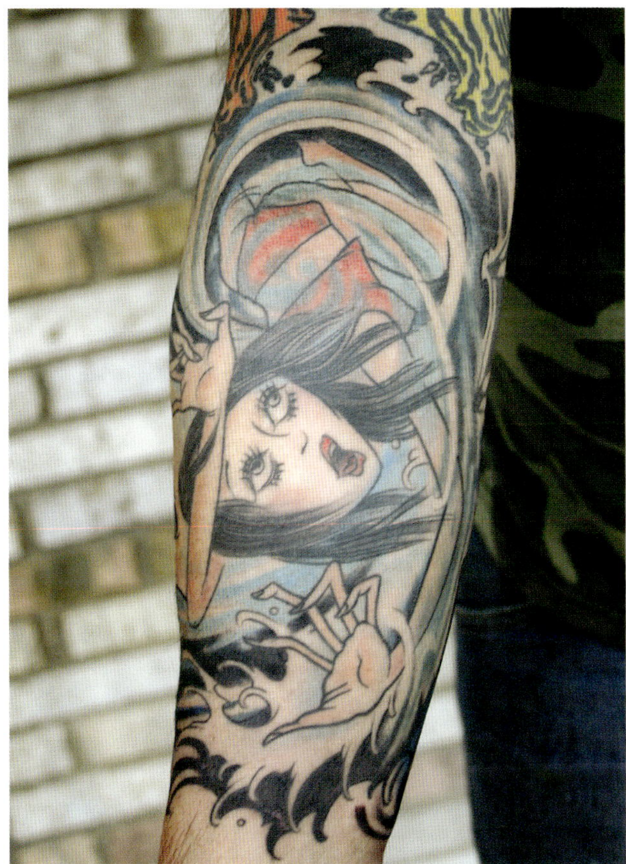

Mark Heggie's unique style is apparent in these sleeves.

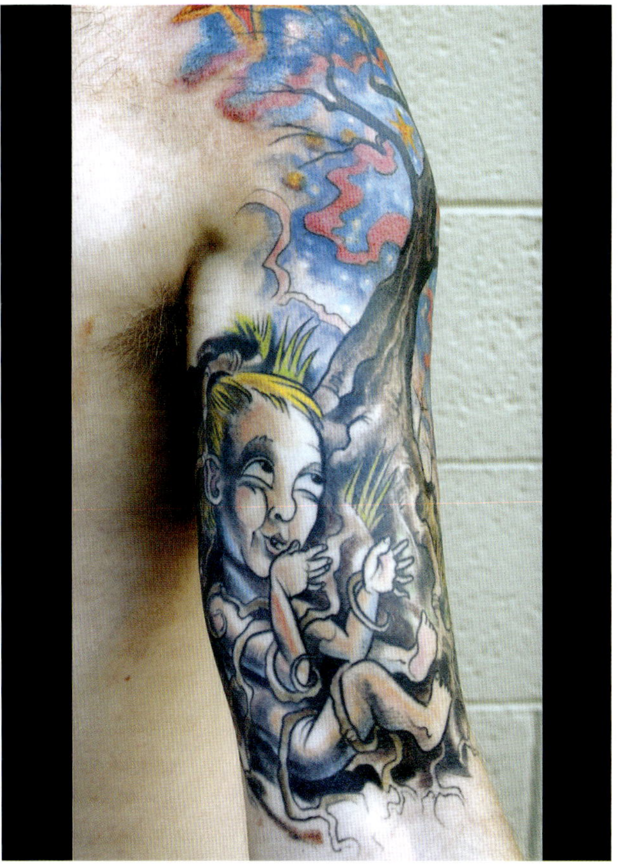

Mark Heggie.

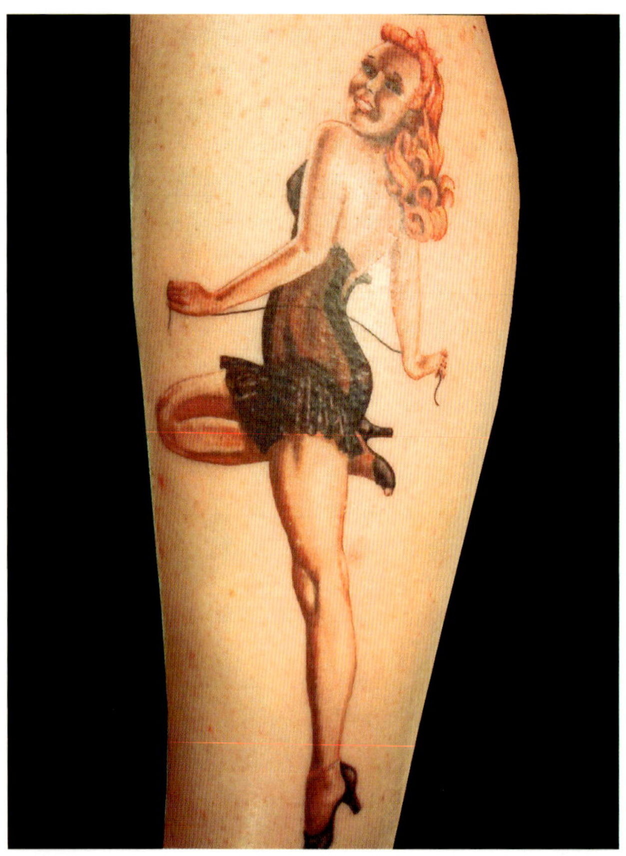

A Vargas style pin-up from John Wayne, Beesting, Ontario, Canada.

"demon," "devil," or "diabolical," and examine the various images that pop up. Save or print a few that appeal to you, and you can then take these images to your artist to use as reference material. These searches might lead you on to many other terms as well. For instance, a general search for "demons" might lead you to some images of Japanese Oni Masks, which are common images for use in traditional Japanese style work. Not only will you have found images that your artist might be able to use as reference in designing your unique piece, but you will have isolated a style of tattoo that can help your artist with designing your background, color scheme, and other elements of the image.

There are many tattoo related websites that can help you locate art. Searching tattoo artists' websites and other tattoo community websites will expand your ideas of what kinds of images might be appropriate for a tattoo. Inked Nation, for instance, is one tattoo community that connects tattoo collectors with tattoo artists in addition to offering libraries of tattoo flash (some of which is free and some is available for a fee), a message board with information on upcoming tattoo events, and a resource library with information on various aspects of tattoo art and the history of the industry. You can find this site at www.inkednation.com.

Another great resource is Deviant Art (www.deviantart.com). It's a Myspace-like community for artists to post and receive feedback about their current projects, and

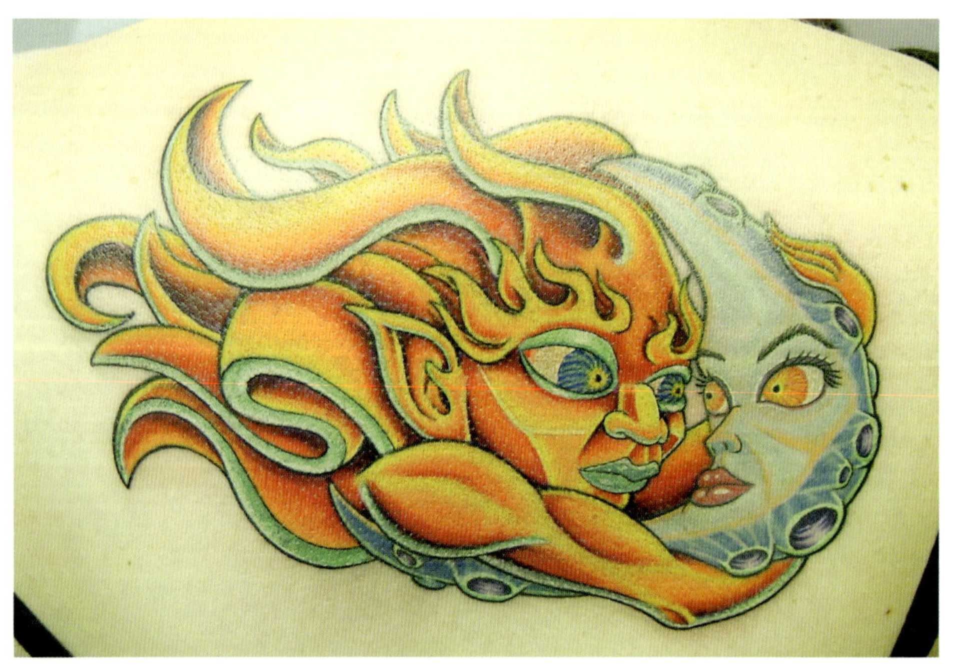

Larry Brogan of Tattoo City Skin Art in Lockport, IL gives us a bold and colorful version of the staple sun and moon tattoo subject matter. Finding an artist who can make your tattoo unique, even if it is subject matter that has been done many times, will make your experience much more enjoyable.

it's a great resource for new and exciting images. While this site is not specifically tattoo-related, it is a great source for ideas and a wonderful starting place for you to find some reference material to take to your artist.

Magazines

Tattoo magazines

Tattoo magazines are useful because they often group images into categories. If you find a magazine that features a category that appeals to you, you can flip through it and find the kinds of images that you like best. Magazines like Skin Art, Tattoos For Men, and Tattoos For Women are great starting points for people who aren't sure exactly what kind of artwork they want for their next tattoos.

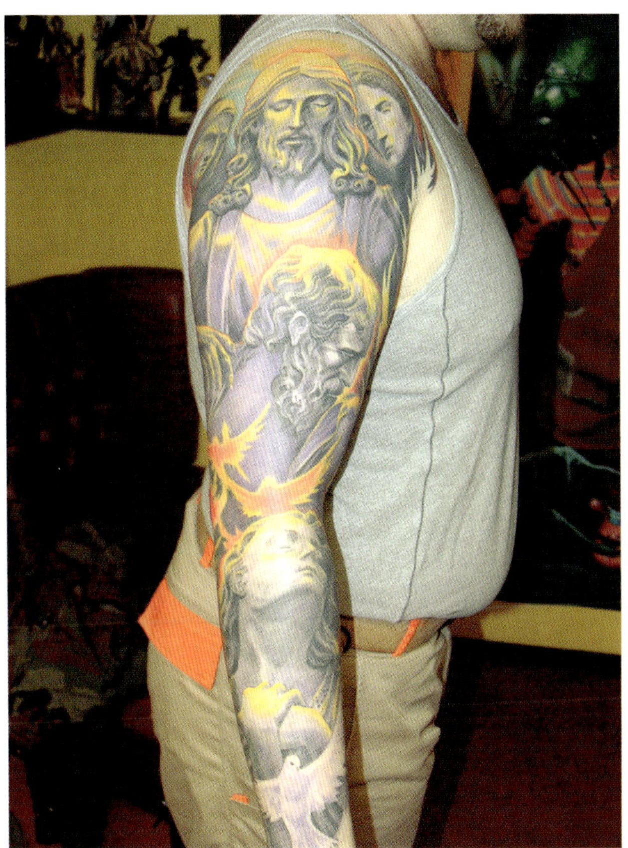

Zsolt Sarkozi is known for being able to achieve amazing effects of three dimensionality.

Tattoo magazines are also helpful for your education as a connoisseur of tattoos. The editors and designers have meticulously selected the images that they publish, so you can get a solid idea of what makes a quality tattoo. This development of your taste will greatly improve your enjoyment of the process of getting tattooed, and it will allow you a lifetime of enjoyment of your ink. These resources are also excellent in helping you to find an artist. If there is an artist whose work you like that you see in magazines, you can usually find their contact information and look them up to get an appointment.

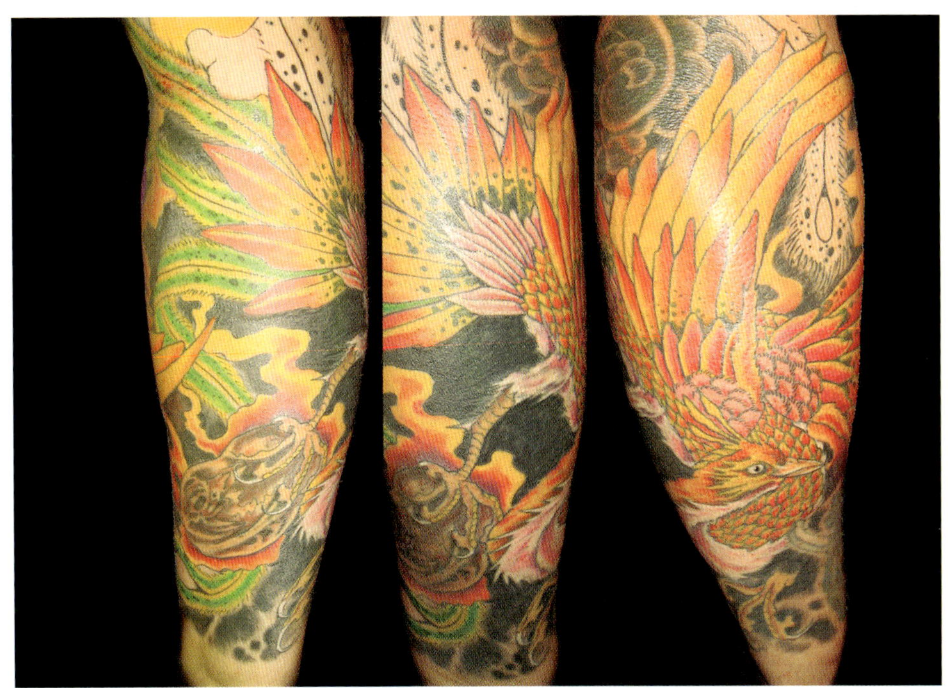

Derek DuFresne, Fleshworks, Victoria, British Columbia.

General magazines

You can use general publications like Vogue, Vanity Fair, Maxim, or similar magazines to find faces, body positions, or

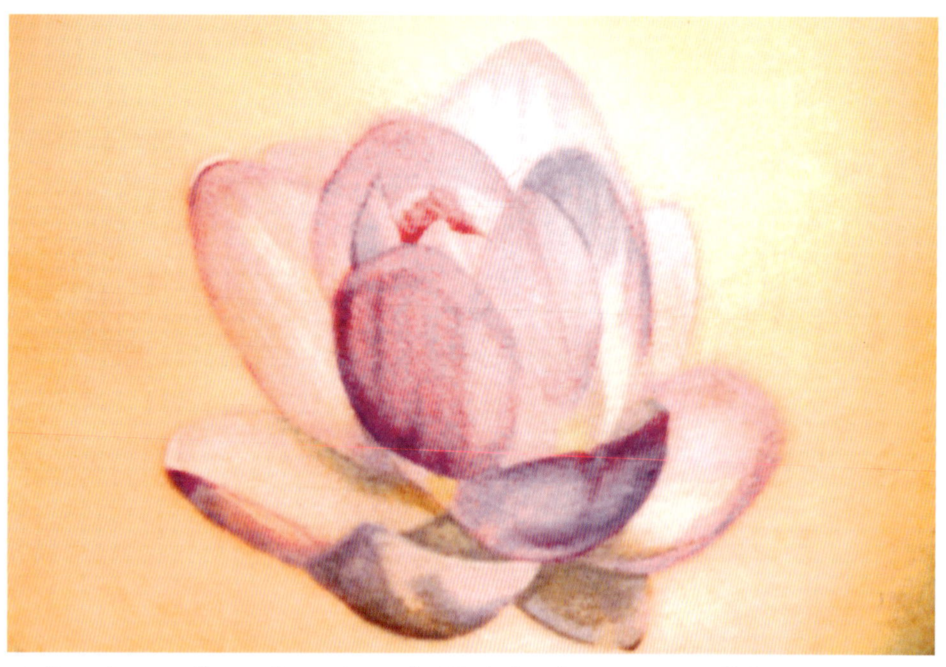

Soft and pretty flower from Amanda Wachob, Blue Moon, Buffalo, NY.

color schemes that you can apply to your tattoo. If, for instance, you are interested in finding a pin-up image, you might flip through a Playboy (strictly for research purposes, of course!) to find different body positions, clothing and hairstyles, and facial expressions to share with your artist. Vargas pin-ups from older Playboys, for instance, are a popular image source for tattoos done in the hybrid style combining elements of photorealism with tradi-

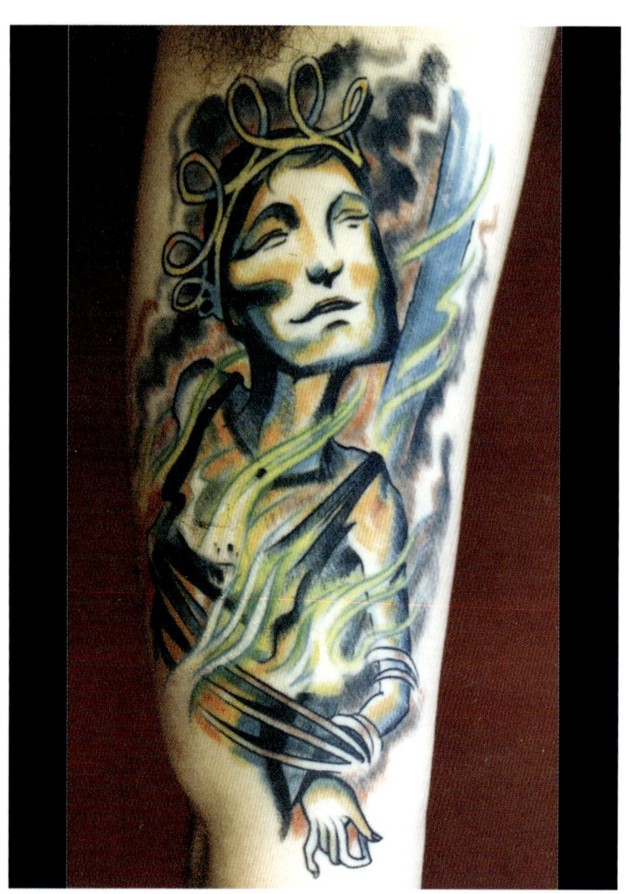

Distinctive painterly work from Mark Heggie, Big Top, Utica, MI.

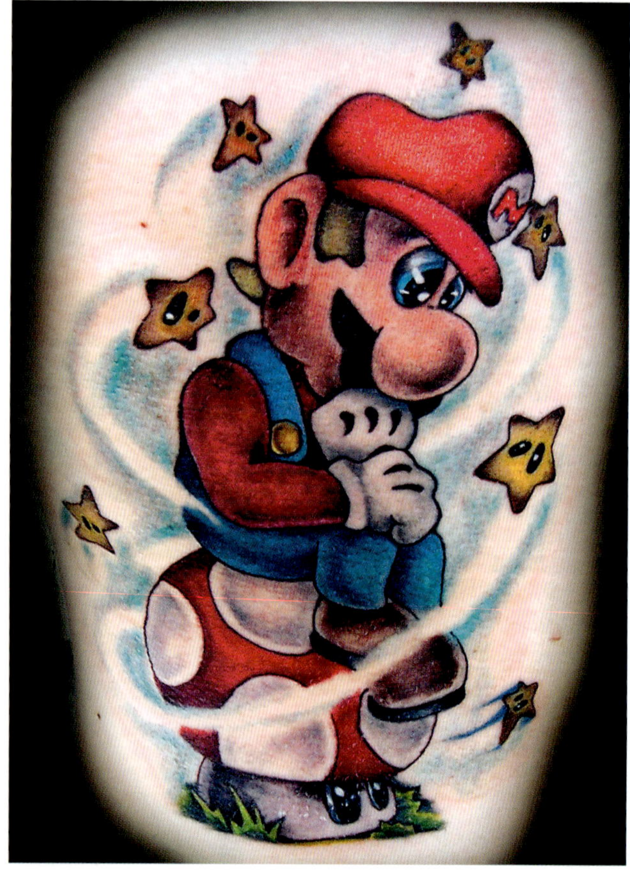

A Nintendo-themed piece from Matt Griffith, 2 Dollar Pistol, Chillicothe, OH.

tional American pin-up imagery. The soft, painterly colors, erotic poses, and clean composition of these images make for some striking tattoo work.

Examining design elements in your favorite magazines, such as color schemes, particular kinds of line work, or creative layouts in ads can give you ideas that you might bring to your artist when you go for your consultation about a piece. Even if you don't find exactly the image you want, you

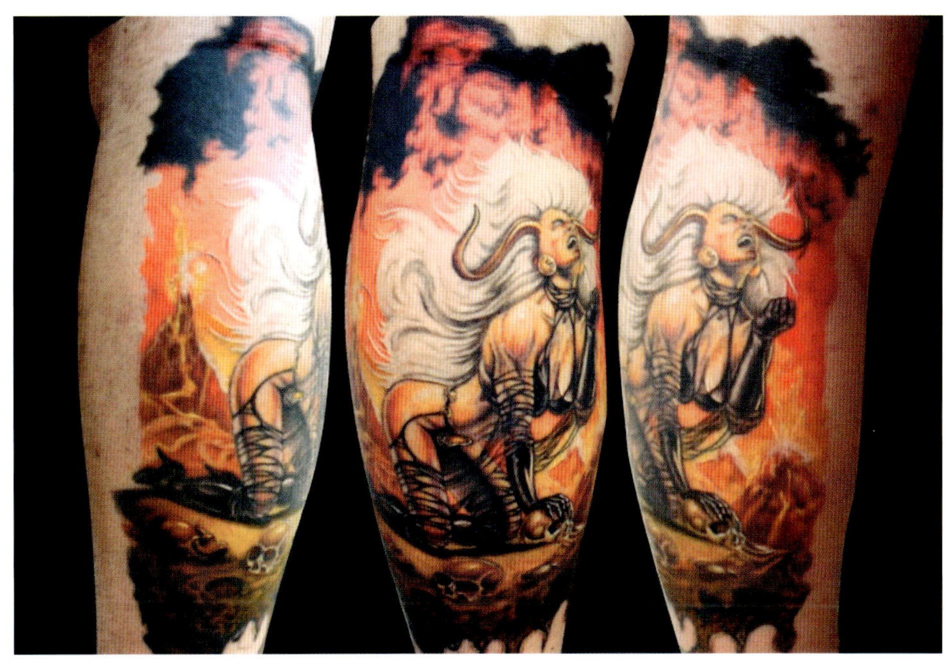

A sexy and colorful piece from John Wayne of Beesting in Ontario, Canada.

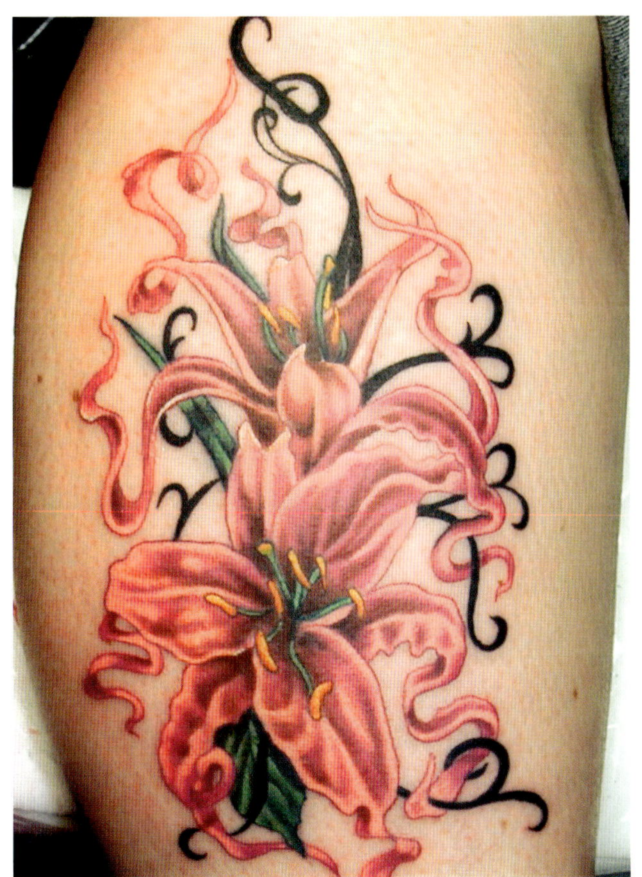

Bold but feminine work from John Wayne, Beesting, Ontario, Canada.

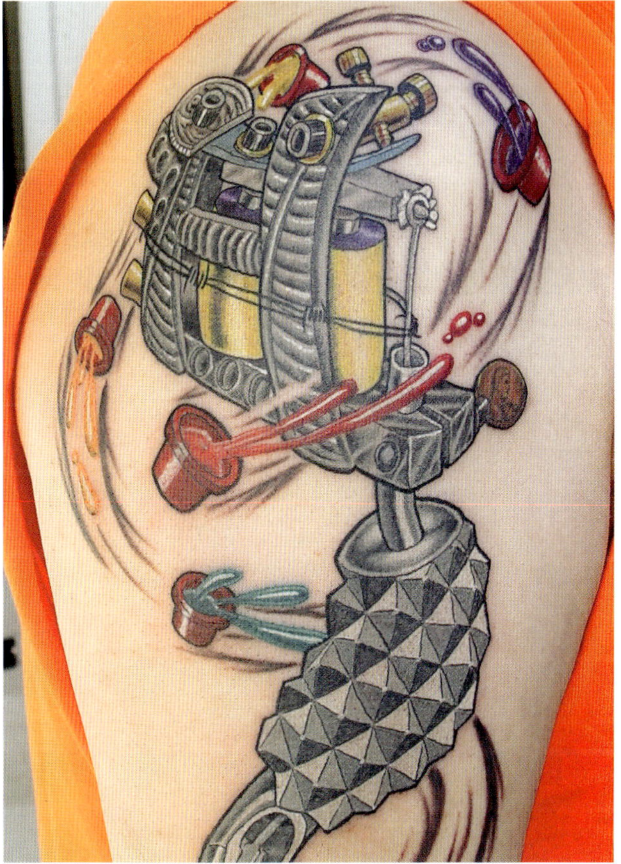

A tattoo machine from Larry Brogan.

might find a style or element that you like by looking through your favorite magazines with your eyes peeled for appealing images. These ideas can be helpful in planning background colors or unifying images to bring together a larger-scale work like an arm or leg sleeve or a full-back tattoo.

We've also seen great tattoos come from art magazines like Juxtapoz or other similar journals that focus on graphic images and design elements.

Art Books

Many people who are attracted to tattoo art are also interested in art generally, and you may already have strong opinions about artwork that you would like reflected in your tattoo design. If you have a favorite artist or a favorite period in art history, finding some images reflective of that style of art might be a good starting place for your conversation with your artist. Some artists, such as Megan Hoogland from Cactus Tattoo in Mankato, Minnesota, even specialize in fine art reproductions.

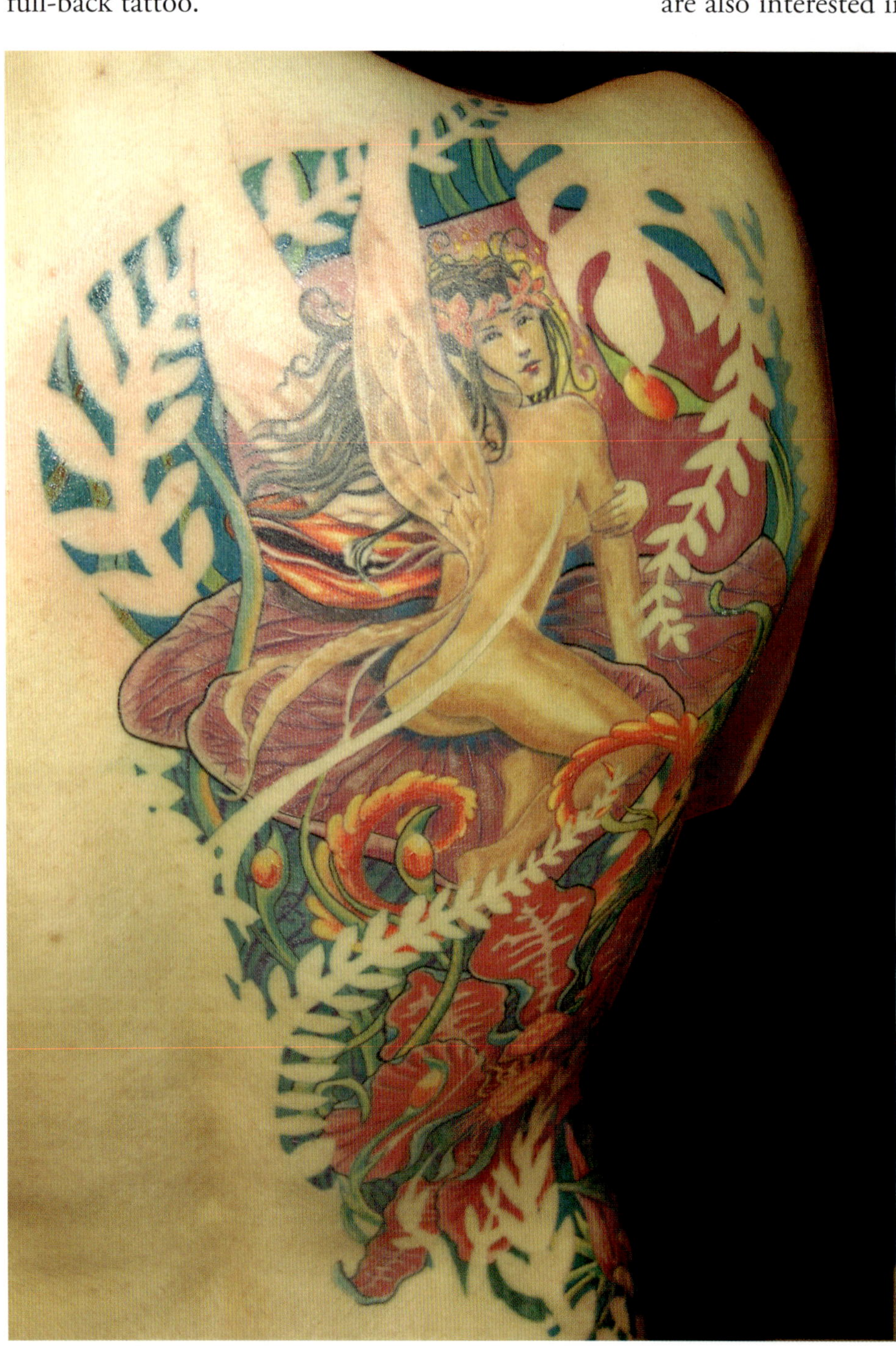

Unique composition from Zsolt Sarkozi, Dark Arts, Budapest, Hungary.

Sometimes traditional art books can serve as useful reference. Even if you don't decide to get a tattoo that is an exact reproduction of a piece of art, you might find inspiration for a theme that you can take to your artist for his or her own unique interpretation. If, for instance, you appreciate classical artwork from the Greek and Roman eras, you might try to incorporate themes from classical myth into your tattoo design. Looking to art and art history books can provide you with a wealth of information about design that can inspire you to develop some truly unique themes for your tattoo artwork.

Television and Film

The world of cinematography is a rich resource for anyone looking for an interesting image for a tattoo. Because cinematographers carefully plan their dramatic lighting, seek out unusual angles for close-up shots, and utilize other techniques to manipulate and enhance viewers' visual experiences of film, movie stills are often excellent sources for portraits or scenes for a tattoo. Websites such as www.hollywood.com offer collections of movie stills that you can scan through to find a portrait or other scene that might translate well into a photorealism style tattoo, such as those done by Nate Beavers of I45 Ink in Houston, Texas, Brandon Bond of All Or Nothing in Atlanta, Georgia, and the other artists who are doing photorealism style work.

Folk Art

Another popular source of reference material is folk art. From the Day Of The Dead skeleton imagery of Mexico to traditional Japanese scroll paintings, many of the themes we have come to associate with tattoos have origins in folk art. Instead of going to someone's interpretation, why not seek out the original? A Google Image search for "day of the dead" or "Japanese calligraphy" will bring you a wealth of inspiration for your next piece, and going to the original sources can help your tattoo to have an air of

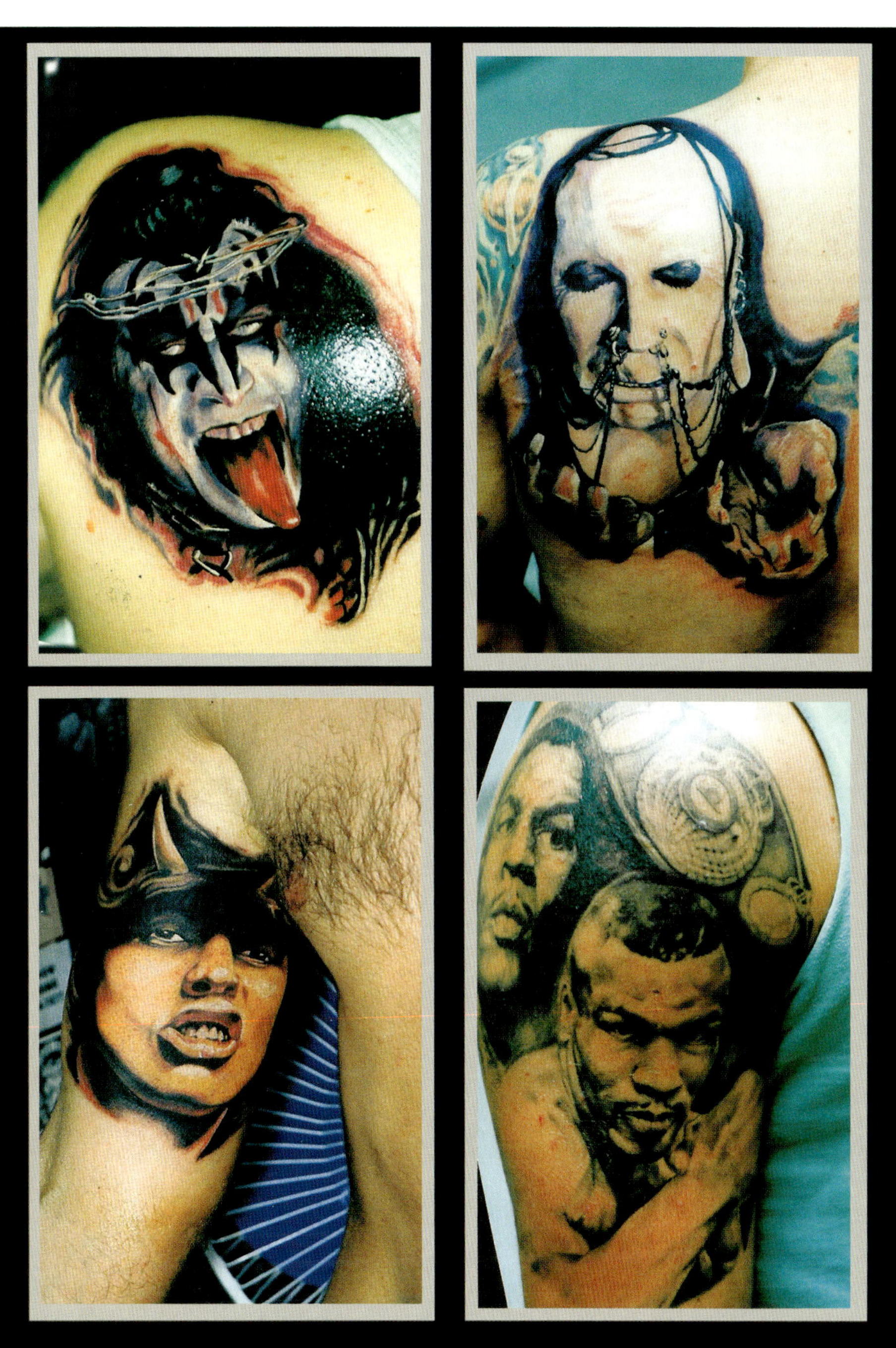

Portrait style work from Zsolt Sarkozi, Dark Arts, Budapest, Hungary.

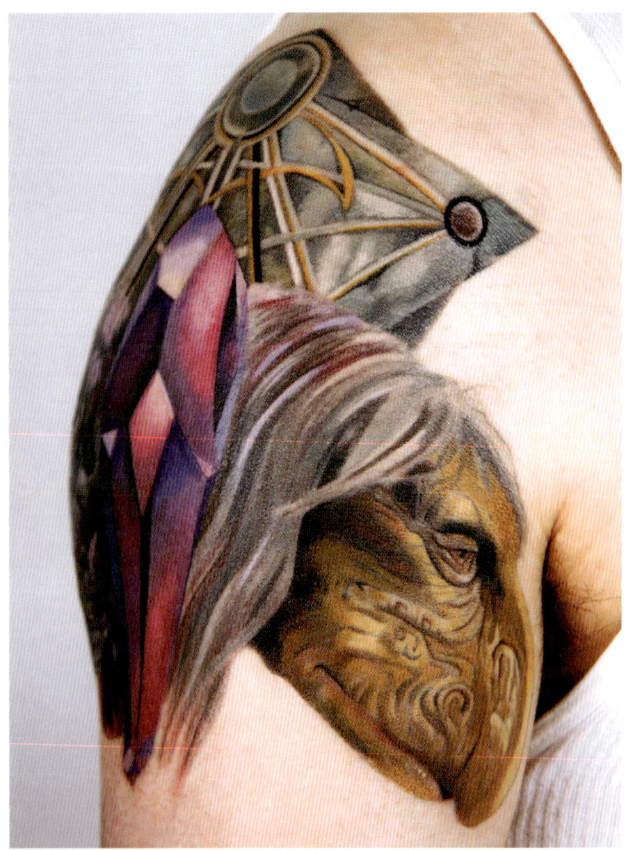

Amanda Wachob, Blue Moon, Buffalo, NY.

authenticity that might make it stand out from others completed in a similar style or with similar themes.

What To Expect From Your Artist

At an initial consultation with an artist, you will likely discuss your ideas and your own vision of the final product. If you have collected material from any of the sources we recommend, you can show those to your artist and discuss what you'd like to see. Often after the initial consultation, artists will ask for you to leave him or her an art deposit. Usually, these deposits are percentages of the cost of the tattoo, and the money will go towards the cost of applying the tattoo should you choose to get it done. This art deposit assures the artist that you are invested enough in the piece and avoids a situation where he or she spends hours preparing a preliminary sketch for a client who disappears. If the client decides not to come back or to go elsewhere, at least the artist will be partly compensated for his or her time in preparing the design.

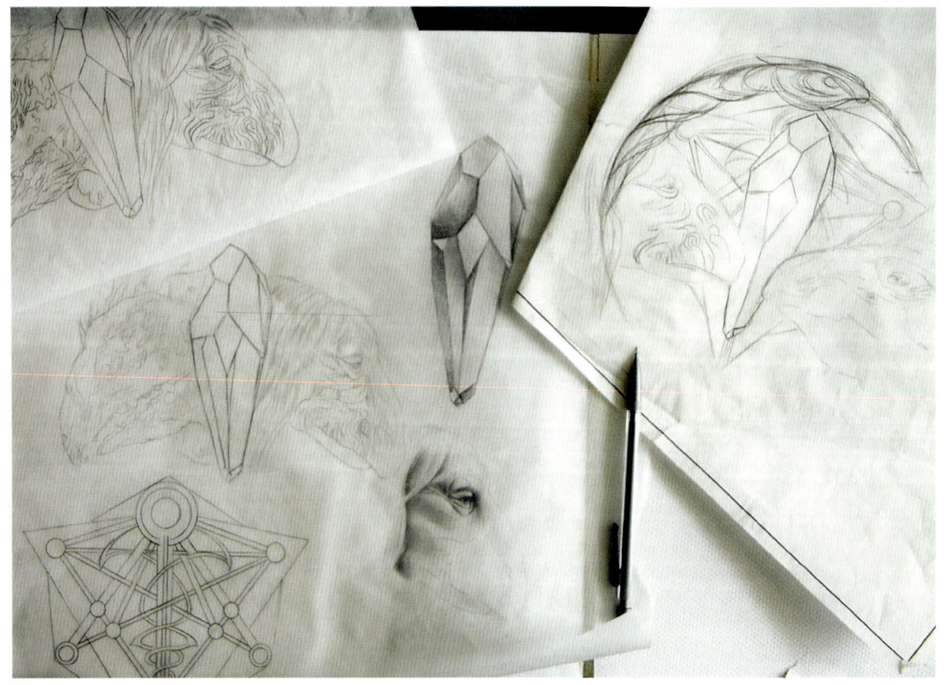

Amanda Wachob's preliminary sketches for the tattoo above.

Generally, the artist and client will either schedule another appointment to discuss the artist's progress with the design, or the two might decide to schedule a time to start the tattoo, and any last-minute tweaks to the design might be addressed on the day of the appointment.

Some artists might render a drawing to completion for you, including color and shading; however, it is more common that he or she will present you with a line drawing, which is what the artist will use in preparing the stencil that will be applied to your skin. The line drawing that he or she prepares will give you an idea of what your tattoo will look like, but you might not see exactly what it will look like until the work is finished. This lack of certainty is one of the disadvantages of custom work over flash; since the flash designs are pre-packaged and usually are drawings that have been rendered to completion, the artist is able to show you exactly what your tattoo will look like at the end of the process. If you have chosen a custom artist whose work you admire, however, you should be confident from the work you have seen in his or her portfolio that the finished product will be satisfactory. If you have doubts about the artist's plans for your color or shading, address them before he or she applies the stencil.

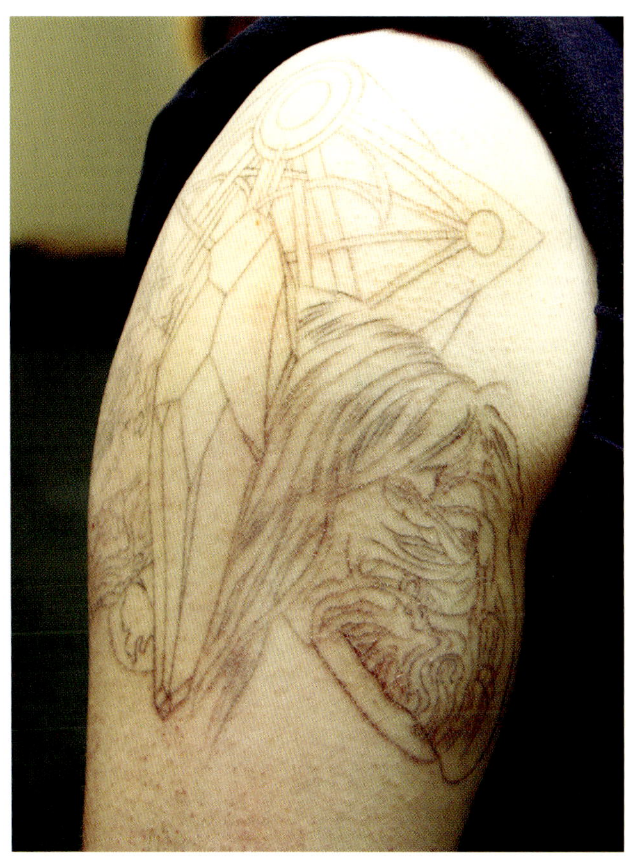

The lines applied to the skin before color.

After you approve the design, the tattooist will apply the stencil using stencil paper to leave a carbon outline on your skin to give him or her a guideline in starting the tattoo-lining process. The artist will usually give you a mirror to look at the placement of the design, and the two of you might decide to adjust the stencil or re-align it based on your aesthetic decisions. Some artists skip the stencil paper and either begin applying the tattoo directly onto the skin in a technique known as "free-handing." This is a highly advanced skill, as the artist will more or less be making up the design as he or she goes along. Many artists are excellent free-hand artists, but make sure you

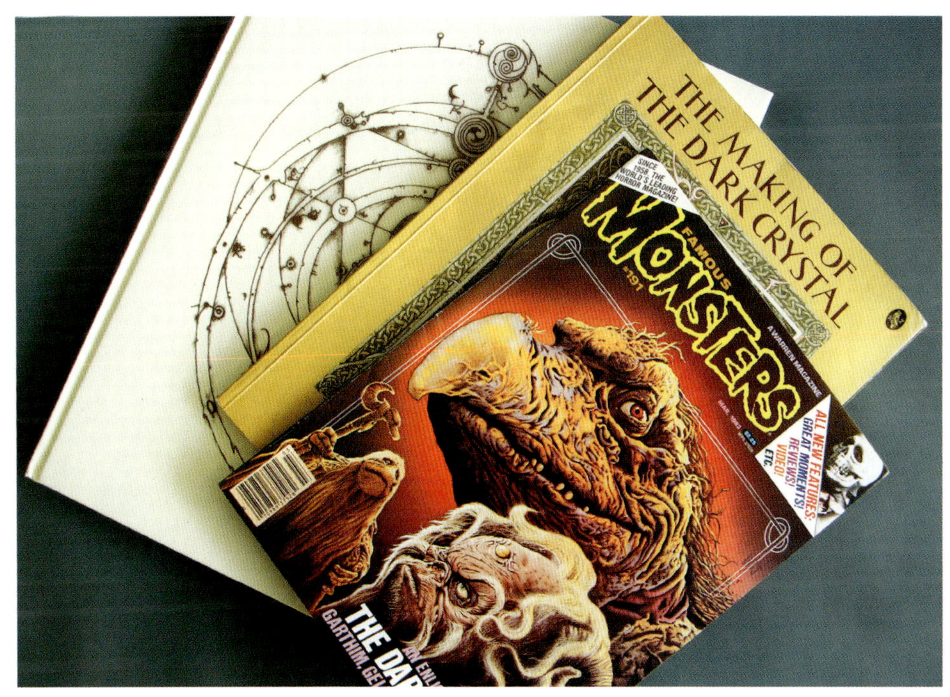

Reference material.

have seen examples in the artist's portfolio before you allow someone to experiment extensively with freehand work on your skin. Other artists will draw directly on your skin and then begin the tattoo after applying their sketch.

While these steps are typical interactions in the tattoo industry, every artist is different, and no standard procedure is ideal for everyone. In order to give you a firsthand idea of one custom artist's approach and one client's experience, we caught up with Amanda Wachob and her client Jeremy Tsitsinas to find out what this process was like for them.

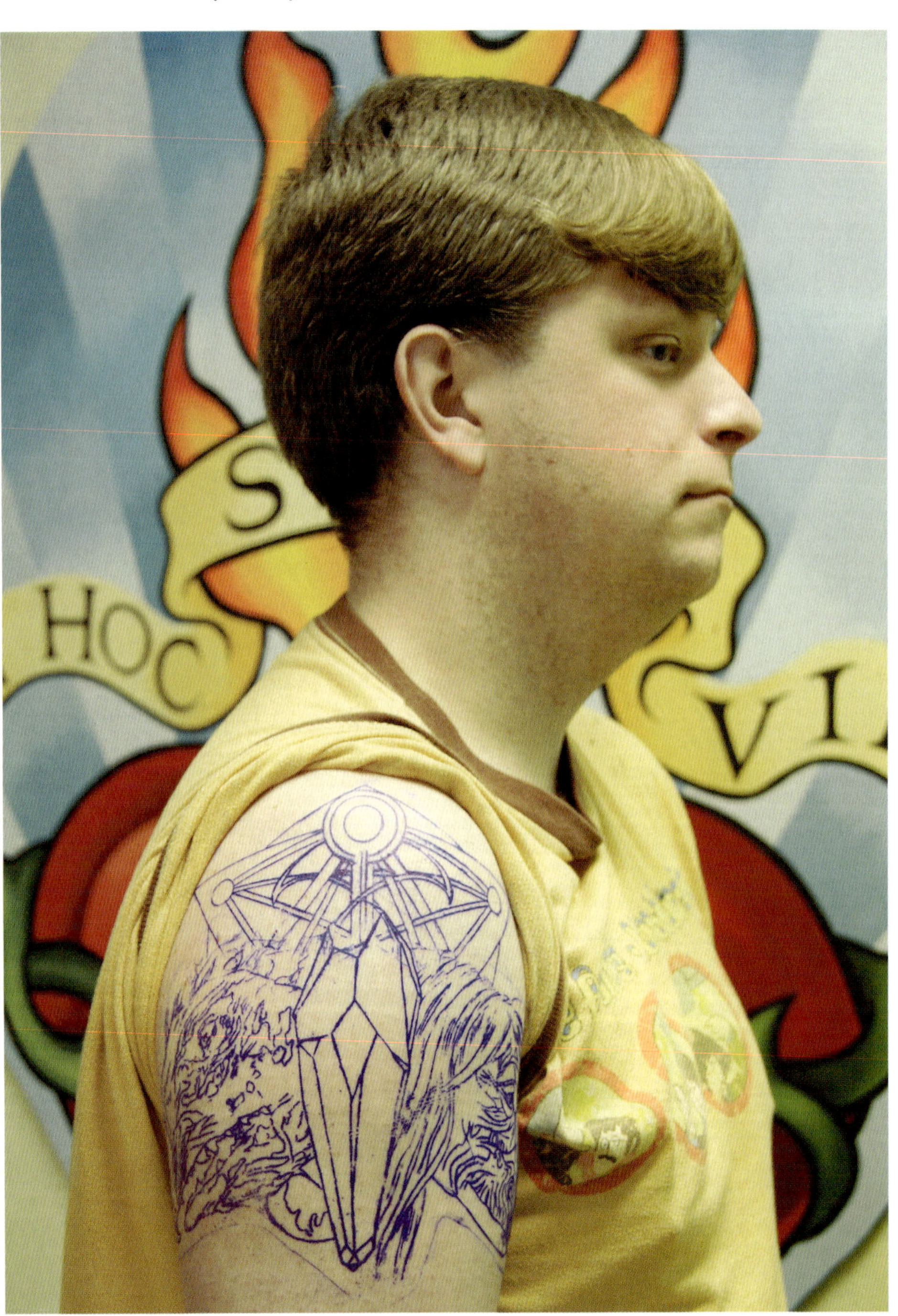

Amanda Wachob's client Jeremy with his preliminary stencil.

Artist and Client Q&A: Amanda Wachob

Amanda Wachob of Blue Moon in Buffalo, New York, is a unique tattooist who is also well-known for her spectacular, luminous paintings. Wachob's tattoo style is a painterly blend of photorealistic elements with surreal color schemes and settings, and her clientele seeks her out for her original interpretations of their ideas.

We asked Amanda about her process in working with a client, and she was generous enough to share these images of a recent piece based on the film The Dark Crystal. Here's what she and her client had to say:

JS: How did you decide that Amanda was the right artist for you?

Jeremy: I was at a tattoo convention in Toronto in 2005, and I saw a sleeve that she had done. The color and detail of the work was unlike anything I've ever seen in terms of a tattoo. Her mastery of color and the proximity of her shop to my hometown made me choose her for my design.

JS: And Amanda, what were your first impressions of the project?

Amanda: He came to me with the idea based on The Dark Crystal, and he said that he eventually wants to expand the design into a full sleeve. I thought that the best way to begin a piece of this scope was to use the Skeksis and the Mystic flanking the Crystal to illustrate the duality of good and evil, which is a pervasive undercurrent in the film. I got started by researching the designs of Brian Froud, whose visions were instrumental in creating the look of the creatures in the film. Plus, this gave me an excuse to watch the movie for the hundredth time! From there, I began sketching some basic ideas…

JS: And Jeremy, what about the Dark Crystal subject matter? How did you decide that was your theme for the piece?

Jeremy: The film with the genius of Jim Henson, Frank Oz, and Brian Froud, is one of the most enjoyable fantasy films I've ever seen. Also, the character Kira was the first "girl" I had a crush on as a kid…

JS: So it had a lot of personal significance for you, then, and it seems like fun subject matter for Amanda as well. I guess that's an important element in an interaction when you're working with an artist, making sure that both of you are interest-

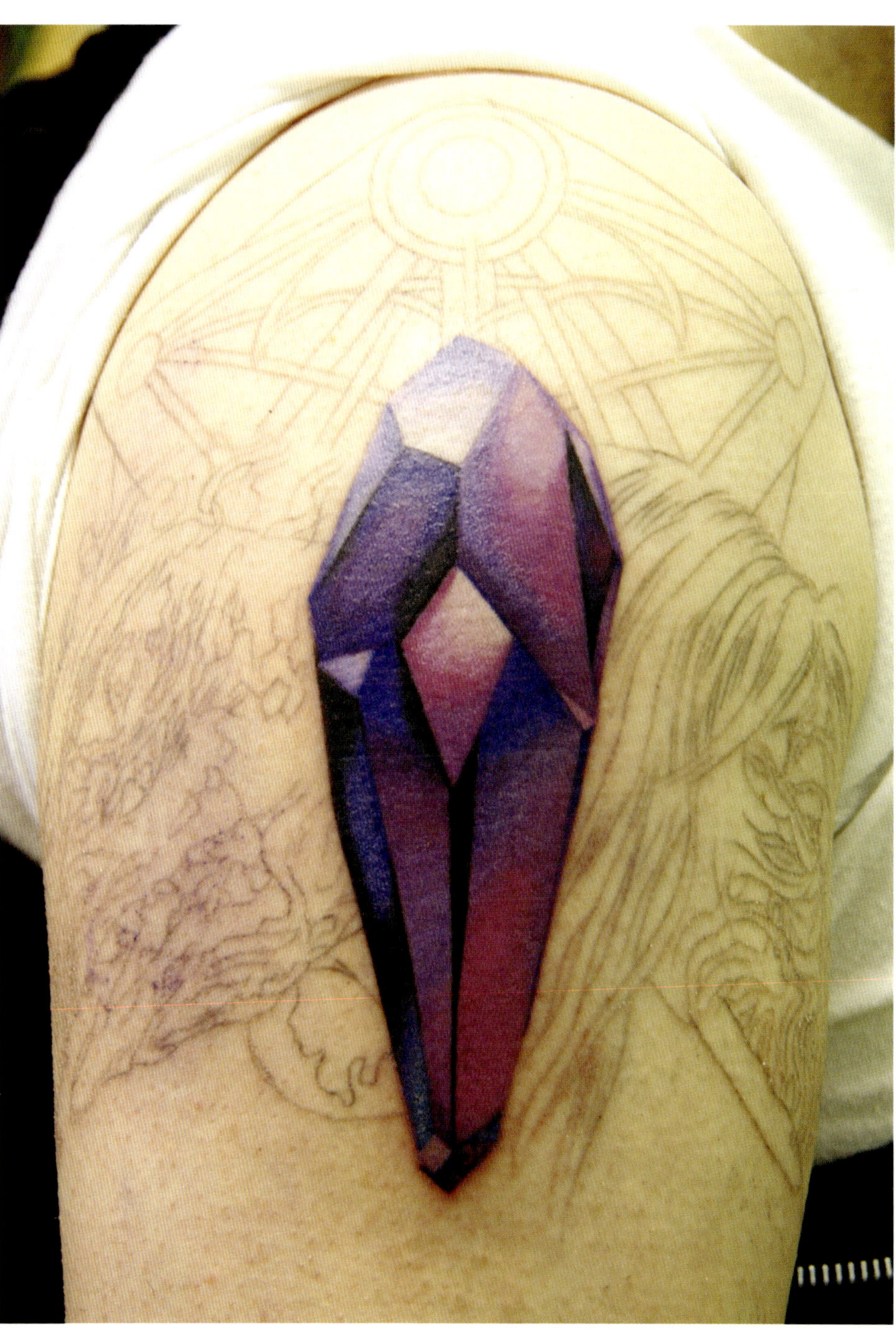

Jeremy's tattoo after the first color session.

ed in the project. How did that translate into working with Amanda on the design?

Jeremy: I explained the idea behind the tattoo, and Amanda did an amazing job transferring my ideas into a wonderful design based on the caduceus.

JS: So, Jeremy, you have other tattoos?

Jeremy: Yes.

JS: So was it different working with Amanda than other artists?

Jeremy: Yes. Aside from the fact that her artwork is so high-quality, this was the first time that the artist was responsible for the majority of the design. In the case of the other artists I've worked with, I provided the design, and I counted on the artist to replicate it or refine it. The Dark Crystal piece is something I've wanted since I first got inked, but until I was introduced to Amanda's work, I had not trusted in the technical ability of another artist in terms of the color work required for the design.

JS: And how was Jeremy for you, Amanda?

Amanda: He was a dream client. He gave me complete artistic freedom, and he had enough faith in my vision and in me as an artist to let go of the reigns.

JS: So your choice of working with her had a lot to do with trust in her ability to interpret your vision? It sounds like you both put a lot of thought into it.

Jeremy: For sure.

JS: So what do you guys think makes Amanda unique?

Amanda: I have a limited scope as to other

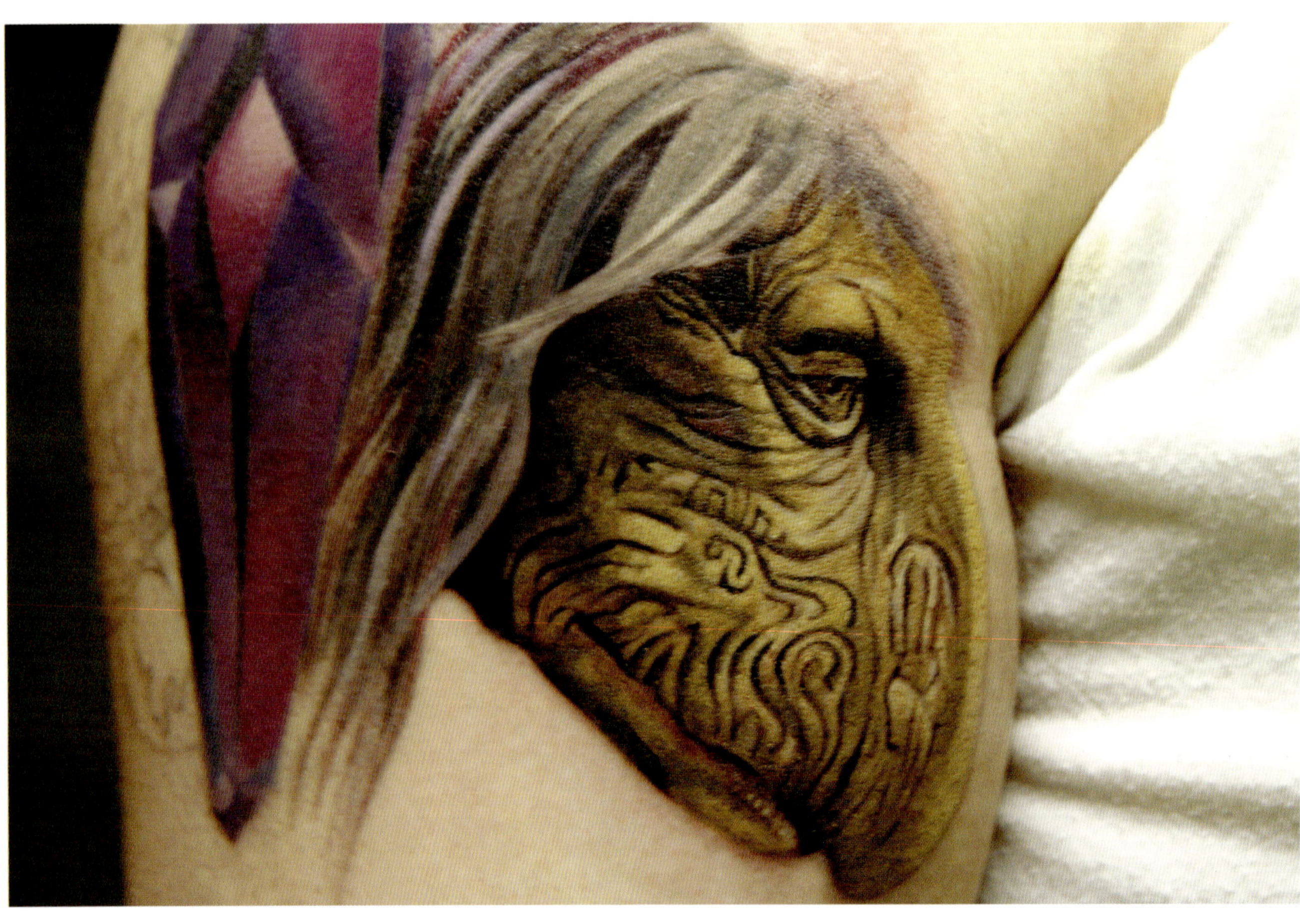

The tattoo after the second color session.

tattoo artists' processes, but I think what sets me apart most is that I approach tattooing from a fine arts perspective. I am a painter, and my goals are similar for tattooing and painting. I am in it to create art, not to generate a quick profit. I work slowly and meticulously, creating something that I can be proud of and something that my client will be pleased with for years to come.

* * *

This interaction is one that is ideal...a patient client and a passionate artist meet and agree over mutually satisfying subject matter. While many of us decide to get a tattoo rashly or on the spur of the moment and fail to consider how the artist-client interaction can make the process more enjoyable and the final product more exciting, becoming more educated about the artists available, the various techniques and styles that they might use, and the wide array of themes that are available for interpretation as a tattoo will guarantee you an experience that is memorable and a product that will please you for many years.

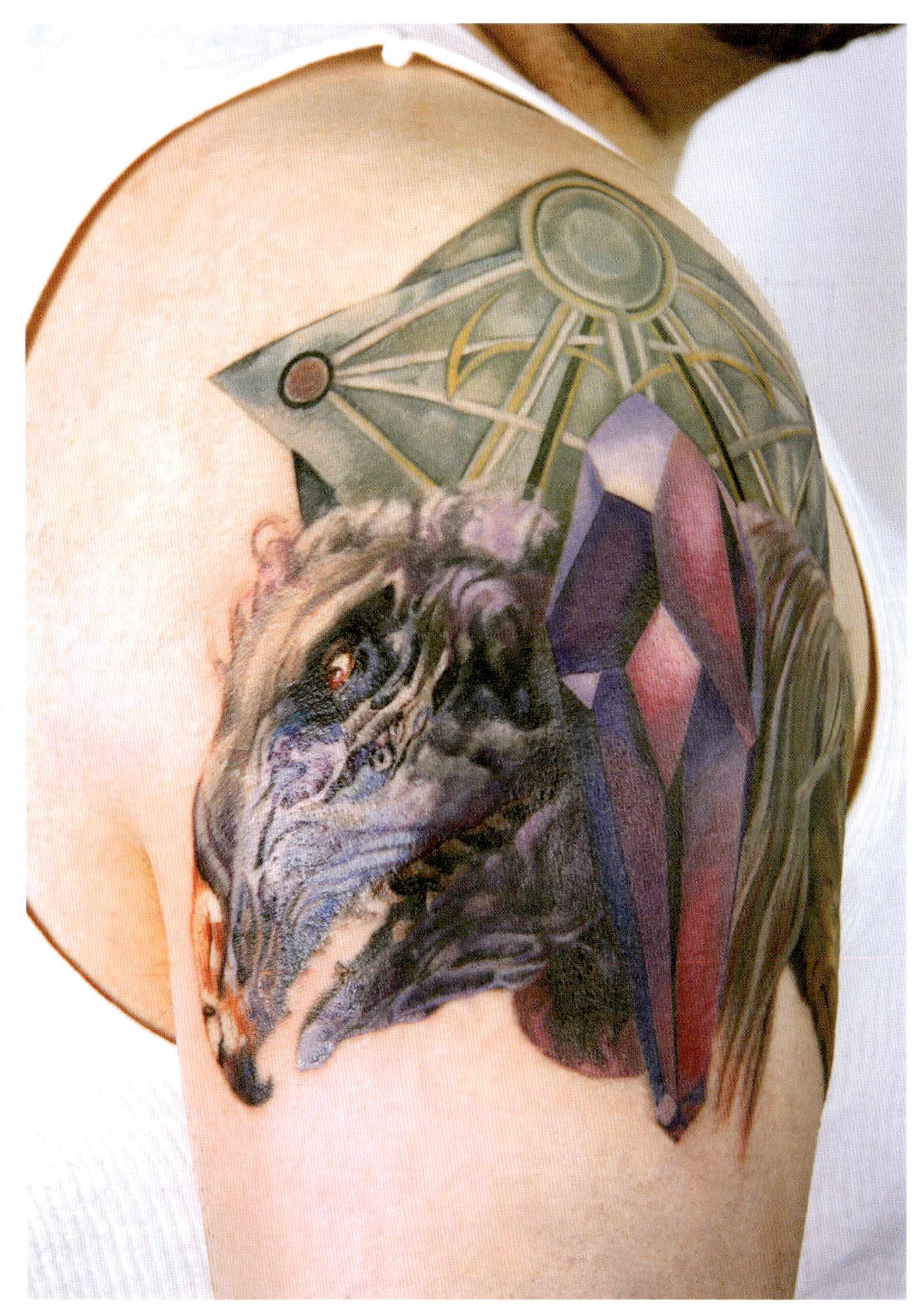

Jeremy's tattoo after the final session.

Chapter Three

Traditional American

A Timeless Classic

When most people hear the word "tattoo," the first images that come to mind are the skull, the dagger, the heart with a banner that reads "MOM." These classic designs are not only standard images for tattoo art; they have infiltrated pop culture and advertising. From the use of classic tattoo designs for jewelry to graphics for corporations, the influence of Traditional American tattoos reaches far beyond the realm of tattoo art. It is a style that has deep roots in American working class culture, and it remains one of the most popular styles of tattooing.

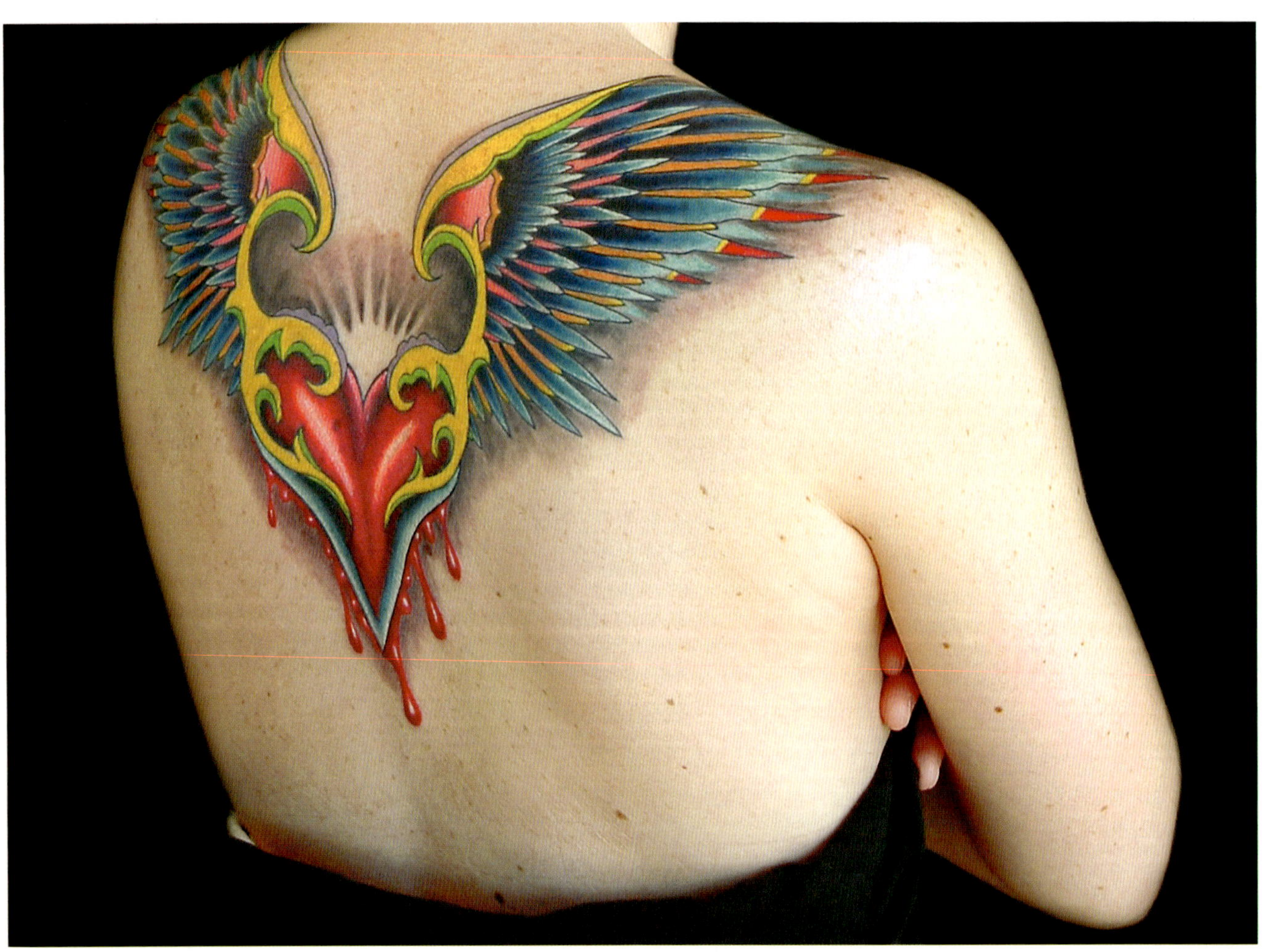

A close-up of our cover girl's tattoo by Brandon Bond of All Or Nothing, Atlanta, GA.

Known for its dark outlines, its bold, primary colors, and its classic appeal, Traditional American work is the basis of many newer styles, and its timeless elegance and symbolism make it an excellent style for any tattoo collector. Because of its wide range of influence on other styles, it also makes an excellent starting point for our investigation into the most popular styles of tattoo art today.

If you are looking for a place to begin your search for the subject matter for your next tattoo, you might investigate the various themes that are common in Traditional American work, even if you are not a fan of the style's aesthetics. You will notice that the kinds of images that appear in Traditional work appear again and again in other tattoo styles, which pay homage to the long history of tattoo art by referencing Traditional work.

Many people who are fans of Traditional American work are true devotees, disdaining all other styles of work. It is not uncommon to find a collector covered in tattoos completed only in Traditional American style artwork. Perhaps because of its rich history or its reputation for being the style that is best able to withstand the test of time, Traditional artists and Traditional collectors are some of the industry's most devoted members.

The style that most of us think of as Traditional developed in the United States in the second half of the nineteenth century. The earliest recorded mentions of tattooing in the U.S. can be found in the records of ships' logs and seamens' diaries and letters. American sailors became enamored of the practice after initially encountering tattoos in their travels to areas where tattooing was a common cultural expression, such as among the Polynesian islanders whose word "tatatau" gave us the English word, "tattoo." While we will cover the designs and origins of these tribal tattoo practices in the Tribal chapter later in this book, it is important to note here that their influence lead to the birth of Traditional American tattoos.

In his memoirs, Herman Melville wrote about the popularity of tattooing among his shipmates on board a United States Navy vessel in the mid-

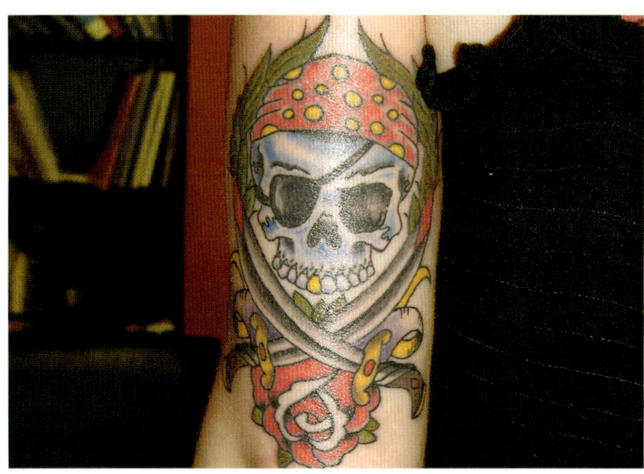

The pirate theme is also common in traditional work, fitting with the nautical history of this style. Adam Patterson, Body And Soul, Jersey City, NJ.

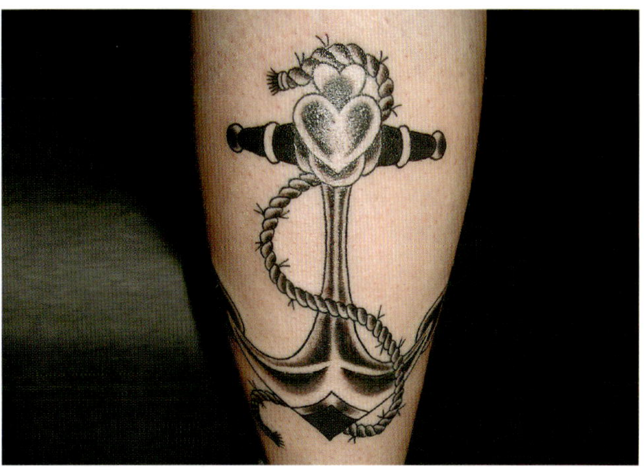

The anchor is a classic traditional American piece. Here Adam Patterson has rendered the image with black & grey tones, which is unusual for a traditional tattoo.

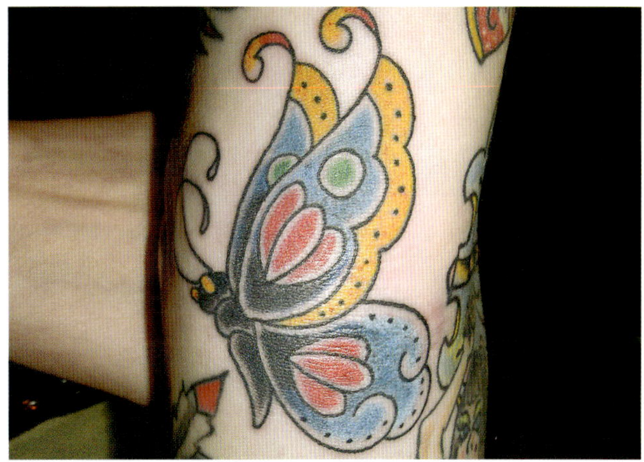

Adam Patterson of Body And Soul in Jersey City, NJ, has re-interpreted this butterfly with a uniquely traditional style.

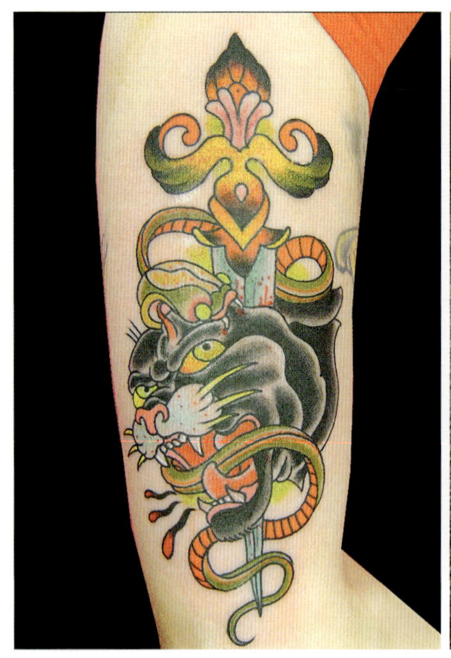

Panthers, snakes, diamonds and daggers are all common in the traditional oeuvre. Mario Desa, Chicago Tattoo, Chicago, IL.

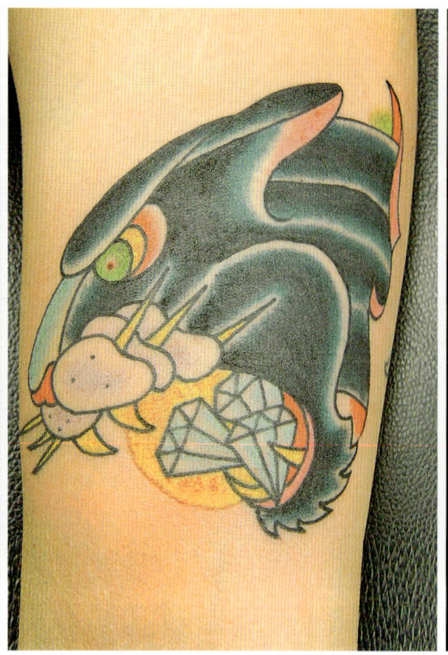

Mario Desa, Chicago Tattoo, Chicago, IL.

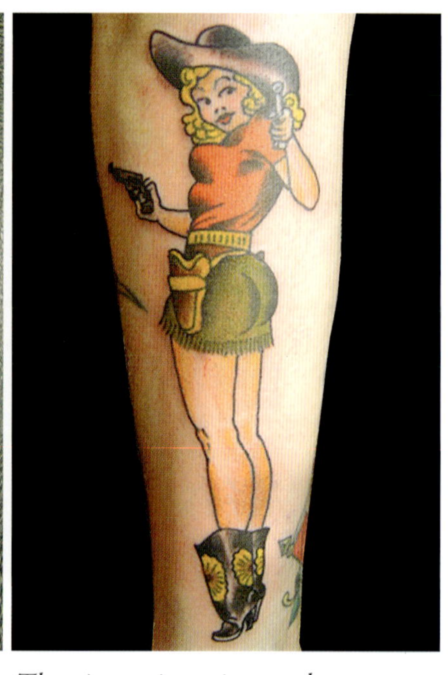

The pin-up is an image that many people think of first when they hear the word "tattoo." This classic cowgirl beauty is from Mario Desa.

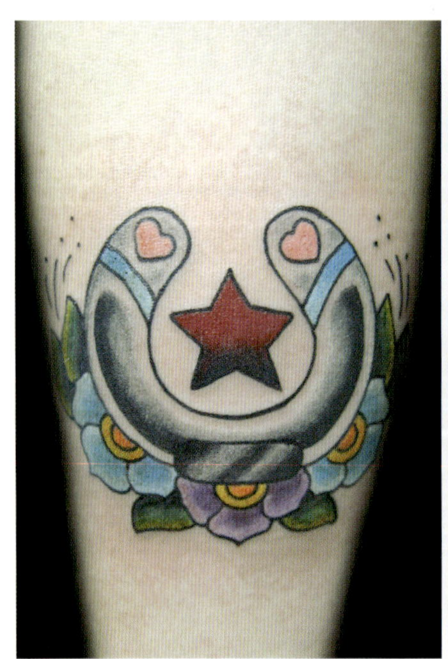

Lucky horseshoe from Kirk Shepherd, Fleshworks, Victoria, British Columbia.

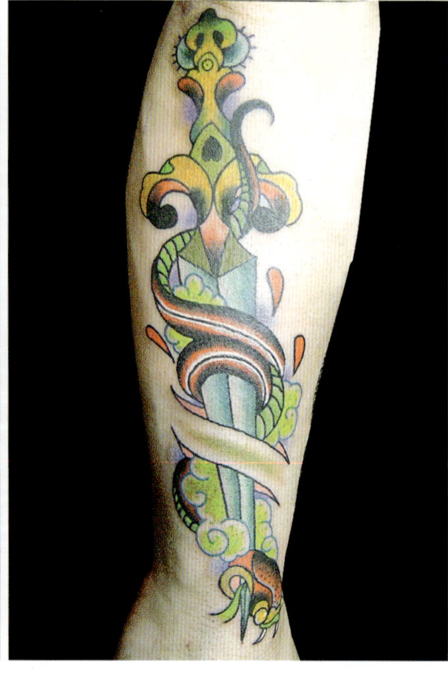

Mario Desa, Chicago Tattoo, Chicago, IL.

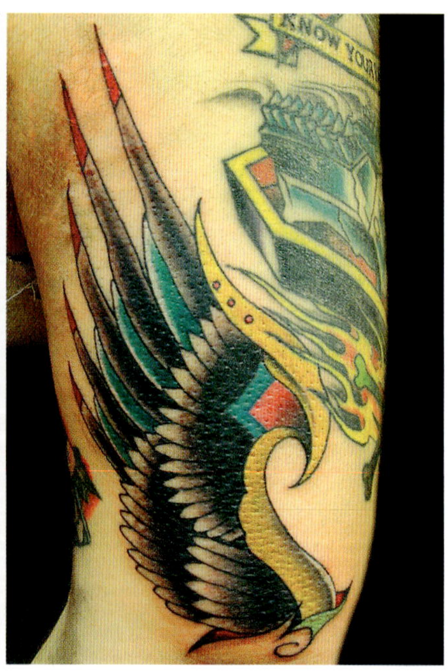

Traditional wing from Brandon Bond, All Or Nothing, Atlanta, GA.

nineteenth century, reporting that the seamen referred to the art of making tattoos as "pricking," and that some of his shipmates excelled in the art and had a collection of tools and inks that they carried on board with them. In addition to the sailors who practiced the art on board ships, tattooists began practicing professionally in port cities to serve the community of sailors who would seek out new tattoos to commemorate stopping in a port town. By the beginning of the twentieth century, a flourishing tattoo industry had developed in New York City, especially around Coney Island and in other areas that were common destinations for the busy sea trade.

The Traditional American style evolved from a stock set of images that these sailors and the tattooists who served them developed through the years. The designs served as a means of silent communication between seamen who did not know one another, describing their service time, their adventures, and what kinds of hazards they had survived. They also functioned as talismans to invigorate their strength or protect the sailors from the many dangers that frequently took the lives of their fellows. For instance, a dragon symbolized having sailed to China, a turtle meant the sailor had passed over the equator, an anchor boasted a crossing of the Atlantic Ocean, a barn swallow symbolized traversing more than 5,000 miles at sea, and a sailboat signified the circumnavigation of Cape Horn. The sailors often would tattoo a pig on one ankle and a cock on the other; as neither of these animals could swim, the belief was that the creatures would carry the sailor quickly to shore if he should fall overboard in the event of an accident. A light house, often with the name of a hometown inked somewhere in the design, was supposed to bring good luck in the sailor's journey and promise a safe return home to his family. A heart with flames represented marriage or eternal love, and the words "HOLD" and "FAST" on the knuckles of both hands promised to give the sailor the courage necessary to lace the ship's ropes securely during a storm.

Many of these classic tattoo images, such as the brightly colored barn swallow, the anchor set against a background of waves, and the sacred heart, have endured the past two centuries and remain popular not only in the Traditional American style, but also in other genre's interpretations or reinventions of these images, particularly in New School or Hybrid versions, which we will

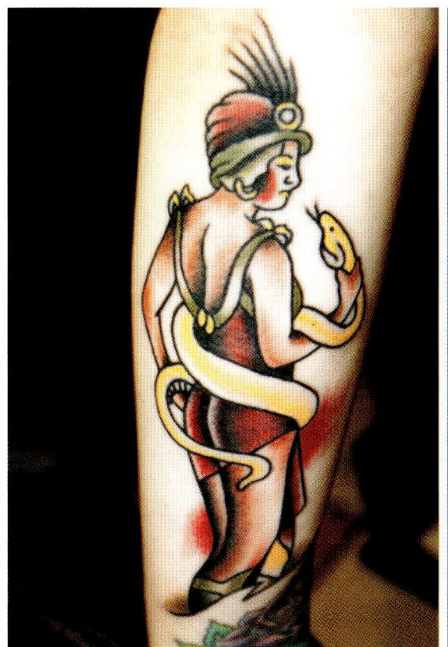

A traditional pin-up from Cory Rogers.

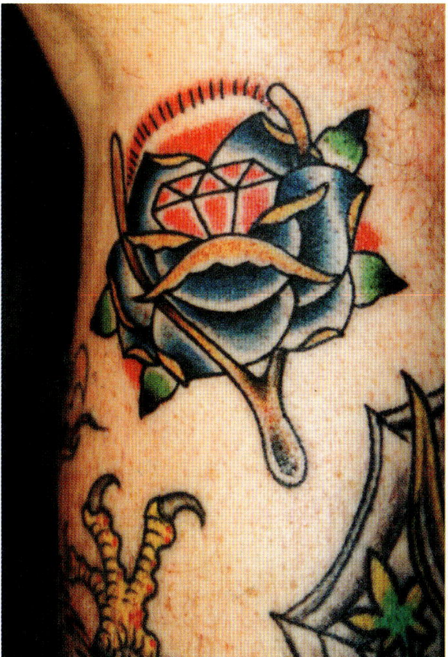

Flattened and stylized roses are common in traditional work. Cory Rogers, 713 Tattoo, Houston, TX.

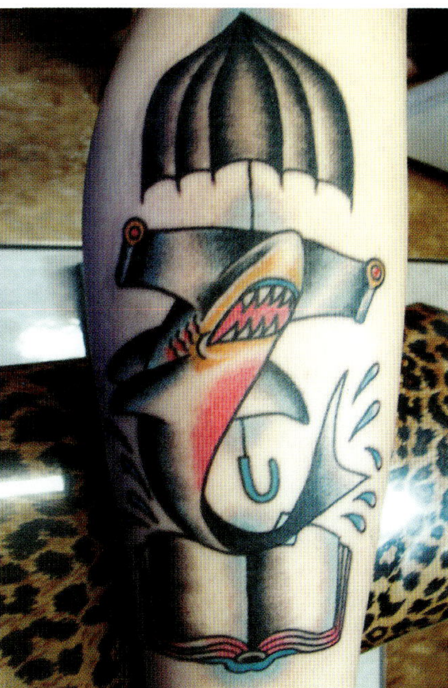

Rogers experiments with recombinations of figures that are traditional classics, as in these surreal pieces.

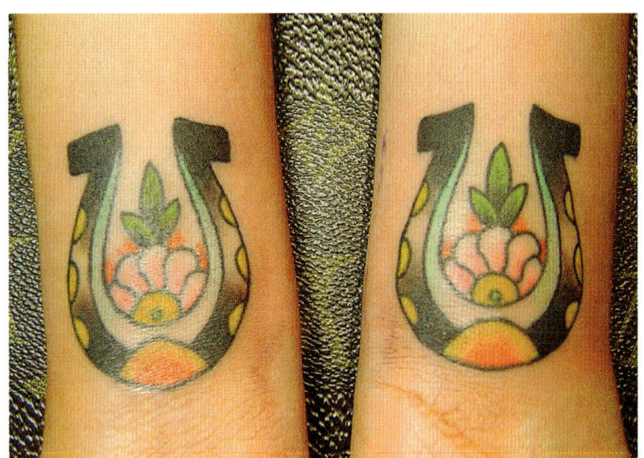

Horseshoes for luck from Mario Desa.

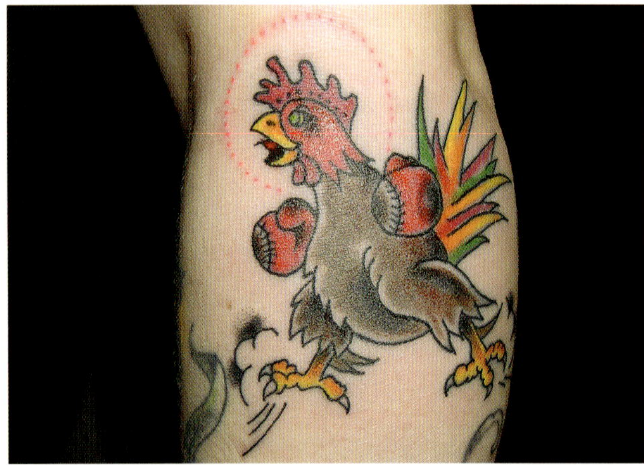

Adam Patterson, Body And Soul, Jersey City, NJ.

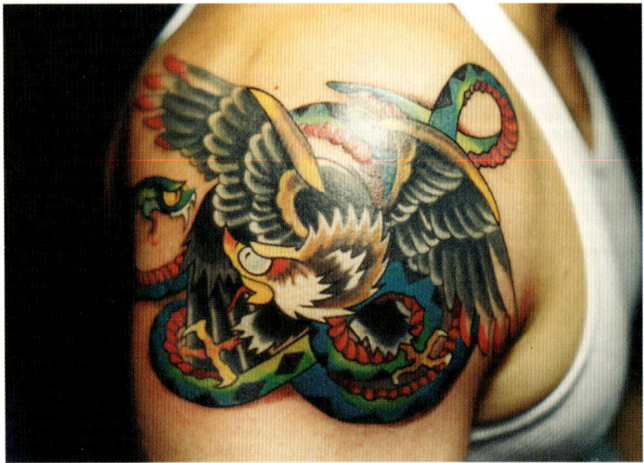

Tattoos featuring patriotic themes are common in traditional tattoos, and here Amanda Wachob has done a gorgeous rendition of the American eagle.

cover in later chapters. These classic designs will likely remain popular for as long as people are getting ink, as their deep roots in tattoo history connect us to a valuable tradition, and their pithy, symbolic meanings are often seen as universally applicable to the human experience.

Not only do artists working in other styles utilize traditional imagery in their own creations; other artists attempt to modernize Traditional work to create designs that many in the industry regard as "Neo-Traditional," using the same subject matter, poses, and color schemes as Traditional tattooing, but adding interest using more modern perspectives and techniques. The tattoo created by Brandon Bond for our cover model, Heidi, is one example of a Neo-Traditional tattoo in that it utilizes the layered wings and sacred heart symbolism as well as the bold, black lines common to Traditional pieces; however, Bond employs more modern color work to heighten the drama in the piece.

While the subject matter is one of the first markers of a Traditional American tattoo, these images have a very distinctive style. Traditional tattoos are known for their bold, black outlines, their clean line work (when performed well), their vivid colors, and their employment of straight black shading. Certain colors are common in Traditional work, particularly red and gold tones. The images are not meant to appear realistic. They are usually one-dimensional, stylized, and they often employ multiple layers to render a sense of depth instead of using three-dimensional perspective, as in Amanda Wachob's American eagle. Notice the layering of the feathers and the straight black shading. While the eagle is not meant to appear realistic, it is instantly recognizable. The Traditional American style is excellent for iconic pieces such as a military or other patriotic tribute piece.

Traditional American artwork often features a rose, and the petals are stylized, pointed, and rendered without an attempt at realism. Artists will often layer colors in these roses, such as red and yellow or red and black, to add interest and to draw the eye across the multiple layers. Another area where traditional artists use stylized lines is in the hair of pin-ups. The pin-up beauty is one of the most common themes in Traditional American art, and their hair is usually drawn in fat rolls that are meant to represent curls. The cheeks of the pin-up girls or of profile portraits, often are rouged with red circles to indicate color. The faces are not shaded, which give them a perfected, idealized effect. The charm in a Traditional American pin-up generally lies less in the face of the girls and more in their unique costumes, as in Mario Desa's cowgirl.

Artist Q & A: Cory Rogers, Traditional Master

We caught up with Cory Rogers of 713 Tattoo in Houston, Texas, to talk about the Traditional American style. Over the last decade, Rogers has become recognized throughout the tattoo industry as a tattooist who has mastered much of the intricacy of Traditional American work, and so he offered us some interesting insight into the style's longstanding popularity, durability, and unique aesthetics.

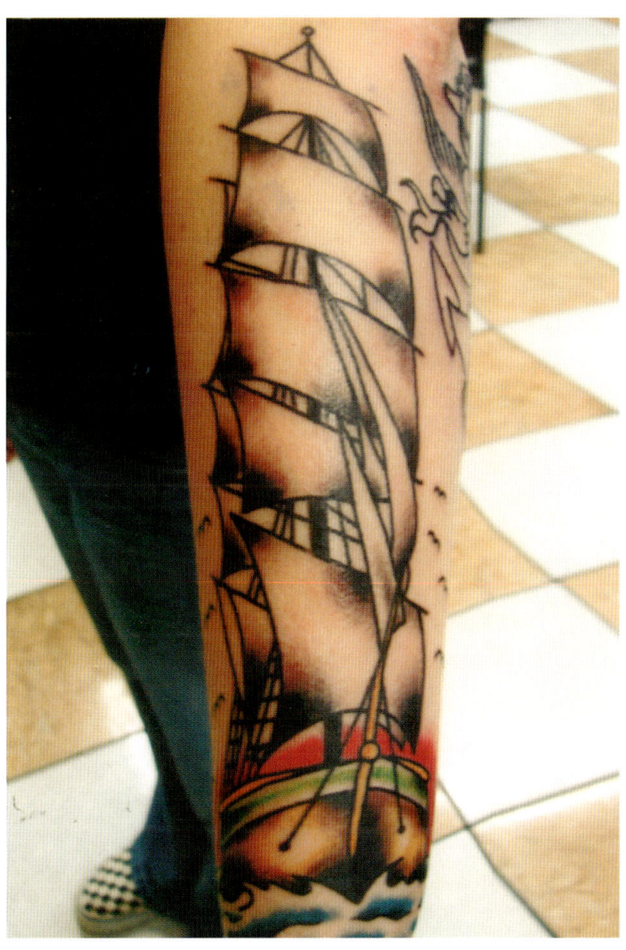

Because of the deep roots of traditional tattooing in sailing, boats are common subjects for tattoos in this style. Cory Rogers, 713 Tattoo, Houston, TX.

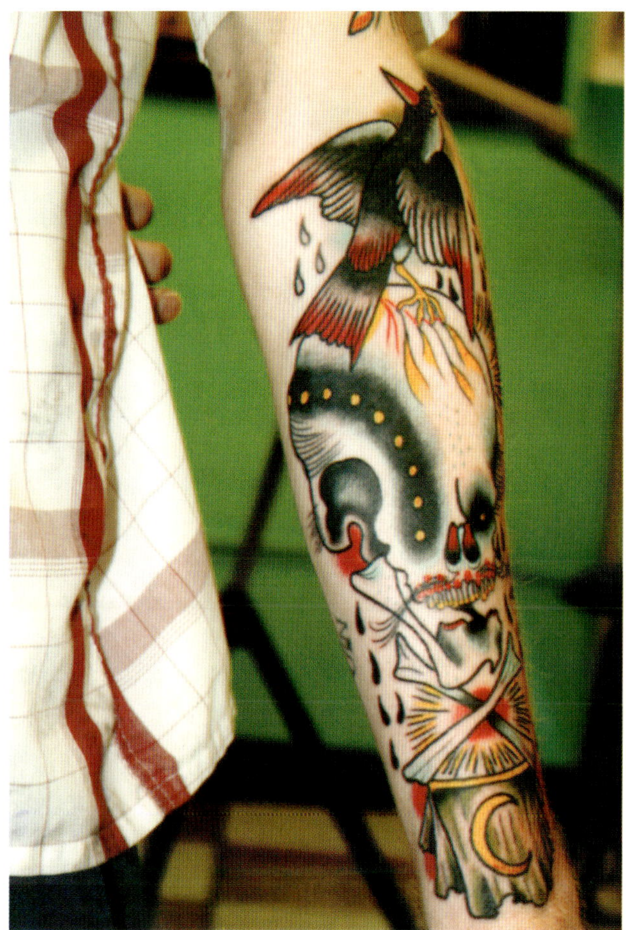

Cory Rogers.

JS: This style of work has been around for a long, long time, but it doesn't seem to be going anywhere. If anything, its influence has spread. What do you think accounts for the Traditional American style's continuing popularity?

Cory: People are becoming more and more educated on tattooing and its history. American Traditional tattoos read really well and age well. And most of all, Traditional tattoos just look like tattoos…these images are what you think of when you hear the word, "tattoo."

Traditional tattoos have to be done right, as everything shows. Your lines have to be on point, shading has to be just right, and the color has to

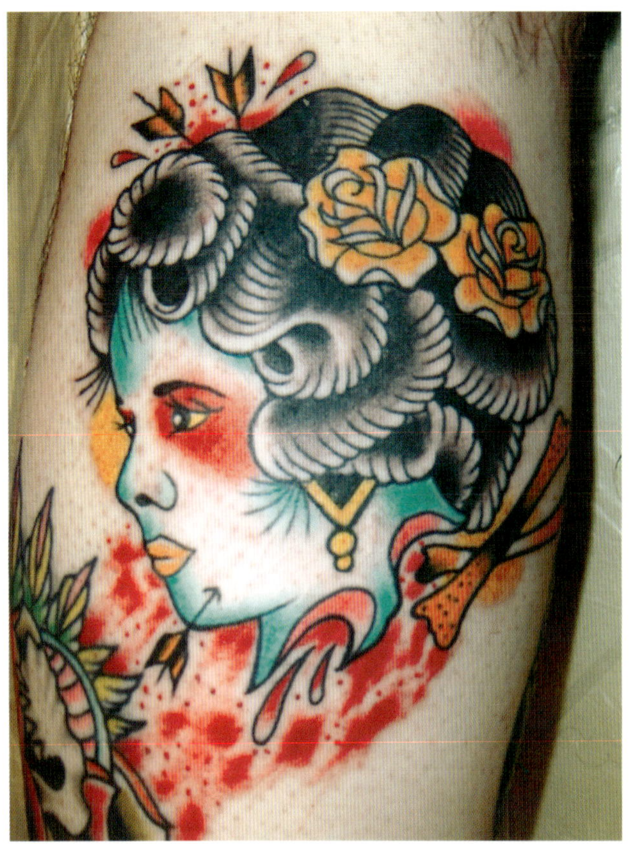

A female portrait in profile with the stylized hair and the straight red for rouge effect. Rogers has heightened the drama in the severed head piece.

be solid! As people come to respect the industry more and more for its artistry, they are also coming to respect the skill necessary to put these tattoos on the skin.

JS: What do you mean by "read well"?

Cory: You could see a Traditional tattoo across a room, and you would always know what it represents. They are simple and bold and lack a lot of detail, which makes the images really clear.

JS: What originally attracted you to the American Traditional style?

Cory: Working with Eric Doyle and Carson Vester molded me into the way I tattoo now. Doing guest spots at Chris Trevino's place and Nick Ley's shop makes me stay on my toes.

JS: What kinds of clients seek you out? Is there a particular type of person, do you think, who prefers Traditional work?

Cory: Traditional work has deep military roots, and I think a lot of the military folks keep the popularity going. Lately, I tattoo a lot of other tattooers, especially at conventions. I am lucky to have the best clients. They give me a lot of artistic freedom, which makes my job more interesting.

JS: I guess that makes sense, that tattooists would like the Traditional style…so what makes you different from other tattooists? What's your process like?

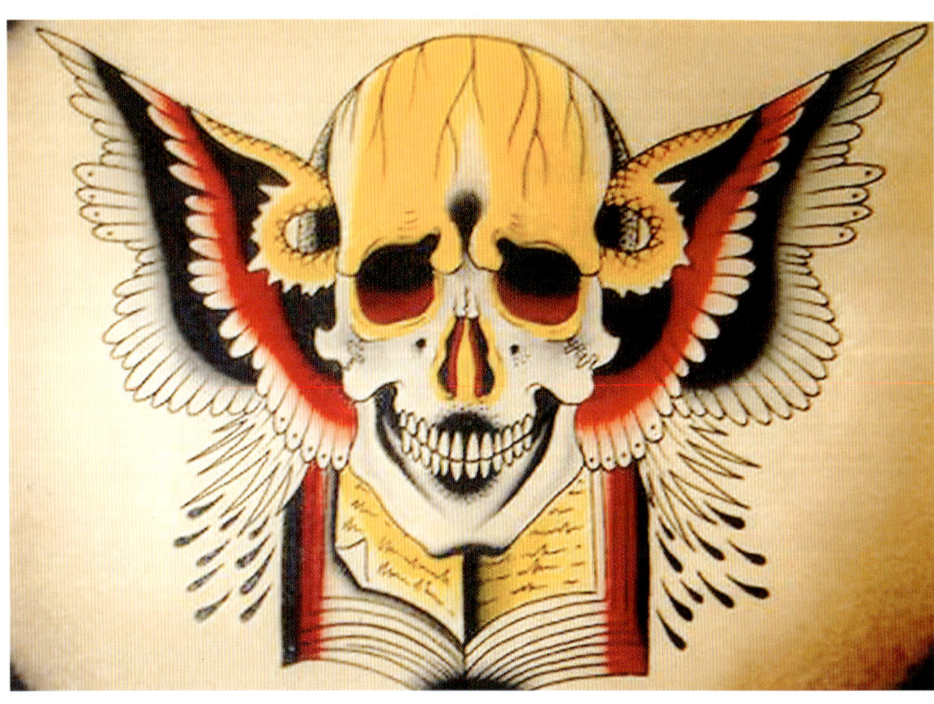

The color scheme and the layered wings are beautiful examples of traditional style from Cory Rogers of 713 Tattoo.

Cory: Usually, the way it works is that my client comes in and I first take a tracing of the area they want tattooed. The next thing we do is get down to discussing the ideas. Nine times out of ten, this part is a fast and easy process. I am usually able to have a drawing done in a day or so, which makes the process go a lot faster. Most of my clients give me a basic idea of what they want, and then they tell me to just run with it. That's all I need to get started - a basic idea.

It is hard, though, to stand out nowadays. Customers are sometimes asking for the same image again and again, and it gets hard to do the same image 10 times and make it interesting every time. I think some of my trademarks, though, are that I use a lot of black, red, and yellow. I like doing weird objects and Biblical images…real creepy stuff, too. I am also known for doing skulls of all shapes, which is something I really enjoy.

JS: You've touched on something we're hoping to teach people with this book…don't get the same thing as everyone else! There's nothing worse than walking down the street and bumping into someone with your same tattoo.

Cory: Especially when there's so many options out there, and such great art.

* * *

And now that we've heard an artist's point of view on the Traditional style, we thought it might be interesting to get the perspective of a client. Heidi, whose lovely visage graces the cover of this book, has a beautiful Traditional tattoo on her back that was executed by Brandon Bond of All Or Nothing in Atlanta, GA. We asked Heidi about the process of getting her tattoo and working with Bond to provide a client's eye view of working with an artist.

Heidi did quite a bit of research to find her artist, and even got on an airplane to be able to get her tattoo. Here's what we found out when we talked to her about her process.

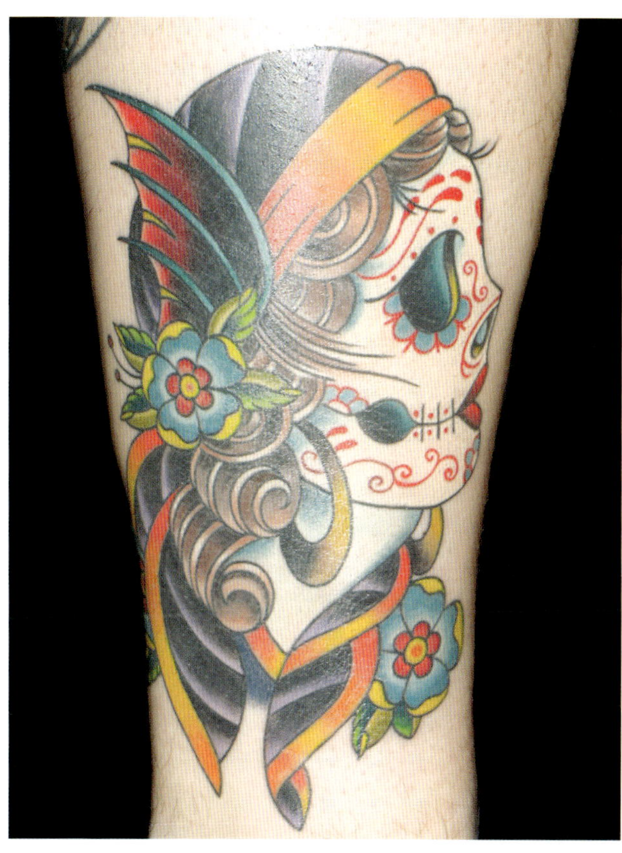

Sugar skulls from the Mexican Day Of The Dead festival are also common in traditional pieces, such as this one from Nate Beavers of I45 in Houston, TX.

Heidi Q & A

JS: How did you choose Brandon to do your work?

Heidi: I read an article about All Or Nothing in a tattoo magazine, which I had bought to do some research on the tattoo I was planning on

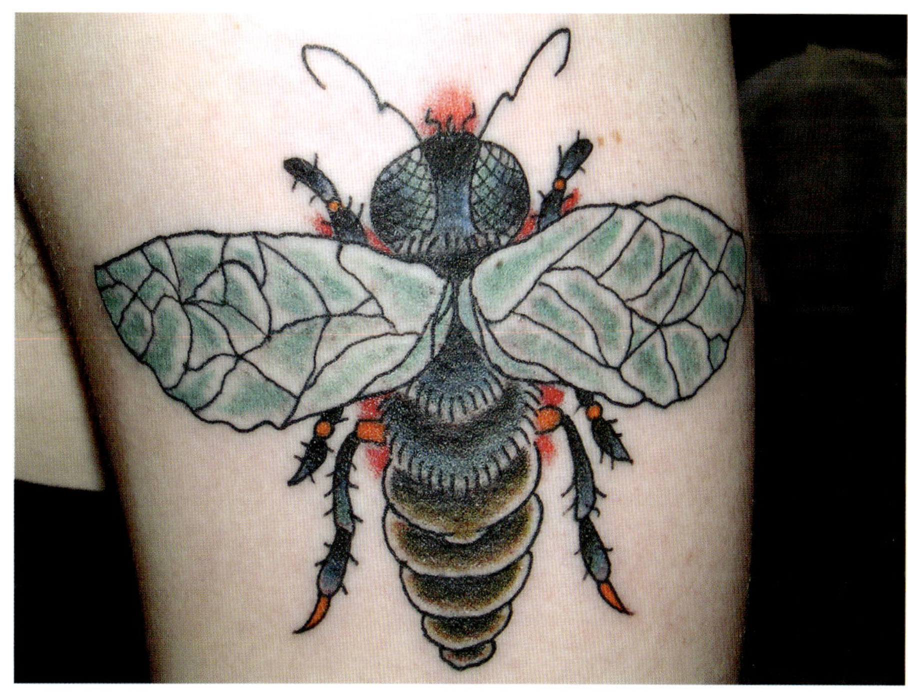

Adam Patterson of Body And Soul has chosen some unusual subject matter, the honeybee, for this tattoo, but he works it in the traditional style, flattening the perspective and using colors common to the traditional American palette.

getting. I saw Brandon's work, and I thought it was some of the most beautiful art I had ever seen. I researched All Or Nothing even further, and I found even more of his beautiful work. I totally fell in love with his art, but I was very disappointed that his shop was in Atlanta, GA, since I live quite a distance from Atlanta. I contacted Brandon, and much to my surprise, I found out that people actually travel to get tattooed by him.

JS: Yeah, that's pretty unusual! But, if you like the artist, I think it's absolutely worth it to take the time to make your way to him or her.

Heidi: Yeah, it was a surprise, but it was not long before I was looking into buying tickets. After a few emails back and forth, I found myself on a plane heading to Atlanta to get tattooed!

JS: What was it like working with Brandon?

Heidi: He was great. I know it might sound like a cliché, but I can honestly say that getting this tattoo was a life altering experience for me. It opened a door to a world that I never knew existed...a world I had always been looking for in a lot of ways...kind of a part of my life that was missing. For helping me find out all these things about myself, I will never be able to express my gratitude to Brandon.

JS: Wow. That sounds like it was a pretty deep experience...

Heidi: It was amazing.

JS: How closely did you work with him in designing the piece?

Heidi: I am by no means an artist, but I knew what tattoo I wanted. I did make a feeble attempt to draw a picture of what I wanted, and I sent that to him. I wanted it to be about the size of a 5x7 picture.

JS: You ended up with something much bigger!

Heidi: Yeah. Eventually, Brandon and I both had a good laugh about my drawing. I hope he threw it away. Maybe the guys in his shop take it out and use it for comic relief sometimes...

JS: It sounds like you had a great experience there, and it is nice to have that kind of chemistry with your artist.

Heidi: Yes. I laughed a lot during the process, which made it all the more fun.

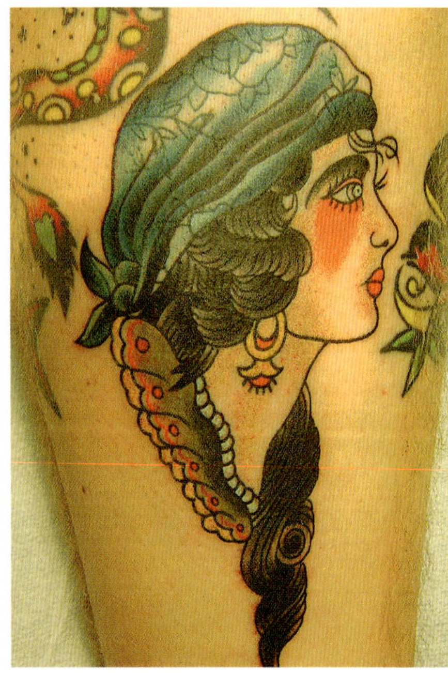

Profiles of beautiful women with highly stylized hair and rouged cheeks are traditional staples. This piece is from Mario Desa of Chicago Tattoo in Chicago, IL.

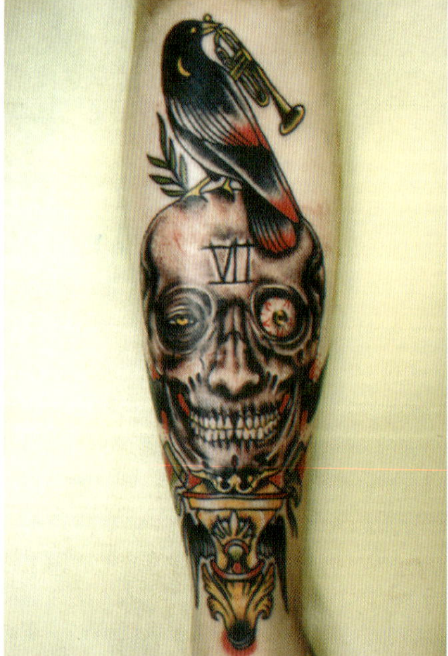

A few examples of traditional interpretations of the skull from Cory Rogers.

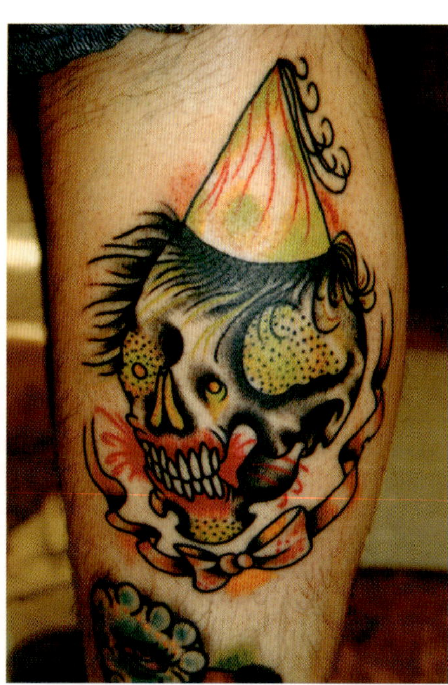

A few examples of traditional interpretations of the skull from Cory Rogers.

When I arrived at All Or Nothing and saw the huge back piece that Brandon created for me, I was shocked at the size he wanted it to be. I had a split second of hesitation, but when I really looked at what he had drawn, I knew it really was the tattoo for I'd always wanted. I knew it was the image for me. There was no doubt in my mind whether or not I was going to get it, exactly the way he created it for me. There is a lot of personal meaning for me in this tattoo, and he captured every bit of it and more.

* * *

So by now, you should have a solid understanding of the underpinnings of the Traditional American tattoo art and also have a little background of the history of this style. If you are particularly enamored of tattoo culture, have a connection to the military, or are a fan of bold color work, clean lines, and simple designs, then Traditional work might be for you.

Perhaps the greatest advantage of the Traditional style over other styles is that Traditional work will withstand many years. While it is possible to have your tattoos touched up to keep them looking good, natural wear and tear and natural changes in the skin will make the tattoos break down over time. All tattoos will fade with time; however, the bold, clean lines of Traditional American work and the saturation of color will keep the image intact through the years, even as it fades. The straight black shading that artists working in this style use will also aid in keeping the image recognizable through time. A common expression in the industry is "Bold Will Hold," meaning that the bold lines, shading, and colors in traditional work hold in the skin through the years. While the ways that the artwork will fade is not something that many of us consider when we are getting our tattoos, it is worth thinking about if you do not want to end up with a big, embarrassing blob that your grandchildren will mock.

Next we will move on to Asian work, which is another style with a deep history and distinctive tradition.

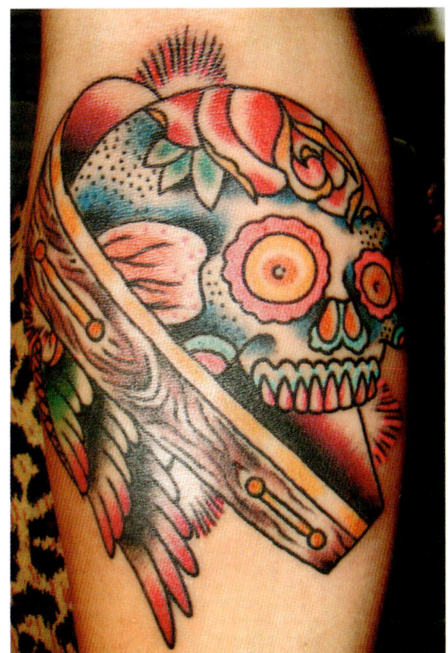

The influence of Mexican Day Of The Dead folk art is apparent here. Cory Rogers, 713 Tattoo, Houston, TX.

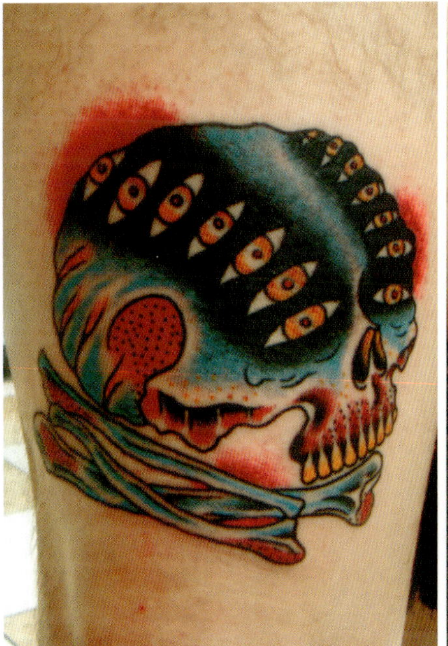

Cory Rogers.

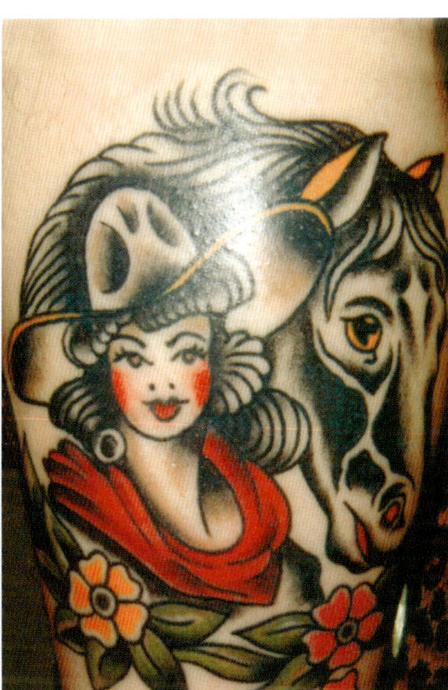

Cory Rogers adds personality to this pin-up by adding a horse in the background, giving the tattoo a Western theme.

Chapter Four

Asian

Beauty Of The East

Asian tattoo designs are some of the most popular images people seek to get tattooed today. The imagery is beautiful, powerful, and diverse, and the themes often juxtapose elegant compositions with strong imagery to render an appealing set of design possibilities.

We have seen how the rich, interesting history behind Traditional American tattooing informs our understanding of the art and images that have evolved into the modern style. The history of tattooing in Asia is equally important to understanding the long-lasting popularity of the style. The

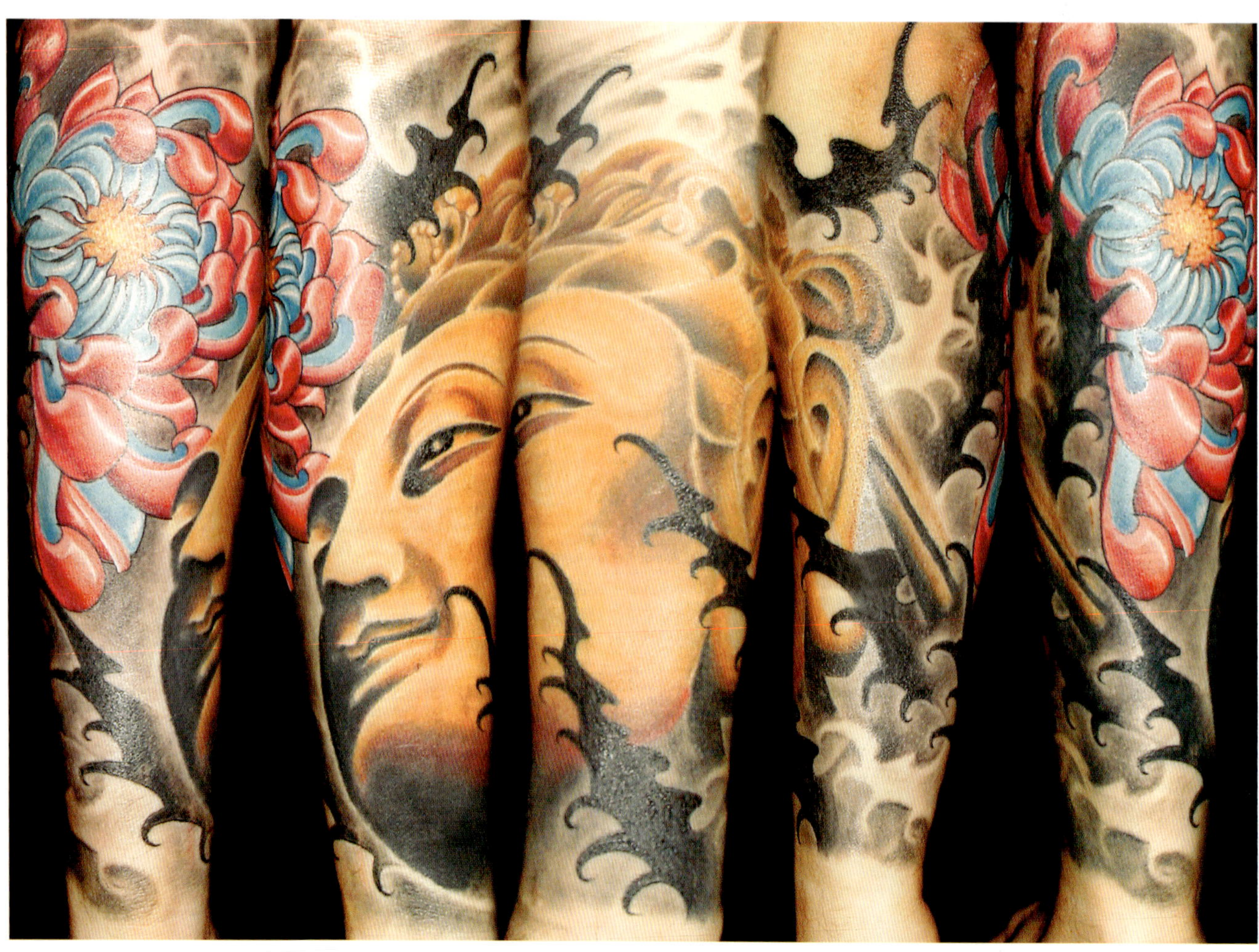

Buddha by Brandon Bond, All Or Nothing, Atlanta, GA

tradition of skin art in Japan is even older than the American tradition, having begun in Japan approximately 10,000 years ago. The earliest Asian tattoo images have more in common with the early Polynesian tribal style of artwork that we will discuss in a later chapter; however, the presence of ink in skin at such an early date in Japan and other Asian countries gives modern designs emerging from this heritage a historical and cultural weight that is another element to consider when you are deciding to get a tattoo completed in this style. History buffs and people attracted to the art and culture of Japan may find themselves drawn to this style of tattoo for its elegant beauty, simplicity, and its association with a long tradition of artists. Ranging from small, delicate pieces to elaborate, bold body suits, the Asian style of work juxtaposes myth, grace, and beauty in an elegant, unique art form that promises never to go out of style.

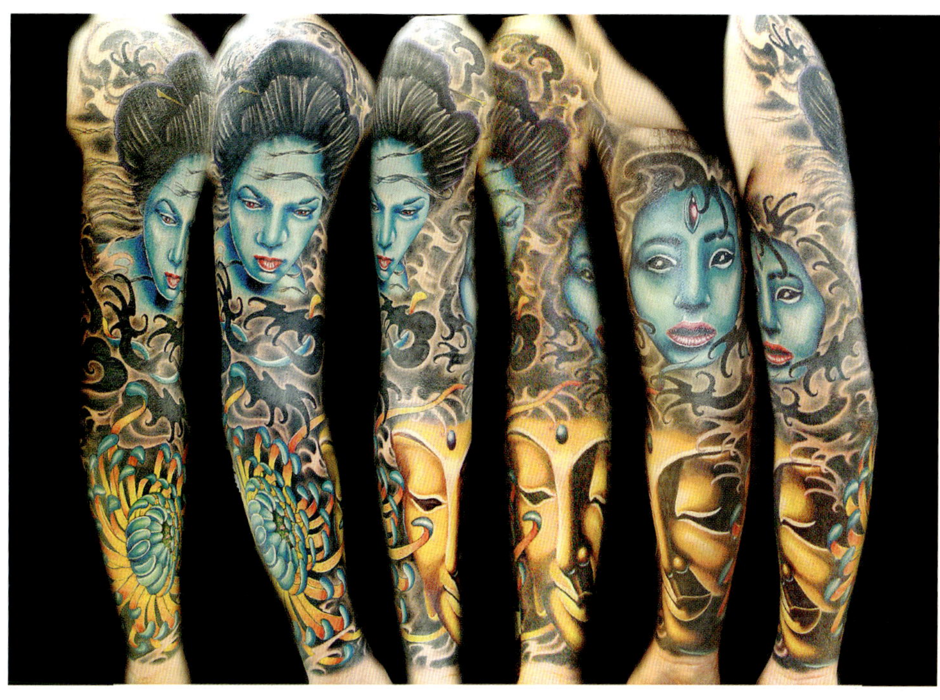

A dynamic sleeve by Brandon Bond, All Or Nothing, Atlanta, GA.

The perception of tattoos and tattooists has changed throughout the centuries in Japan. Just like in the Western world, in modern Asia, especially in cities with the most contact with Western marketing and people from other countries, tattoos are becoming more and more acceptable; however, there was a time when tattoos were used in this part of the

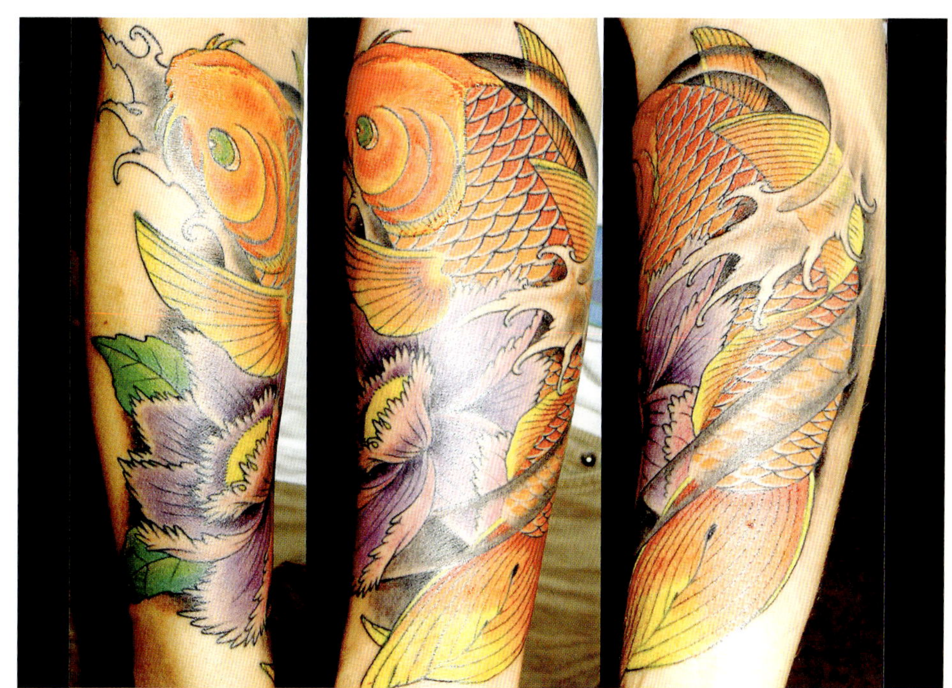

Koi fish by Federico Ferroni.

world as punishment for crimes or to mark someone as a slave. During the Kofun period in Japan, for instance, from about 300-600 AD, tattoos were used to represent criminality; this heritage has had a lasting effect, and tattoos are still often associated with the criminal underworld in Japan. Tattoos also have a long association with the Japanese mafia, and entrance to some tattoo shops is barred unless you have connections through an underworld society. If you are interested in knowing more about the Japanese underground, there is an interesting novel by Kanehara Hitomi set in the modern tattoo and body modification subculture of Tokyo called *Snakes And Earrings*, which traces a young girl named Lui through her body modification journey in all its gory detail.

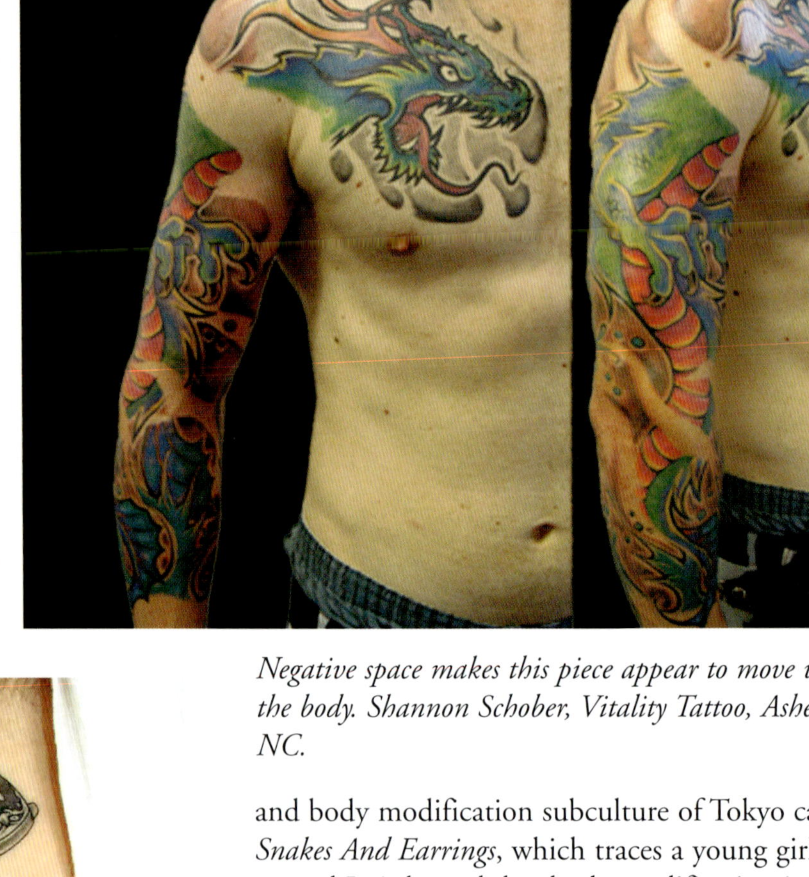

Negative space makes this piece appear to move with the body. Shannon Schober, Vitality Tattoo, Asheville, NC.

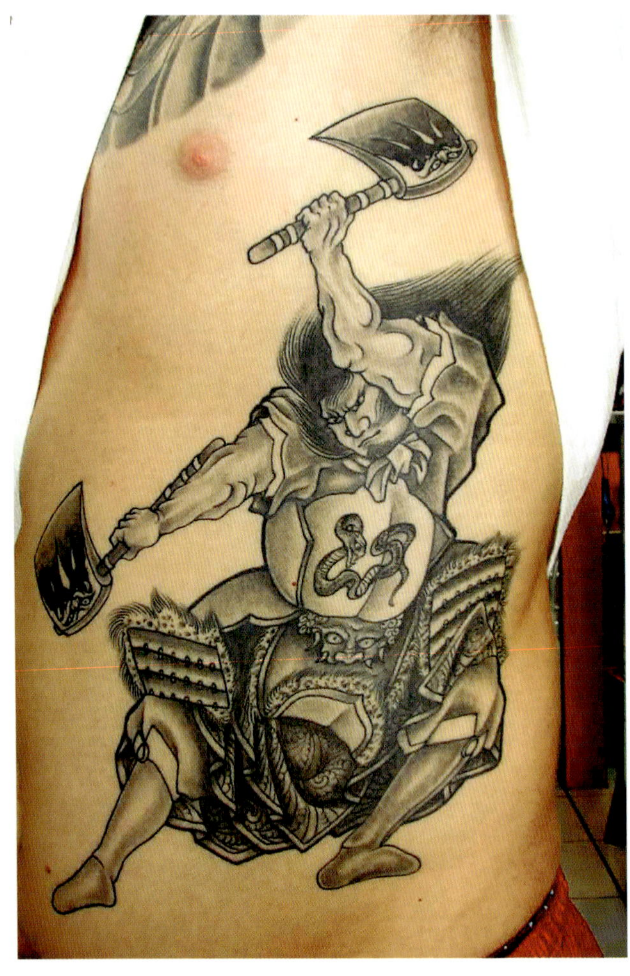

Warrior themes are common in Asian style pieces. Federico Ferroni, South Beach Tattoo.

Historically, Japanese artists used the traditional hand-poked method, and it is still possible to find some artists in modern-day Japan who work in this style. One such artist is the legendary Horiyoshi III, who sometimes appears at conventions in the United States where it is possible to watch him work. The traditional hand technique is called "tebori." Most contemporary artists, however, use the modern electric tattoo machine for a faster, less painful experience.

Although the traditional methods are less common now, the training that a tattoo artist must undergo in Japan and other Asian countries is an intense, rigorous apprenticeship. Generally, the artist will train for several years under a tattoo master, often even living in the master's house. Like in Western tattoo apprenticeships, part of the training includes cleaning the tattoo studio, watching the master artist work, learning about the mechanics of the machines and learning how

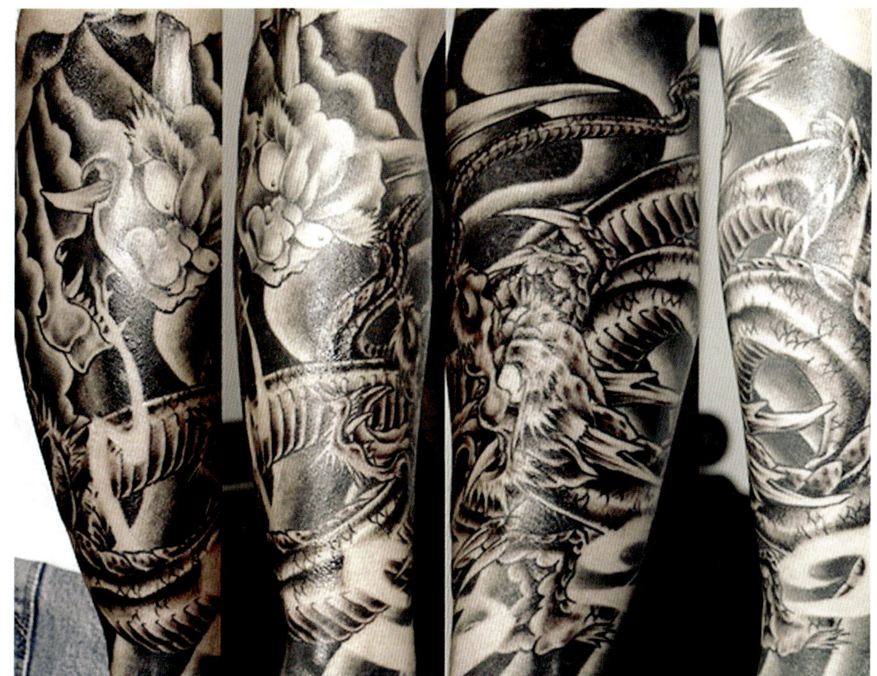

A wind god fights a dragon in this black and grey version of an Asian sleeve by Dave Attonito of Good Clean Fun, Snellville, GA.

to build his or her own needles and machines, completing rigorous drawing exercises, making and combining inks, and eventually tattooing his or her own skin. The difference between the Western and Eastern tattoo apprenticeship, however, is that the Eastern is much more time-consuming, generally taking several more than the 1-3 years that are standard in the United States.

Usually, upon completing the apprenticeship in Japan, the new artist will be given a tattoo name by the master. This new name will most often combine the word "hori," which means "engraver" in Japanese, with a part of the master's name or some other important word. If you become familiar with tattoo artists who are popular in the industry today, you will likely hear names like Horiyoshi or Horitaka when you read about international artists, and you can tell by the "hori" in the name that they were trained traditionally in Japan.

Japanese tattoos (called Irezumi) developed into an intricate modern art during the Edo period, from about 1600-1868, when designs became more complex and tattooing techniques became more advanced. The combined influence of woodblock print designs and the release of the artist Kuniyoshi's 108 Heroes of the Suikoden, which was a collection of illustrations representing Robin Hood-style "noble bandits" that were all covered in intricate tattoos, contributed to this increase in the popularity of tattooing. The designs we think of as Japanese or Asian style have their roots in this tradition.

These tattoos were grand compositions covering the entire body, often leaving only the hands, feet, and head uncovered.

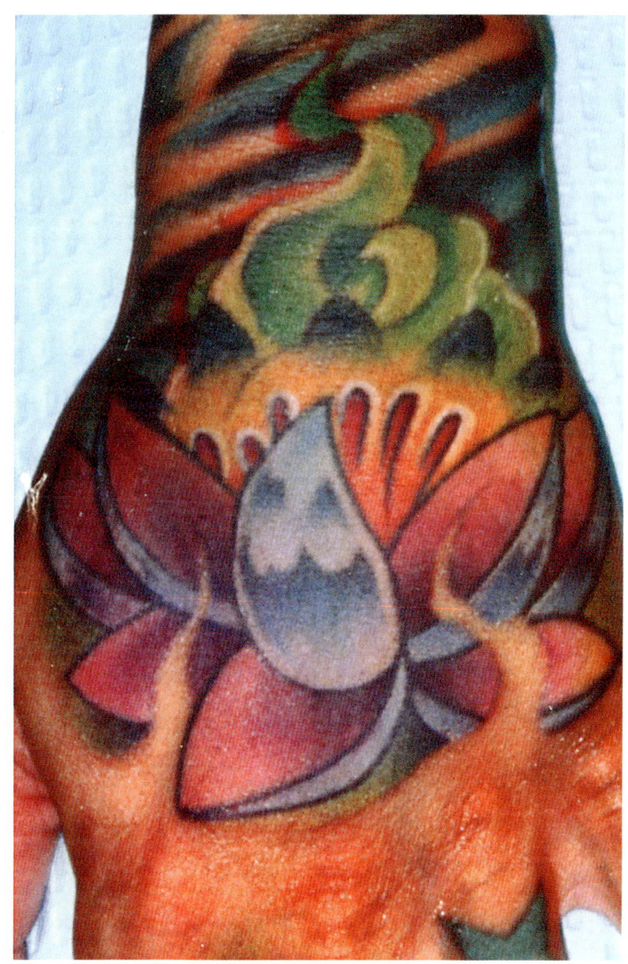

Sarah Peacock of Artfuel in Wilmington, NC, offers this delicate, modern interpretation of the lotus flower.

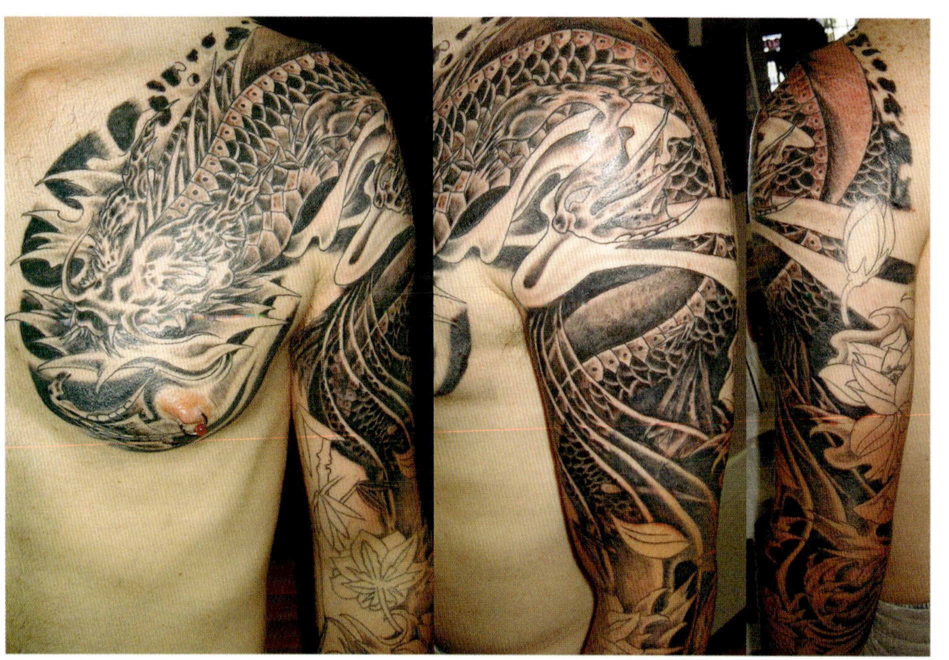

Derek Dufresne's vision of a traditional Japanese half-sleeve using black and grey.

Designs were detailed, and therefore they are expensive and require a lot of time. The commitment to planning the art required to complete these large-scale pieces takes a highly skilled artist, which explains why many of the most extraordinarily talented tattooists work in this style.

Japanese tattoos are characterized by themes such as the koi fish, the Buddha, geishas, samurais and other heroes, figures from Japanese myth, beautiful flowers, black finger waves representing water,

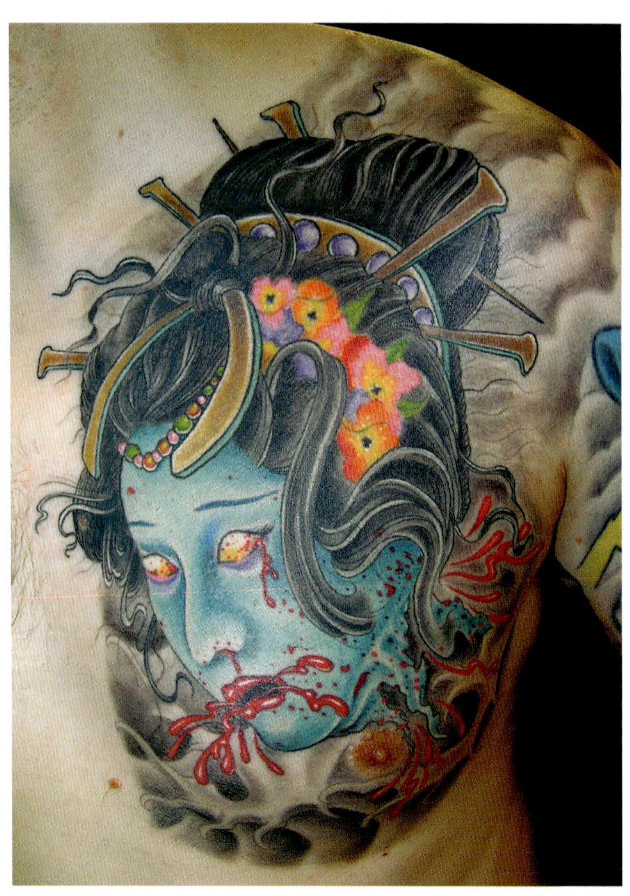

The severed head of a geisha has become a popular image for tattoos in recent years. All Or Nothing's Brandon Bond.

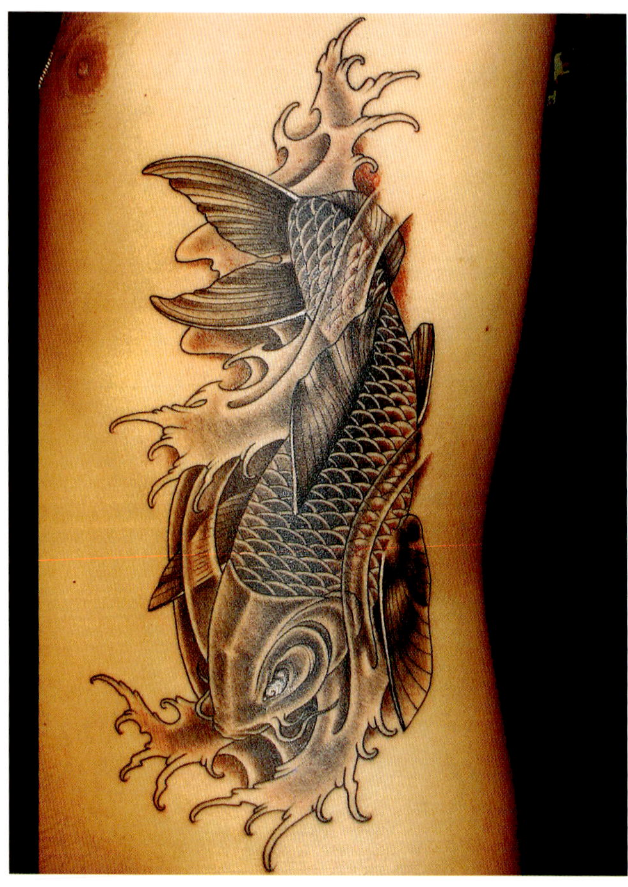

Koi fish with Japanese-style water in black and grey by Federico Ferroni of South Beach Tattoo.

and soft grey shaded wind bars or clouds. The culminating effect of these elaborate compositions is a bold but delicate image, often spanning large areas of the body and complimenting the body's natural shapes and motion.

Many of these images are rooted in myth and rich in symbol. The koi fish, for instance, is revered in Japanese society because it was believed that once a koi advanced past a particular point in the Yellow River, it would magically transform into a dragon. This myth

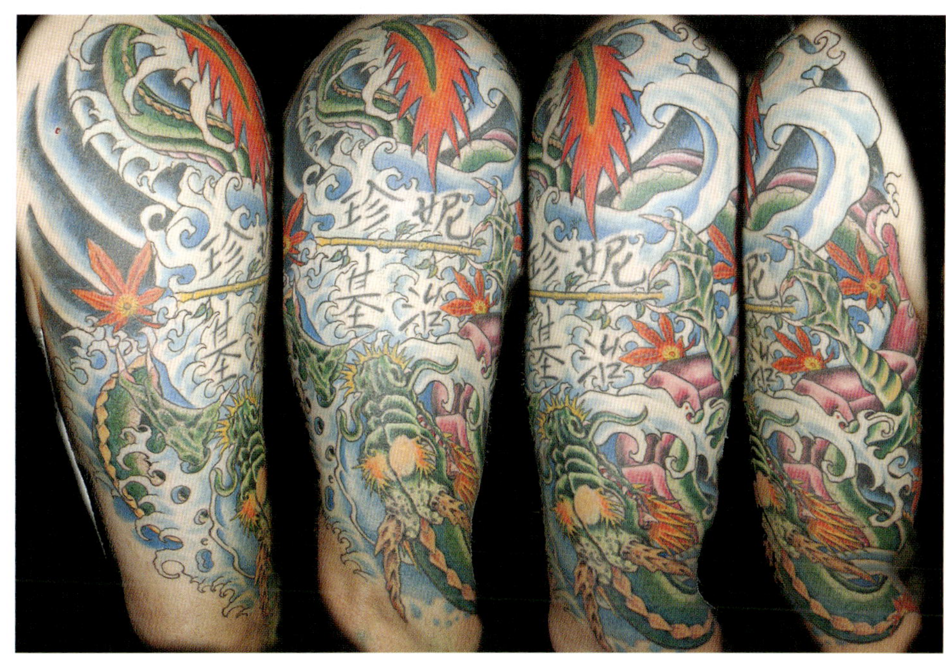

Kanji is also popular as tattoo on its own, and it adds interest to a more complex design when it is incorporated into a larger piece.

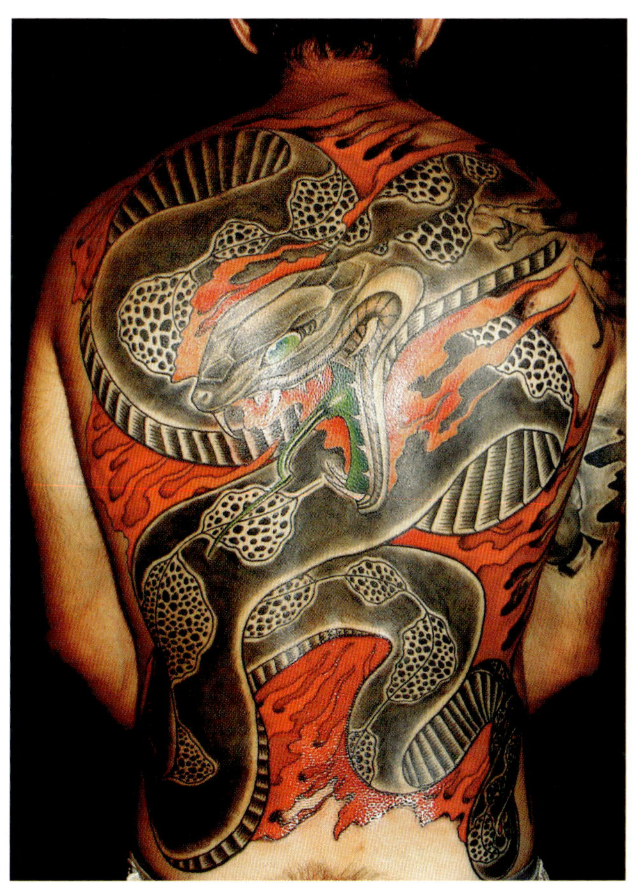

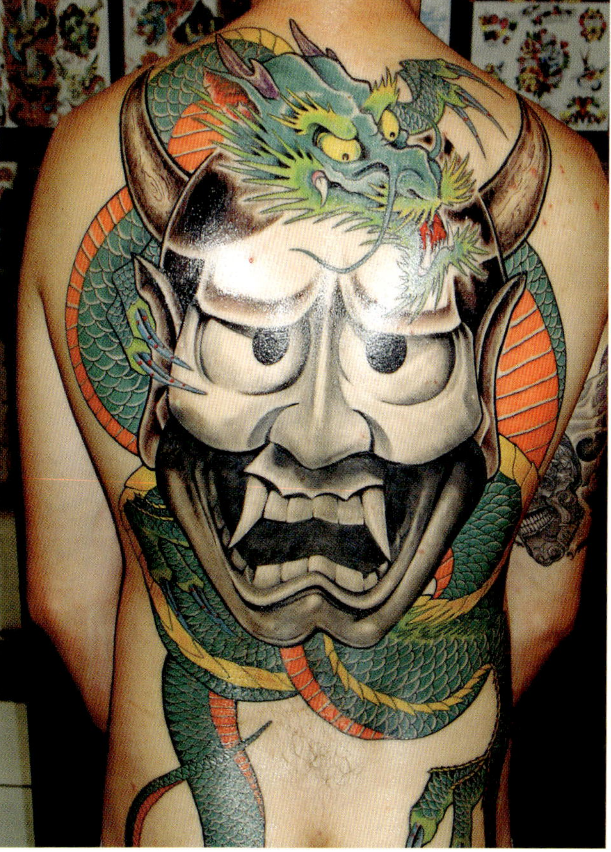

Federico Ferroni of South Beach Tattoo creates a modern, bold interpretation of the traditional Japanese back-piece combining simple elements in an intricate, powerful design.

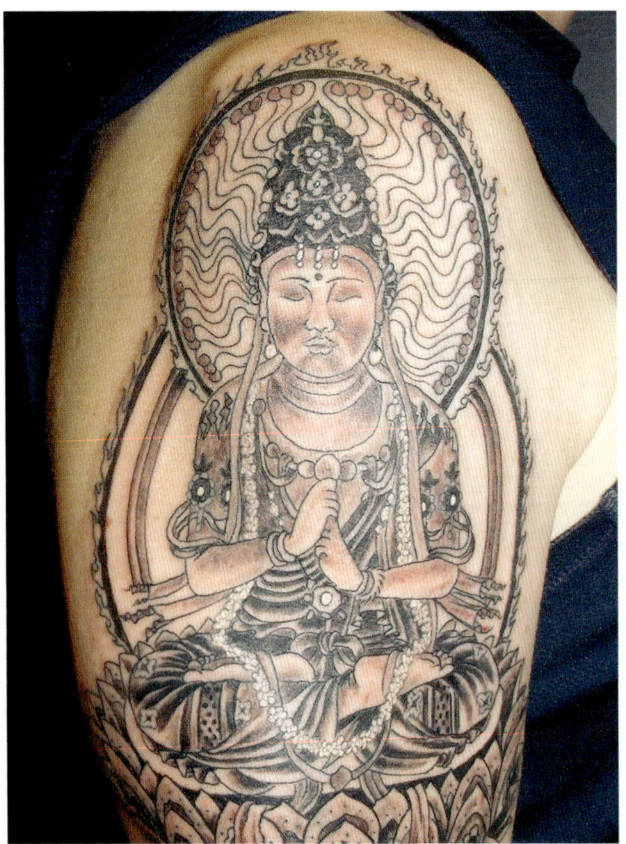

Derek Dufresne's Buddha reads well from a distance, but also features intricate details.

has resulted in the koi being associated with ambition, perseverance, and strength. The Oni masks that are often misrepresented as demons by Westerners are symbolic of wordly passion. The dragon, which is practically omnipresent in Japanese tattoo artwork, is believed to bring good luck to its wearer.

Another popular tattoo theme emerging from Japanese tattoo art is the kanji, the equivalent of western "lettering." Generally tattooed to appear to have been drawn in calligraphy, kanji figures are incorporated with other Japanese images or stand alone. While kanji tattoos can be beautiful, if you do not speak Japanese, make sure you do not get a tattoo with a mistaken meaning! There are several websites, most notably www.hanzismatter.com, that are entirely devoted to making fun of Westerners with kanji tattoos that are either meaningless or have an embarrassing meaning. It's worth the time to check with a native speaker before getting a kanji tattoo.

One tattoo artist specializing in the Japanese style is Derek Dufresne of Fleshworks in Victoria, British Columbia. While he does not work exclusively in the Asian style, he is best known for large-scale, Japanese-influenced pieces. We caught up with him to find out about his attraction to this style and its influence on the West.

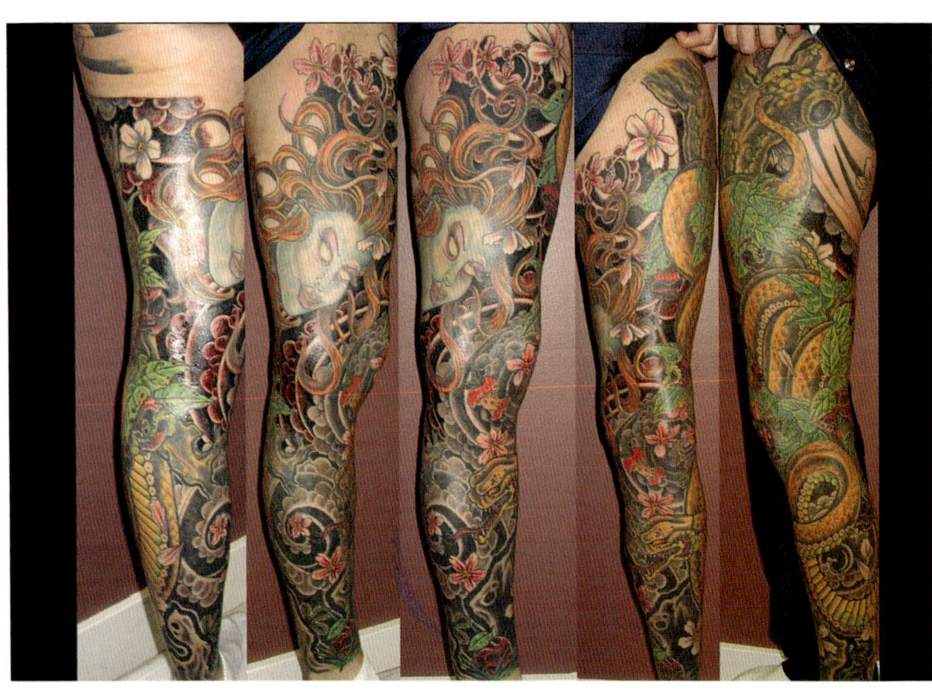

Even when Derek Dufresne's image is not based in Asian myth, the influence of Asian style on his custom artwork is undeniable. The option to design a tattoo with Asian elements is always available, even when the ideas being represented are Western.

Derek Dufresne Q & A

JS: You are an artist primarily known for work in the Japanese style. We were curious about whether or not you always worked in this style or if you have become attracted to it through the years of your career. What attracted you to the Asian style originally?

Derek: I've always been drawn to that style artwork and tattooing. There really is nothing sweeter, in my opinion, than a well-planned out, well-executed Asian sleeve or back-piece, or ultimately, body suit. The way the designs flow with the body, the use of negative space…the flowing waters and finger waves, dragons, foo dogs, ghouls, koi, big crazy flowers…I don't know, I just love drawing these things with a little bit of my own take on them, and I think they make the best tattoo designs.

JS: What do you think makes Asian style work so popular today, even in Western countries?

Derek: It's a timeless tattoo style. These images won't make for a trendy tattoo. It can be worked in or around any existing work quite easily. Because of its flowing coverage, simple designs, and unisex subject matter, Japanese tattoo designs are a style that appeals to all kinds of people.

JS: So even though you get all kinds of people, not everyone wants Asian work. Have you noticed what kinds of people are most likely to get a Japanese piece?

Derek: Serious collectors. Working almost totally by appointment has weeded out the impulse clients for me—you know, the ones who are just walking by and decide on the spur of the moment that it would be cool to get a new tattoo. My studio is a few blocks out of the busy downtown touristy area, so that also helps cut down on the quick, trendy tattoos you see in most street shops.

JS: So you think that folks come to you for the Japanese-style stuff are committed and interested in having a real piece of art, not just a trendy accessory?

Derek: A tattoo is a lifetime commitment. There are so many tattoo artists out there right now that it is really important to do your research as a collector.

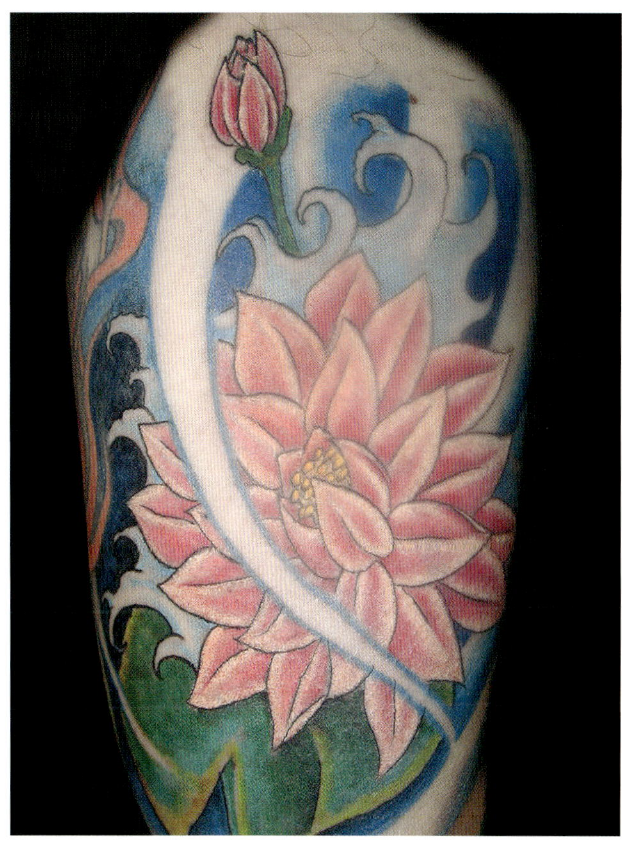

Peony by Brandon Bond, All Or Nothing, Atlanta, GA. Notice the use of Japanese-style water in the background, which further contributes to the Japanese milieu.

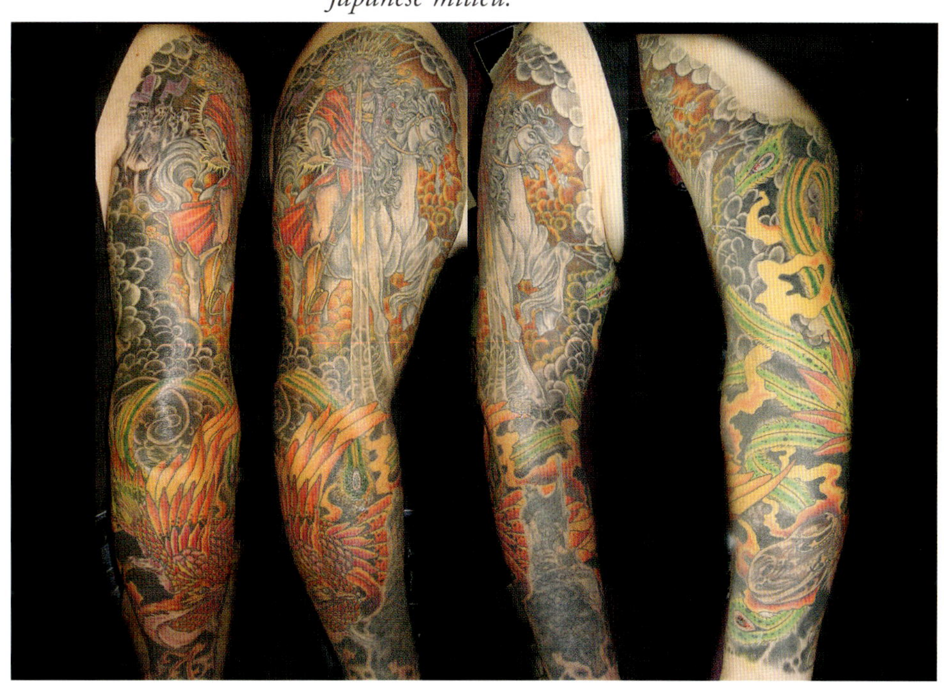

Derek Dufresne.

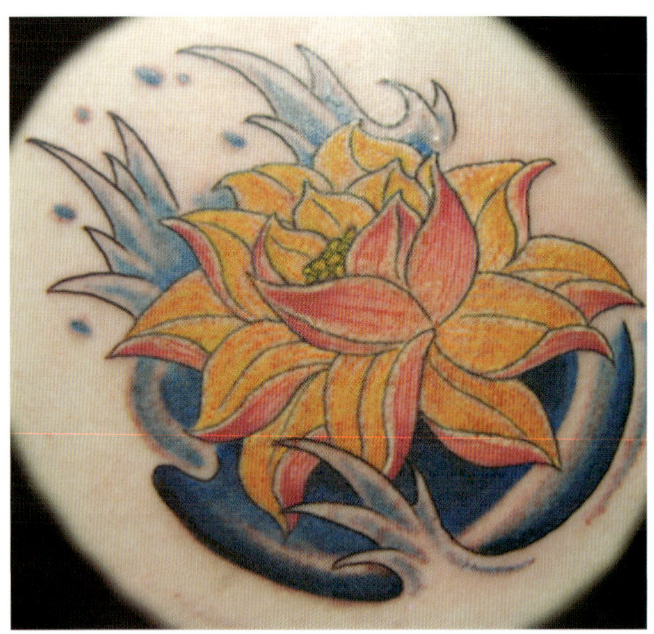

The lotus is a popular image in Asian work, both in compositions and on its own.

You've got to look at portfolios and make sure the work is top quality and it is in the style you are interested in getting. My clients are good about doing that…by the time they find me and get to my shop and wait for their appointment, they are usually pretty clear on what they want.

JS: Because we're showing our readers the process behind the tattoos, we're interested in hearing a little about what it's like working with you on a piece. What's your design process like, from beginning to end?

Derek: Usually, I set up a consultation appointment where we sit down and discuss what they want, where they want it, color or black and grey, and other general preferences. We just kind of bounce some ideas around. I've learned through the years that there is nothing worse than spending hours and hours drawing, and then the client comes back to the shop to have a look at what you've come up with, and he hates it. Usually I draw up a rough idea of what I think they want

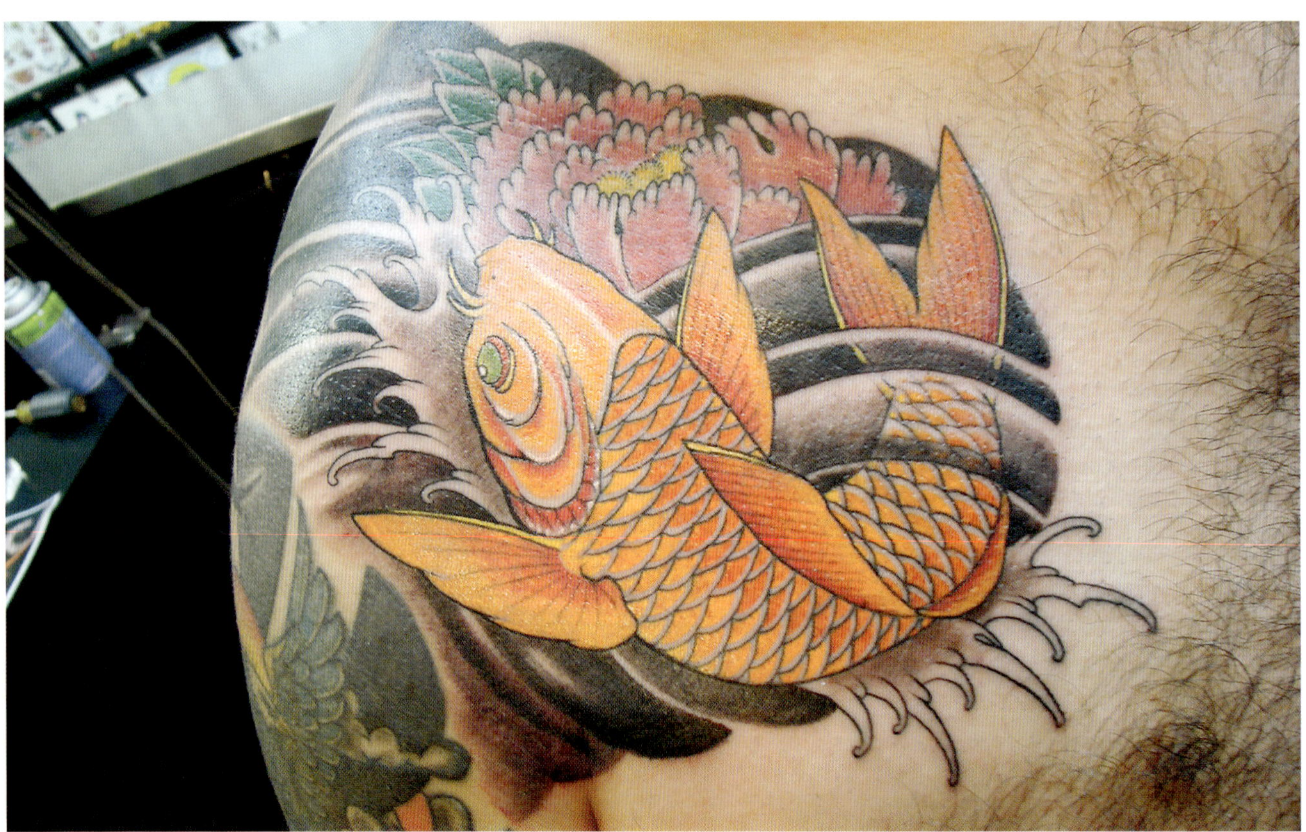

Koi fish by Federico Ferroni.

and have them come look at that first. From there, we make any required changes, and I work up the finished drawing. It saves me a lot of time and saves my clients the disappointment of not getting it right the first time.

Whenever possible, I try to look at real life things for reference for a piece. If there's a koi fish, flowers, birds, snakes, or anything from nature, I look to photographs to get ideas for how to make the images realistic while still incorporating elements of the Asian style my clients expect. Placement on the body is also very important, generally, but especially with a Japanese-style piece. Making sure the piece is going to flow with the person's muscle and body structure to me is almost as important as the artwork itself. Also, the design needs to be readable from a distance. If it's too busy, I try to "simple it up" a little. Less is more with Asian stuff, in my opinion. These designs are beautiful, and they are even more beautiful if they are put on big and bold and simple.

* * *

If you are interested in heavy coverage such as a backpiece, full sleeves, or even an entire body suit, the dynamic, bold compositions of Japanese-style work might be right for you. There is an incredible wealth of mythology, art, and other traditions to pull from in designing your piece, which makes this style to be one of the most diverse traditions. Additionally, the juxtaposition of bold colors with softer elements like wind or large, dynamic elements like dragons with delicate images like cherry blossoms makes for a visually pleasing, unique tattoo.

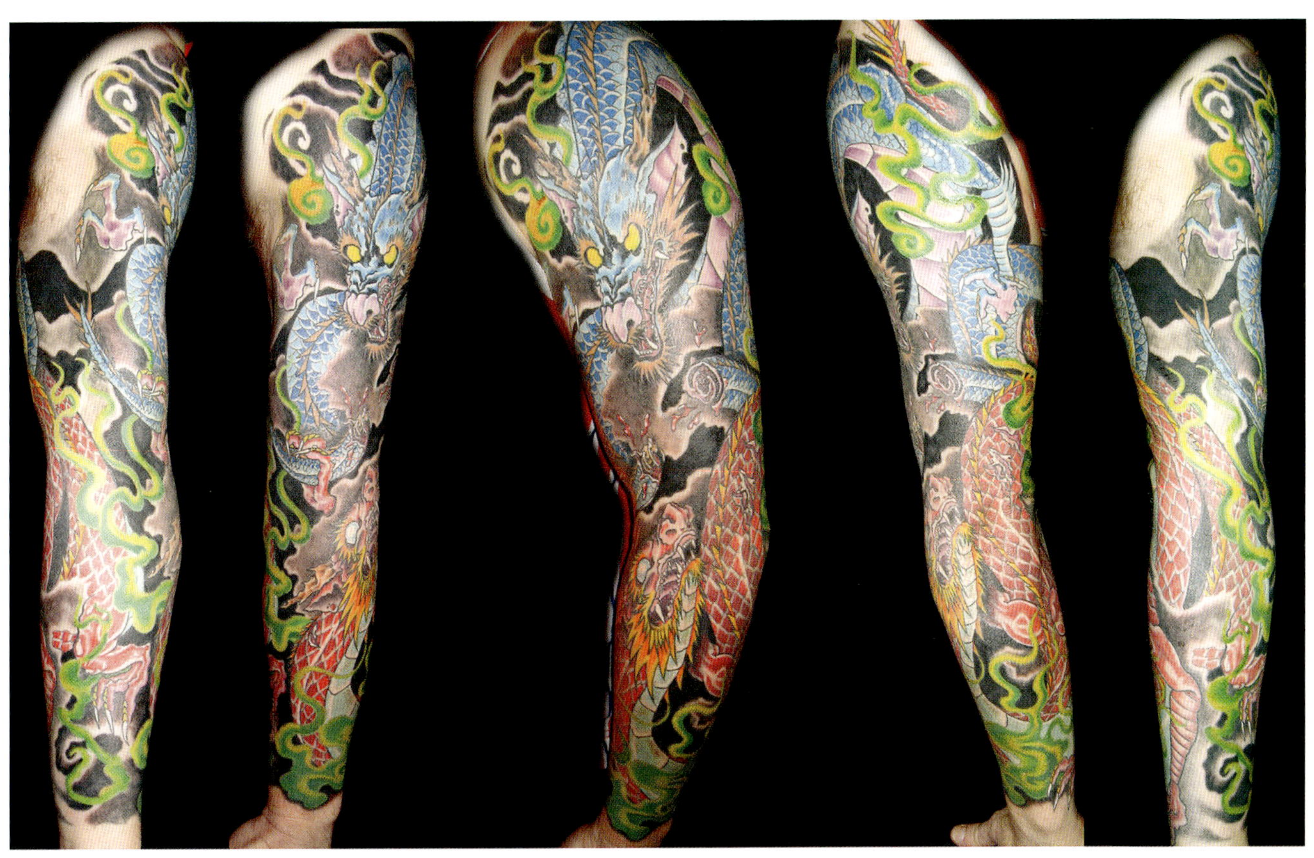

Chapter Five

New School

Fun, Young, and Funky

From bobble-head figures to bubbly pin-ups, New School style tattoos are some of the most fun designs to have emerged from tattoo artistry. While the Traditional American and Asian styles we have covered so far have long, rich traditions and heavy symbolic meanings, New School artwork is often lighter, younger, funkier, and more humorous than these older styles.

New School tattooing is a relatively young style. In fact, it is so new that the term "New School" can sometimes be a bit ambiguous or misleading. It is often applied to many different kinds

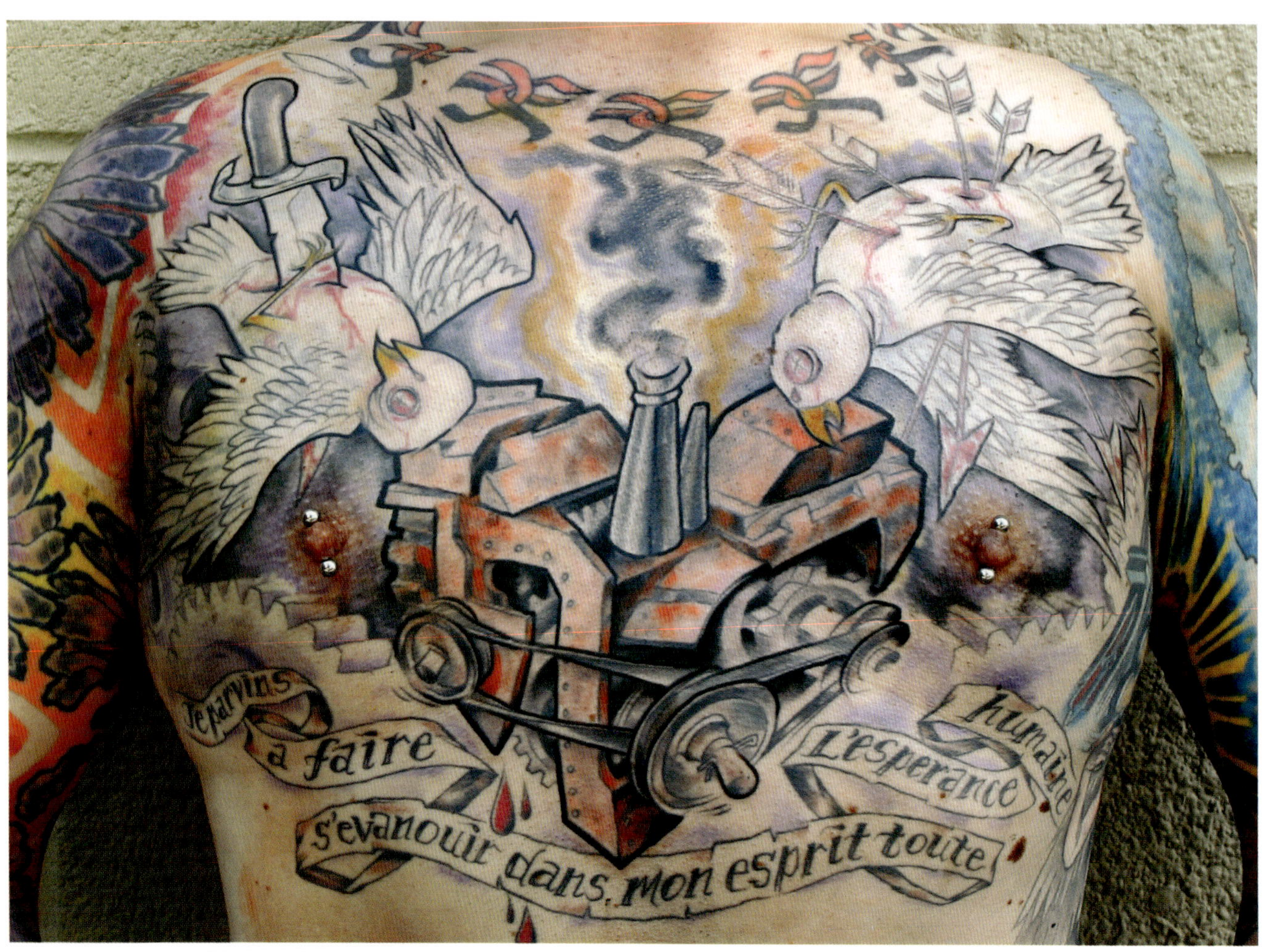

Mark Heggie, Big Top, Utica, MI.

of tattoos, which can make defining exactly what comprises a "New School" tattoo somewhat difficult. After the fine line movement in tattooing reached its zenith in the 1980s, tattooists were looking for new approaches and techniques to challenge themselves and to push the boundaries of tattoo art and to expand their vision of what is possible in a tattoo in an entirely new direction. Artists began producing a different kind of work—using a new palette of bright and funky colors and twists on the traditional tattoo imagery to produce innovative designs that enlivened the indelible art with original, exciting changes. The culminating style of art is hip, fresh, and fun, and although some of its popularity has waned, its witty imagery and wild color work continue to make this a style of tattoo art that many collectors seek out and that many artists enjoy tattooing.

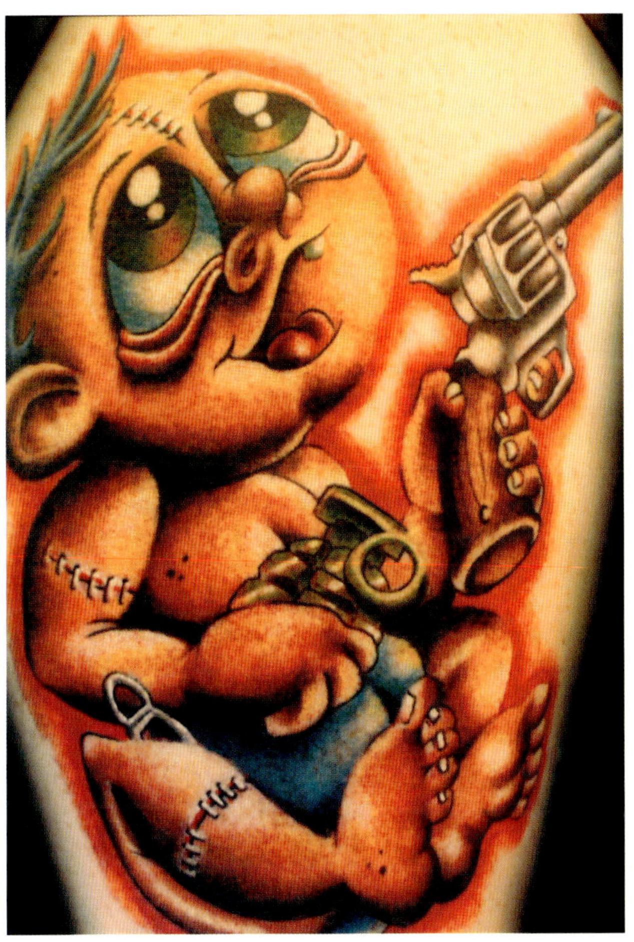

New School art is known for being bold and colorful, and Josh Woods is particularly known as a master of this kind of color work.

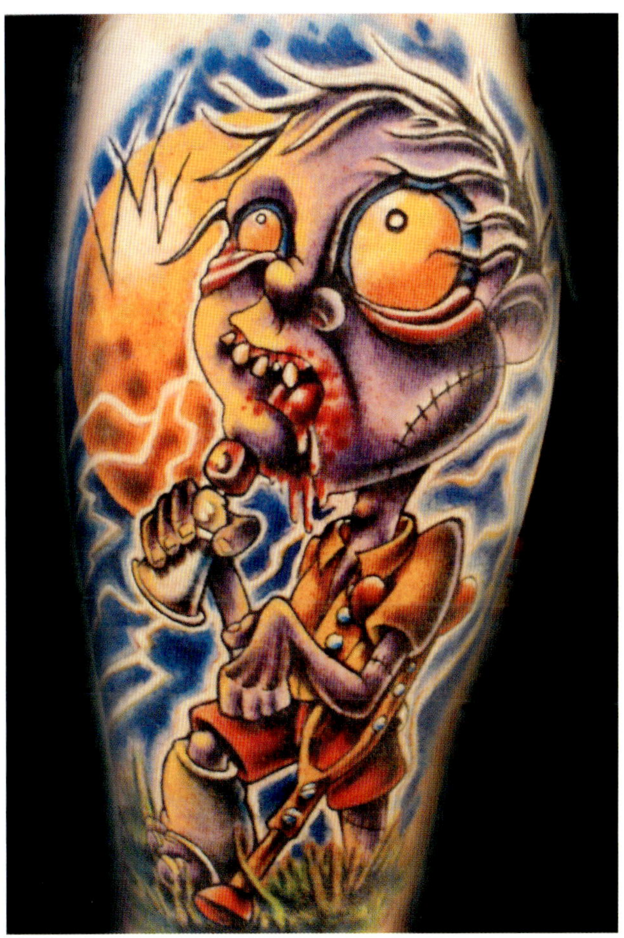

Josh Woods.

One of the characteristics that defines a New School tattoo is that there is often an ironic twist in the imagery that artists select for their designs. Zombies are a popular theme in this style of artwork, but these little unholy, undead creatures are not presented as horrific. Generally, they are cute, bubbly, boldly colored, and have goofy, childlike expressions on their faces. In the work of Jason Ackerman of Lucky 7 in Boca Raton, Florida, for example, the figures are often zombie children, and they are usually engaged in some less than horrific activity, such as the two figures in the disco house party zombie piece where the moldering corpses are sillier than they are scary. Other common New School designs include children doing something distinctly un-childlike, such as hiding bloody knives behind their backs. One instance of this theme is in Jason Ackerman's clever blue devil girl. She is crying, as if she is sorry for something she has done, and she appears to be holding a human heart and some flowers. In spite of the dark theme, the colors are an ironic mixture of soft pastels and psychedelic pinks and greens. Her eyes are large and soft, and her face is elfish and cute.

The influence of Traditional American tattoo art is everywhere in New School artists' designs. Tattooists often incorporate the bold lines and bright, primary colors that mark traditional American style work or reference the traditional American heritage by using traditional motifs with a New School twist. The anchor is a hallmark image in Traditional American tattooing, paying homage to the seafaring founders of the art. One example of a New School re-creation of this theme is Kirk Shepherd's updated interpretation of an anchor with bubbly, cartoony forms. We have also seen many examples in the Traditional American chapter of the pin-up or profile image of a woman's face, and this theme is also popular for New School revisions. One example is Brandon Bond's buxom exaggeration of a classic pin-up, which he rendered with heightened color, increased three-dimensionality, and unusual perspective. The barn swallow is another theme that appears regularly in Traditional American tattoo art, and New School artists often use the Traditional bird as their reference for their pieces, as in John Wayne's barn swallow chest piece featuring an angelic blue bird and a demonic red bird clashing around a New School version of the Traditional nautical star. Skulls and daggers appear everywhere in Traditional American tattoos, but in Bryce Stucke's interpretation of a

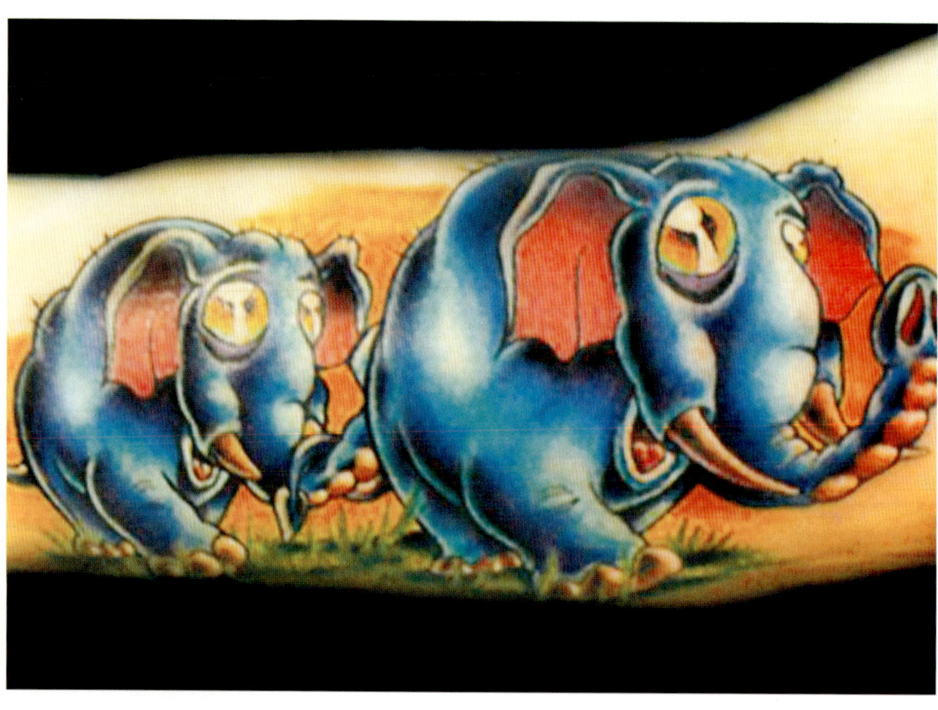

Josh Woods, All Or Nothing, Atlanta, GA.

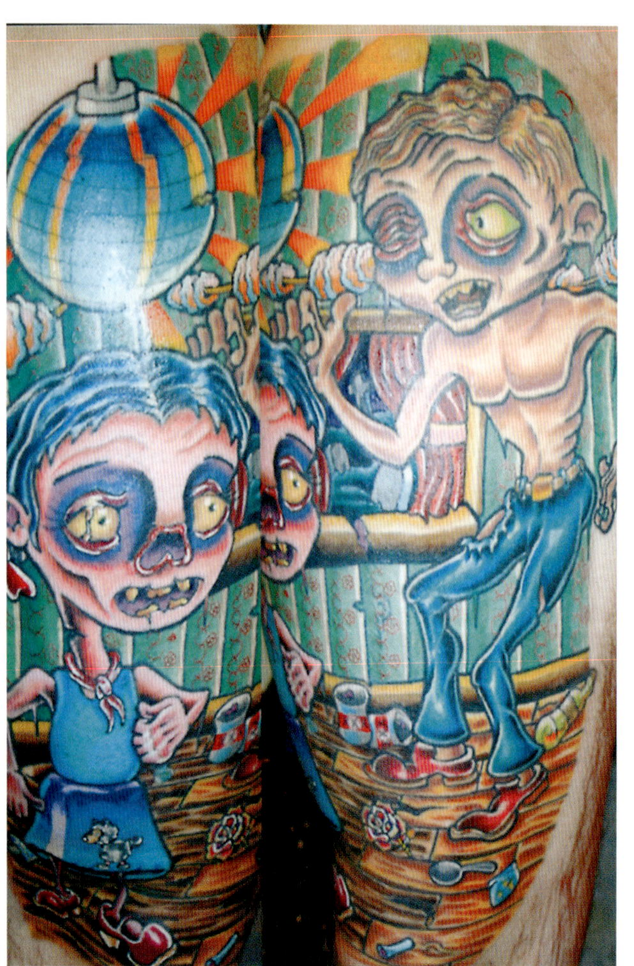

Jason Ackerman, Lucky 7, Boca Raton, FL.

skull and dagger, for instance, he applies the tweaked perspective and bright colors that are common in New School art to the Traditional American themes. The bow in the skull's hair transforms the heavy symbol of mortality into a clever, morbidly funny image of a little girl's skull, beautifully preserving the symbolism that makes Traditional American artwork so powerful while lightening up the tone a bit with New School attitude.

These New School revisions of Traditional American artwork breathe new life into the old imagery, keeping it fresh and appealing to new generations of tattoo collectors while maintaining the integrity of the symbolism inherent in the Traditional artwork. This interaction between the old art and the new attitude is perhaps the greatest strength of New School artistry, as it reflects a

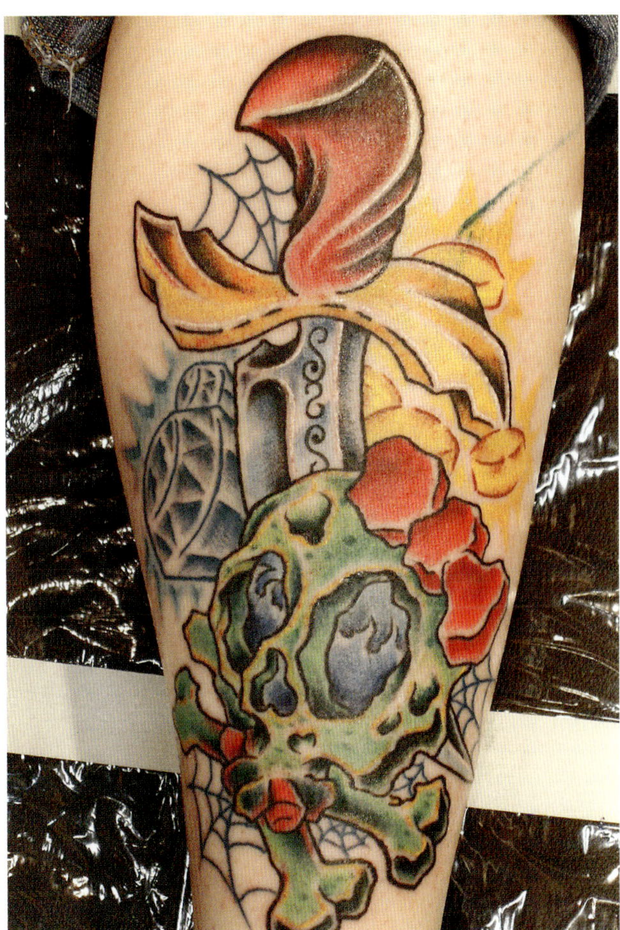

Bryce Stucke, Body Armor, Clearfield, PA.

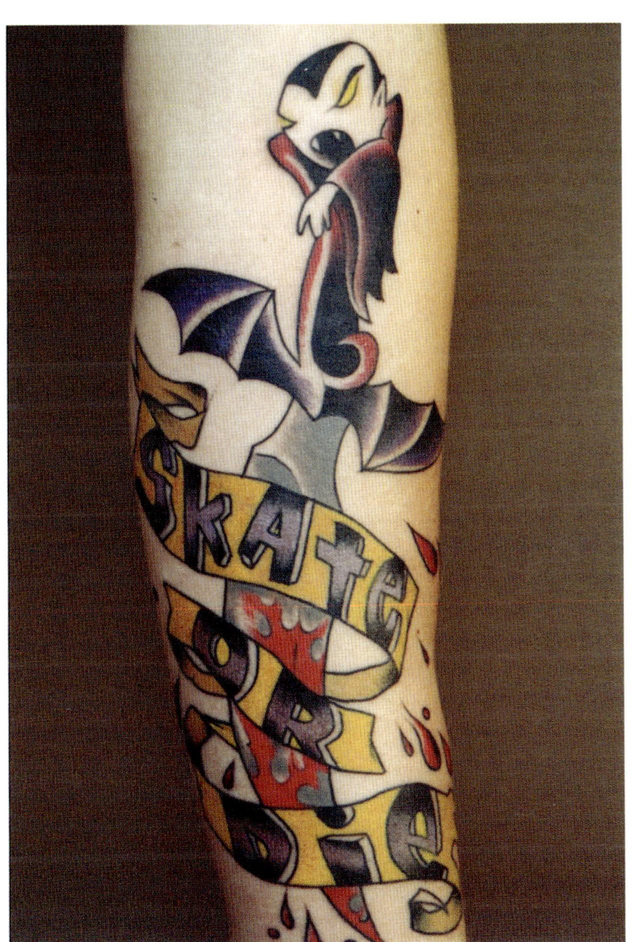

Mark Heggie, Big Top, Utica, MI.

modern mindset with respect to the past. New School artists pay homage to their predecessors without being slaves to the rules of the traditional style. In this way, New School artists preserve all that is powerful and symbolic about tattooing's past by repackaging it in a manner that will appeal to a wider audience.

Another significant influence on New School style is graffiti art. As the graffiti art movement reached its peak in the early 80s, the bright color palette and the experimental use of perspective of the graffiti style spilled over into tattoo designs, and its influence can still be seen in both the subject matter and style of New School art. Some of this influence is apparent in the lettering in Mark Heggie's New School version of the dagger with the words "Skate Or Die," which also expresses a sentiment that is drenched in New School attitude.

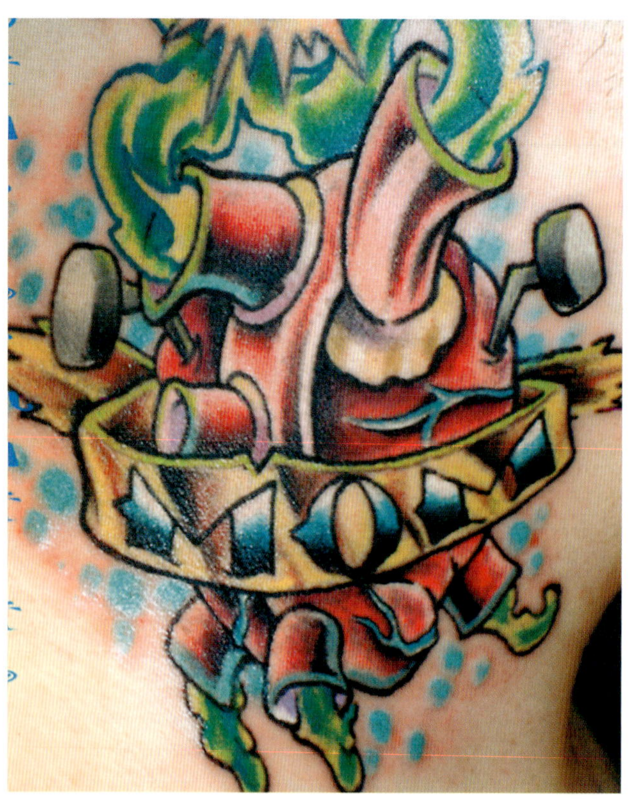

Jason Ackerman, Lucky 7, Boca Raton, FL.

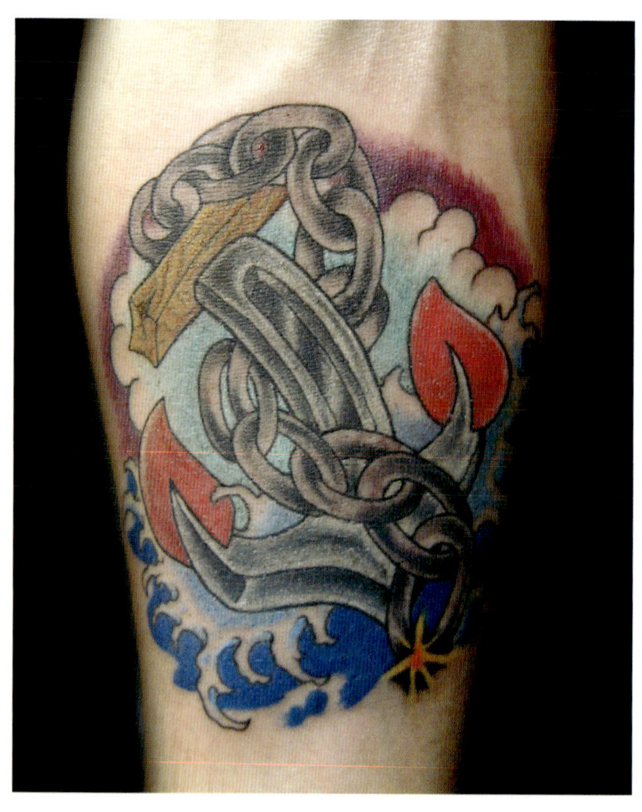

Kirk Shepherd, Fleshworks, Victoria, British Columbia.

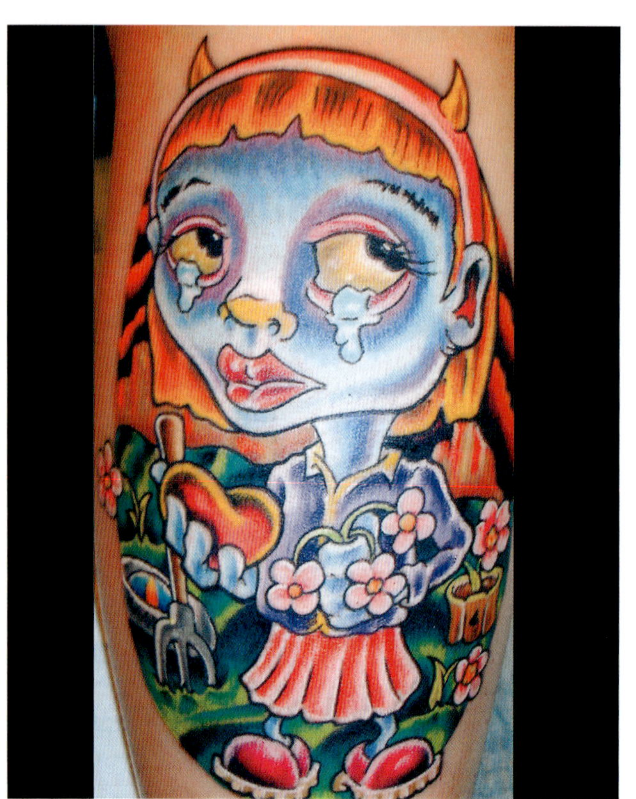

Jason Ackerman, Lucky 7, Boca Raton, FL.

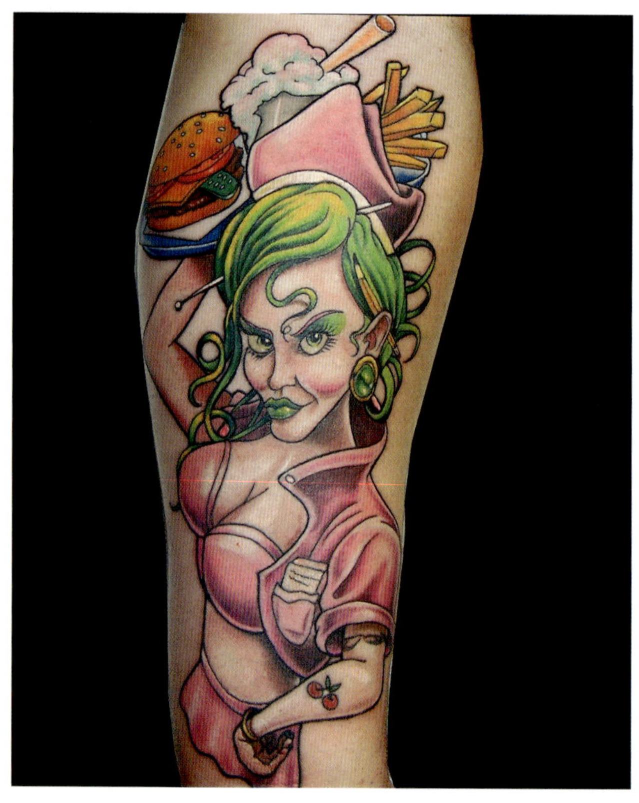

John Wayne, Beesting, Belle River, Canada.

One of the artists on the forefront of the New School tattoo movement today is Josh Woods. He is a young artist who has not been in the industry for as long as many of the other artists we have met; however, his apparent talent belies his short career, and his skills are particularly strong in his New School artwork. Josh works at All Or Nothing Tattoo in Atlanta, Georgia, and we caught up with him to find out more about his ideas on the style, his clients, and his impressions on the state of the art today.

Josh Woods Q&A

JS: As your career develops, you are becoming more and more diverse as an artist, but early on, your portfolio was chock full of New School art. What attracted you to New School artwork originally?

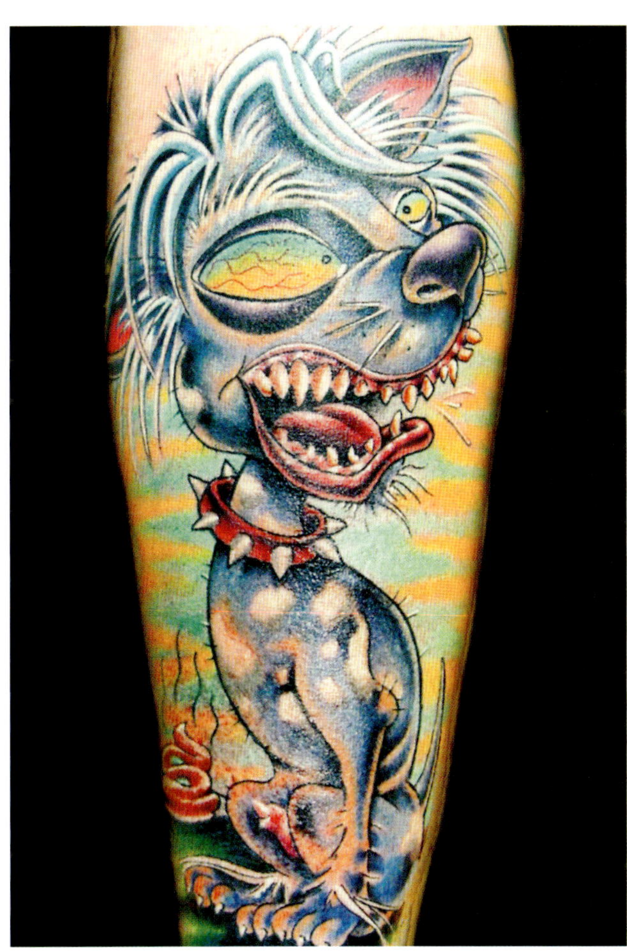

Josh Woods, All Or Nothing, Atlanta, GA.

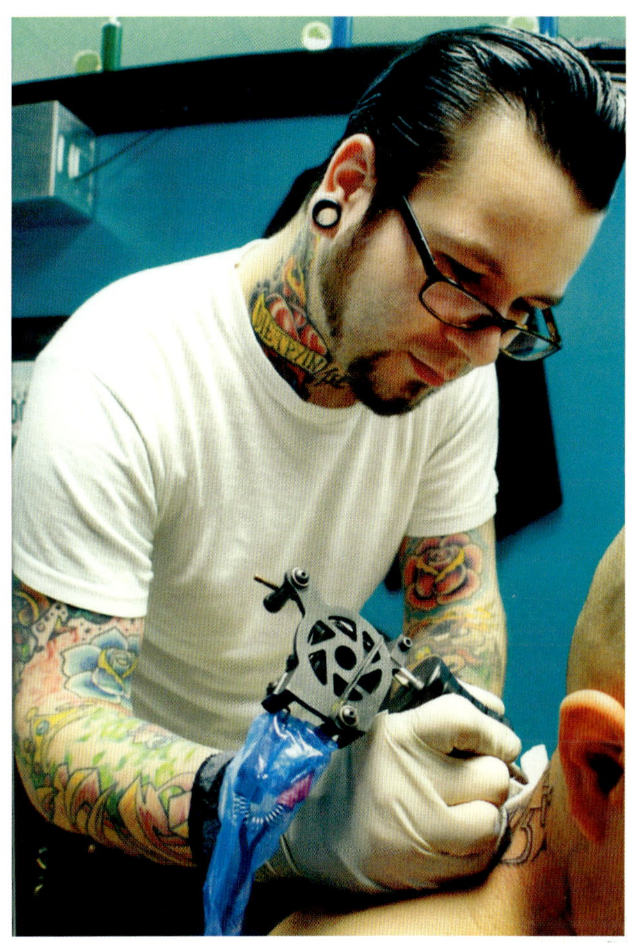

Josh Woods at work.

Josh: I really was always into New School art, even before I started tattooing. My art teachers in high school always used to get frustrated with me because my "cartoonish" style was always more important to me than realistic drawings. I just fell in love with that style at the time, and it followed me into my tattoo career.

JS: Some New School tattooists were also a part of the graffiti scene, and their interest in that style of artwork spilled over into their tattooing. Were you interested in graffiti, or were you drawn to this style for other reasons?

Josh: I never was. To be honest, I've never even tried my hand at graffiti. I've always been very interested in it, but I never found the right opportunity or a location where I could try it out legally. I never had friends who did it or got involved otherwise, and I guess I've just stuck with drawing

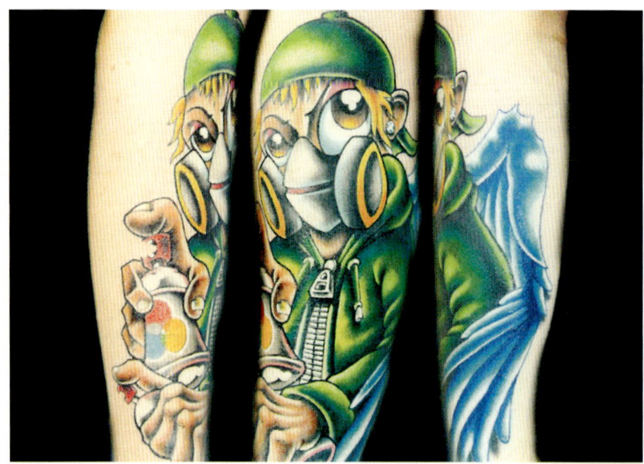

Here Josh Woods references graffiti's influence on New School style tattoo art.

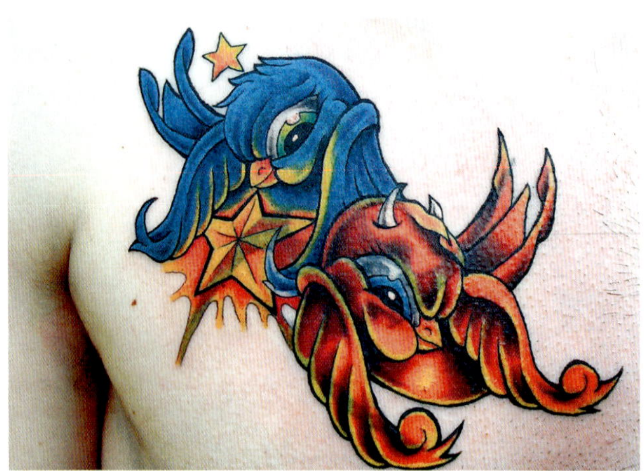

John Wayne's New School take on traditional birds.

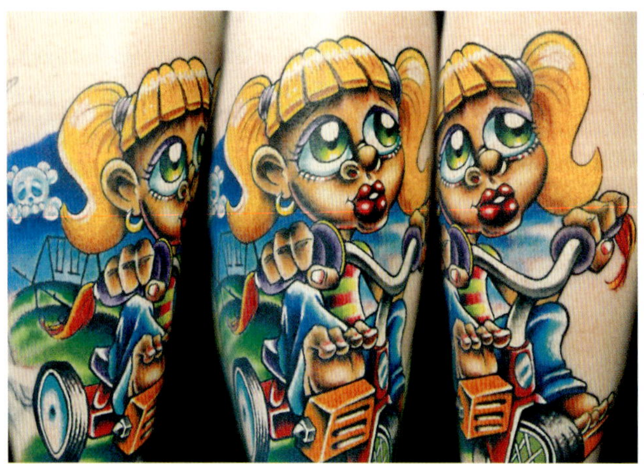

New School art often recreates or reinvents the standard tattoo traditions. In this piece, for instance, Josh Woods presents a cartoon-version of a little girl instead of the classic, sexy tattoo pin-up.

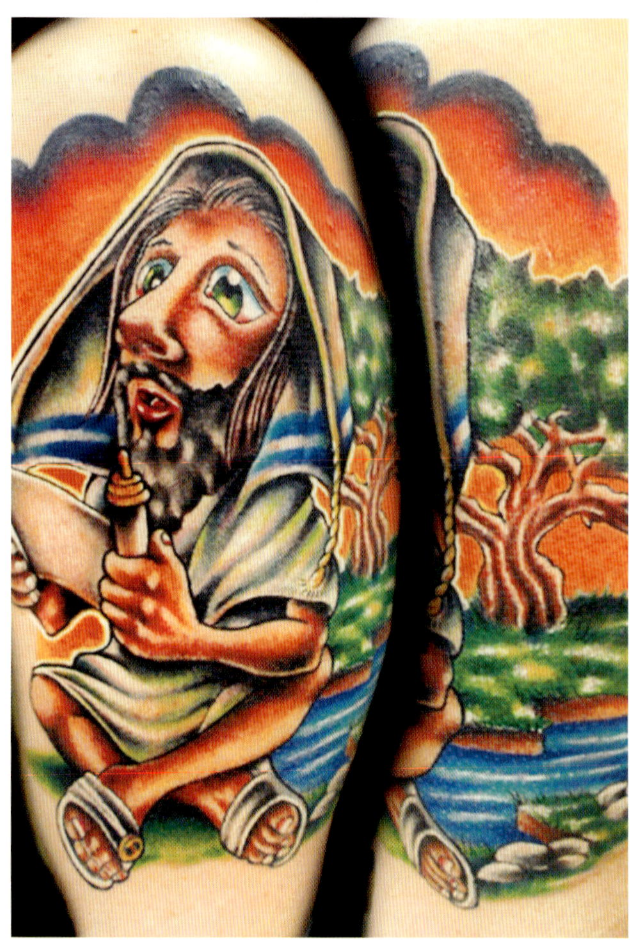

Josh Woods, All Or Nothing, Atlanta, GA.

graffiti on paper. I still think of trying it, but I am always so damn busy with other stuff that I find it hard to start a new medium. I suppose someday, though!

JS: So it was mostly through tattooing that you became connected with the style?

Josh: Yeah. When I became a tattooist, I was able to find a whole new world of amazing artists, and that's when I learned the term "New School." Like I said, I'd been drawing cartoony-style figures since high school, but tattooing put a label on it for me. By just looking through magazines and watching artists working in this style at tattoo conventions, I have been influenced to experiment with and create my own ideas for this style of art. The inspiration I've gotten from the tattoo world has brought my artwork to a whole new level.

JS: I've noticed that you've been doing a little work outside of the New School style lately, testing out photorealism. What has made you want to try new stuff?

Josh: Well…honestly, at first I was just sick and tired of seeing every award at every tattoo convention going to the realism pieces. I felt like I was seeing nothing but photorealism everywhere in the industry. It really is like the new black! Hah!

I realized, though, that I was being immature and lazy. I began to accept the fact that I was never going to get better by hiding in a closet, scared of the rest of the world, while all the artists around me flourished in the new style. After figuring that out, I learned to appreciate every aspect of the art, utilizing as many styles as I could possibly take on. This adjustment in my attitude has helped my artwork as well as my career to grow immensely.

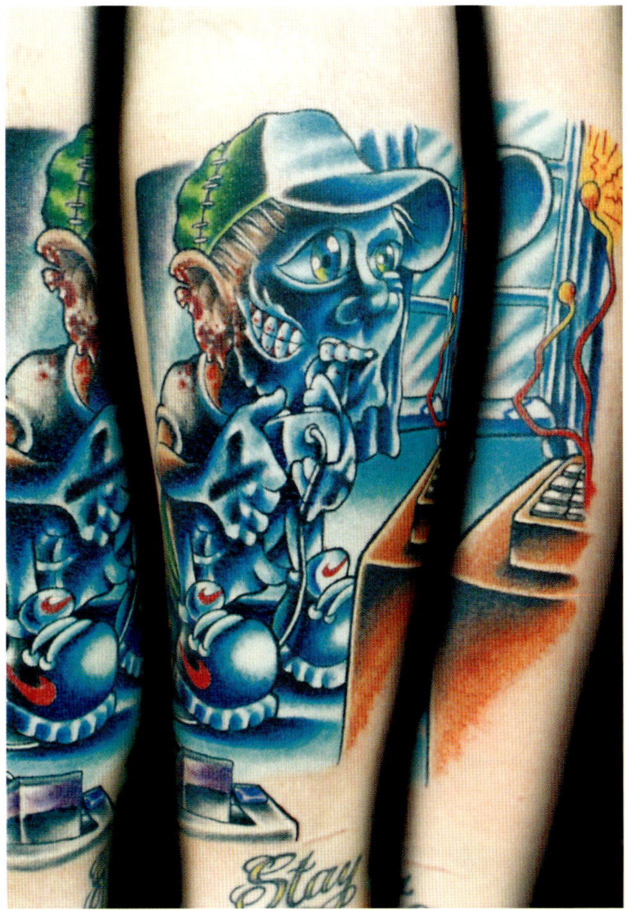

Josh Woods.

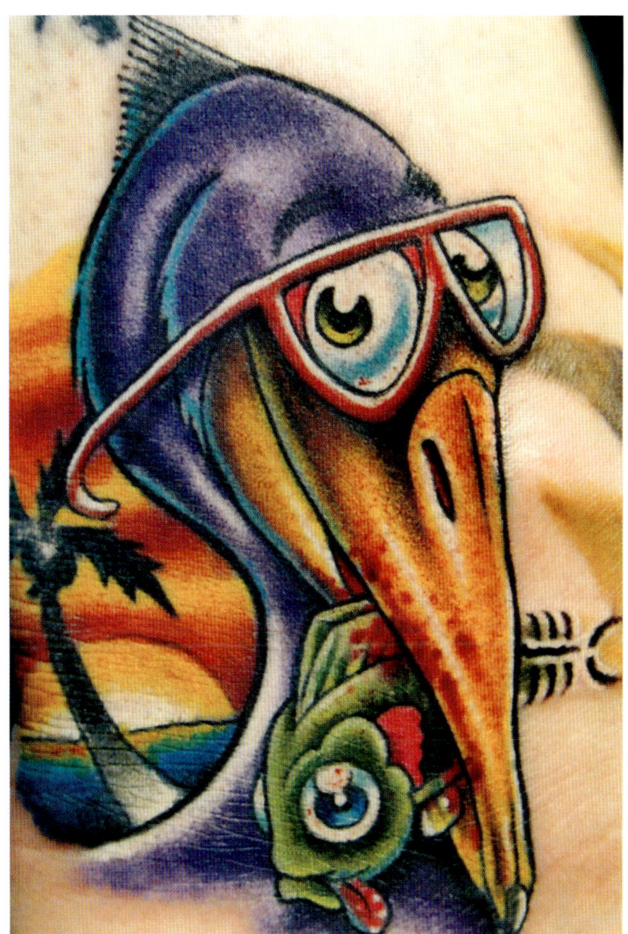

Josh Woods.

Moving to Atlanta and working at All Or Nothing with amazing artists has also helped me with my learning process, and that has helped me grow into doing photorealism. I share a booth with Sean Herman, and we are constantly pushing each other to improve. If we think we got one thing down, we experiment with another. Sean's an amazing person and friend, and we love traveling to conventions together and doing guest spots all over the country. We both enjoy meeting other great artists that help us learn even more.

JS: So even though New School style isn't as popular as photorealism, people still like it. You've still got a following of clients who are interested in your New School stuff. What do you think accounts for its continuing popularity?

Josh: Yeah, it is not huge right now, but it's a style that will always be liked by many. I think it's

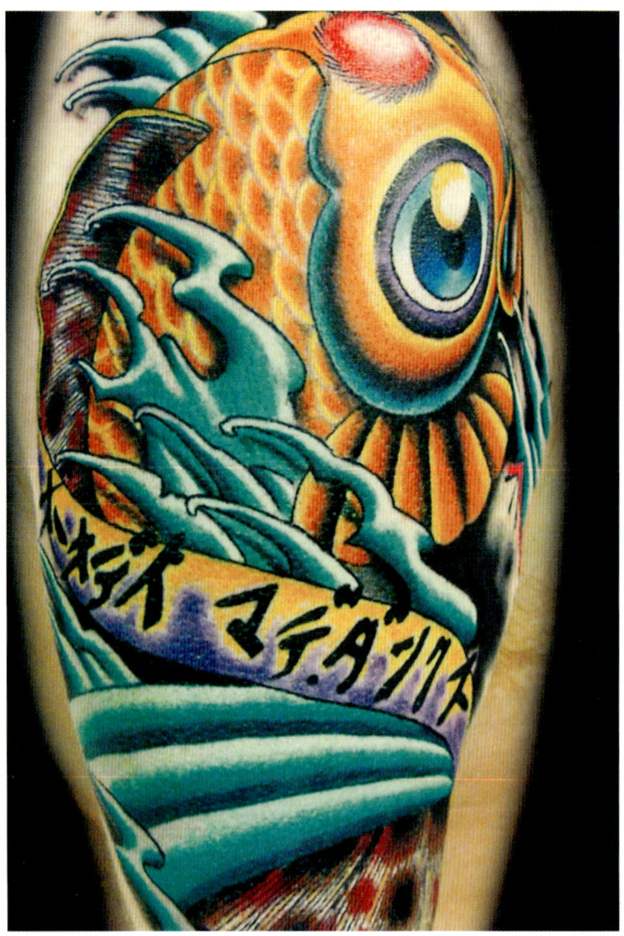

A New School recreation of a traditional Asian standard, the koi.

because of all the bright colors, the animation, the composition and proportions, and also the use of black and color blends. Mainly, I think New School is a gateway to all different types of individuals. There is so much you can do with it and so many different categories to choose from that most people can find a way to relate to it...funny, serious, bold, light, dark...you name it, you can do it with a New School tattoo!

JS: What kinds of clients are most attracted to your work? Have you noticed any patterns?

Josh: I get people of all sorts from all over the world. I get a lot of customers, actually, who fly from all over. Usually, the clients who fly in to be able to get work from me are for New School stuff because that's what I have become known for ever since I broke into the industry. I get clients of all ages and races as well...I just love to tattoo anybody!

JS: And of course, we'd like to know a little bit about your process...like where do you look for reference? How closely do you work with the client? And just generally, what kind of stuff do you consider when you are planning a new piece?

Josh: I almost always use reference when I'm starting a drawing, and usually, I prefer to use a real picture of the subject matter I'm going to be drawing. For example, if the client asks me to draw a dog (a mean dog, a silly dog, whatever), nine times out of ten, I'll look at a picture of a real dog while I'm drawing it or tattooing it. It gives me room to put my own twist on things, plus it allows me to get all of the anatomy and lighting correct. There's nothing wrong with using something that will make your work better as long as you're not downright copying it from someone else's portfolio.

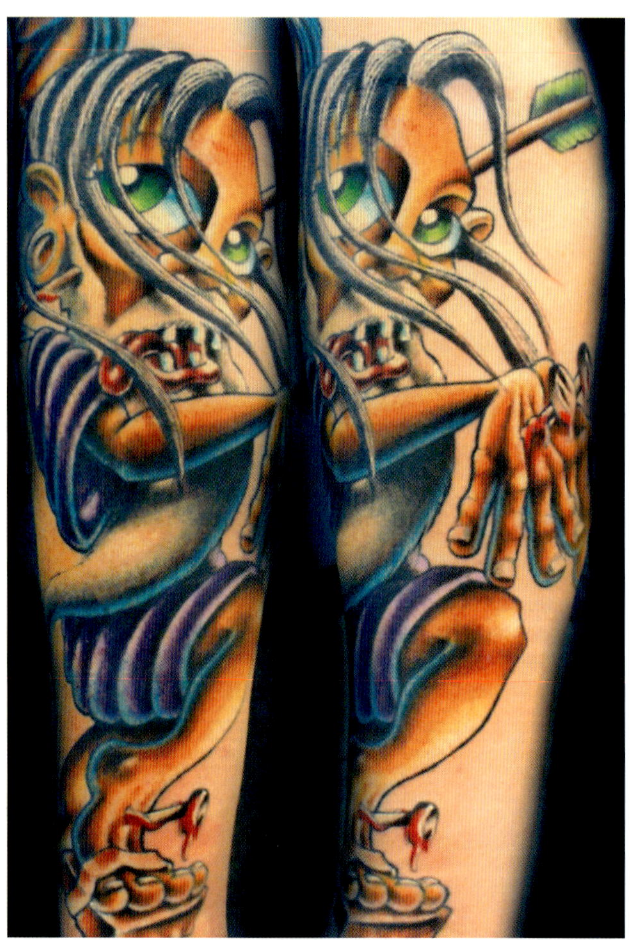

Josh Woods, All Or Nothing, Atlanta, GA.

No one wants to be accused of ripping someone else off. Copying someone's work is just pure laziness, and that is not what I'm about…plus, the work belongs to someone and has specific meaning to that someone. I think that the tattoo industry can only better itself if everyone pushes to make something different instead of recycling the same stuff over and over again!

JS: That makes a lot of sense coming from someone who is kind of a master of New School style, which is all about tweaking, changing perspective, and re-creating old stuff into newer, more exciting images…

Josh: Everyone is influenced by all sorts of art, and these influences show up in the work each artist produces. I let the client tell me or give me whatever he or she wants or needs, from a photo to an internet printout, really anything. However, I think that in the end, most clients are coming to Josh Woods to get a piece of Josh Woods's art. I will not trace somebody else's artwork or do something that is exactly like someone else's tattoo. If that's what the client wants, then there are plenty of artists for that…just not me. I usually never have a problem with my clients, though…they come to me for my style of work, and I give them the best I can offer them. I love my job and clientele because of it. Thanks guys!

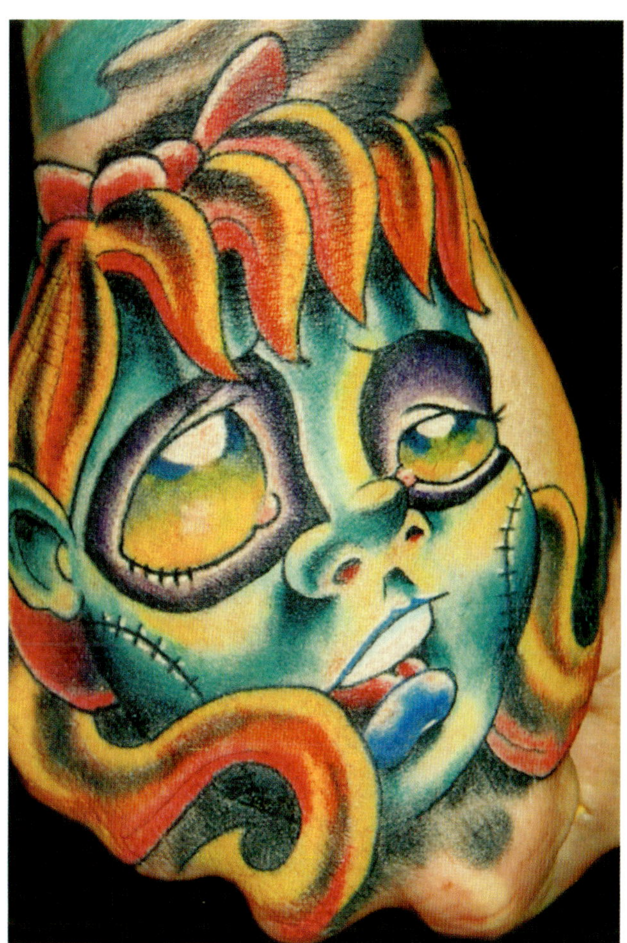

Josh Woods.

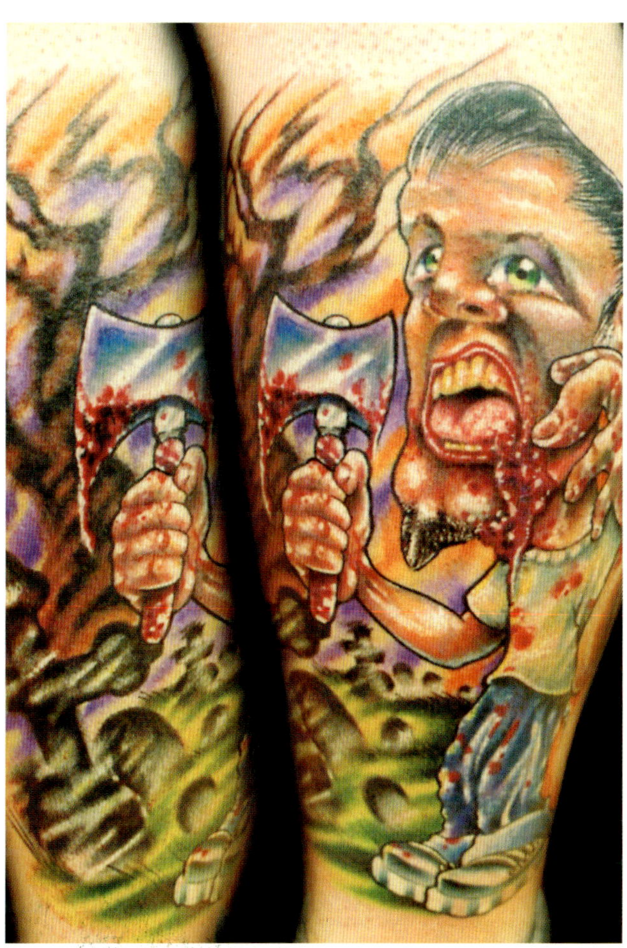

New School art combines elements of horror with cartoon-style design to render disconcerting effects.

JS: One of our goals with this book is to encourage folks always to get unique, custom art. What do you have to say to artists and clients about the importance of creating or seeking out unique work?

Josh: I am always, always giving it my all. I try to put together the best piece of custom art that I possibly can, every time. If you feel that something isn't right, either as the artist or the client,

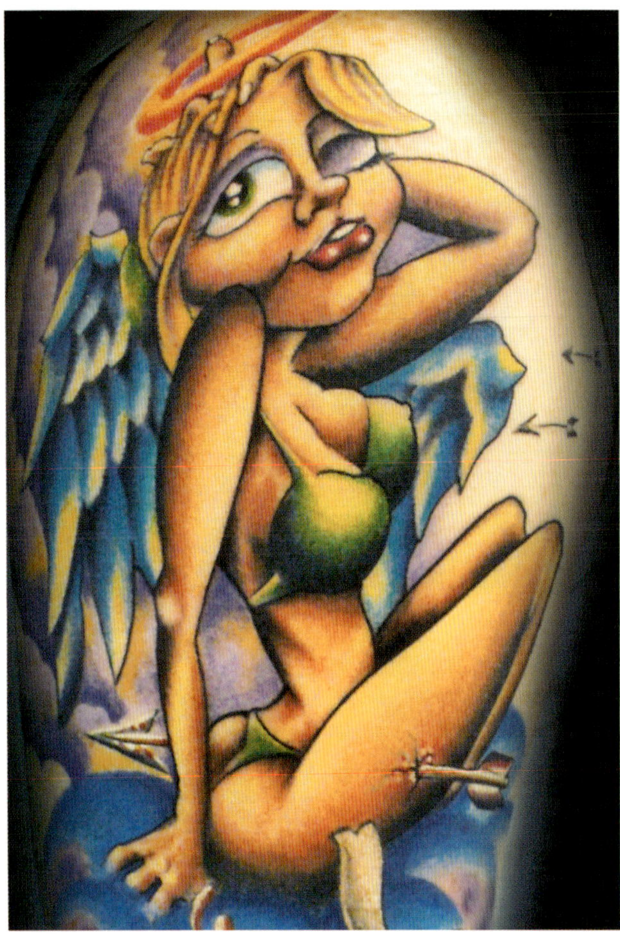

A New School version of a pin up by Brandon Bond, All Or Nothing, Atlanta, GA.

then don't do it! Artists and collectors both… when the piece isn't right, wait until it is. Redraw it, ask other people for criticism or feedback, and do whatever it takes until the final design is truly what it should be.

It drives me nuts to see people just getting a tattoo because they are tired of waiting for the right drawing. People who get crappy tattoos deserve them, really…and tattoo artists who don't put their all into every piece or who are just in it for the money aren't helping to make this industry better.

Those of us who strive each and every day to make this an amazing industry will treat the clients the way they should be treated. It is very important to me to treat my clients with all the respect that they deserve, because they are the ones giving me the opportunity to do what I love. Respect will go a long way in the tattoo industry, so teaching, helping, and listening to every artist and client can do nothing but good things for us all.

* * *

Talking to Josh also brings up another important point to consider about tattoo styles. The New School style emerged during the era of HIV and the increasing concern over sanitation, which also caused a change in the environment of the tattoo world. Instead of being an underground, closed society, the New School era emerged with an openness, a willingness to teach and share information, and a concern with keeping everything in the industry honest and above-board. Josh Woods is an example of this new attitude in

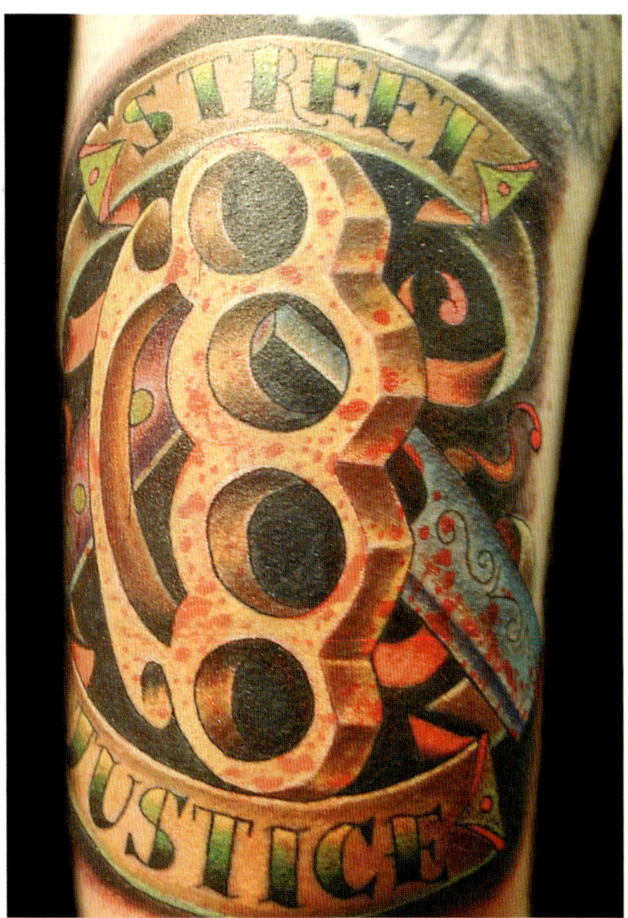

Brandon Bond, All Or Nothing, Atlanta, GA.

tattooing, and working with an artist like him will guarantee that you will have a safe and pleasant experience.

The New School style is light-hearted, often ironic, and grounded in underground culture. These bold, fun images are sure to make a statement.

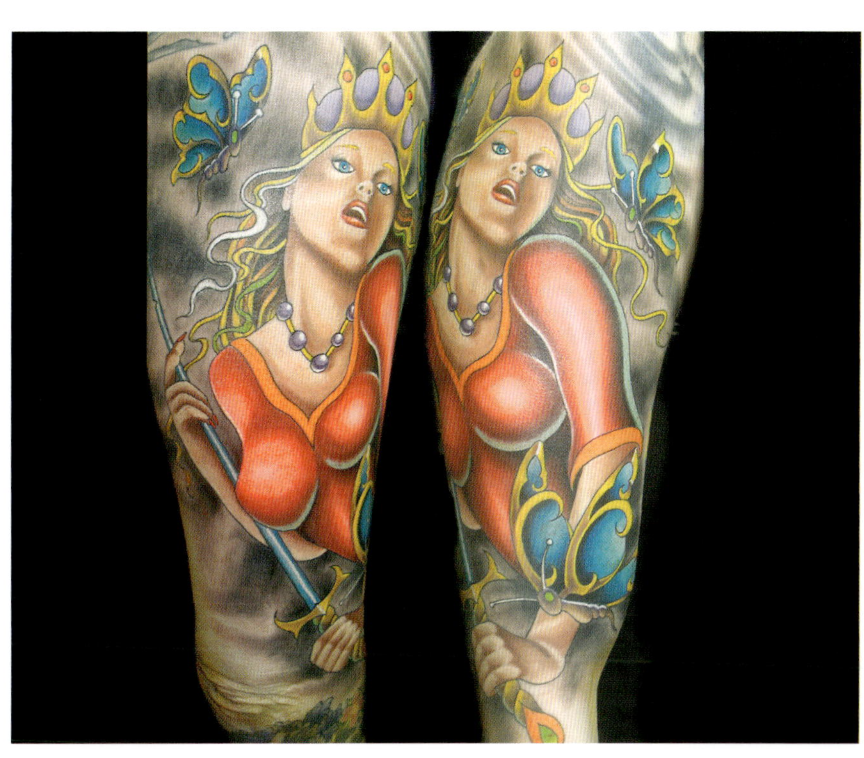

Brandon Bond, All Or Nothing, Atlanta, GA

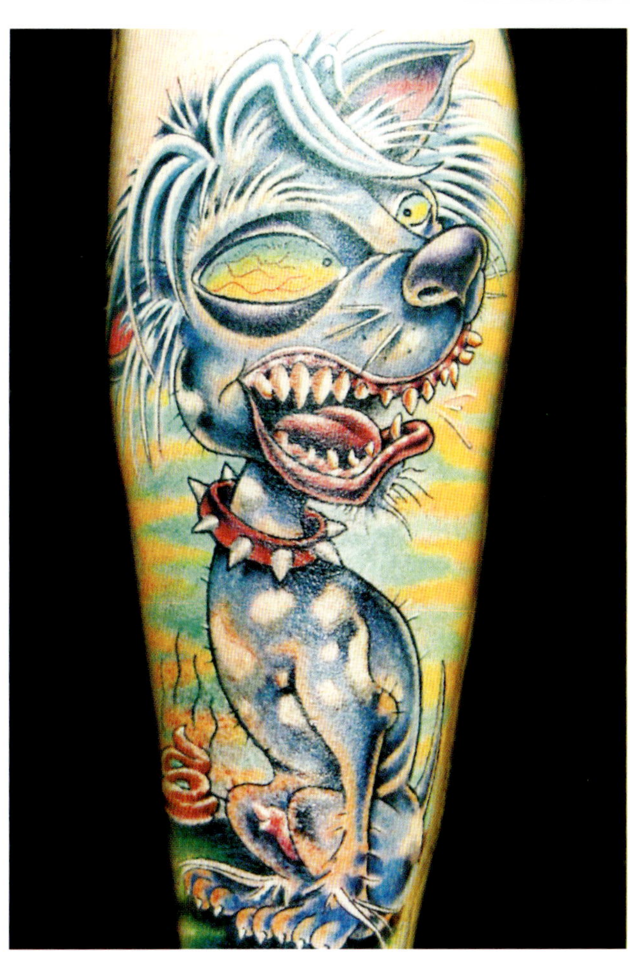

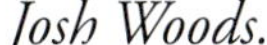

Josh Woods.

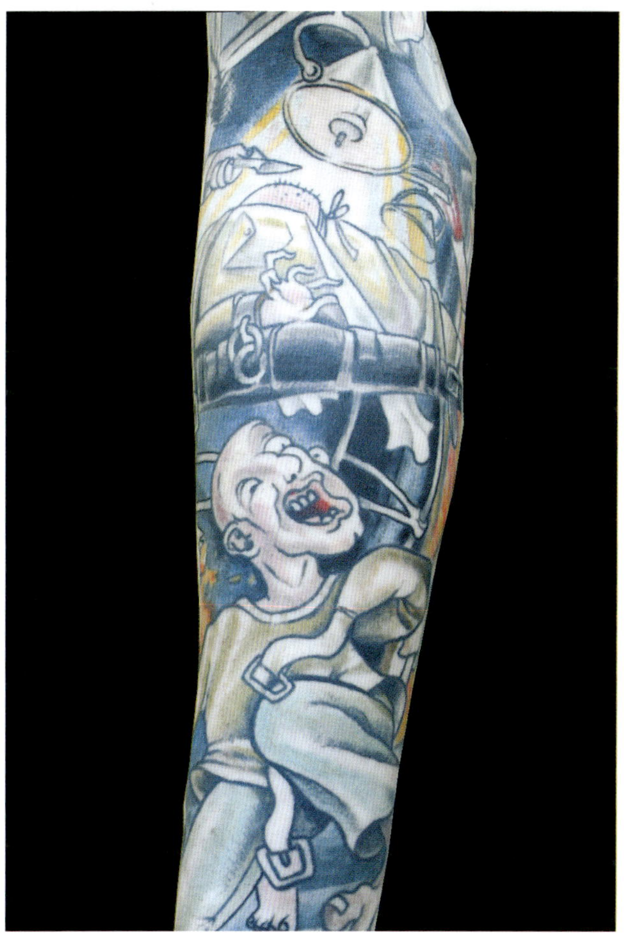

A comic-book influenced sleeve by Mark Heggie, Big Top, Utica, MI.

Chapter Six

Black and Grey

The Dark Side

One of the first questions a tattoo artist might ask you is whether or not you are interested in a piece that is in color or black and grey. The color palette is one of the first things to consider in determining your tattoo design. If you enjoy the realism of portraiture or the dark visual effects possible from an image rendered entirely in chiaroscuro, then black and grey work might be right for you.

The history behind the black and grey style

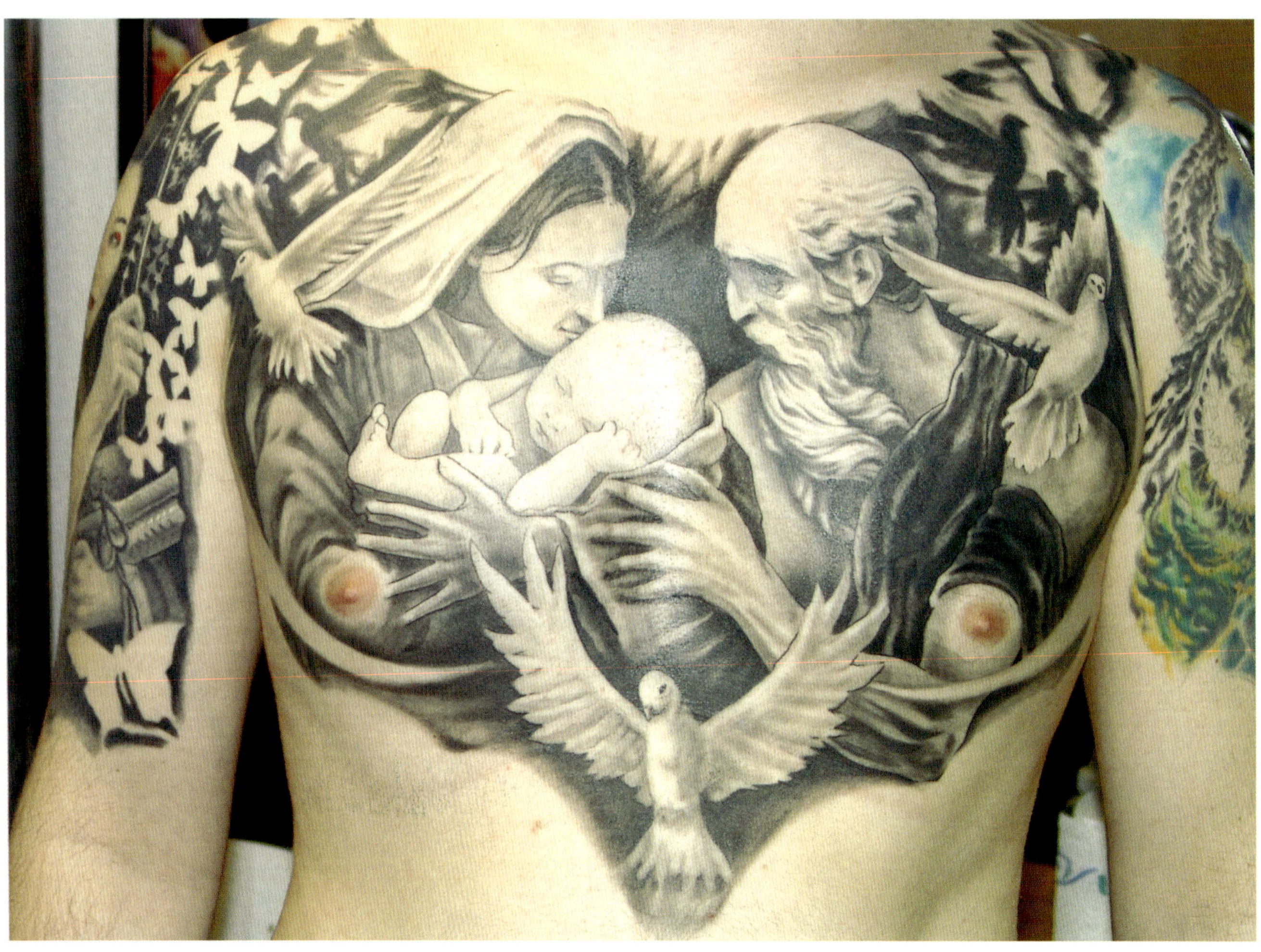

Zsolt Sarkozi of Dark Arts uses his skill for black and grey compositions to create some beautiful religious scenes.

that remains popular today is interesting in that it is generally believed to have emerged in prisons. Perhaps because of tattoo art's long association with outsiders and the criminal underworld, it is not uncommon for people in prison to get tattoos. While the practice is generally unclean and unsafe, it is a reality. Prison tattoos are so common that a Canadian project attempted to provide a safe way for prisoners to obtain tattoos by offering regulated facilities to prevent the

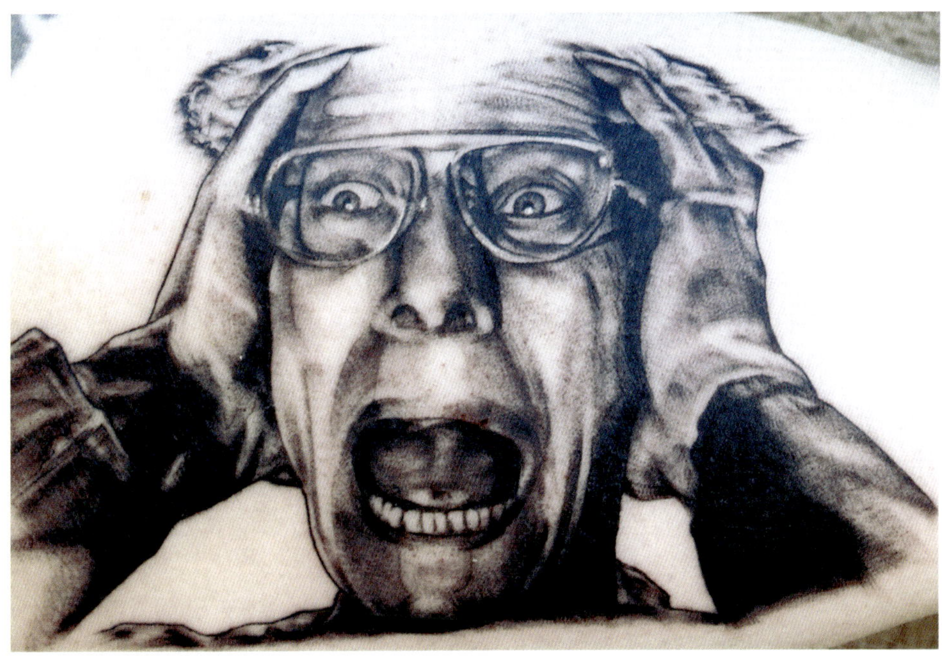

An interesting portrait from Dave Attonito.

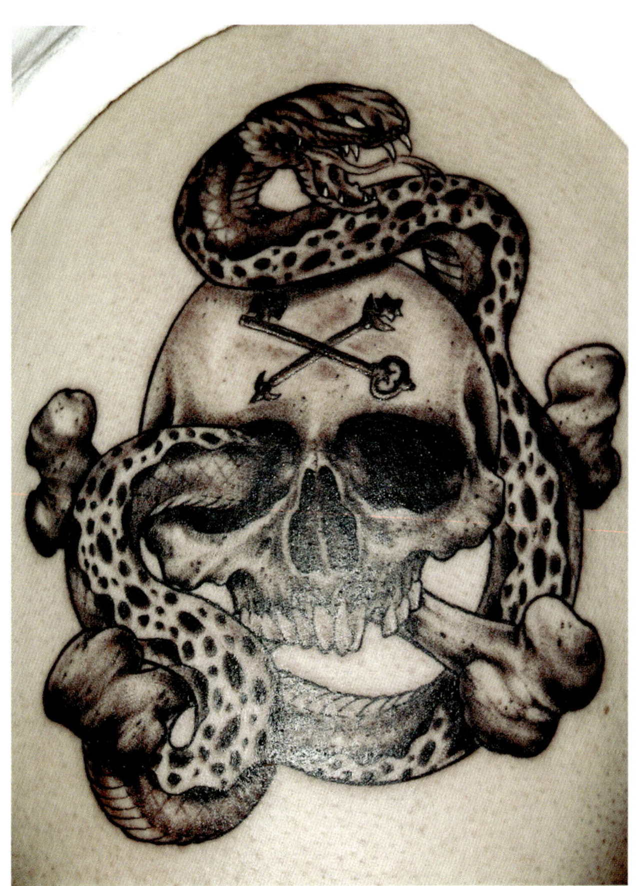

Attonito's take on some tattoo classics.

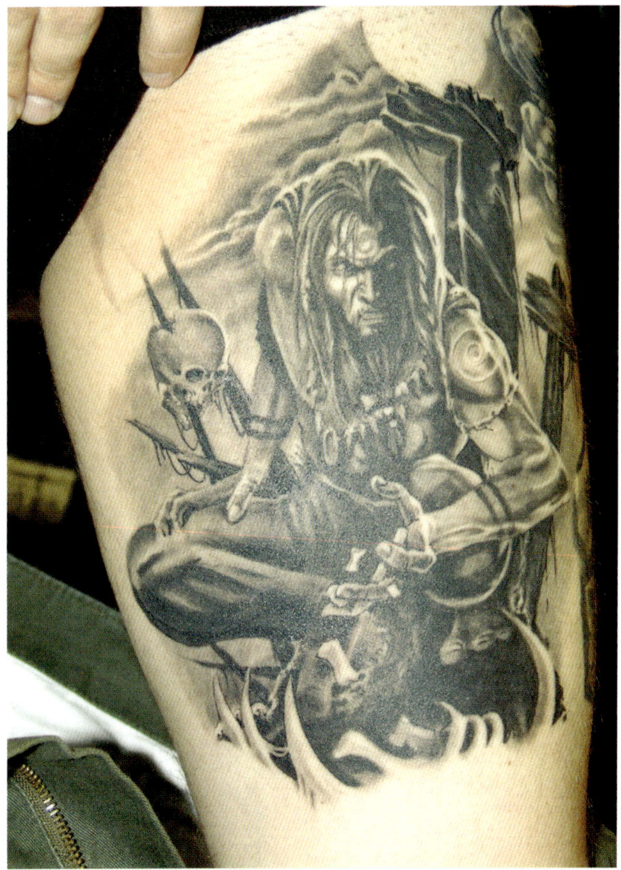

Zsolt Sarkozi, Dark Arts, Budapest, Hungary.

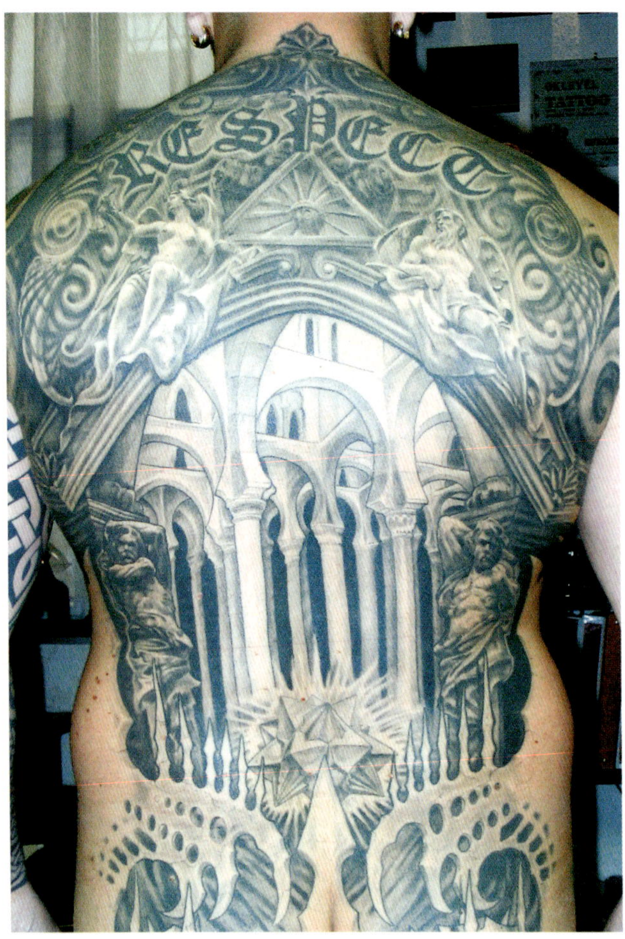

Sarkozi is also adept at using negative space to create a sense of three-dimensionality, as in the negative space gate in this backpiece. Negative space images against a dark background is a useful effect for black and grey pieces.

spread of infections diseases. People in prisons use their ink to identify themselves as members of particular gangs or to present a symbolic storyline of their various crimes and the places where they have served time in prison. One of the most fascinating and elaborate systems of prison tattoo markings has emerged in Russia, where the meanings for various symbols are coded to allow criminals to recognize each other and to read one another's stories without having to exchange a single word.

North American "jailhouse" tattoos often represent symbols that identify members of gangs or otherwise mark a criminal's career. A tear drop tattooed under the wearer's eye, for instance, might represent a murder that the wearer has committed, or it might represent the wearer having served time in jail. A spider web tattoo can also represent either incarceration or drug addiction. Another way that gang members mark themselves as outside of society is by getting tattooed in places that are generally "taboo," such as on the face or hands. It is also common for tattoos done in this style to include text, either in bold black or in a softened black and grey script in an English or Gothic style.

Because it is difficult for prison inmates to get their hands on colored ink or to manufacture their own from the materials available to them, prisoners often resort to using cigarette ash to make their pigments. With homemade tattoo machines and this hand-mixed ink,

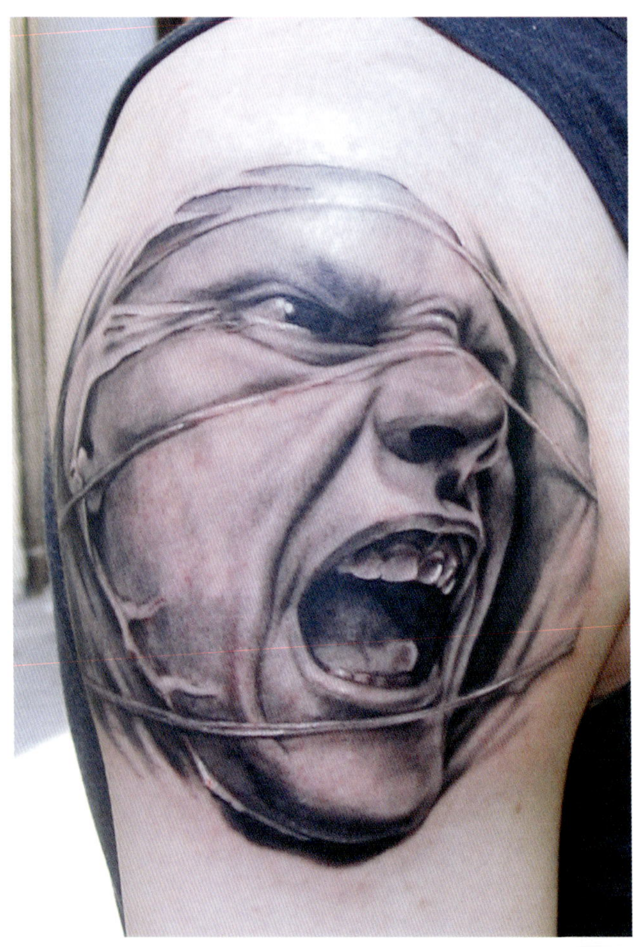

This piece from Zsolt Sarkozi is most striking in its effect of three-dimensionality. The positioning on the body makes Sarkozi's lifelike composition appear to pop out of the arm.

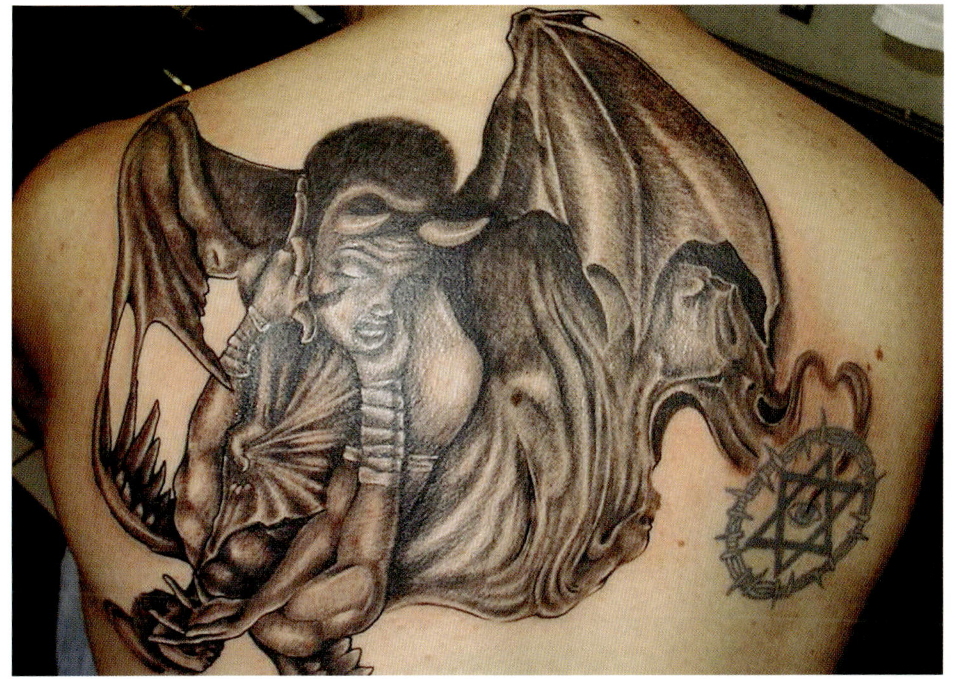

and grey tattoos have also become associated with a particular kind of content. From skulls to demons to zombies, the images most often represented in black and grey style are images from "the dark side." Fantasy scenes from sources like *Dungeons and Dragons* or *The Lord Of The Rings,* pirate scenes, skulls, horror portraits from movie stills, wizards and witches and warlocks…all these themes are common for black and

More dark and demonic work from Federico Ferroni of South Beach Tattoo.

inmates gave birth to the black and grey style that we are familiar with today. From portraits of beloved family members or other heroic figures to religious symbols to signs demarking gang affiliation, some prison tattoos rendered from these makeshift inks and machines are surprisingly beautiful, considering their seedy origins. When tattoo artists outside of the prison world saw the beautiful, symbolic work emerging from prisons, they realized that the black and grey style had much potential for mass appeal and that it was something that they should exploit.

After the tattoo artists working on the outside saw the potential in these images, they began working to develop techniques to refine the style for mass consumption. Popularized by rappers and other musicians, the images have become increasingly common, and tattoo artists subsequently have been capitalizing on their popularity by developing more techniques to make these tattoos clean and unique. Focusing on solid line work and realistic shading, black

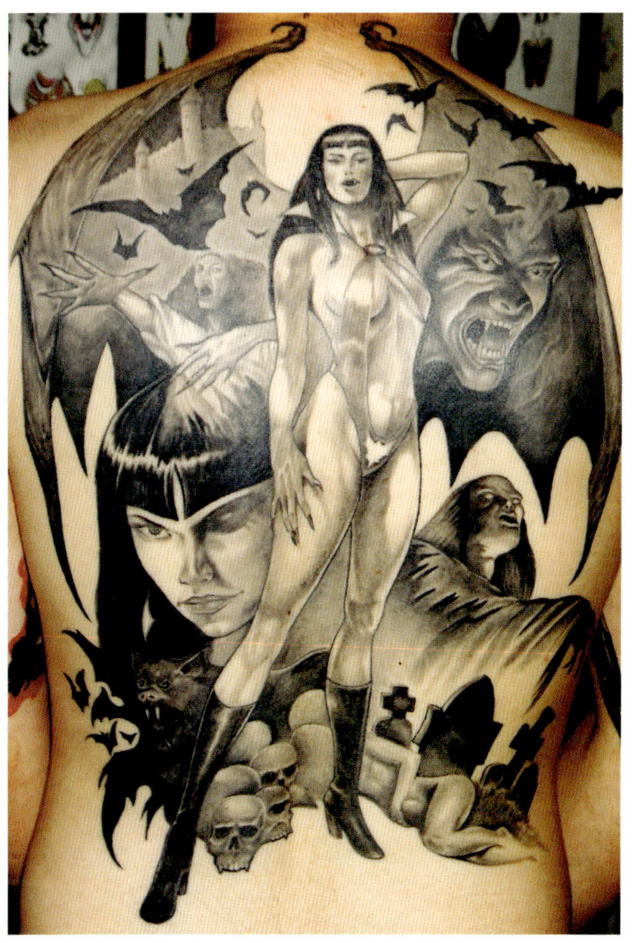

Federico Ferroni of South Beach Tattoo uses stark contrasts to achieve a dramatic, dynamic composition. The subject matter, as in many black and grey pieces, is dark and demonic.

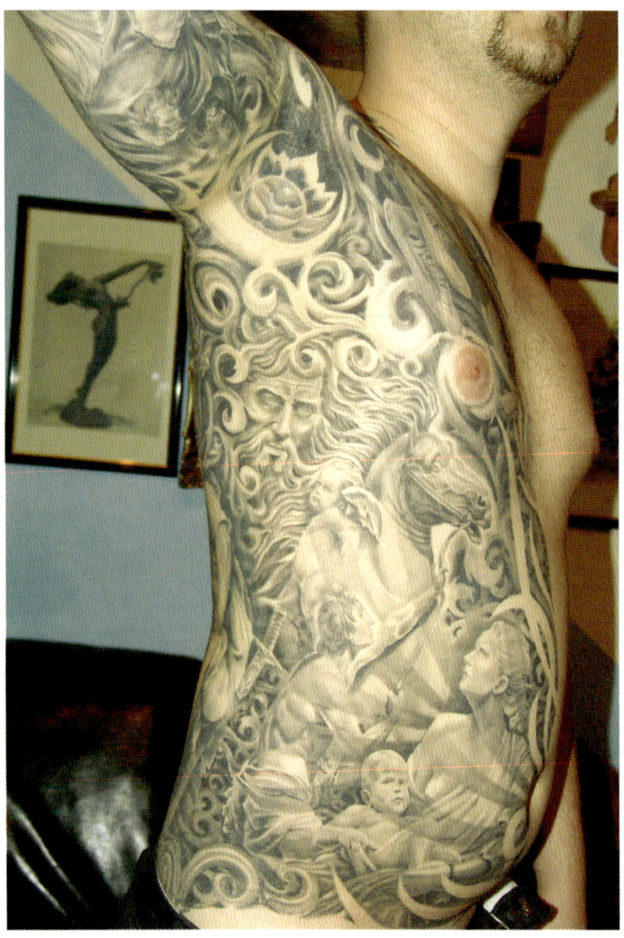

This complex composition (pages 72 and 73), compromising almost an entire upper body suit, is an example of chiaroscuro at its finest.

grey work in this darker genre. An example of these darker images is Beesting's John Wayne's wizard and dragon leg piece, which spans two of the wearer's legs. Also see Federico Ferroni's batlady backpiece, which uses stark contrasts in black and grey to achieve a dynamic composition.

It is perhaps surprising that black and grey is also a common style for religious pieces, such as the gorgeous chiaroscuro from Hungary's Zsolt Sarkozi. With its roots in the underworld and the common themes of dark and demonic subjects, it is surprising that black and grey is used so often for tattoos with a Christian theme. As in Zsolt Sarkozi's religious pieces, however, the soft shading and delicate beauty that a skilled black and grey artist is able to achieve with these subtle tones make the style an excellent choice for work with a religious theme or tattoos that reference classical art. Many of the religious images most commonly used in these tattoos come from Italian or other Renaissance art or Mexican Folk Art paintings of the Virgin Mary, Jesus, or other saints and angels. The unusual or obscure sources of reference for these tattoos make the final products unique and beautiful, and the delicate effects possible in black and grey only enhance these images.

For similar reasons, portraits, tributes, and other memorial pieces are also often done in black and grey as well, and artists using modern techniques and inks are now able to achieve highly realistic effects.

If you are attracted to the black and grey

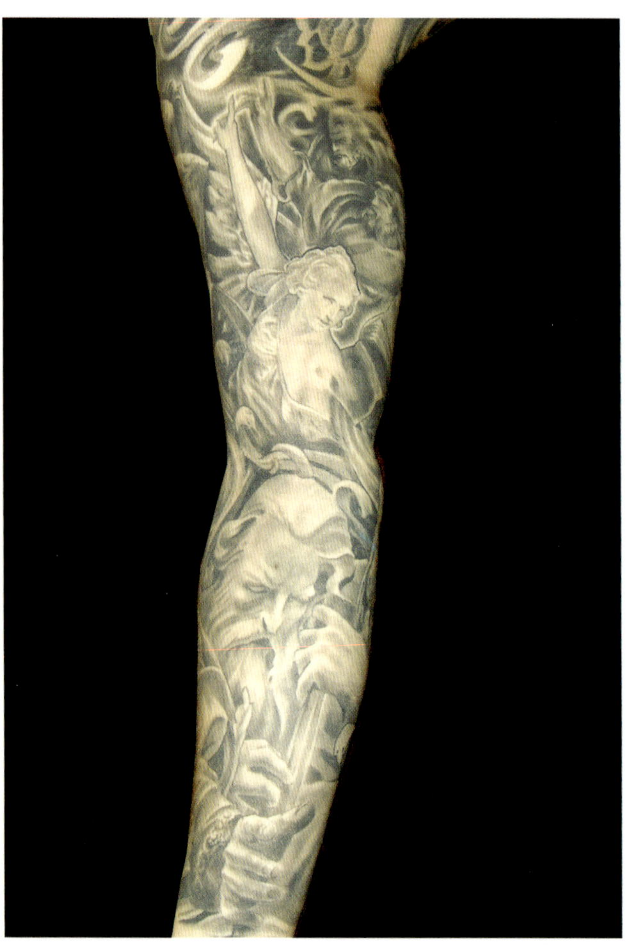

Zsolt Sarkozi, Dark Arts, Budapest, Hungary.

style, it would be worth your time to investigate what artists in your area specialize in black and grey. Particularly if you would like to get a portrait, finding an artist who specializes in black and grey portraiture will be a wise investment of your resources. Just as some artists specialize in color work, many artists prefer to work only in black and grey. These artists are able to achieve amazing effects using negative space, white highlights, and fine gradations in their chiaroscuro. Taking the time to find one of these artists to complete your black and grey masterpiece will be well worth it. One artist who has recently gained much notoriety for her strong black and grey portrait work is Kat Von D of L.A. Ink, whose realistic portraiture has become beloved by many fans. Her fame has also lead to an

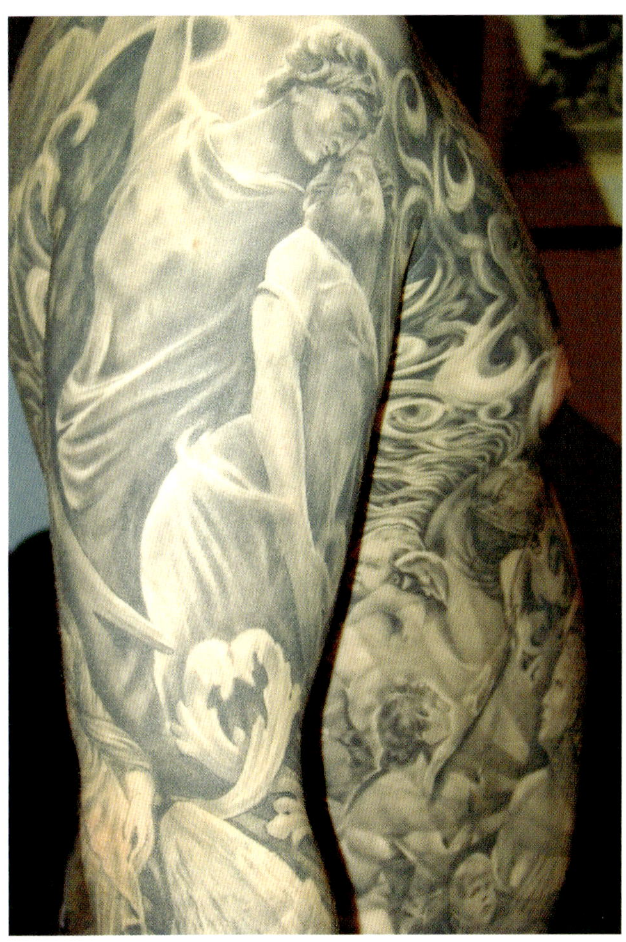

Zsolt Sarkozi, Dark Arts, Budapest, Hungary.

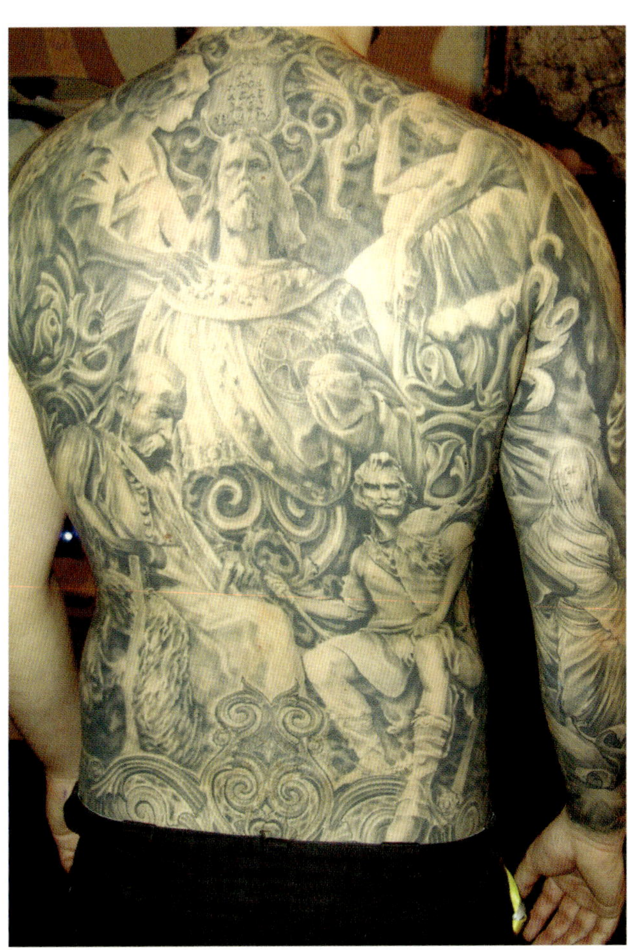

Zsolt Sarkozi, Dark Arts, Budapest, Hungary.

increased knowledge of the style and an awareness among artists of what is possible to achieve with a palette restricted to black and grey as well as a desire to demonstrate that they are capable of rendering portraits as realistically as Kat, so now is a great time to get a black and grey tattoo.

The disadvantage of not taking your time to find the right artist to complete a portrait style piece is that a botched job is difficult to disguise. If you take a picture of a child, parent, or other loved one to an artist and he or she tattoos an unsuccessful portrait on you, your intended tribute can result in an embarrassing insult. Since there are artists who specialize in this style, we strongly recommend you find one if you are seeking portrait work.

In addition to being highly realistic, another of the advantages of black and grey work is that it is known to withstand the test of time better than many other styles. All tattoos will fade with time; however, black and grey work will retain its integrity more consistently through the years than many other styles of tattoo art. A portrait done in black and grey style, for instance, will continue to look like a portrait after many years of fading. A color portrait might be more visually appealing initially, but it might fade irregularly as different colors fade at different rates. A color portrait, of course, could be touched up, but many people choose to stick with black and grey work for its durability and classic beauty.

Touch ups are available, and many artists will touch up their own work for free. Tattoo artists are nomads, however, and the artist who did your work may not always be around. It is possible then, that getting touch ups could be costly, so considering an image's durability is another element to weigh in deciding on the style and design of your tattoo. Like Traditional American tattoos, black and grey tattoos are known to hold up through many years, and they are less likely to look blobby and unrecognizable as your skin ages.

One artist who is known throughout the industry for his gorgeous black and grey work, his realistic portraiture, and his dark and demonic designs is Dave Attonito, the owner of Good Clean Fun in Snellville, GA. We caught up with Dave to find out about his work and his thoughts on black and grey style.

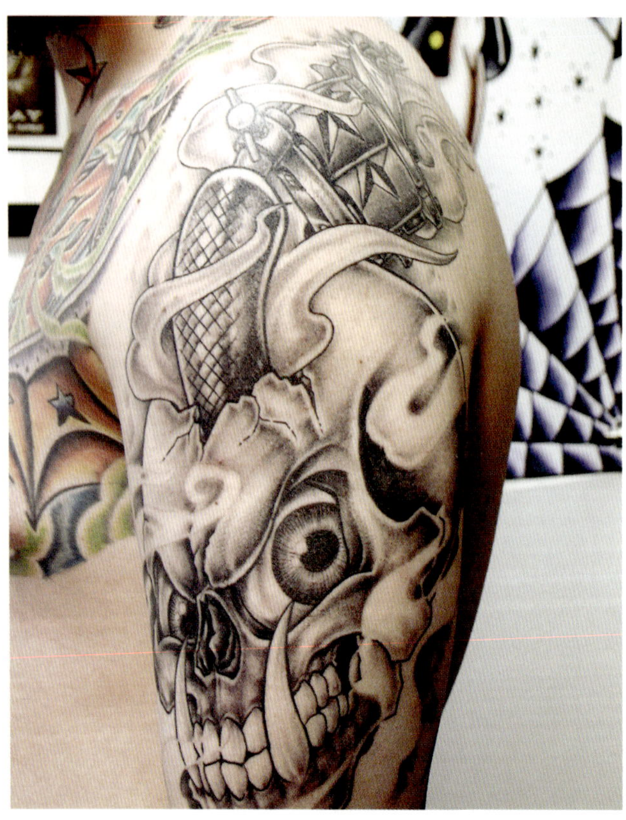

Skulls, snakes, and other images we associate with the "dark side" are common in black and grey work. Here Dave Attonito's soft shading, effective use of negative space, and mastery of details (as represented in the skull's eyes and the cross-hatching on the tattoo machine) bring this imagery to life.

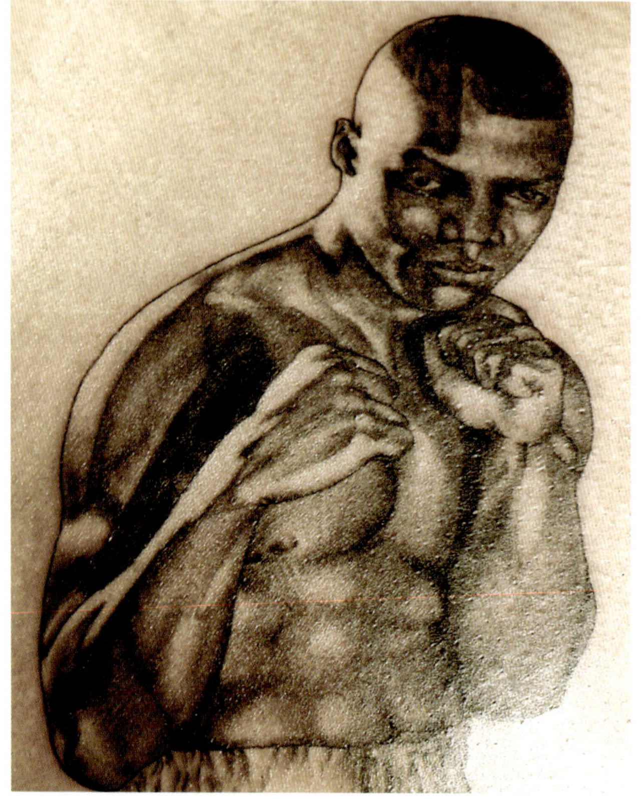

Notice the variations in texture Attonito accomplishes with his shading…the differences between the hair, the skin, and the cloth are particularly striking in this piece.

Dave Attonito Q & A

JS: While you also do some beautiful traditional American work, it seems to me that you are most well known for your black and grey tattoo designs. What first attracted you to that style?

Dave: I guess I have always been attracted to black and grey artwork. Even before I started tattooing, my preferred medium for artwork always has been pencil or charcoal. I have always enjoyed drawing more than painting.

JS: I guess that makes sense...your preferences for fine art overlap in your tattoo tastes. Your focus on drawing and black and grey work is clear in your fine art and flash designs as well.

Since you do so much work in this style, though, I wonder if you wouldn't get tired of it? What keeps it interesting?

Dave: I think part of it is that I continue to get better at it with each new piece. If I ever felt that I had stopped growing as a tattooer, I would probably just stop tattooing. There are black and grey artists out there whose work I still look up to, and every time I go to their websites, I think about throwing away my machines. But as long as I feel like there's room to grow, it keeps me interested in the art.

JS: So it's the challenge, then? To keep improving and watching yourself grow?

Dave: As soon as you think that you are the "best," you are NOT...and you are not going to ever get any better with that attitude.

JS: What do you think makes black and grey tattoos remain popular?

Dave: I think that black and grey tattoos will always be popular. Traditionally, black and grey is the style that is most commonly associated

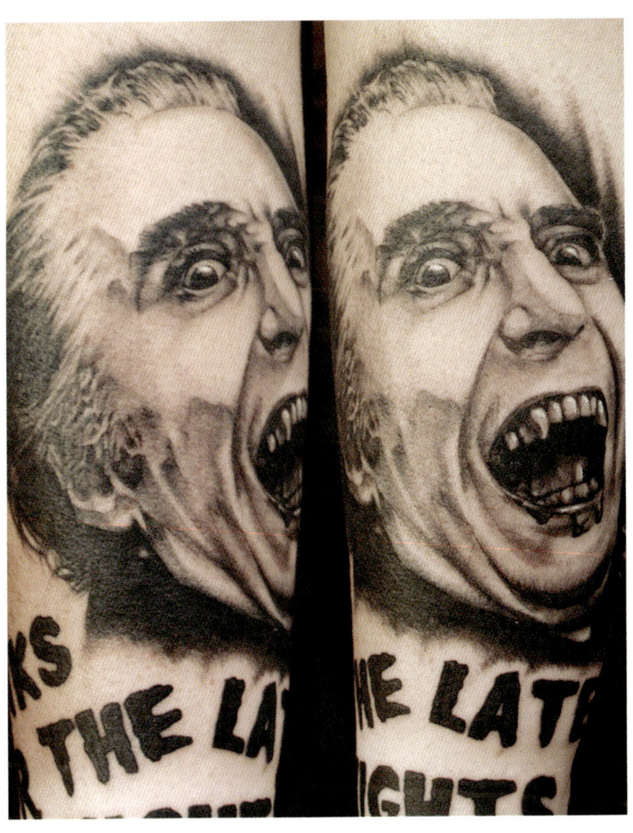

Two vampires from Dave Attonito. Notice how the black shading in the background sets off the softer tones. Pairing light and dark in this manner achieve dramatic effects.

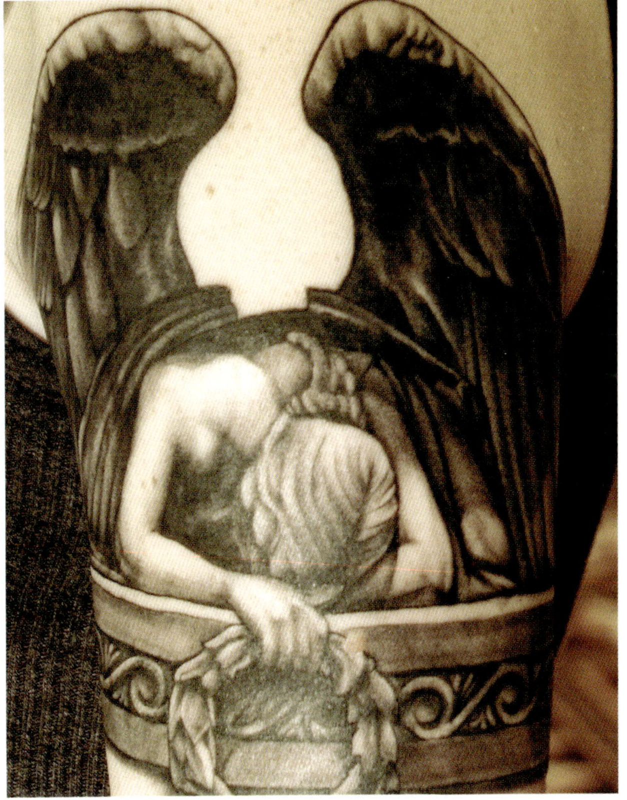

Attonito's sad angel is a unique twist on the tattooed armband. Again, his talent for rendering texture with chiaroscuro is apparent in the various effects he achieves in the wings, hair, skin, plant, and architectural elements.

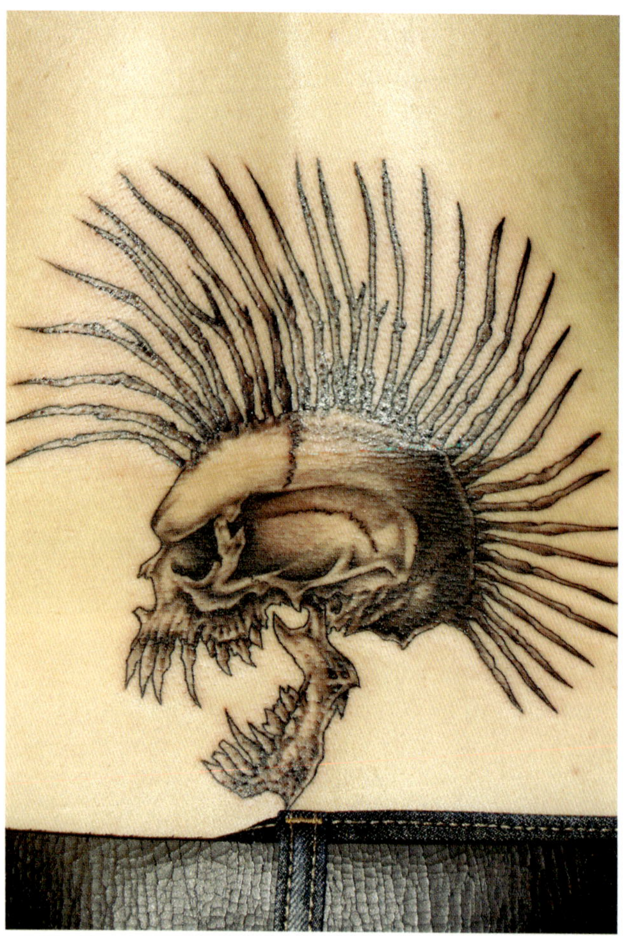

How punk rock is this bone-mohawk skull, rendered in Attonito's clean lines and soft black and grey?

with portrait style tattooing. One of the things that I find very pleasing about black and grey tattooing is that as the tattoos age, they tend to look even nicer if the client takes good care of the tattoo. The greys soften up some over time and really settle into the skin nicely.

JS: Yes. The durability of a black and grey piece is definitely something that attracts clients. What else do you think makes a client seek out your work, in particular?

Dave: I get people of all ages and from all backgrounds, so there really isn't any particular kind of customer who seems to seek me out more than any other.

JS: Maybe that's because black and grey style is classic, and when it's done well, it can make for some really elegant work. That kind of classic beauty appeals to everyone.

We also want to know a little bit about your process as an artist. We're encouraging our readers to become more familiar with the work behind the tattoo, and it's been interesting to compare the various ways the artists we've spoken to work with clients. Can you tell us a little bit about how you work?

Dave: I often use reference material for my tattooing. I find reference everywhere: on the internet, in books (I think it is really important for any artists to have a good reference library), magazines, DVDs, and other places. If I can't find the reference I need for a particular piece, I will sometimes photograph it myself.

The relationship with the client usually depends on the particular client. Sometimes,

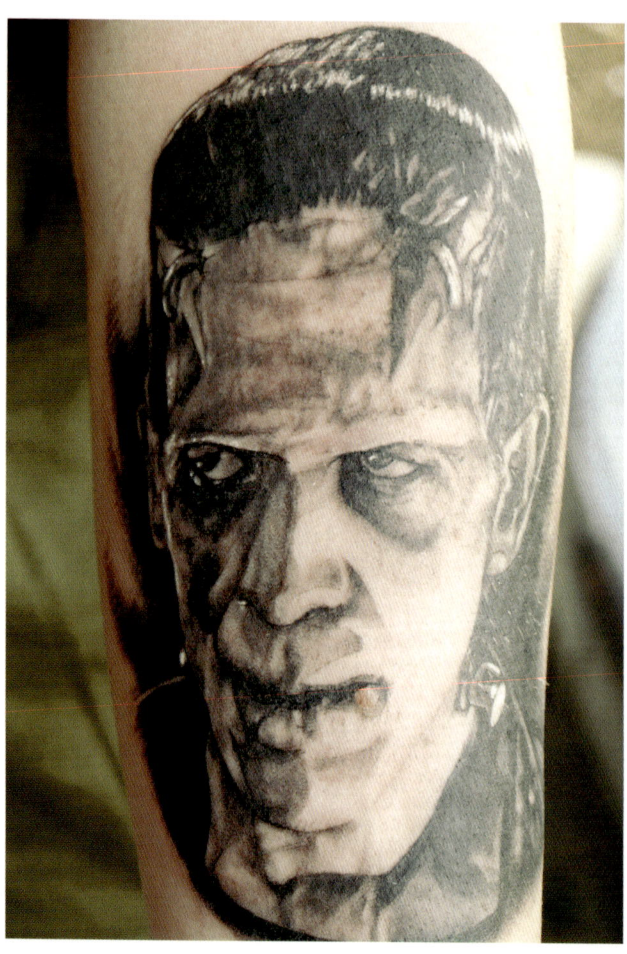

Using his virtuosic skill with black and grey realism, Attonito captures Frankenstein, making this classic of horror beautiful. Using figures from horror movies as reference for a tattoo is becoming more and more popular.

they want to be deeply involved in the drawing process (and sometimes, they want to be a little *too* involved!). Other times, they give me total artistic freedom.

The most important things to me to consider in putting the artwork together are how the tattoo will fit the area, how it will age, and how readable the image is.

JS: I'm sure your clients appreciate that attention to things they might not think to consider...placement and aging and readability aren't usually on a client's mind. That's another thing for clients to consider, too...finding a really experienced tattoo artist is advantageous, as you guys know to think about these things.

I also wanted to ask you about the content that seems to come up in black and grey so often. While there's portraiture in black and grey and the occasional religious piece, very often, black and grey work is dark or demonic. Why do you think that is?

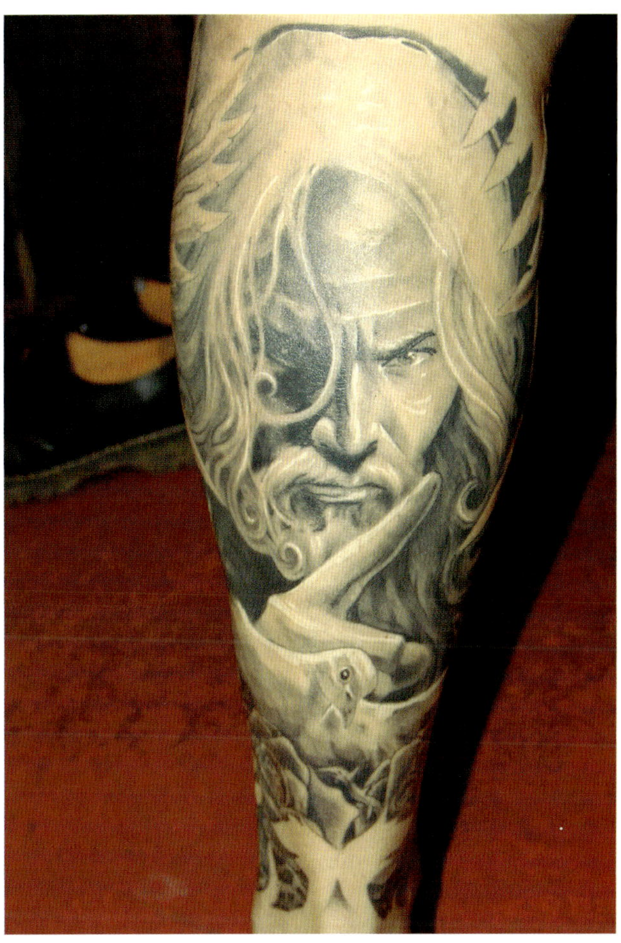

Dramatic light and dark contrast and intense realism from Zsolt Sarkozi.

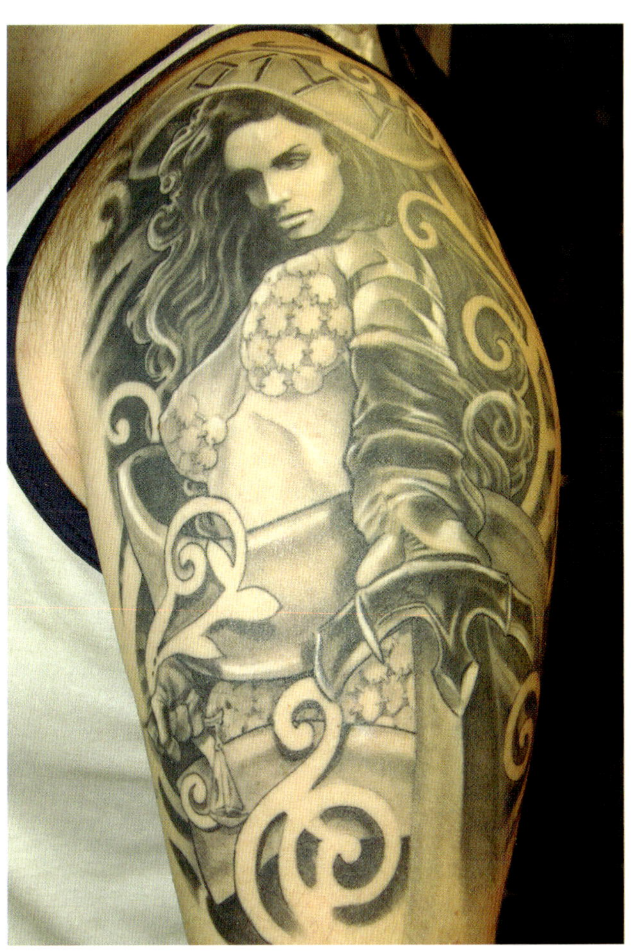

Zsolt Sarkozi, Dark Arts, Budapest, Hungary.

Dave: I think that the lack of color lends itself well to the scarier tattoos. Just like horror movies look great in black and white—it's somehow just a little creepier.

* * *

While we're talking about black ink, we will next consider tribal artwork, which is usually rendered entirely in solid black ink.

Chapter Seven

Tribal & Biomechanical

The Ancient Art

It seems like almost everyone has at least one tribal tattoo. From Pamela Anderson's tribal armband to Mike Tyson's shocking facial tattoo to Dennis Rodman's prominent tribal style chest and shoulder work, celebrities have helped to make the tribal style one of the most commonly requested types of tattoos in shops today. The prominent, sexy tribal designs gracing the lower backs of young women, derisively referred to by some as "tramp stamps" or "ass antlers," further demonstrate that the allure of the simple black ink tattoo designs is not going away.

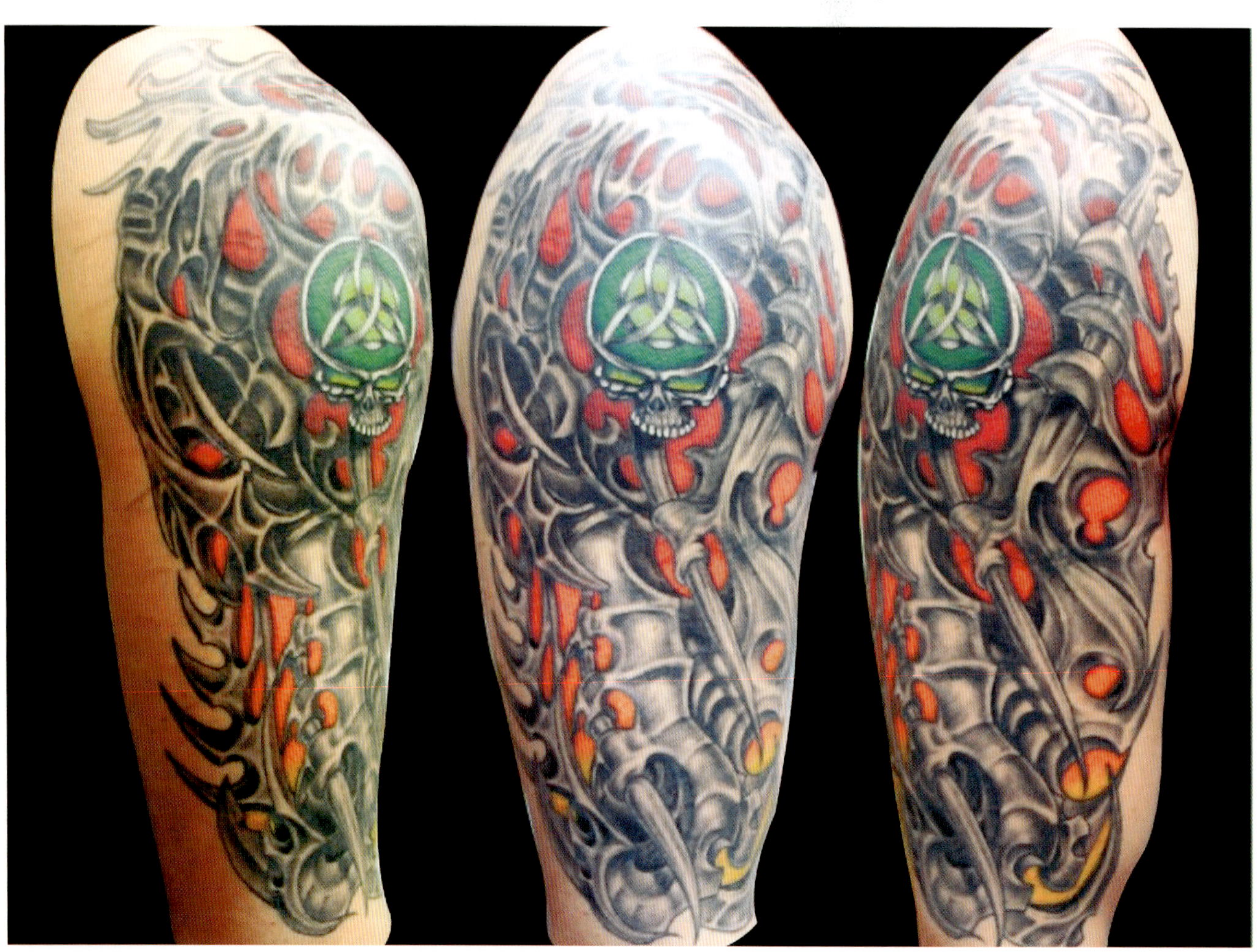

John Wayne offers a biomechanical half-sleeve, which enhances the musculature in a manner similar to tribal with a much more intricate design and bolder color work.

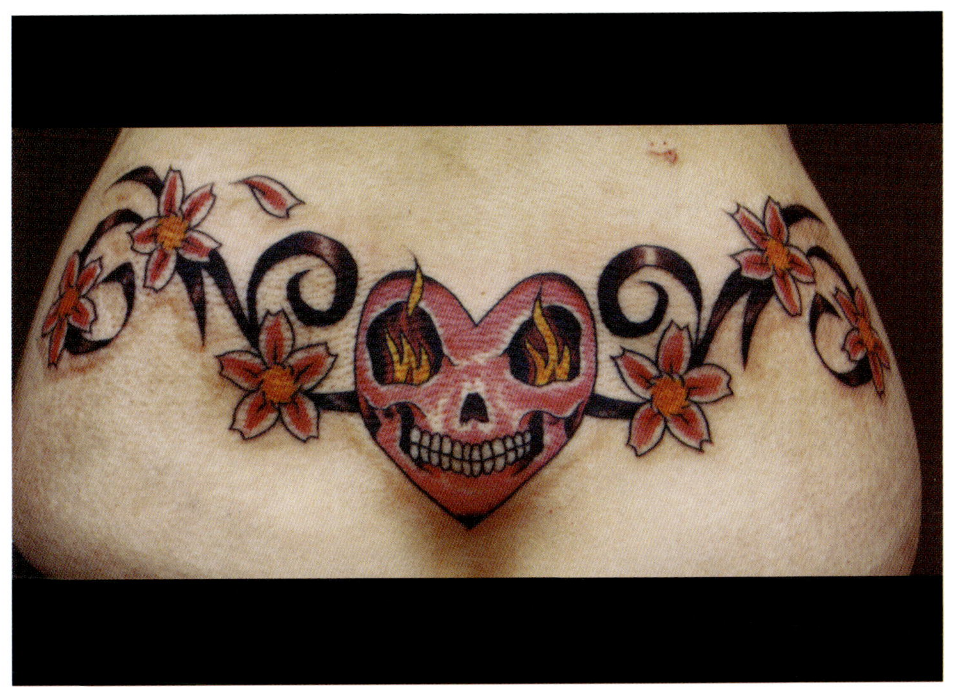

Here Mark Heggie has used a black tribal background to unify this unique color piece into an elegant lower back tattoo.

Tattoos based on tribal designs saw a rise in popularity during the late eighties and early nineties, and much of this popularity continues today. The boldness and simplicity of the designs make for a beautiful body enhancement, which perhaps accounts for much of the style's popularity. Tribal designs traditionally were rooted in cultures that used them either to identify a person as a member of their society or as talismans to protect the wearer from bad spirits, illness, or other spiritual danger. This ancient history and connection to the mysterious makes tribal artwork a powerful, universally pleasing design source for your new tattoo.

It is somewhat surprising that a style originating in obscure, small islands with cultures so very different from our own has gained such popularity. From the time Captain James Cook and his crew aboard *The Endeavor* landed in Tahiti in 1769, the Tahitian ritual of inking their bodies using a sharp instrument dipped in soot from their lamps has fascinated Westerners.

For this reason, the most widely known and imitated tribal tattoo style is the Polynesian, which has developed over several thousand years in Tahiti and other Pacific islands into an intricate, geometrically patterned design style. Since the warm climate in these islands made clothing rare and sparse, many of these cultures used tattoo art as their primary means of decorating their bodies. In the tribal cultures that perfected this style of tattoo, the placement, composition, and type of design indicates much about the wearer's social status.

A few cultures still practice tribal tattooing today. One notable example

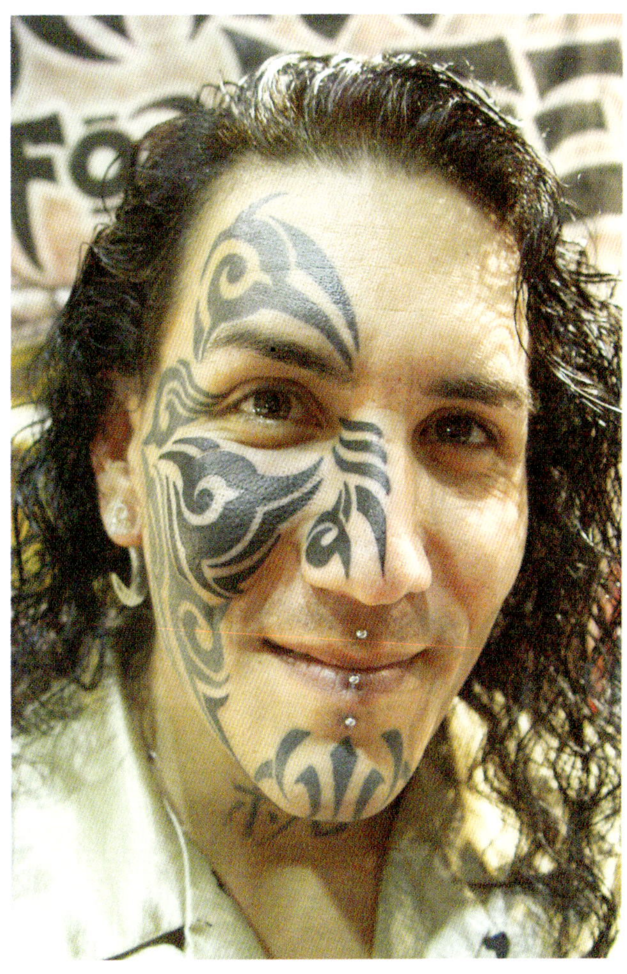

Larry Brogan offers a modern interpretation of the tribal elders' practice of facial tattooing to represent rank.

is the Malaysian island of Borneo, where it is possible to find artists working with traditional tattoo tools and creating authentic tribal designs. Other cultures from which we borrow tribal designs include the Japanese, Hindu, Chinese, Native American, Egyptian, Mayan, Celtic, Aztec, Hawaiian, Inuit, and mystic traditions like that surrounding the signs of the Zodiac.

The tattoos we have come to think of as tribal

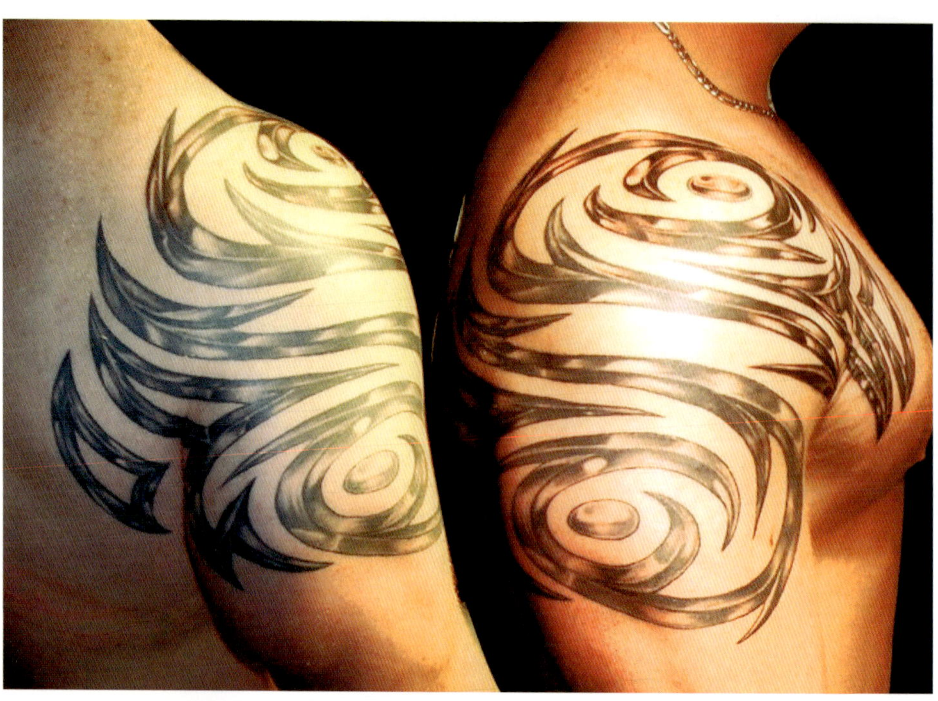

Well-place tribal design enhances the body's natural shape and movement. The artist in this piece has spread the design beyond the arm to include the chest and the back, enhancing the wearer's natural musculature. John Wayne, Beesting, Ontario, Canada.

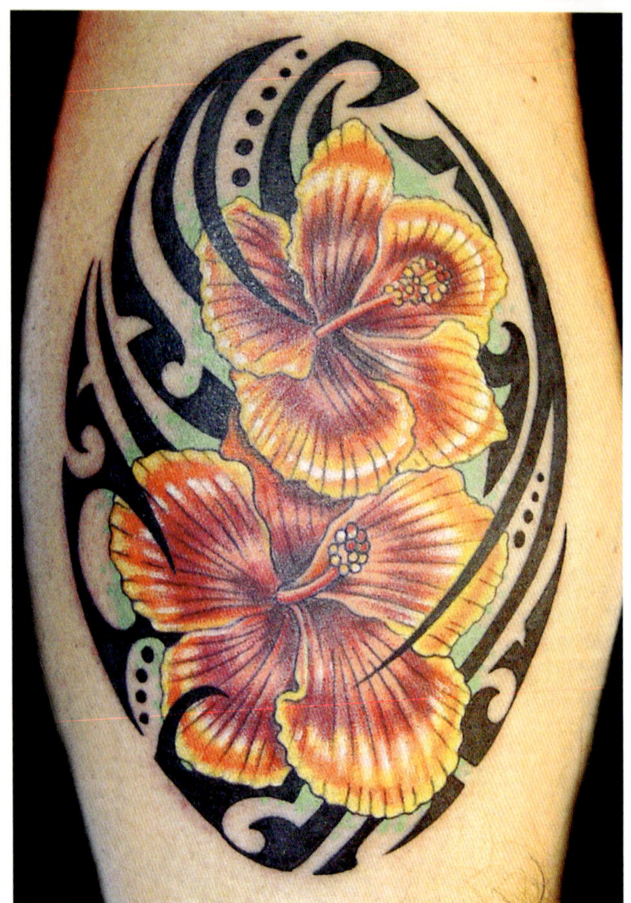

Nate Beavers uses a tribal design both in the foreground and background of this floral piece, which nicely sets off the bright colors in the tropical flowers.

do not have the cultural significance of these authentic tribal pieces; however, the style and design are based on the images of this type of tattoo, and they can be designed to enhance the body's natural shapes and movement. And while modern tribal tattoos lack the symbolic meaning that was intrinsic to the tribal originals, some of them do reference themes and images that were common in ancient art. Tribal suns are popular, for instance, and they were also common in ancient societies who worshipped the sun or revered fire as a critical element for survival. Modern tribal versions of dragons and other mythical creatures, flowers, animals, and other designs have origins in ancient art that can provide layers of meaning to your modern tribal design for your tattoo.

Tribal designs are also popular for use as background for other images, such as a flower or butterfly. The thick black lines make an excellent background for a soft color piece, adding visual interest and a contextual counterpoint to femi-

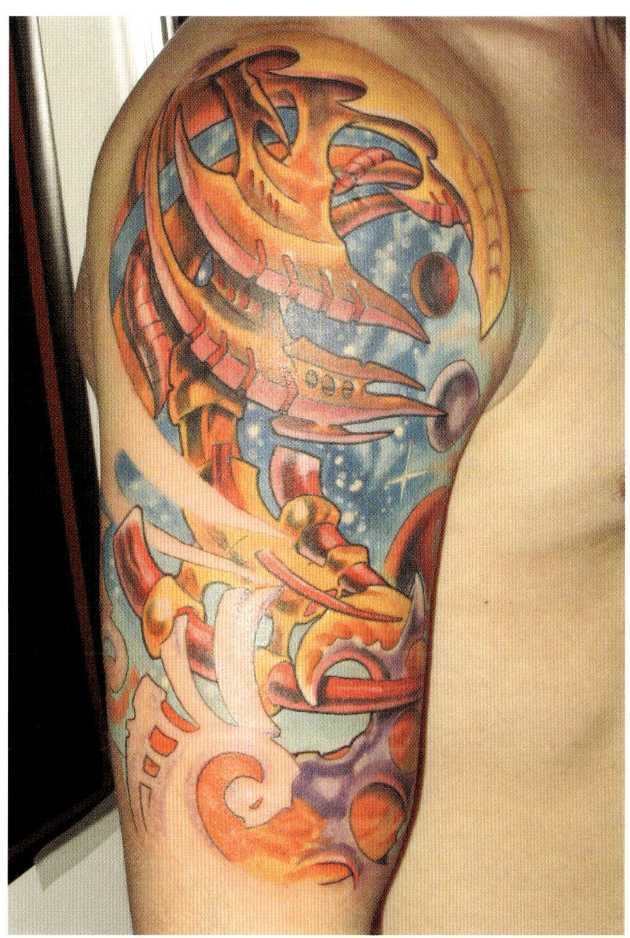

Zsolt Sarkozi's biomechanical design uses negative space and large, geometric shapes to flow with the musculature of the wearer's body in a a manner similar to tribal work; however, this piece uses bold colors and an outer-space theme to make the piece even more unique.

nine, delicate pieces, such as in Kirk Shepherd's tribal background for a flower design or Nate Beavers's use of tribal in both the foreground and background for his tropical flower tattoo. Tribal line work also works well as an enhancement to other color work, such as in Shannon Schober's use of a tribal style design as a dagger in his heart tattoo.

One way to make your tribal tattoo more meaningful is to do a little research on the tribal styles of many different cultures and to find out more about the significance behind the designs. If there is a culture that is particularly meaningful for you or an area of the world most close to your own family heritage, you might find out what kind of body art or other artwork is common to that culture. Designs in traditional clothing, weaving, painting, pottery, or other folk art that have cultural significance might make an excellent reference source for a tribal tattoo.

In addition to being strong images for enhancing the body's natural shape, tribal tattoos are excellent options for darker skin tones. While tiny details and bold color work will show up on very pale skin, they are not as effective in darker skin shades. The bold, spacious designs possible with tribal art give people of color many more options for larger tattoos and heavier coverage.

Another style emerged as a kind of adaptation, or sub-type, of tribal. The biomechanical style enhances the body in a manner similar to tribal pieces, yet tattoos rendered in this style often

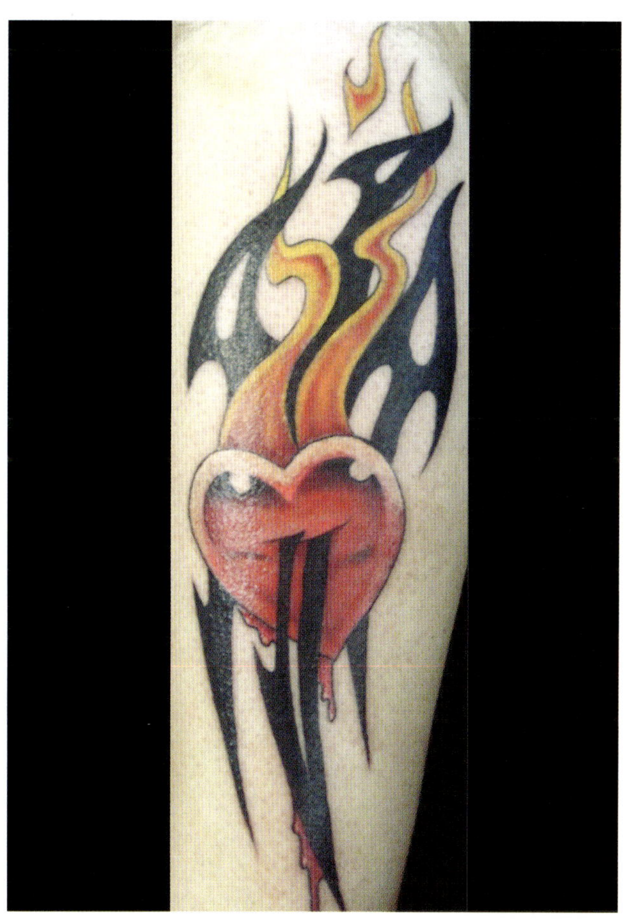

Shannon Schober of Vitality Tattoo in Asheville, NC, uses the tribal as a backdrop for this heart, but also adds interest by running the tribal piece through the heart like a dagger.

include color and more detailed patterns and folds. John Wayne and Zsolt Sarkozi both provide examples of biomechanical work, demonstrating both the similarities to the tribal style as well as biomechanical's own unique qualities. Notice that Zsolt Sarkozi incorporates an outer-space theme in his biomechanical piece, which adds the interest of subject matter to the tattoo while still using negative space and large, geometric shapes to flow with the wearer's natural musculature.

The ability to enhance the body's natural shapes and to be designed around particular body parts is one of the reasons that tribal work remains so popular. It is easy to adapt a design to encircle an arm, a belly button, a nipple, or other circular shapes. Curving lines can seductively enhance a woman's lower back or tailbone area, or bold concentric designs enhance a man's muscular chest or shoulders.

If you are considering getting a tattoo in the tribal style, look for an artist whose portfolio demonstrates clean lines and creative design. Because many tribal tattoos are composed entirely of black ink or shades of grey, it is easy for a tribal tattoo to come off looking very similar to other tribal pieces. Artists who specialize in tribal style or who enjoy drawing geometric designs will make sure that your tattoo will be uniquely yours, so it is helpful to find someone who enjoys this kind of work to avoid getting a tattoo that seems generic.

Cory Ferguson Q & A

One artist known for his unique tribal designs is Cory Ferguson. Cory has been involved in the industry since 1993, when he started making needles and doing other grunt work around the shop where his father worked as a tattoo artist, and he has been tattooing independently since May of 2000. Cory now owns his own shop, Enlightened Art, which is located in Oakville, Ontario. We spoke with Cory about his interest in tribal art and his thoughts on the style's mainstream popularity in spite of its exotic origins.

JS: What was it that initially attracted you to the tribal style?

Cory: About five years ago, a client approached me about doing a Polynesian style

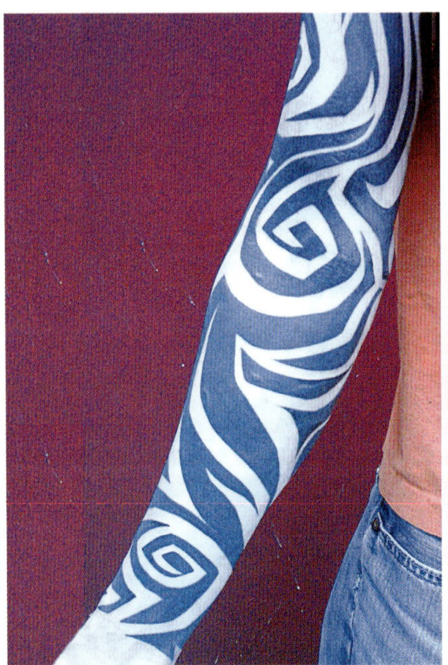

Mark Heggie of Big Top Tattoo in Utica, MI, makes this tribal sleeve unique by tweaking some of the edges to give the uniform design an abstract feel.

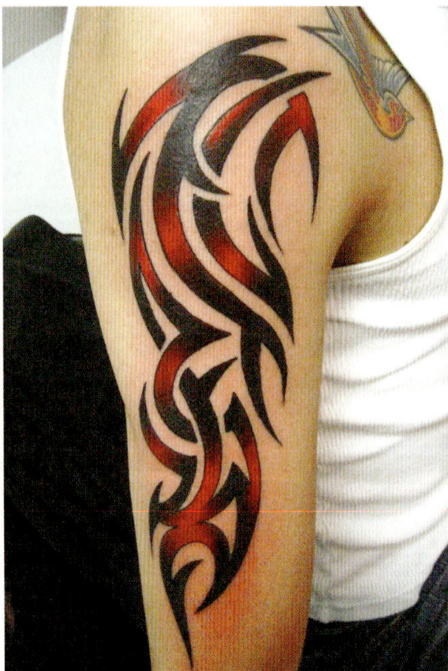

Here Hard Knox artist John Sweeney includes red with the classic black tribal to make this piece unique.

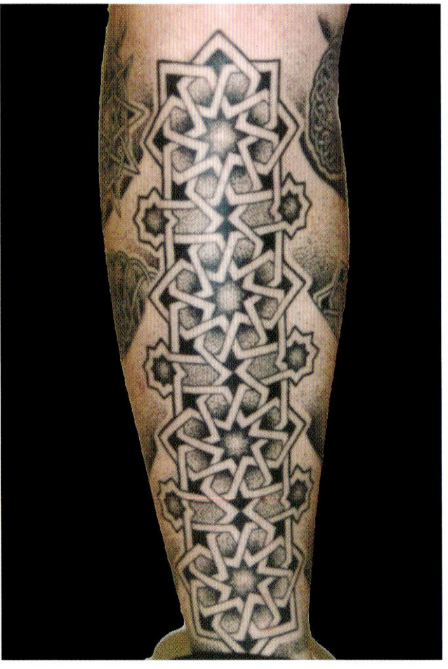

This shin piece combines hard edges with softer effects using the shading rendered from Cory's stippling technique. The softened edges provide an interesting contrast with the more angular shapes.

backpiece, and at the time, I had never done anything in the tribal genre before. So, I figured I had to do a lot of research to understand all of the dynamics of the style and to make sure it was done exactly right. It was, after all, a backpiece! That's a lot of time for the client and a big project for me, so I wanted to figure out how to do it right.

So after I started learning about the basics of designing tribal artwork and how it was done, I was completely hooked. I thought that the play between positive and negative space was really clever, and I loved the fact that, in a sense, there are two designs to every tribal piece…one is the image that is tattooed in black, and one that is left with the skin tone. If you ignore one and just focus on the other, the tattoo will never look right. You have to be conscious of both parts when you are designing at all times in order to create a proper tribal design.

A good piece of tribal often has the effect of an optical illusion because the eye tends to see either one design or the other. If you are looking at the black design, the negative space one sort of disappears, and if you then focus on the negative space design, the black ink becomes more of a background to it. The eye seems to focus on only one at a time, which creates some really interesting effects that are really pleasing to the eye.

JS: You take advantage of these effects as well, especially when you use the dotwork technique that you have become known for. I'm calling it "dotwork," but I'd like to know what term you would use to describe your trademark style? How long have you been using it? And do you know of any other artists who work in this style?

Cory: I started doing dots not long after I started doing the Polynesian-influenced stuff. In general, at that time my tattooing just took a major turn towards blackwork of all kinds. I would say "dotwork" is the term I use most in referring to that style, but some people call it stippling or pointillism. Basically, it is using dots spaced out in varying degrees of density to convey shading and grey tones. I enjoy the challenge of using only one color ink, black, to create so many

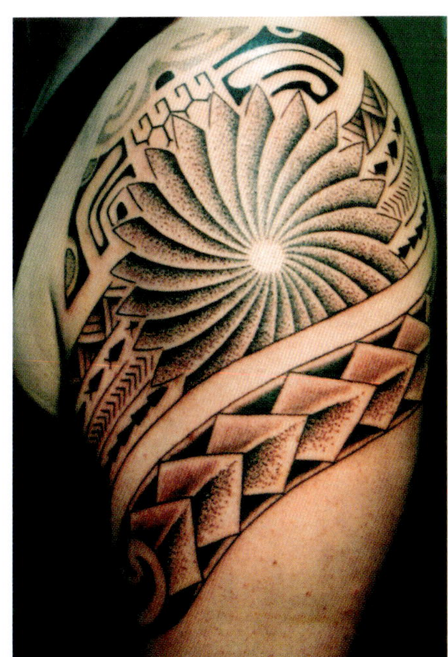

The fanning petals of the flower image in the center circle around a point rendered entirely from negative space.

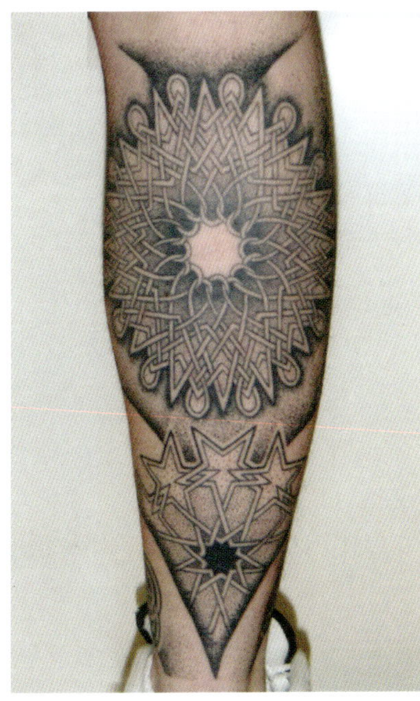

The crispness of Cory's lines, as evidenced by his clean stars and the neat overlapping lines in the knot, allow him to render some eye-pleasing effects in this piece, which feels like an optical illusion.

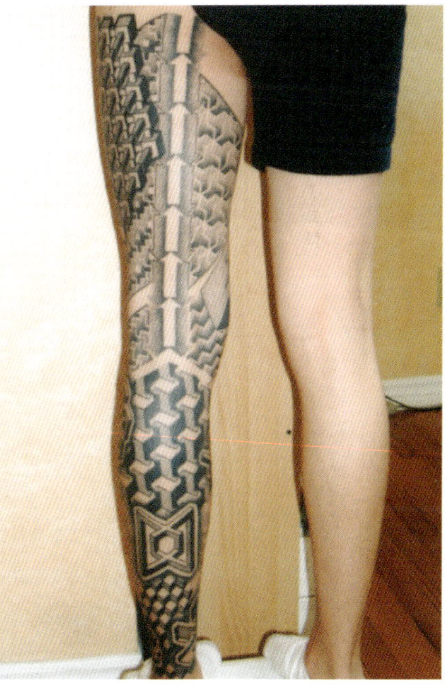

A leg sleeve using Cory's trademark stippling effects to create striking geometric patterns.

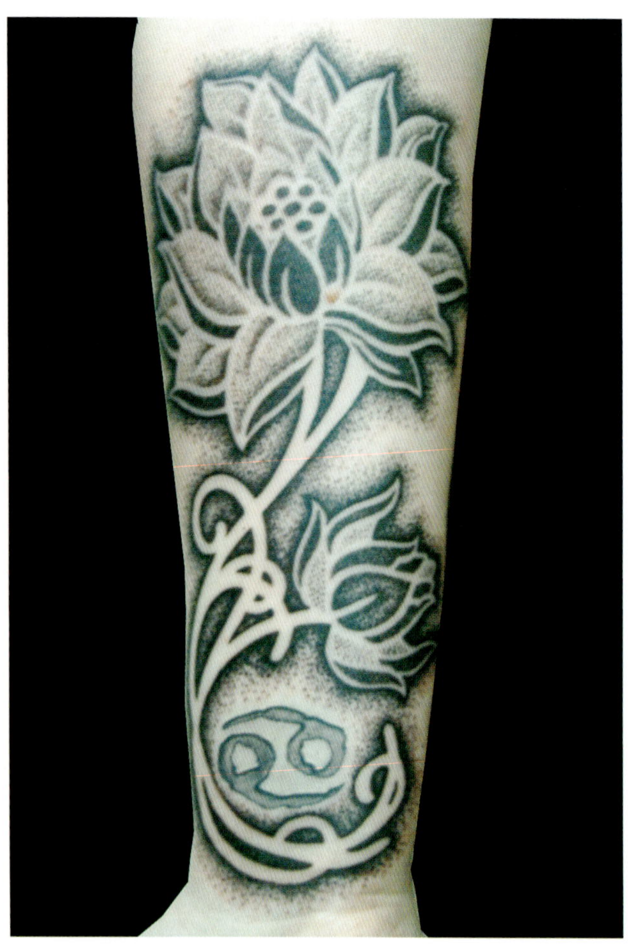

Here the contrast between the black space and the negative space that Cory discussed in his interview is most apparent. Notice how the details he achieves by using his dotwork technique adds interest to this tribal flower.

different gradations and tones in a tattoo. I more or less attribute the beginnings of this style to Xed Lehead from Into-you Tattoos in London, England. Now, however, there are many people doing the dot thing. I hear about more all the time, but as for my inspiration and influences in developing my own techniques using dotwork, I would have to cite Xed and French Thomas at Into-you as the main ones.

JS: What do you think makes tribal tattoos stay so popular? Especially for a style of tattooing that has such obscure roots, it's become really popular in the Western world.

Cory: I wouldn't say that it is the most popular style any more, but at the same time, the tribal style never really goes away. The fact that it is evolving and progressing right now is keeping it alive and exciting. I think that when it is done right, tribal can be really flattering to the body, and it has sort of a timeless quality. Instead of taking a subject matter and putting it on a person, it seems to make the person more of the subject matter, and the tattoo is more or less accenting or decorating what is already there. To me, it sort of works in the way that an animal naturally wears its stripes or markings.

JS: Some tattooists seem resentful if asked to do tribal pieces and talk negatively about "packing black." You, on the other hand, have found a way to make tribal pieces much more interesting than the basic black design. What do you think of attitudes towards tribal in the industry?

Cory: Yeah, I would agree that in general peo-

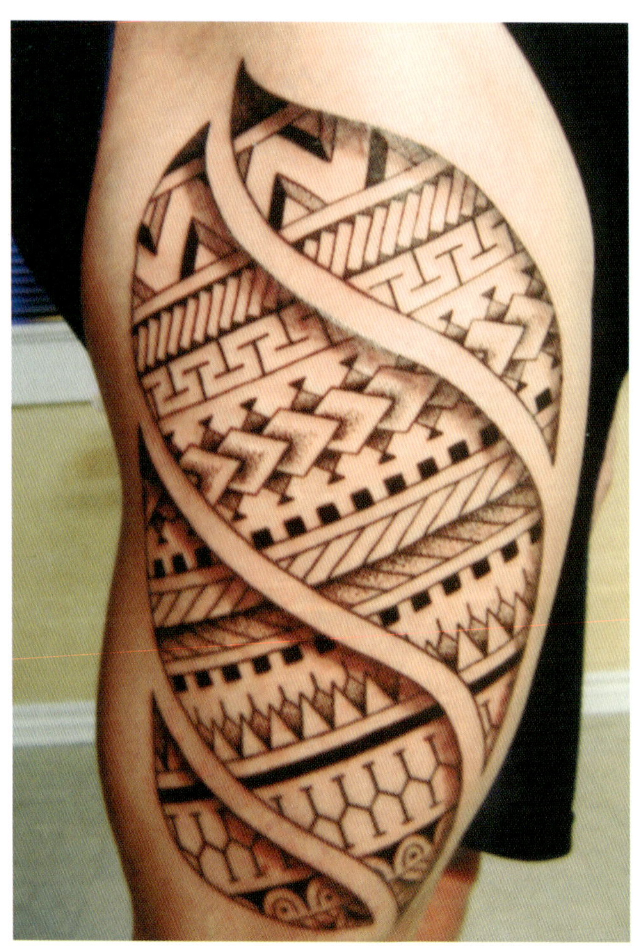

The details in this piece from Cory Ferguson are set off by the large blocks of tribal shapes, adding visual interest to the piece.

ple in the industry can be pretty down on tribal. I would guess that this probably comes from having to pump out your "typical" tribal designs from flash, which is often poorly drawn and lacks creativity, proper flow, and the right play between positive and negative space, which for me are the things that make a good tribal piece a lot of fun to do. For some artists, after the outlines are done, the time you have to spend filling them in can be boring I suppose, but for some reason, I don't mind it. In some ways, the lack of detail can be Zen-like. I don't really need to think too hard when doing it, and my mind can wander on to other things. At the same time, I am still concentrating intensely on not just filling it in, but making sure it is extremely solid and done as gently as possible so that it will heal quickly and be as black as it possibly can be. I am very obsessed on how

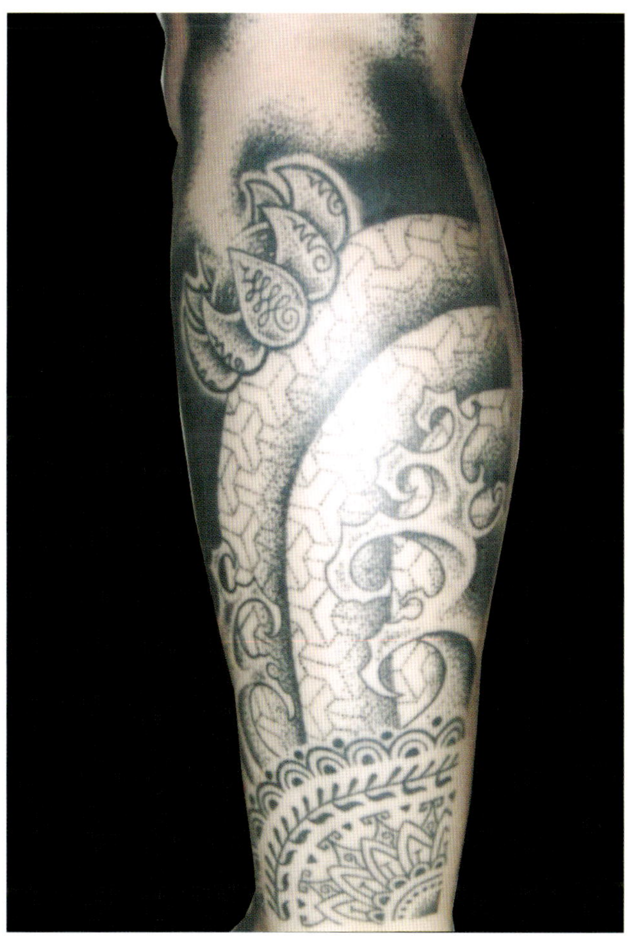

Here Cory juxtaposes elements of Asian design with his signature tribal style to create a delicate, unique piece.

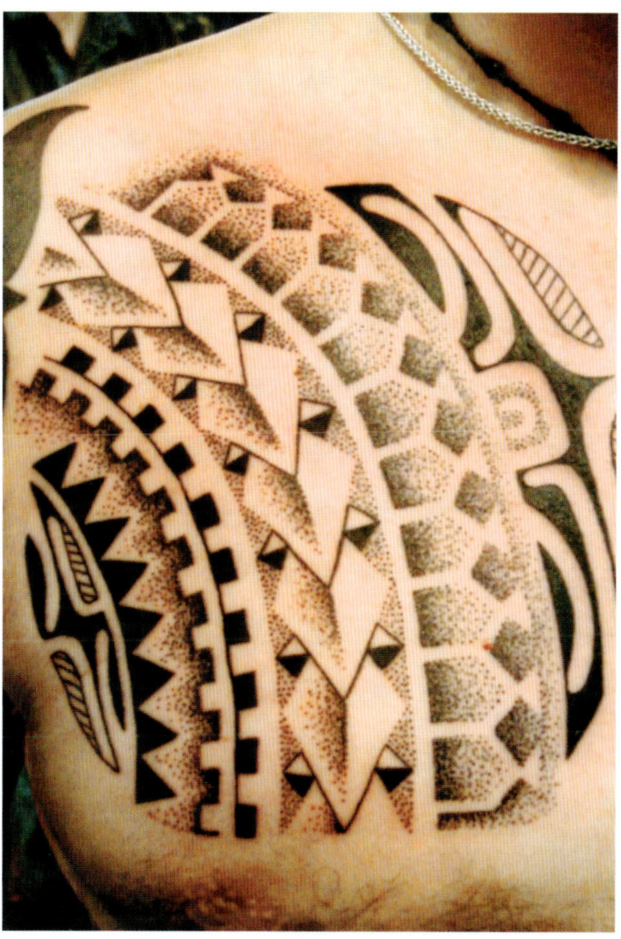

This piece recalls traditional Polynesian tribal work, and the shape of the tattoo truly enhances this wearer's natural musculature in his chest.

solid I can get it, so I'm not happy with just black. It's gotta be really black.

JS: What kinds of clients are most attracted to your work? Do people come to you already aware of your unique style, or do you have to sell them on your custom approach?

Cory: In the beginning, I generally had to really push this kind of style on the people who were coming to me asking for tribal armbands when those were really popular, but those days are long gone for me. At this point, most people come to me to get my style or because they hear I am the guy to come to for tribal. Tribal brings in a weird mix of people for me. People from all across the board, of course, but I find that I get a lot of the tough guy tribal dudes, like the cops or the body builders. And then the dotwork/geometric/Buddhisty kind of stuff that I do attracts the com-

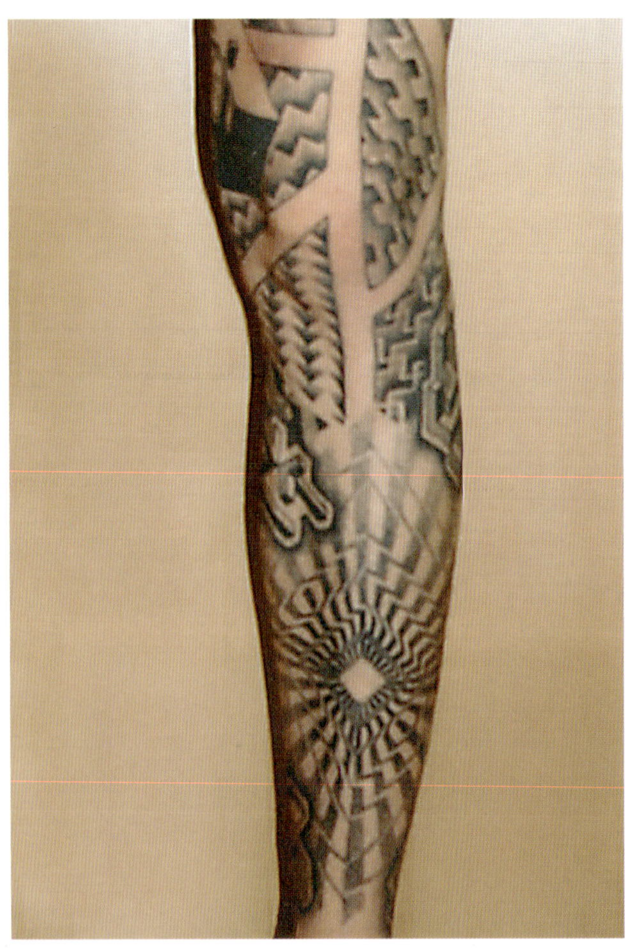

Cory creates the impression of many different shades of black and grey using the dotwork technique.

plete opposite—a very spiritual and hippyish kind of crowd usually seeks out those pieces.

JS: Do you work exclusively in blackwork, or do you also tattoo in other styles? Which styles do you prefer?

Cory: I prefer blackwork the most, but I am also doing a lot of Japanese stuff at the moment, which contains a minimal amount of color. For the most part, though, I am still working with a lot of black ink. I have been doing portraits for a few years now as well. So I am basically dividing my time between my tribal dotwork style and Japanese work with the occasional portrait thrown in from time to time. I avoid color as much as possible, but I can do it when I need to and I doubt I will ever stop using it entirely. I try to use what I learn from each style to help me out with the other. I am also doing a sort of mixture of Japanese and tribal/dotwork with a lot of water and windbar backgrounds done in dots, and I sometimes try to integrate tribal patterns into these designs as well. It results in a more flowing, organic kind of style, which is a nice change of pace from the geometric straight line grid pattern tribal stuff, which can be a struggle to form to the body's natural curves.

JS: Some of these patterns in your designs are intricate, and they seem that they might be quite difficult to tattoo. Do you think that these geometric styles can be more difficult than other styles of tattoos?

Cory: I think it depends on what you get used to. For me personally, I have become accustomed to tattooing repetitive pattern work…the kind of stuff that messes with your eyes. I don't find this style to be any more difficult than the every day

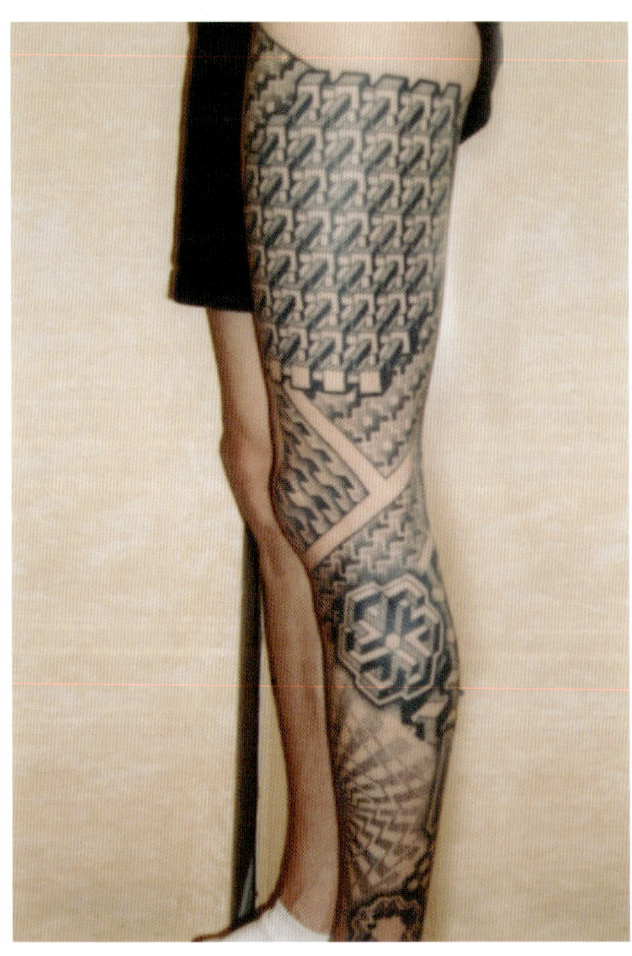

Notice also how the geometric patterns flow with the body's natural musculature.

challenge of getting the ink to go in the skin exactly how you want, regardless of the intricacy of the design. I do get other tattooists looking at my work and saying, "Better you than me!" but I think it just means that the optical effect is doing what it is supposed to do. In reality, I don't think that these techniques are any more difficult than any other kind of advanced tattoo technique. All this new color realism portrait stuff with a million different skin tones looks absolutely mind boggling to me, and I would not have any idea of where to start with a piece like that. But the people that are out there rocking that stuff every day probably don't find it to be so hard.

JS: Where do you get your inspiration?

Cory: I get my inspiration everywhere…from other tattooists, to art, books, architecture, textiles, nature. Some of my favorite stuff to use tends to be Asian influenced patterns and symbols, mathematical geometric designs like optical illusions, and crop circles.

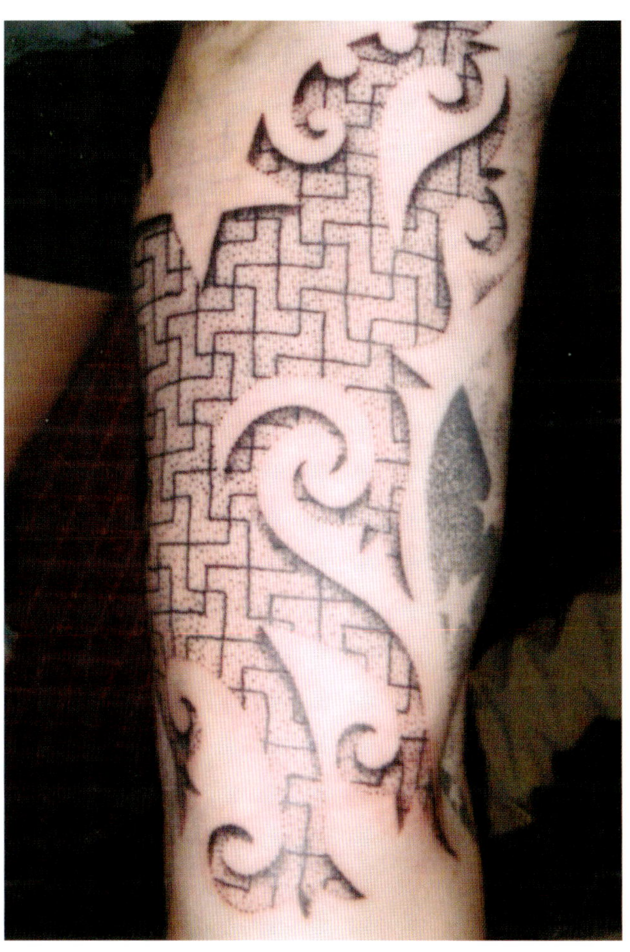

Cory Ferguson, Enlightened Art, Oakville, Ontario

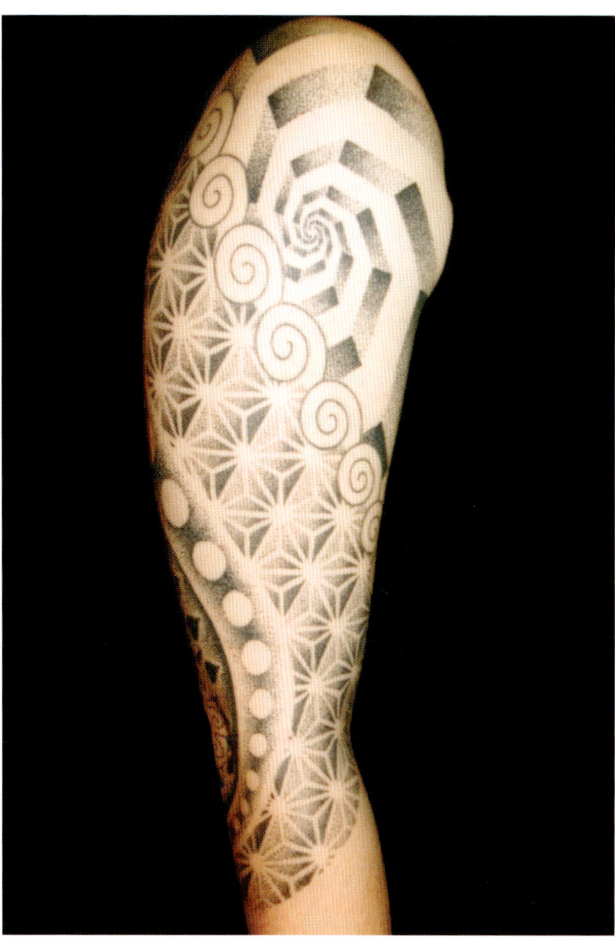

This tribal sleeve illustrates how effectively tribal work can cover a large amount of the body. Tribal imagery works well for sleeves and back pieces or any area of the body where you are interested in getting heavy coverage. The flowing lines in this piece compliment the natural musculature of the wearer's arm nicely.

* * *

Now that we have covered many of the basics, the next styles we will discuss are among the most exciting, cutting edge movements in the tattoo world. Color photorealism and Hybrid tattoos are the newest tattoo styles we will cover, and they comprise some of the most interesting work going on in the industry today.

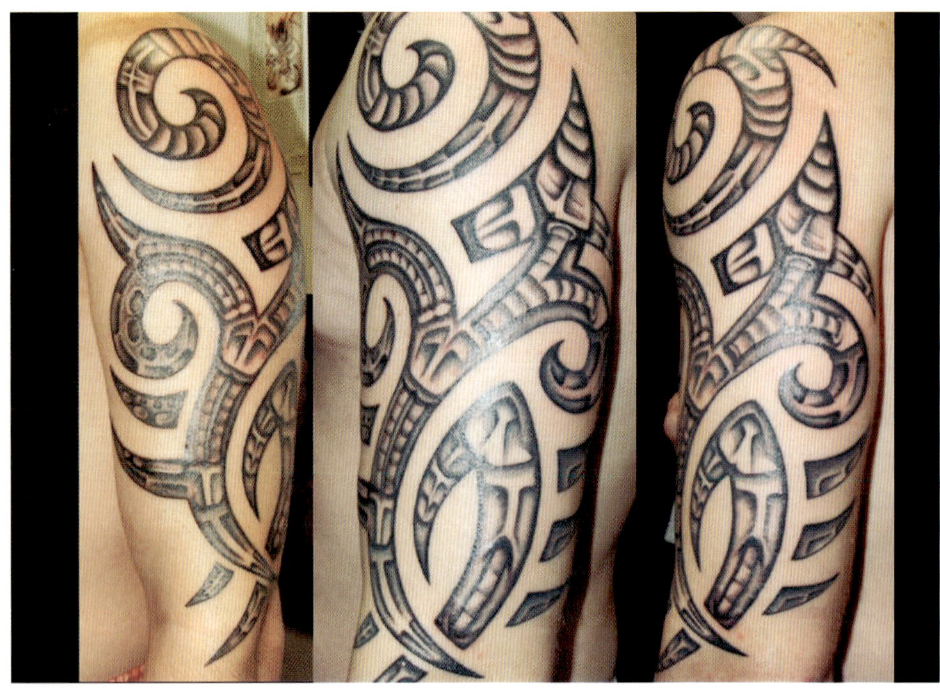

Increasing the complexity of the design by adding additional layers of geometric pattern is one way to make your tribal tattoo more unique, as in this piece by Shannon Brown, Local Color, West Chester, PA.

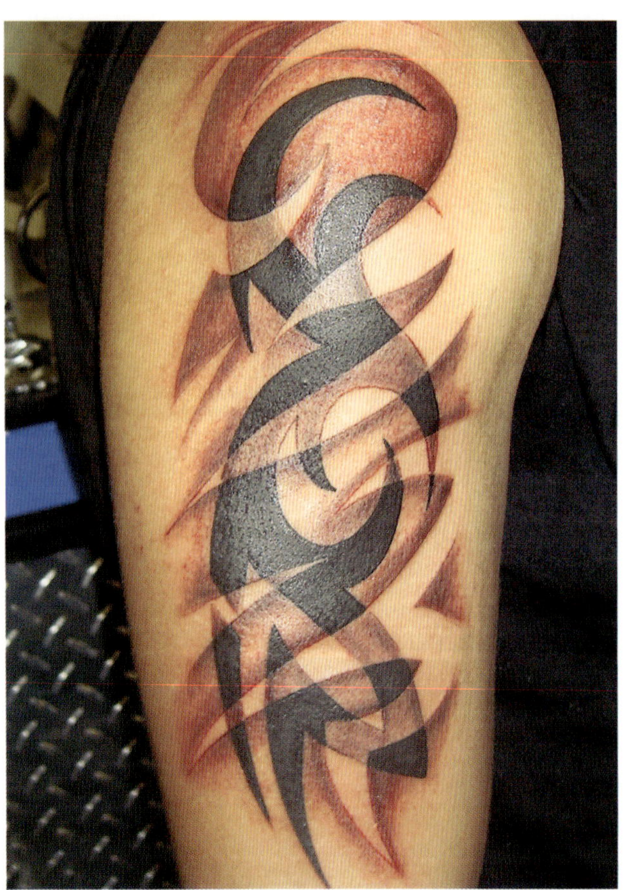

A modern take on the geometric designs common in tribal pieces using negative space and soft shading to heighten visual interest. John Sweeney, Hard Knox, Yonkers, NY.

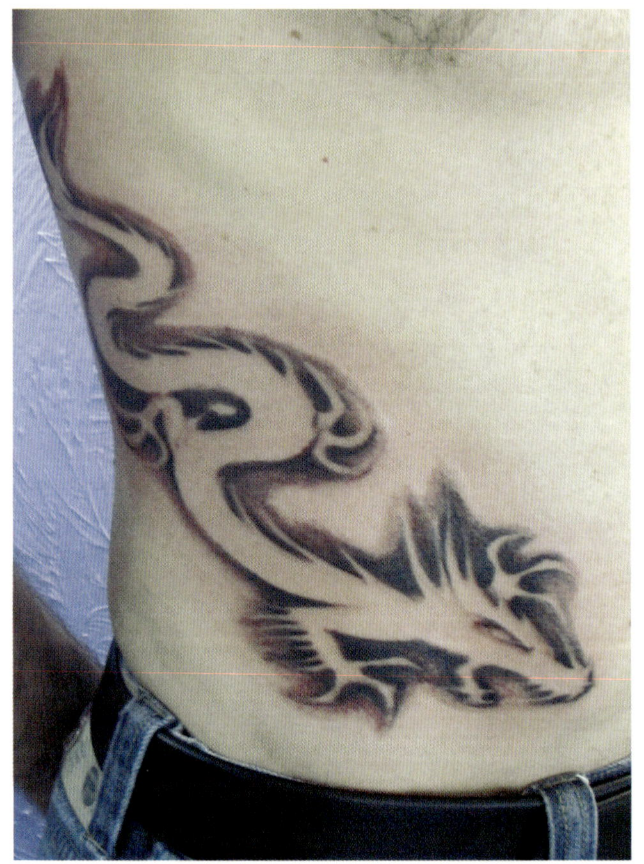

This tribal dragon is rendered through negative space and soft shading, which makes it a unique take on a commonplace tattoo. Also, the placement on the body increases its effectiveness. Shannon Schober, Vitality Tattoo, Asheville, NC.

An obvious enhancement of the body using an elegant tribal design by Shannon Schober, Vitality Tattoo, Asheville, NC.

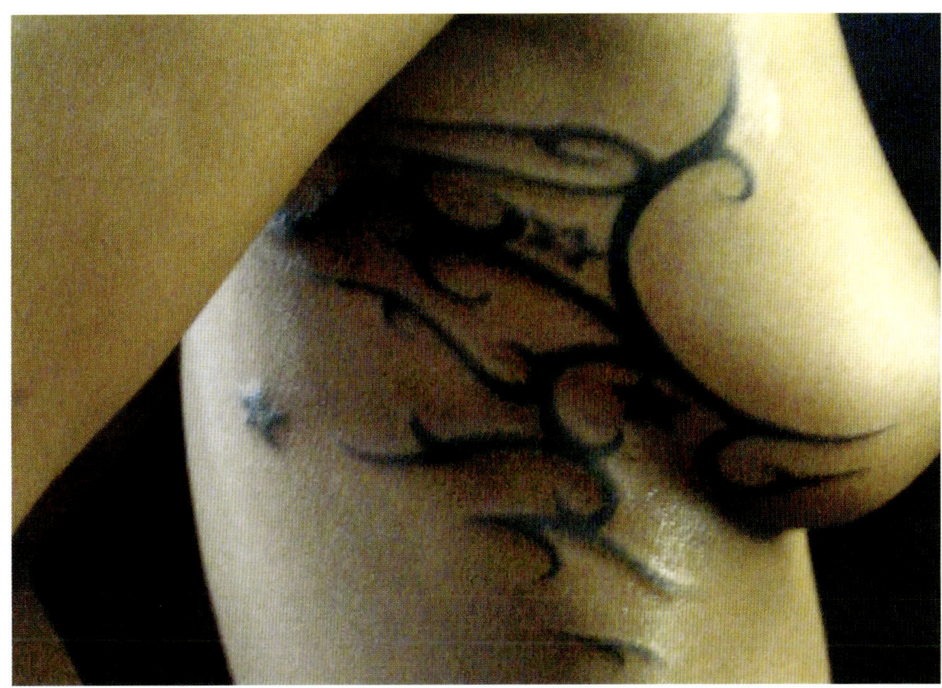

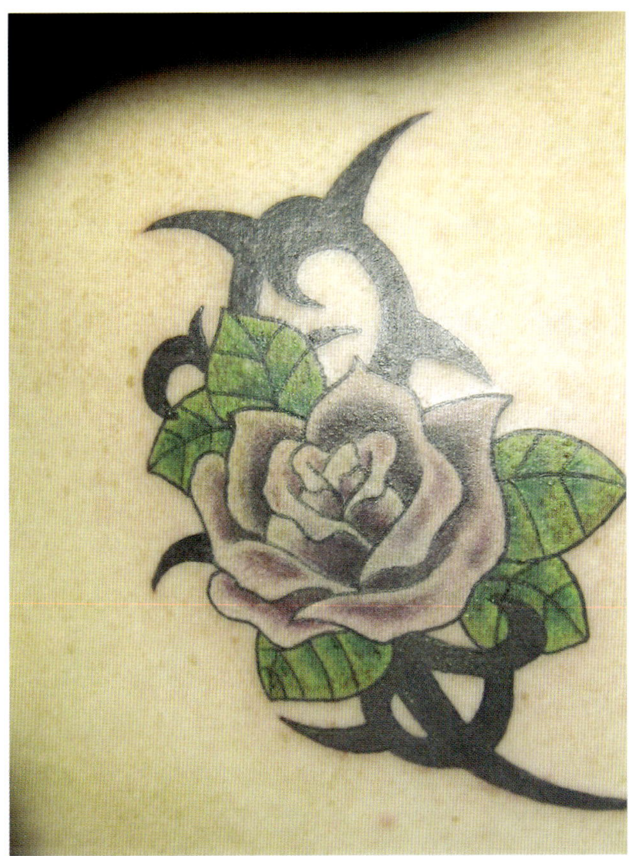

The bold, black designs common in tribal pieces make an excellent backdrop for color pieces, especially in feminine designs like flowers or butterflies, as in this piece by Kirk Shepherd, Fleshworks, Victoria, British Columbia.

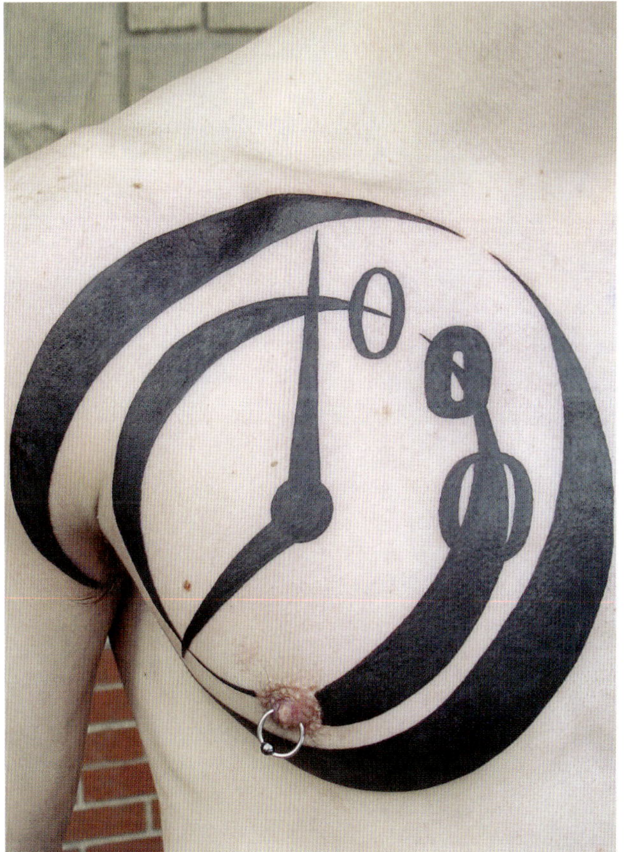

In this unique design from Larry Brogan of Tattoo City in Lockport, IL, he uses the bold shapes common in tribal designs to render a familiar image. The result is a striking, unique tattoo that flatters the chest of its wearer.

Chapter Eight

Photorealism

Tattoo Art's Cutting Edge

One of the more exciting types of tattoos that has been increasing in popularity over the last few years is the hyper-realistic, psychedelic, wildly colored school of color photorealism. The increasing quality of inks and machines as well as the attraction of highly skilled artists to the tattoo medium has made it possible to achieve some amazing effects on skin, and the artists working in this new style of color photorealism are producing some of the most exciting work to

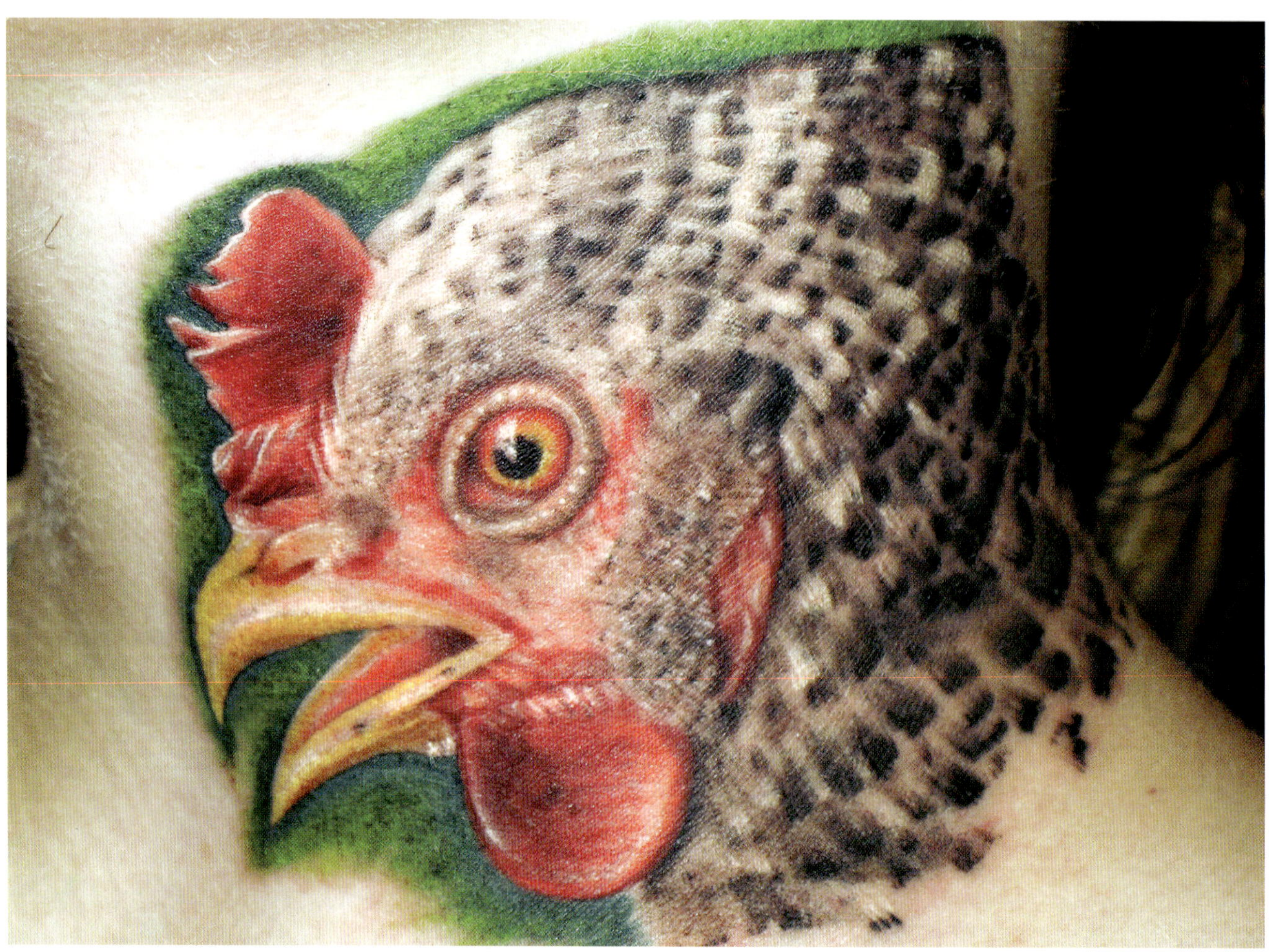

The green background makes the colors pop in this striking, highly realistic chicken head. Sean Herman, All Or Nothing, Atlanta, GA.

come out of the industry in many years. Some members of the tattoo media have even referred to this new breed of artists as comprising a Renaissance of tattoo art, a development of new possibilities through advancements in the technology that has grown up alongside the industry and the artistry that is at its heart. These developments promise to recreate what we consider to be suitable subject matter for tattoo art.

This Renaissance of photorealism has developed alongside the increasing acceptance and widespread popularity of tattoo art in mainstream society. What once was considered taboo and kept in the backrooms is now visible in boardrooms and classrooms. Tattoos are appearing in advertisements, on television, and on celebrities other than the rock stars who traditionally wore tattoos as signs of their badass, outsider status. Because tattoos are reaching a broader audience, the subject matter is changing along with the style. The photorealistic tattoos that are becoming more and more popular are evidence of the changing state of tattoo art.

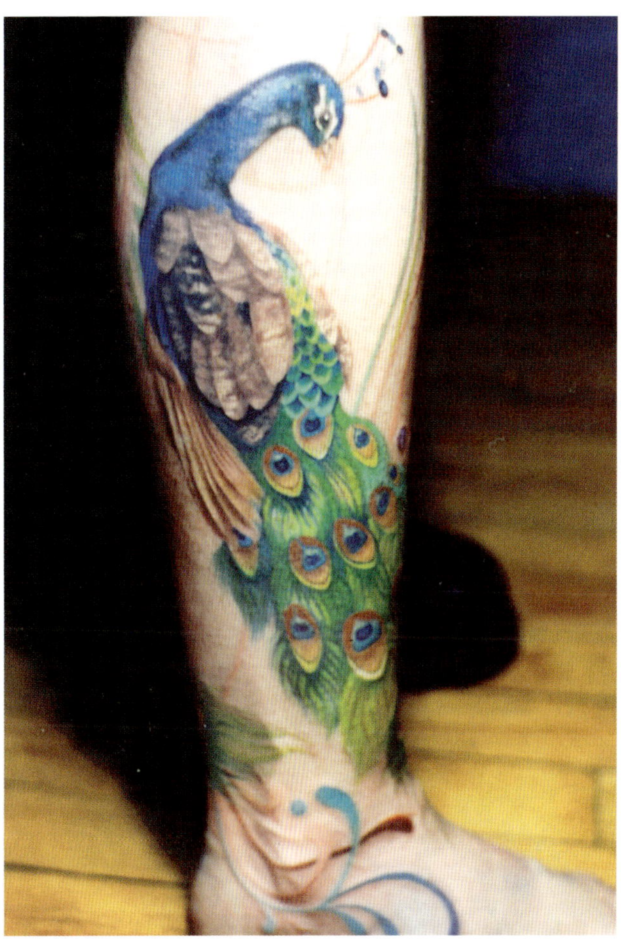

The details in the feathers, the bold colors, and the graceful positioning on the body make this photorealistic peacock from Amanda Wachob striking.

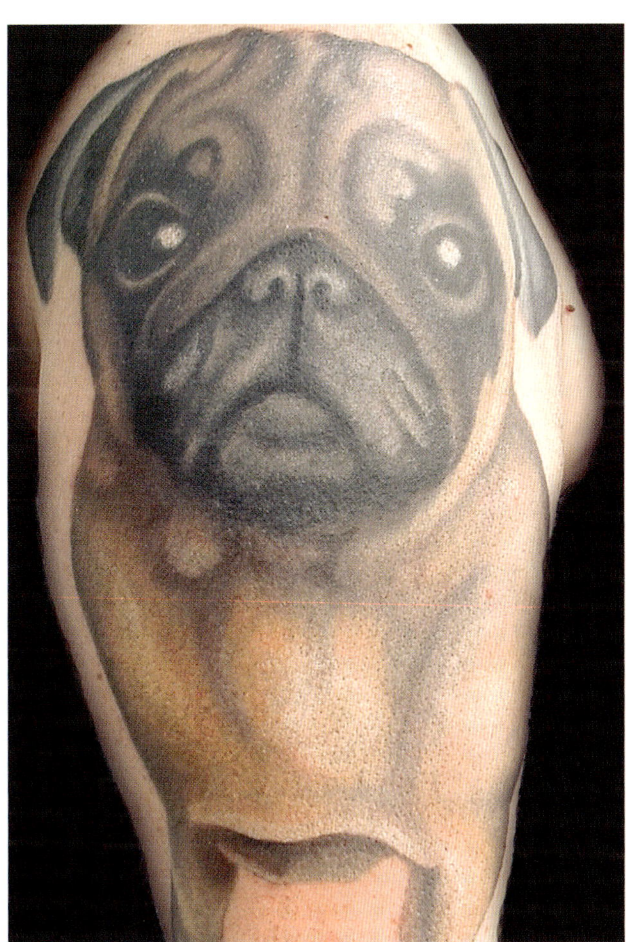

Brandon Bond, All Or Nothing, Atlanta, GA.

One of the many advantages of this style of tattoo art is the high impact on the viewer. These kinds of tattoos are so far outside of what most people think of as tattoo art that the images are sometimes shockingly, unbelievably real to people who are not familiar with the art. The images are eye-catching, head-turning, bold and unique, and they are sure to provoke a reaction from viewers seeing this style of artwork for the first time. Wearers of photorealistic tattoos are often approached by strangers and asked, "Is

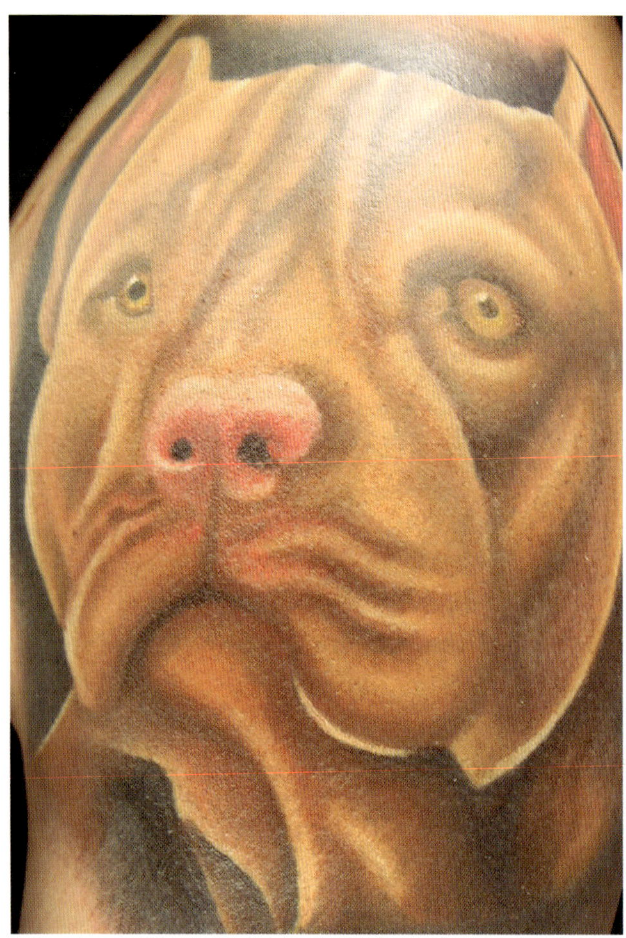

Notice the heightened eye color in the pit bull's eyes. This enhancement of color is one of the advantages of color realism over black and grey portraiture. Brandon Bond, All Or Nothing, Atlanta, GA.

it real?" The images artists are capable of creating in this style are truly breathtaking, and it takes some adjustment for the uninitiated to see that these images really are tattoos.

One of the more popular subjects for these kinds of tattoos is to replicate images from horror movies, particularly faces taken from still frames. In Brandon Bond's *Grudge* face, for instance, he replicates the creepy little boy from the horror movie with heightened colors in a tattoo that not only preserves the tone of the movie, but creates a meaningful, beautiful image that makes a great component of the sleeve it helps to comprise. If you are an old school horror fan or another sort of film buff, selecting a still frame from your favorite movie is a great starting place for your image search for reference. If you bring these images to your artist in your initial consultation, you can discuss the various options your artist might consider to enhance the reference material, such as manipulating the colors, zooming or cropping aspects of the image, or otherwise tweaking it to heighten the drama of the piece.

One of the most common effects that tattooists who work in this style will use to make these images appear so dramatic is zooming. Instead of presenting an entire scene from a film, for instance, the artist selects one image, zooms and crops and focuses, presenting one element of the image in great detail. In Brandon Bond's pit bull portrait, for instance, he focuses on the face of the dog instead of presenting its

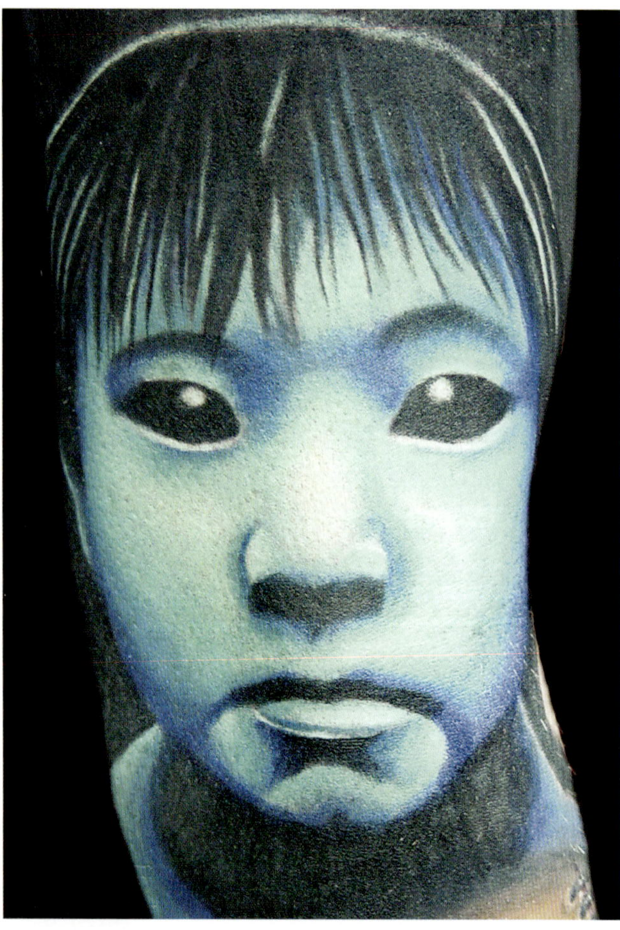

Brandon Bond is known for his bold, beautiful blues and his striking photorealism. This figure is from a still of the creepy kid from the movie The Grudge.

entire body. By zooming in on the dog's face, he is able to focus more detail on the aspects of the animal that are more unique and preserve the dog's character—the eyes, the wrinkles, and the pink nose all stand out more when they are given more space in the image. This heightens the drama of the composition, and it allows a tattoo artist to accomplish some virtuosic displays of his color work. The pit bull tattoo is soft and painterly while remaining true to the dog's unique face. Zsolt Sarkozi's interpretation of the Joker from the *Batman* series of comics similarly uses zooming and cropping to draw attention to the most dramatic features. Sarkozi also employs negative space to draw attention to the eyes, hair, and menacing smile. These techniques guarantee that the eyes of the viewer

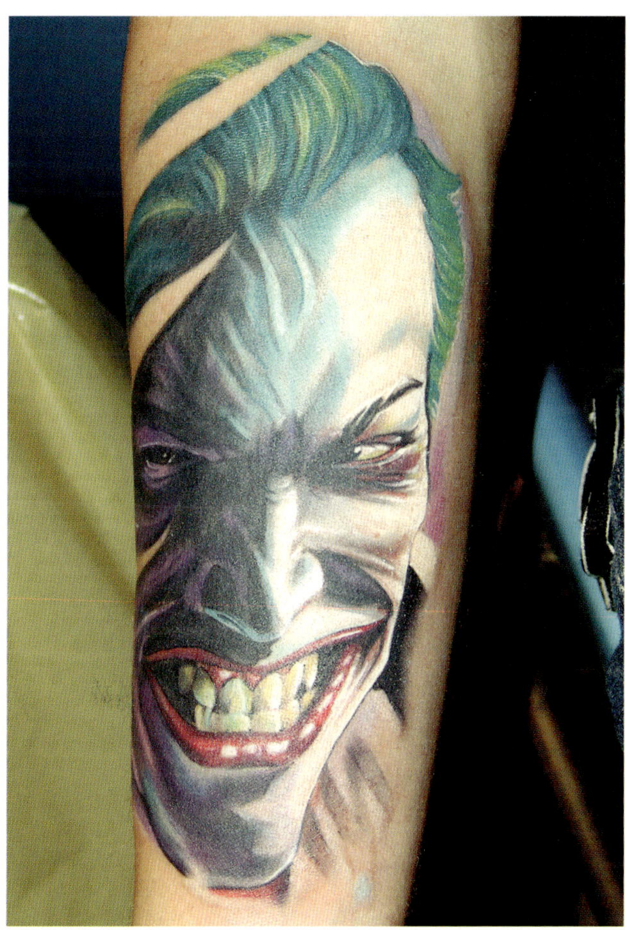

Black and grey master Zsolt Sarkozi's signature use of negative space to create the illusion of depth in a scene is also effective in his interpretation of Batman's Joker character.

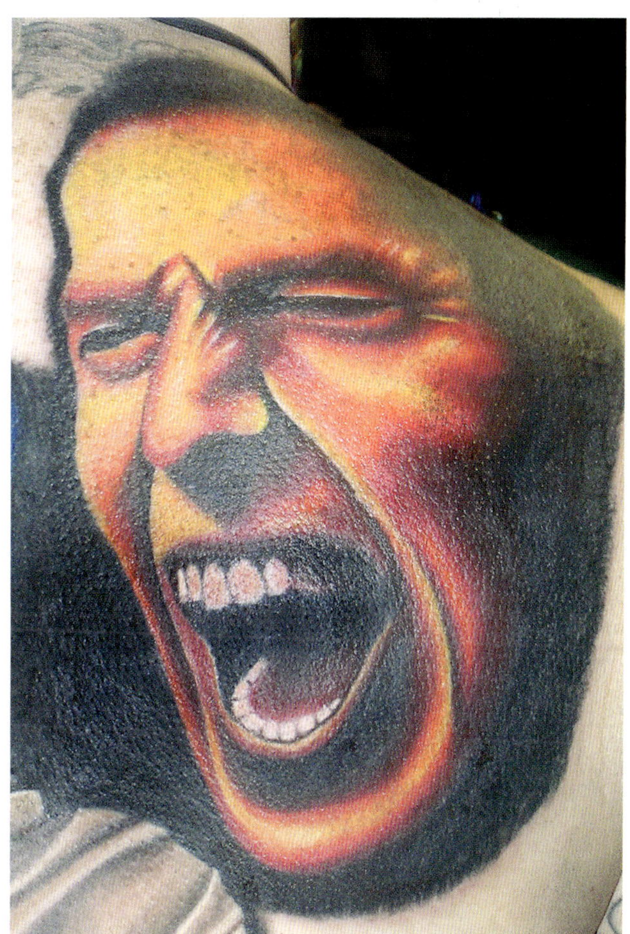

Brandon Bond of All Or Nothing in Atlanta, GA, heightens the red and orange tones in these portraits to render a hyper-realistic effect.

focus on the most important parts of the images, making the impact of these tattoos high.

Photorealism has long been an aspect of tattooing, most often in the black and grey portraiture we have already covered. While artists working in this traditional style of black and grey are able to achieve highly realistic effects using shading and by manipulating the impression of a light source and shadow in their designs, these portraits are much more subtle and do not achieve the high drama of the current trend of color photorealism. From the provocative subject matter that many artists choose for these tattoos to the realistic impressions of texture, aggressive contrasts in color, and hyper-realistic three dimensionality of these

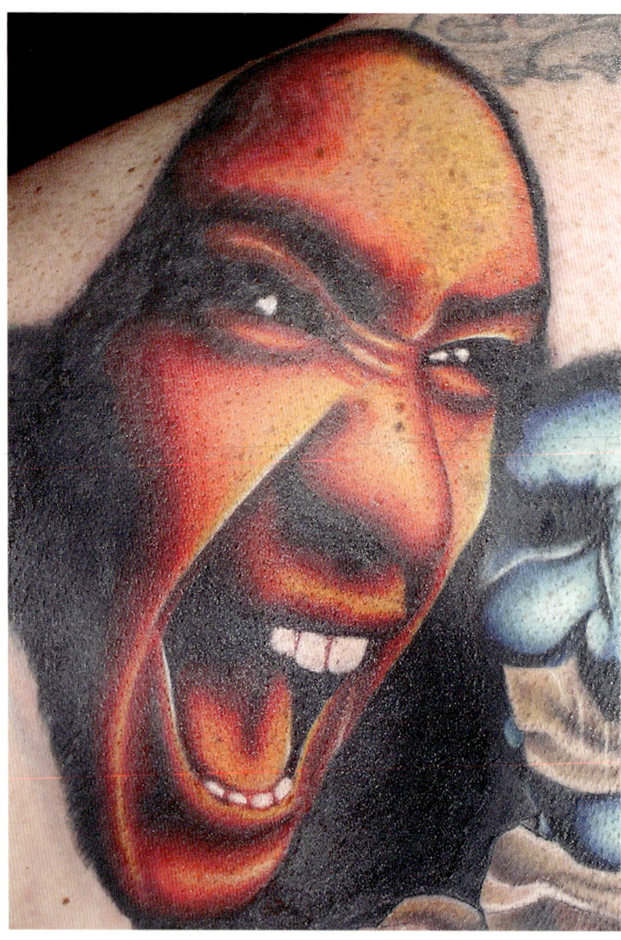

Brandon Bond of All Or Nothing in Atlanta, GA.

astonishing, painterly effects using skin as their canvases. Tattoos completed in this style often explore spatial dynamics in an image, tweaking forms in a manner similar to the manipulations in forms we discussed in the chapter on New School artwork, presenting an enhanced vision of reality. The artists create images that are realistic, but they are also much more.

Because of the high impact of this style of artwork, many artists have jumped on the bandwagon and attempted to become photorealistic tattoo artists, exploiting the opportunity to make money off of a few talented artists' innovations. The images that these newer artists produce can be striking; however, if you are considering getting a tattoo done in this style, it is worth looking for an artist with some experience

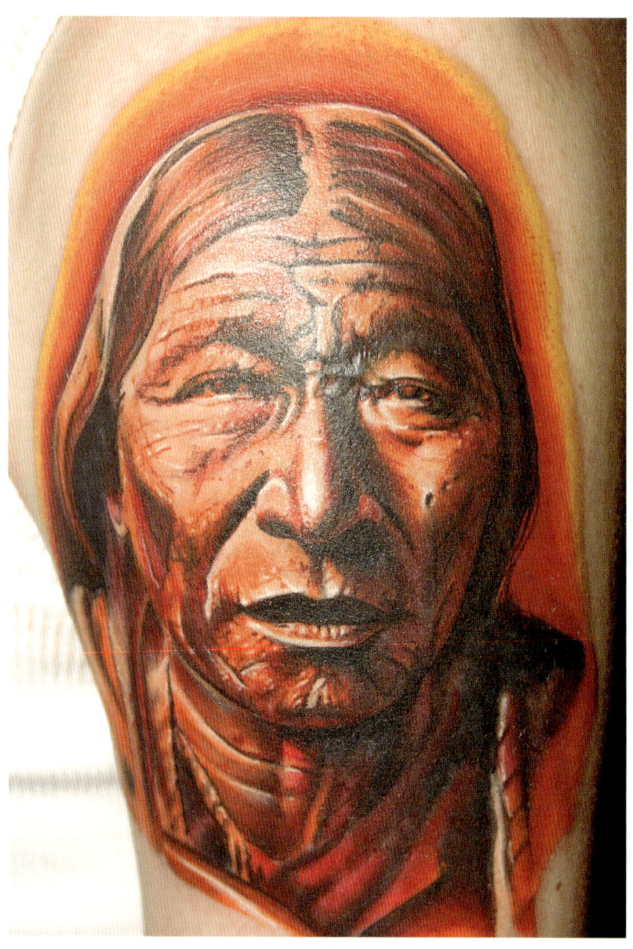

Here Zsolt Sarkozi has created a highly detailed, realistic image with heightened rusts, reds, and oranges.

pieces, the developments in cutting-edge photorealism have brought tattoo art into the avante garde.

Another difference between traditional black and grey portraiture and color photorealism is that the images are often not quite "realistic." While most artists refer to this style as "photorealism," which is why we have chosen this term for our purposes in this chapter, the colors in the images are often tweaked using Photoshop or other color-enhancement techniques to give artists options to experiment with color variations that are a far cry from "realistic." The style is, in fact, something more like "hyper-real," allowing artists extraordinary room for creative expression and freeing them up to achieve some and with a portfolio that demonstrates he or she is proficient in the style. Different colors of inks fade through time, and it is likely that these color portraits will fade into a blobby mess if they are not done by artists with experience working in this style. It will definitely be worth your time and energy to do your research to make sure you find an artist whose work has proven to withstand the test of time.

One artist who is a forerunner of this style is Nate Beavers, owner of I45 Ink in Houston, TX. While Nate is known for his creative New School designs, his black and grey portraiture, and his use of traditional elements in many different kinds of tattoos, in recent years he has become most well-known for his high-impact photorealism, his use of Photoshop to manipulate his colors, and his recent experiments with pairing photorealism with traditional American elements. Nate is widely regarded as one of the leaders in the photorealism style of tattoo work, and we were lucky enough to catch up with him and to have the opportunity to talk with him about his work and his thoughts on the style, and here is what we found out.

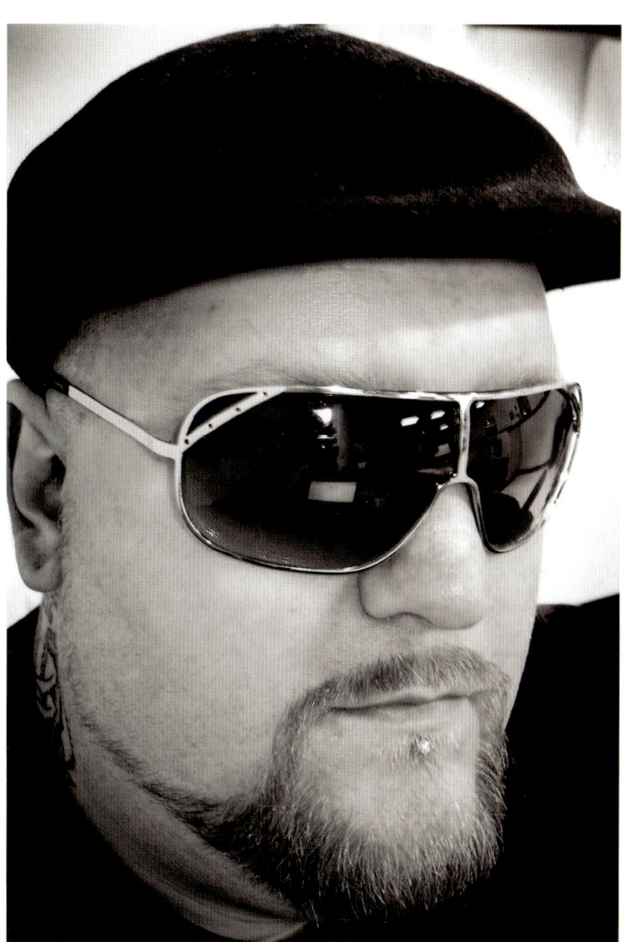

Nate Beavers, I 45 Tattoo, Houston, TX

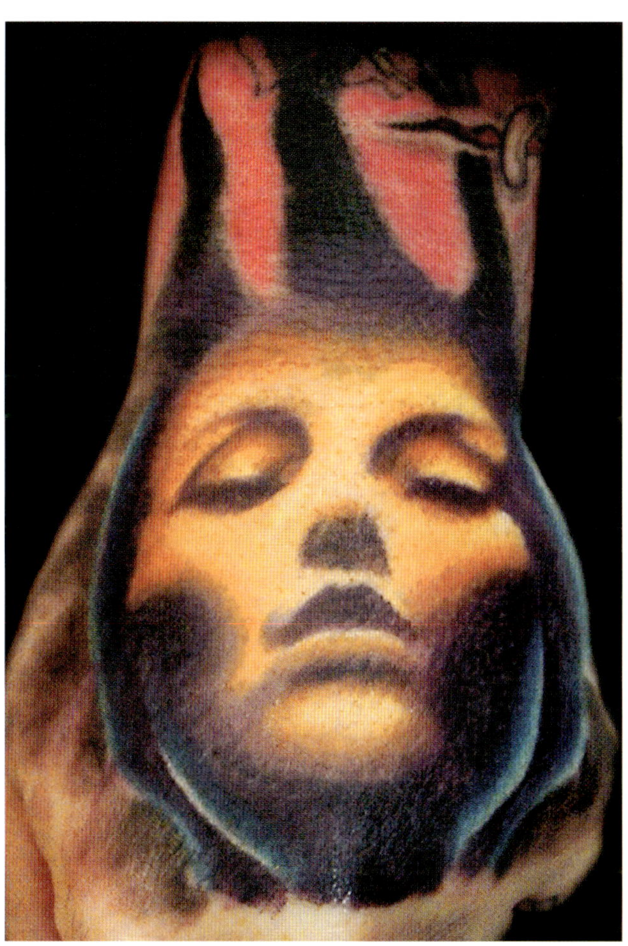

Brandon Bond is known for effective use of the human hand as a canvas.

Nate Beavers Q & A

JS: This new style of photorealism that you have been experimenting with for the last few years is really blowing up in the industry. It is becoming one of the most popular styles of tattoos. What do you think has made this cutting-edge style of art so successful?

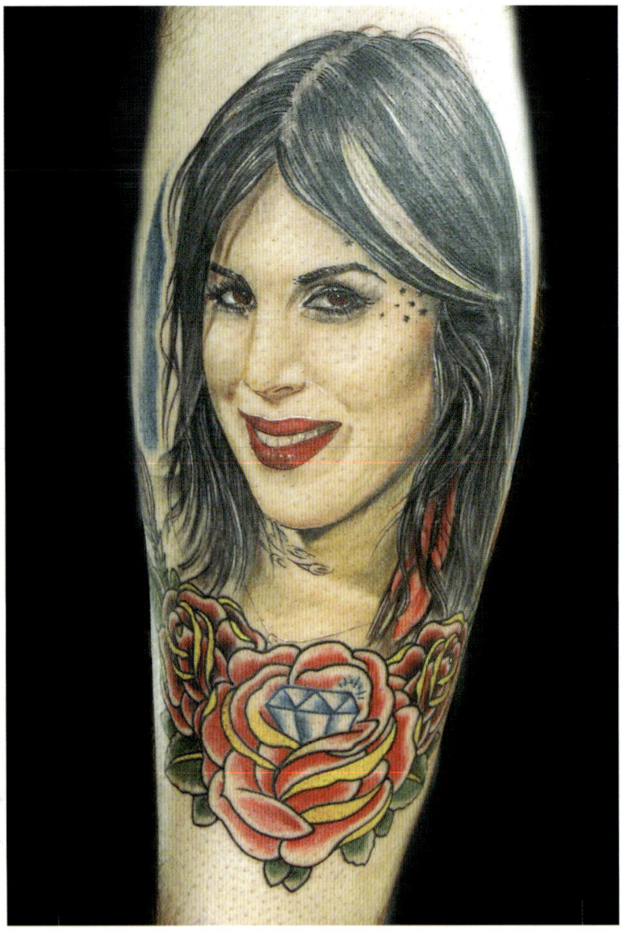

Nate's incorporation of traditional elements in this portrait of Kat Von D.

JS: Yes. That's the "other" style you are known for...crazy hybrid compositions...

Nate: Yeah. The hybrid stuff is fun for me to draw, but the photorealism is just straightforward enough to catch the eyes of everyone and anyone.

JS: I think you're dead on about the high impact and about the mass appeal. Some of these images are really beautiful, and even if you aren't crazy about tattoos, it is hard for anyone to deny something as beautiful as your vampire half sleeve, for instance.

One of the things that we're exploring in this book is the relationship between the tattoo artist and the client as well as the artist's process. It seems like the process might be pretty different in a tattoo done in this style. We were curious about what

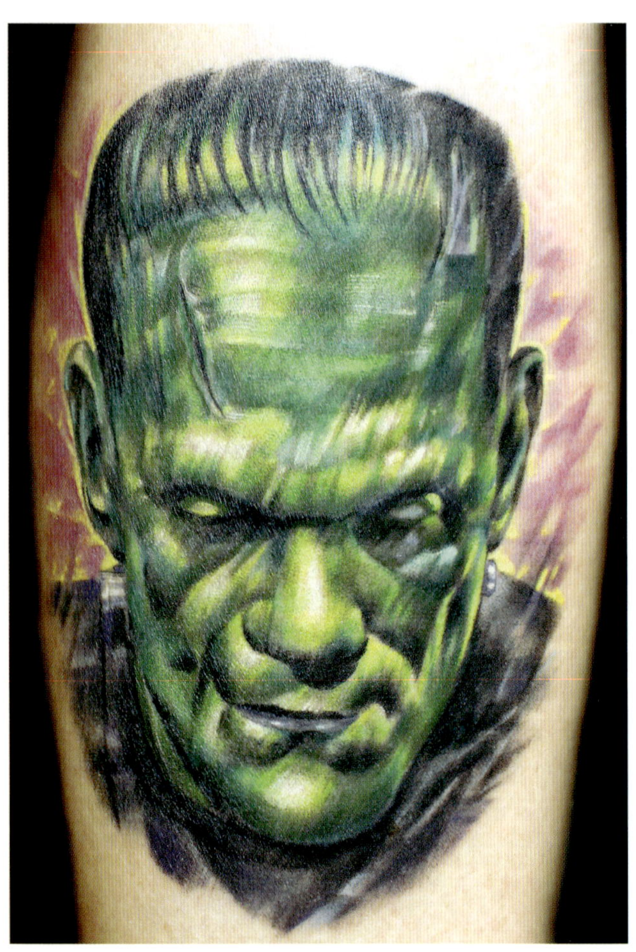

A painterly version of Frankenstein.

Nate: I think these kinds of tattoos have more of an impact visually, and it is harder to pull off than other kinds of tattoos. People respect the skill it takes to be able to do photorealism well. There is way less room for error when dealing with portraiture. If the nose is wrong, it sucks. If one of the eyes is off, then the portrait has a lazy eye or crossed eyes. Every piece has to be dead on, or the piece as a whole suffers drastically. I think the realm of people without any tattoos or knowledge of good work are generally more impressed by photorealism because it appeals to the masses more so than a crazy two-headed snake with panther legs choking a Cyclops chicken...

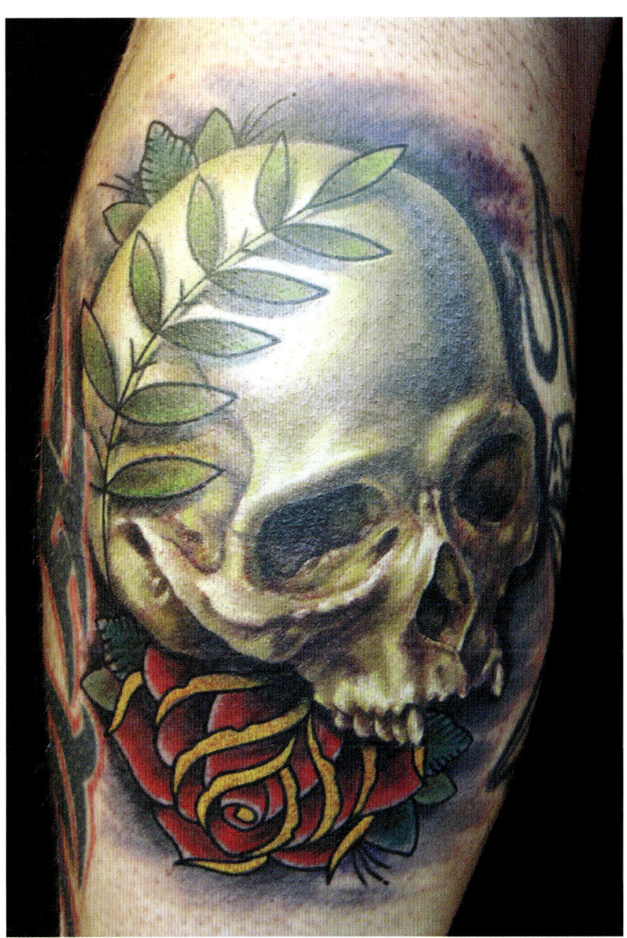

Here Nate masterfully blends the high drama of photorealism with the stylized beauty of traditionalism.

your process is like when you're designing a piece in this style?

Nate: I start with an idea of the main image involved, and then I search for the perfect picture to use for reference. I use a lot of photo reference for the pieces that I tattoo, but then I usually intertwine some of my own drawings into it. I definitely like to use Photoshop as a tool to get it set up. I use Photoshop to layer images that become the foundation for the end product for the tattoo. I also use it to tweak the colors and to experiment with variations in the darkness and lightness. I've been learning more and more about Photoshop as I've been doing this kind of work, and it is an awesome tool to have.

JS: And how closely do you work with your clients when you're planning a tattoo?

Nate: I try to get inside their heads and come up with something that I think they're wanting to see done but aren't able to put down on paper themselves. I usually take a ton of notes on the details they are sure they want to include in the piece, and I like to have a lot of time to think it over, even if it's just for a while, just in my head, before I start drawing…kind of to see what comes up. One good thing about getting more established in the industry, is that recently I have had a lot of clients tell me to just do whatever it is that I want to do, and that is always the best possible scenario, for sure. It gives me a chance to experiment and try out new ideas, which I always appreciate.

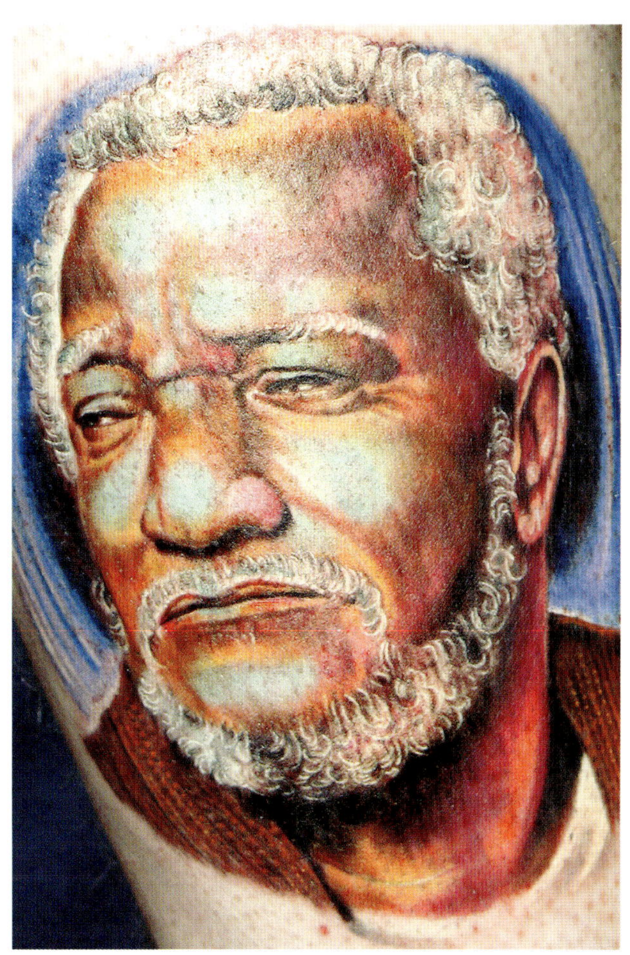

Nate is known for his realistic hair, as in this tribute to Fred Sanford.

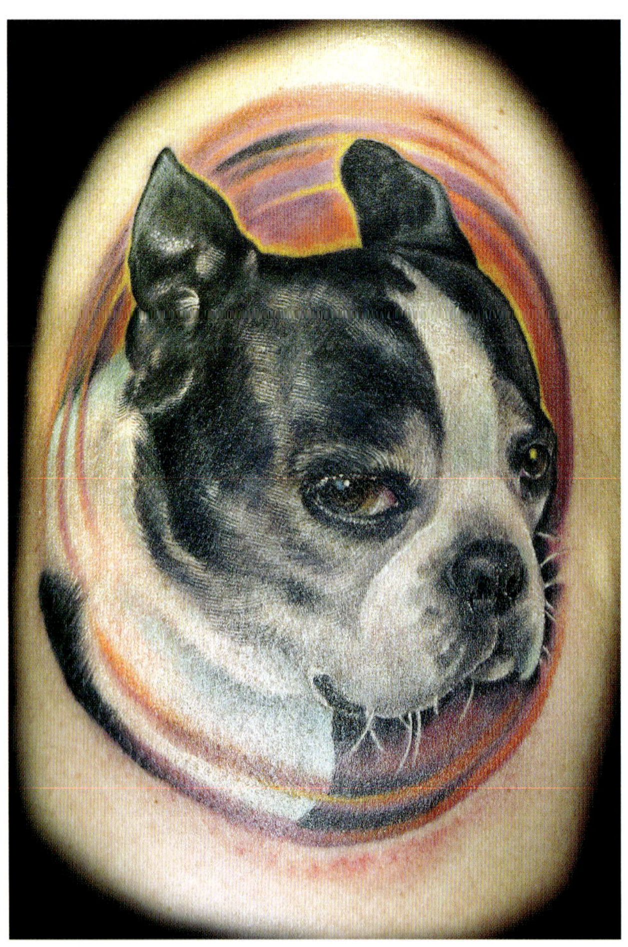

Notice the details in the hair in this Boston Terrier portrait.

JS: Yes, I guess that is one of the advantages of having had a long career. It gives you the chance to sometimes get a blank canvas that you can fill up however you want, and you probably get a lot more freedom from your clients about the design.

Nate: Yeah, and I won't always budge on elements of design that I think are necessary. If I think something will look better, I usually insist on it, or tell them I won't put out work that doesn't reflect my skill level and suggest someone else who might be a more appropriate artist for the tattoo they want.

JS: So speaking of your clients, have you noticed that your style of work is attractive to a particular kind of person?

Nate: I have noticed that a lot more of the serious collectors have been wanting my work, especially the photorealism stuff...more seasoned tattoo veterans and less of the newby tattoo fans. That is good for me because they tend to handle it well and they usually have sought me out for my style instead of just stumbling into a shop and wanting to get something done on the spur of the moment. I hate to start a decent sized tattoo that someone won't be able to handle. It makes the process drag on for way too long, and it makes it hard for me to take it as seriously as it should be, because at some point, I usually just want to get the piece done and get the fussy client out of my sight before I get upset. It happens...we get frustrated...

JS: There seems to have been a Renaissance in tattooing in the last 10 years or so, especially in the art of the photorealistic tattoo. It's changing from

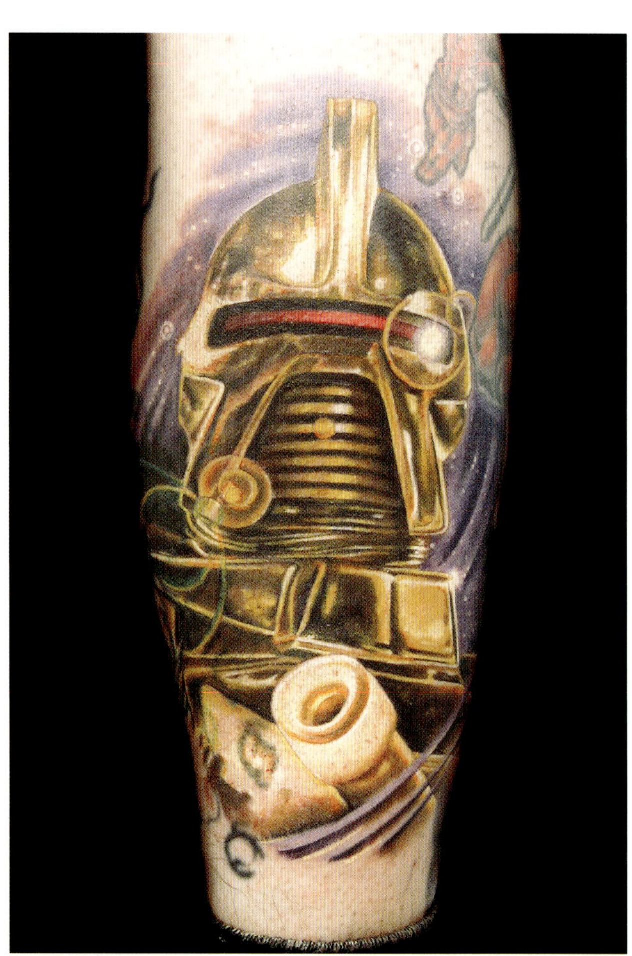

Cylon figure from Battlestar Galactica. Notice the metallic textures Nate achieves using the techniques of color realism.

straight portraiture to something much more interesting. Being one of the forerunners of this movement, what do you think explains its development?

Nate: Honestly, I think it's that regular portraits were getting kind of boring. I started to add stuff to the realistic pieces I was doing to make them more than just another portrait…to add some movement and emotion to it all.

JS: Do you think the term "Renaissance" is appropriate for what's going on in the industry? Folks toss that word around a lot when they are talking about your work…

Nate: I have heard that word used several times by many tattoo enthusiasts, and I guess they are right. Tattoo work has become more of an art movement. From inside the industry, it sometimes seems that we're in a kind of race,

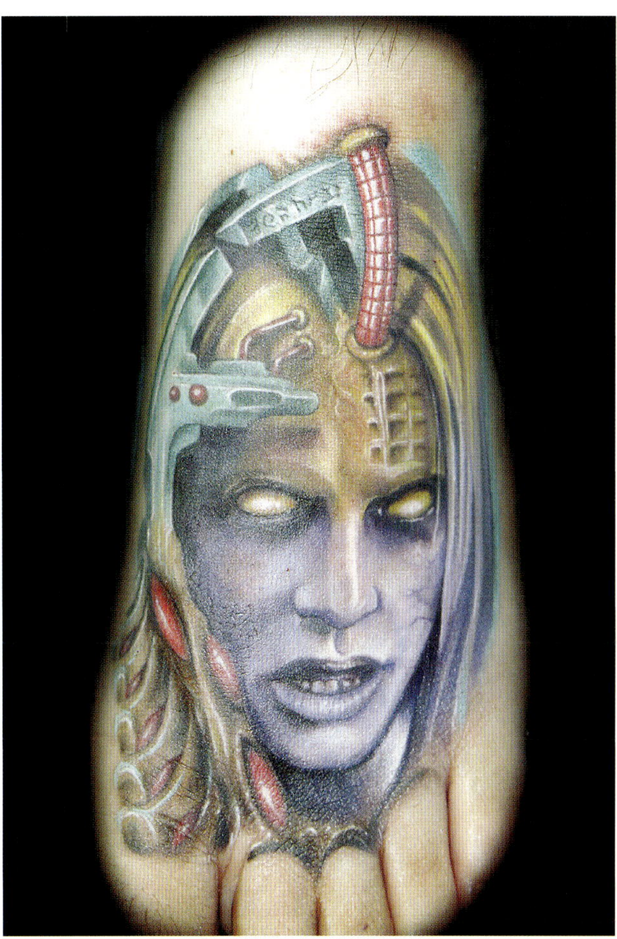

Here Nate fuses the biomechanical style with his colorful photorealism in an interesting foot tattoo.

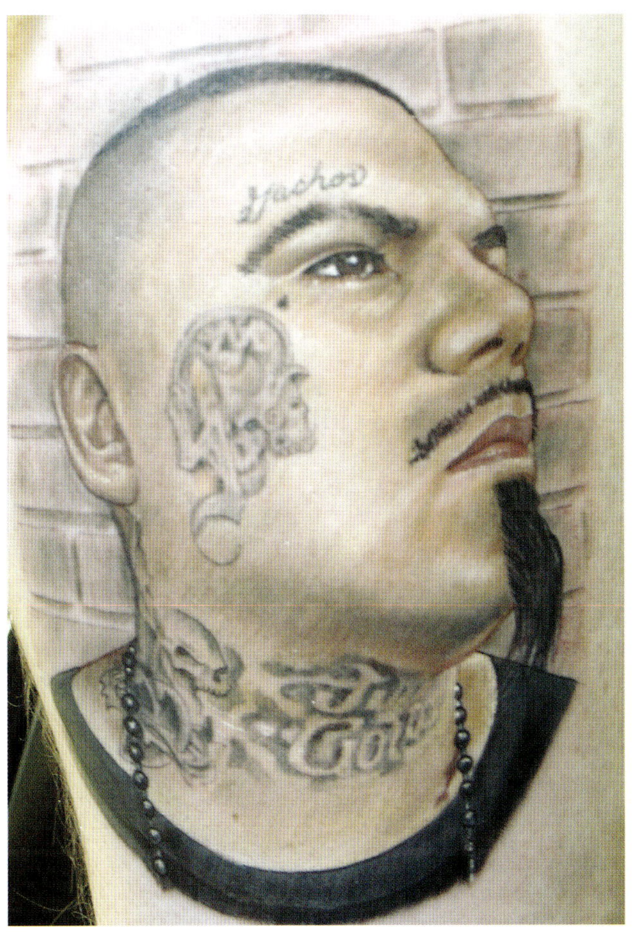

Nate's color portrait of rapper Juan Gotti. The brick background is unique.

that the process has progressed through an underlying competition to do the most realistic, innovative, boundary-pushing tattoo possible. It's sparked some insanely good things, from the photorealism stuff to the biomechanical thing that seems to be coming back around in a major way. There is a lot of exciting work out there, and a lot of great artists coming up.

JS: So it is a pretty exciting time for you to be in the industry…and it's a pretty exciting time for collectors to be getting new tattoos…

Nate: Yeah.

JS: Looking through your portfolio, I have also noticed that you've started doing a lot of mixing of styles in recent pieces, combining, for instance, stylized flowers reminiscent of traditional American work with the wild colors and experimental angles of this newer photorealism. What's going on with that new mix?

Nate: My goal is to create a formula to make a cool tattoo out of any image every time. That is every artist's goal, I think. I want to put out a picture of what I see in my head, but it isn't always easy to translate the mental stuff to paper. I just keep morphing and mixing things until I get there. I will always try to do better, more unique, more beautiful and higher-impact tattoos, and I'm always searching for obscure reference. That's what's up. I'm always changing, so who knows…I might just get into another style altogether!

JS: You mentioned the level of difficulty involved in putting on these kinds of tattoos. Are there any tips you have for folks interested in getting a tattoo in the photorealistic style?

Nate: I always suggest www.TattooNow.com to people who are looking for an artist. Some of the best artists working in the industry today are on that site, and you can locate an artist based on the state that they're in, so it's good for people who are interested in finding someone local. I do a lot of business on Myspace, too, which is becoming a great place to find artists in your area or to find artists you like and to follow them to see when they might be on tour near you. The library is always the best place to search for reference for both the tattooist and the client. I try not to use Google too much, even though it's the easiest and quickest source for reference. The images cataloged there are used over and over again, and it would suck if it turned into a source of images that weren't much more unique than flash. That's

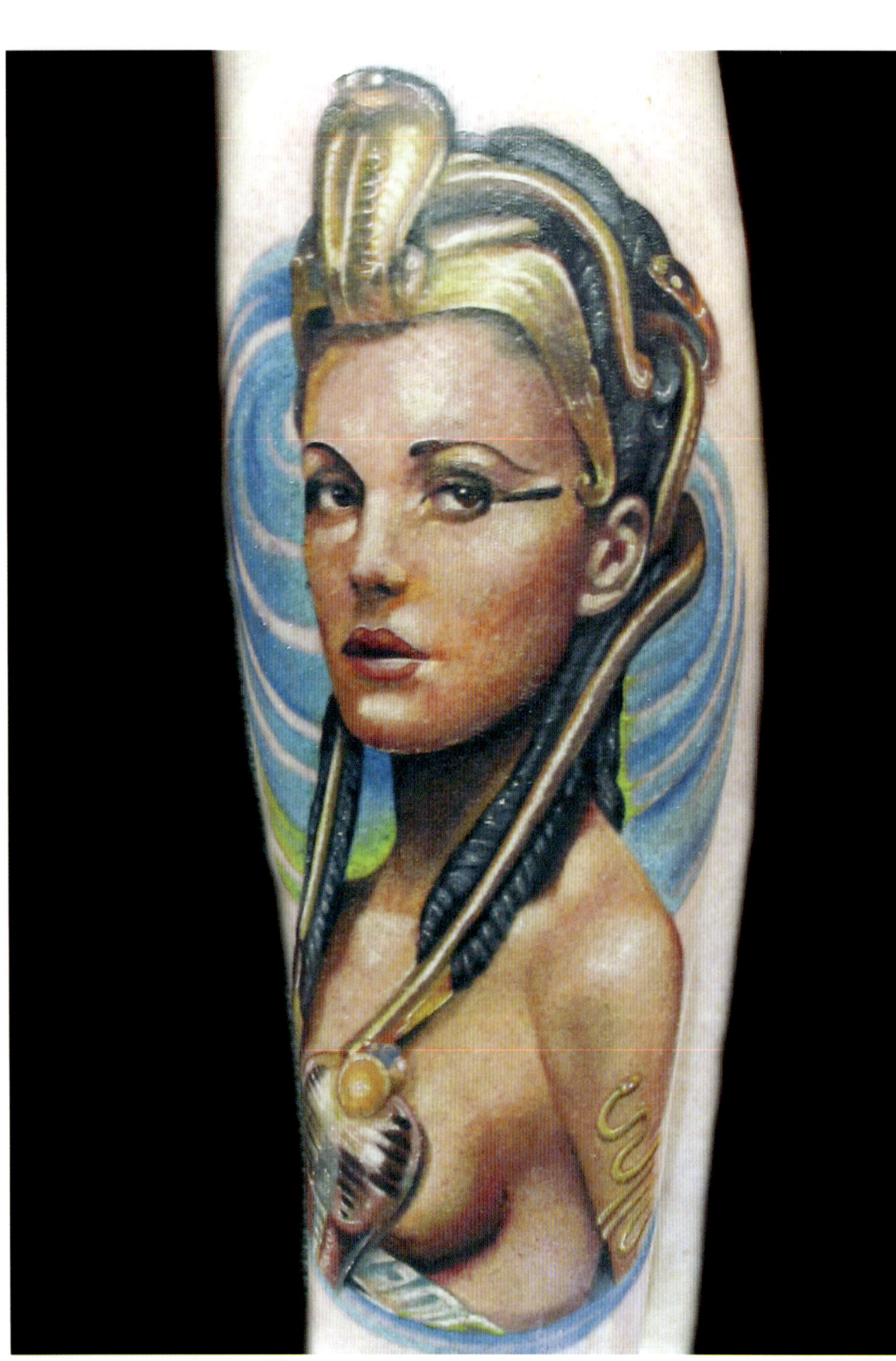

Nate's version of Cleopatra.

not what this photorealism stuff is about..

When I do use Google to find a reference piece, I just do an image search and type in key words to lead me in the right direction…like if I want to do a scary female face, I type in "scary bloody chick" and see what I find. Sometimes I'll search through model's sites or fetish sites to see what's out there. You've got to keep an open mind and put in a lot of time to find good reference, but there's a lot out there, and it's worth it to look.

* * *

Photorealism is one of the most impressive tattoo styles, and the cutting-edge techniques and imagery required to produce these masterpieces are improving all the time. As these techniques continue evolving, work emerging from this school of art promises to get better and better. If you follow the careers of tattooists like Nate who are working in this vein, you will see tremendous growth through each piece they create.

The next style that we will cover is also an edgier style that veers from much of the traditional work we have investigated so far. Hybrid styles are becoming increasingly popular for tattoo aficionados, and mixing the elements in pieces is an exciting way to make your tattoo unique.

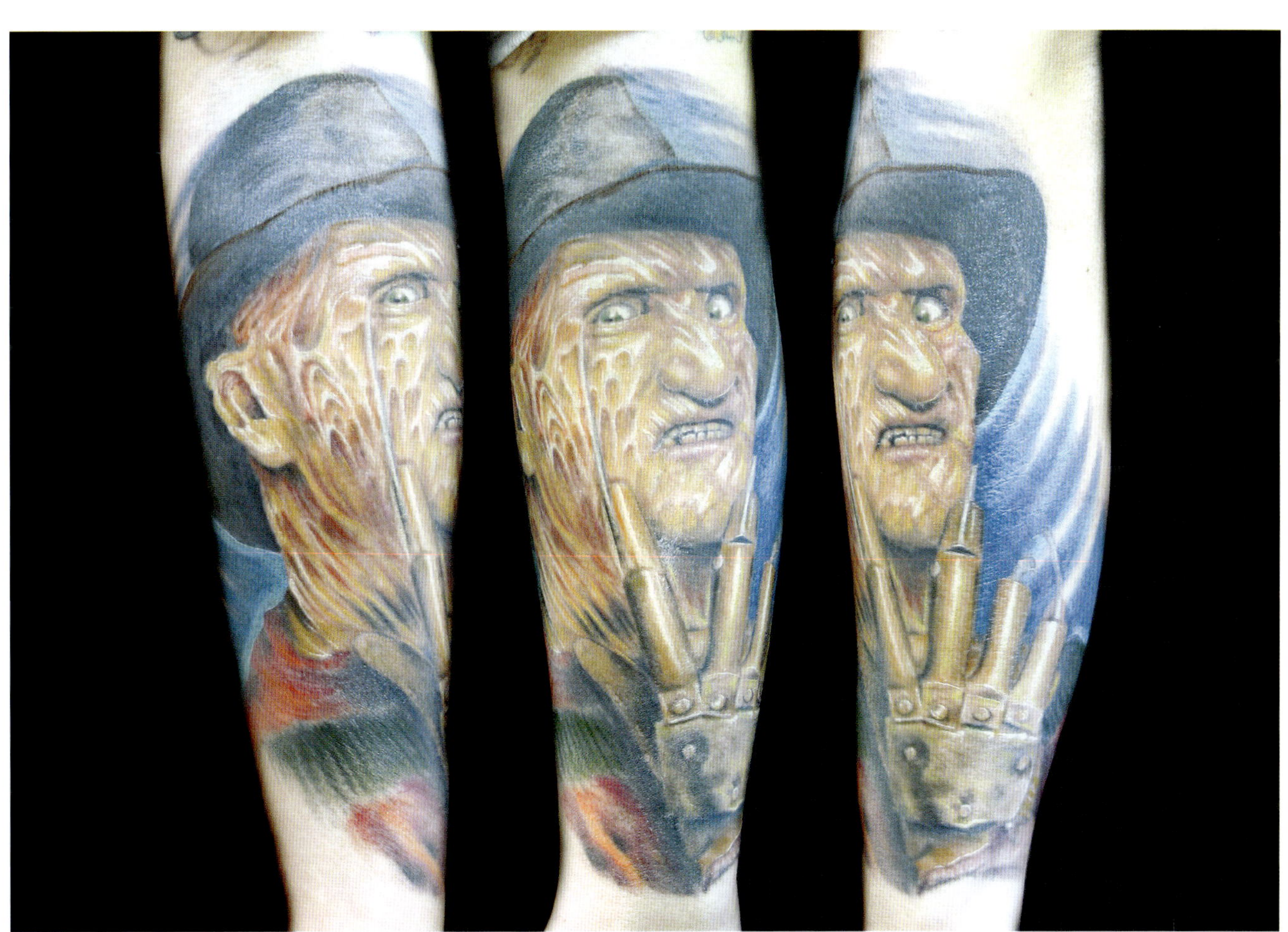

A horror portrait featuring that eighties legend, Freddy Kruger.

Chapter Nine

Hybrids

Weird And Wild

Another style that is becoming more and more popular in recent years is what we might call a "hybrid" style of tattoo. Created either by combining aspects of many different styles of tattoo into the design of a single image or by combining elements from a single style in an unusual way, these tattoos are opening up new avenues of expression for tattoo artists and collectors alike. Hybrid tattoos allow artists to manipulate tired, old imagery into new and

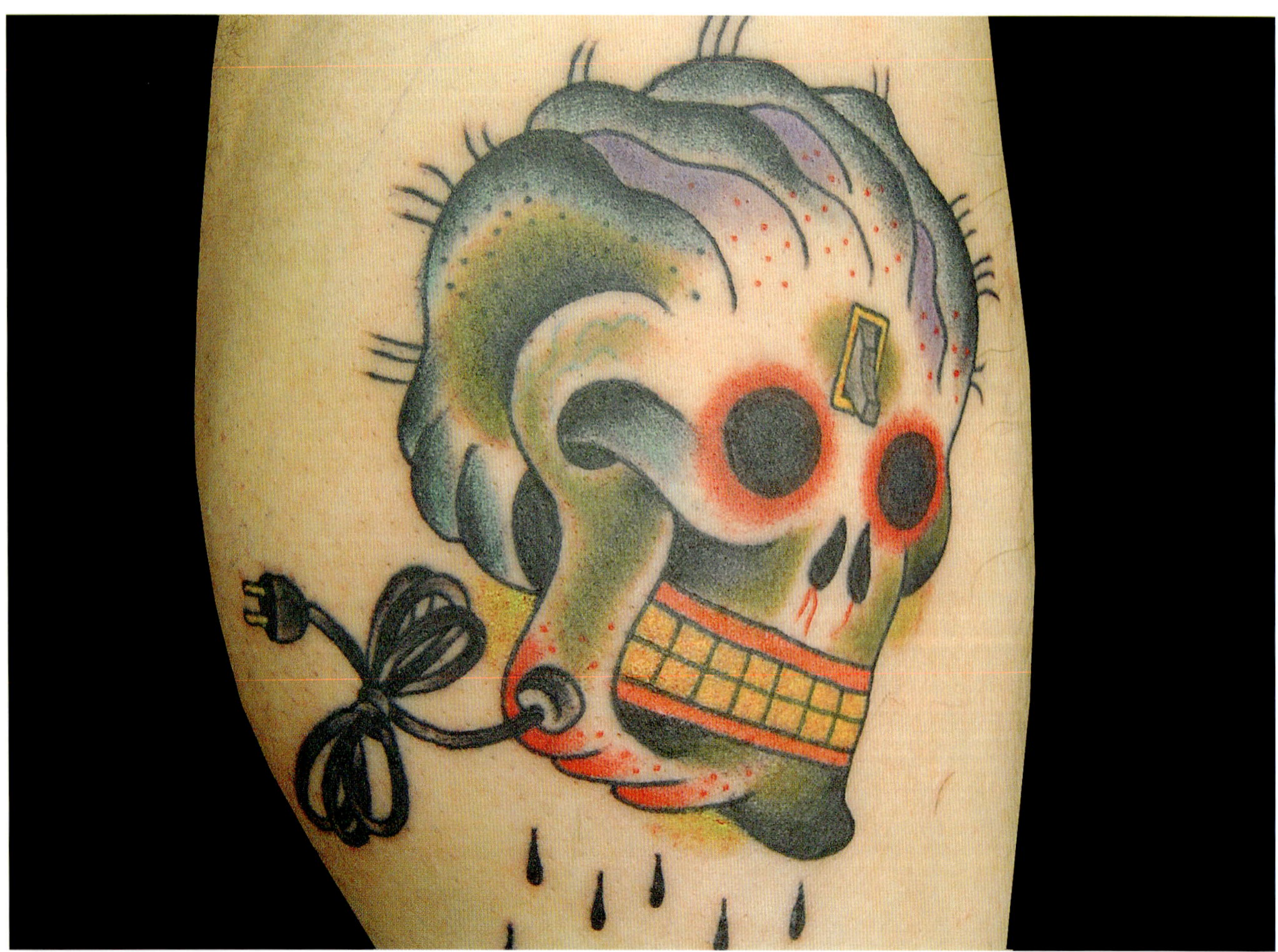

This plug-in skull has traditional style, but its attitude and unusual color scheme are more New School. Mario Desa, Chicago Tattoo, Chicago, IL.

exciting forms; from rearranging elements of older styles of tattoos to create weird new styles to the juxtaposition of the flat, bold colors of traditional work with cutting-edge photorealism, the reinvention of the traditional tattoo through hybrid styles is perhaps the wave of the future.

One of the advantages of creating hybrid images for tattoos is that the finished product will always be unique. Combining some of the more interesting elements of two styles, such as the pin-ups that incorporate photorealistic techniques with traditional American imagery, can create some truly striking images. In the pin-ups executed by Caroline Hedgepeth of Greenville, North Carolina's Skin Grafix, for instance, she juxtaposes the realistic flesh-tones and psychedelic color manipulations of photorealistic tattoos with the seductive, stylized poses and erotic themes that we typically associate with traditional American tattoos. The effect is to preserve the symbolism and authentic feel of a traditional American piece while adding the drama and high-impact of a photorealistic tattoo, thereby granting the wearer the opportunity to have a tattoo reflecting much of the best work in the industry in a single image.

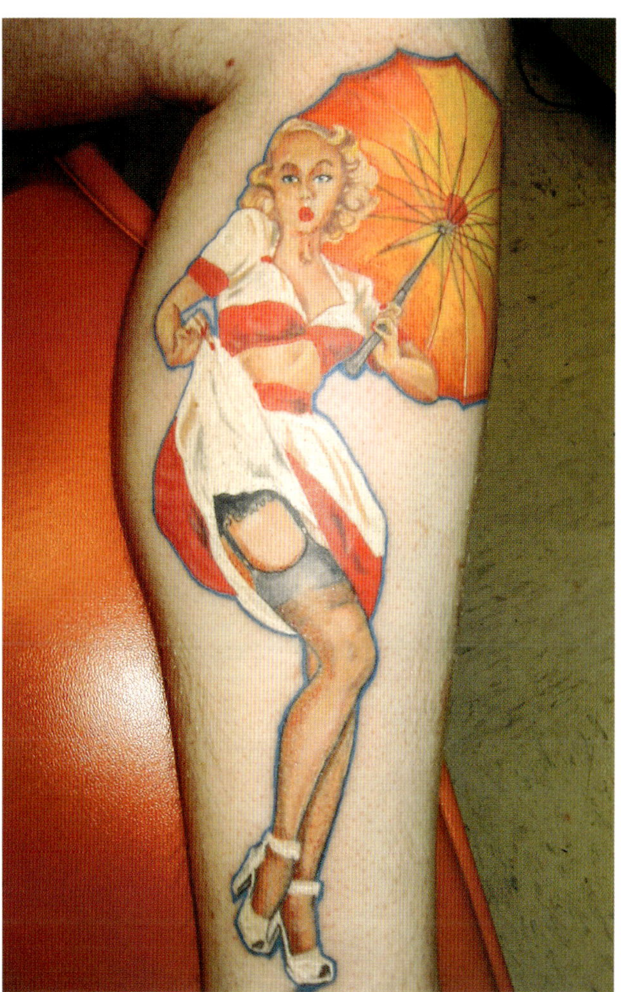

Caroline Hedgepeth of Skin Grafix in Greenville, NC, combines techniques used to achieve photorealistic effects with traditional American subject matter in these striking pin-ups.

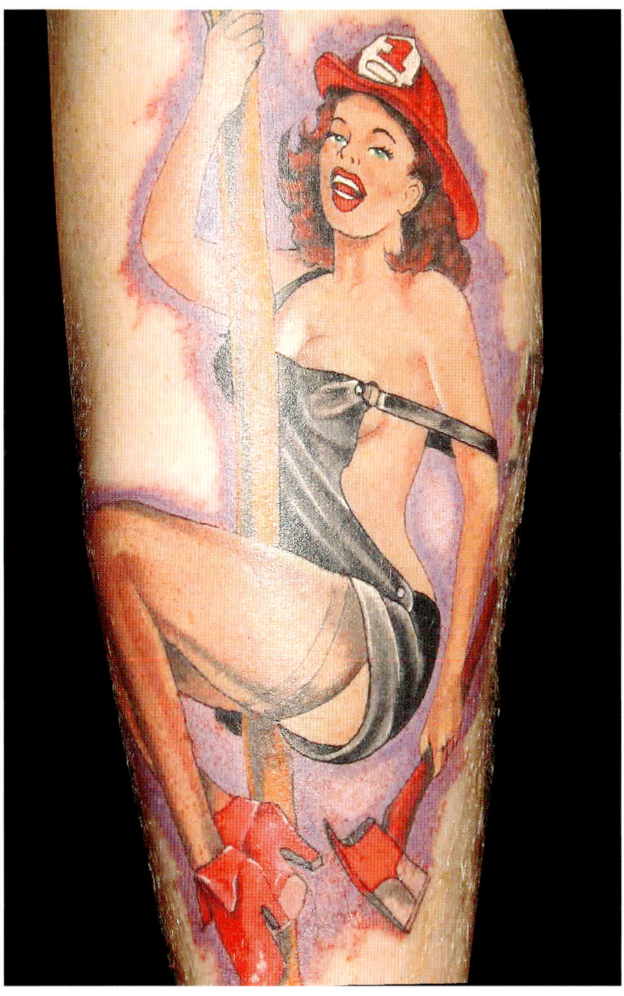

Caroline Hedgepeth of Skin Grafix in Greenville, NC.

As opposed to the mass-appeal that is common in the photorealistic designs that we discussed in the previous chapter, some of the images that are emerging from tattoo artists'

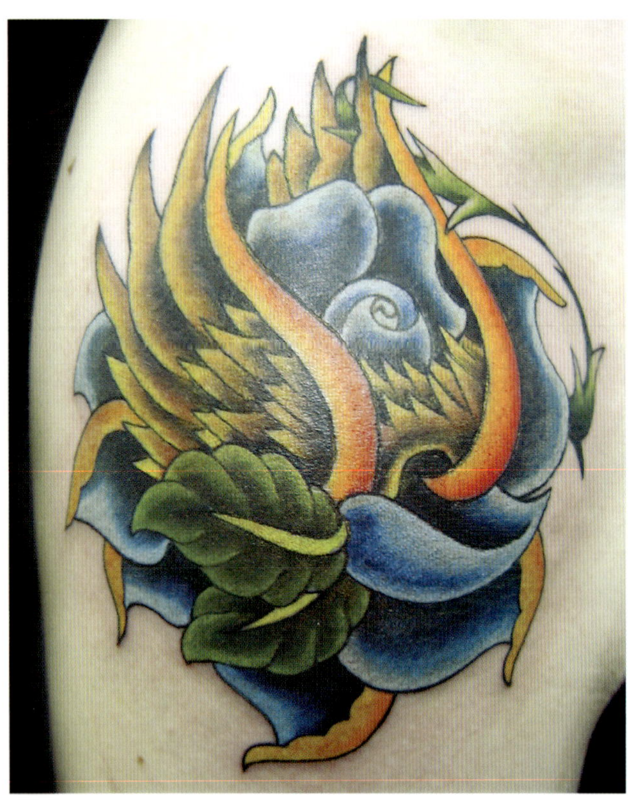

Kirk Shepherd, Fleshworks, Victoria, B.C.

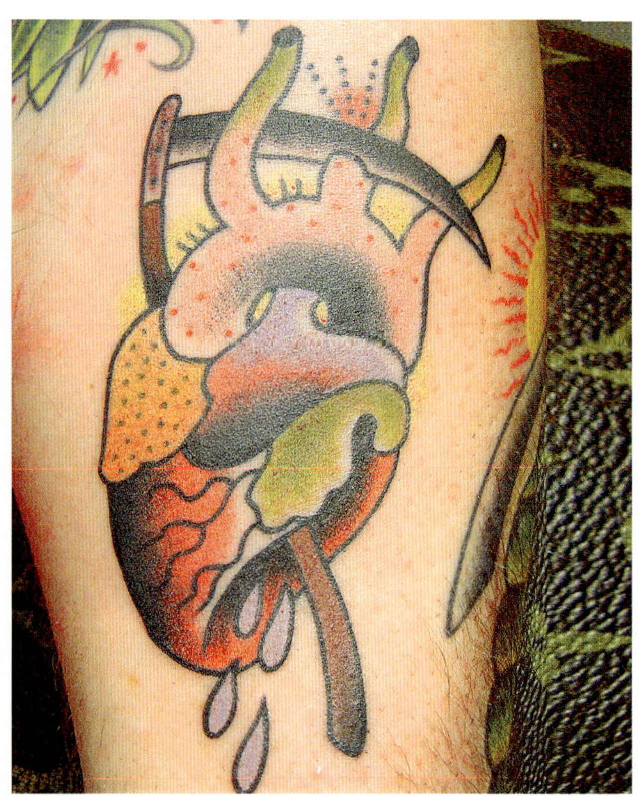

Scythe and heart from Mario Desa, Chicago Tattoo, Chicago, IL.

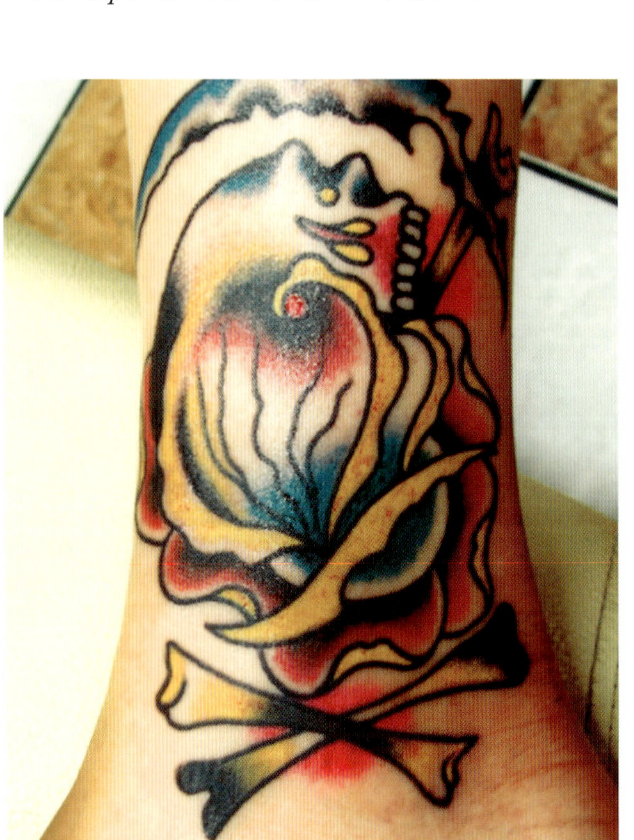

Skull and crossbones reaper rose from Cory Rogers, 713 Tattoo, Houston, TX

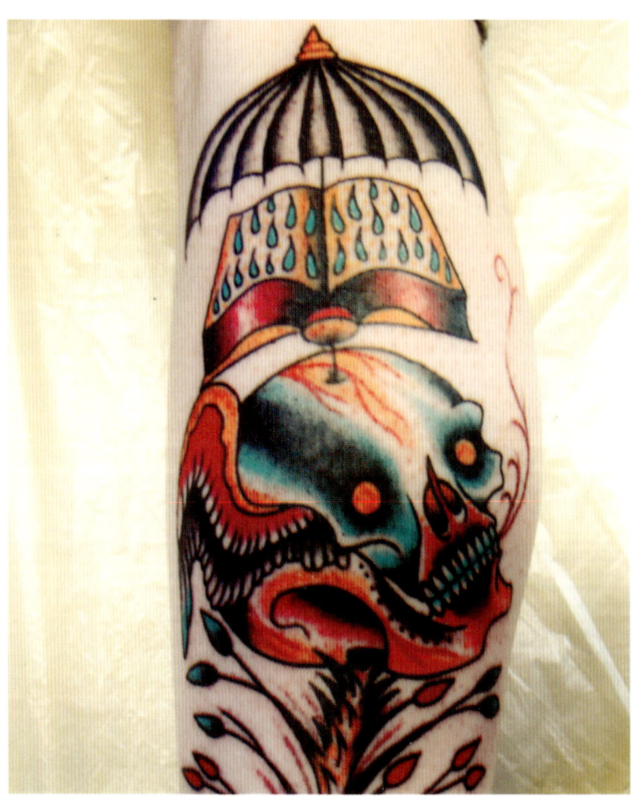

713 Tattoo's Cory Rogers re-creates traditional American classics by breaking down the parts and realigning them in new and exciting ways.

experiments with new stylistic combinations are pretty strange, making them perhaps less appealing to people who are not familiar with tattoo art. While their weirdness can alienate some of the uninitiated, the definitive, defiant uniqueness of a hybrid style tattoo attracts others. Images like Nate Beavers's Chihuahua robot tank, for instance, are not likely ever to be duplicated. This tattoo began when a client requested a portrait of a beloved pet Chihuahua, and Nate took the opportunity to go a little mad in the design. The resulting image is certainly one-of-a-kind, and the wearer can be sure that nobody else will have a tattoo like it.

Other artists who are experimenting with hybrid style work combine elements from a single style that usually we would not consider putting together. These experiments often result in somewhat unsettling, original images that take advantage of the recognizability of the style that they pull from while creating a fresh image.

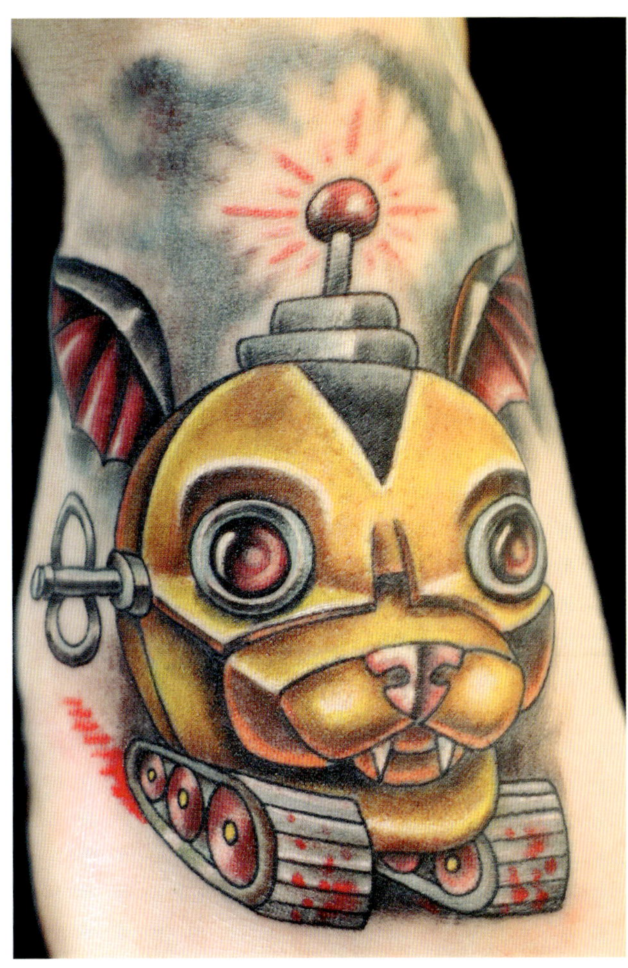

Take one part portrait, one part New School funk, and one part sheer madness, and you get this just plain weird creature: Nate Beavers's wind-up Chihuahua robot tank.

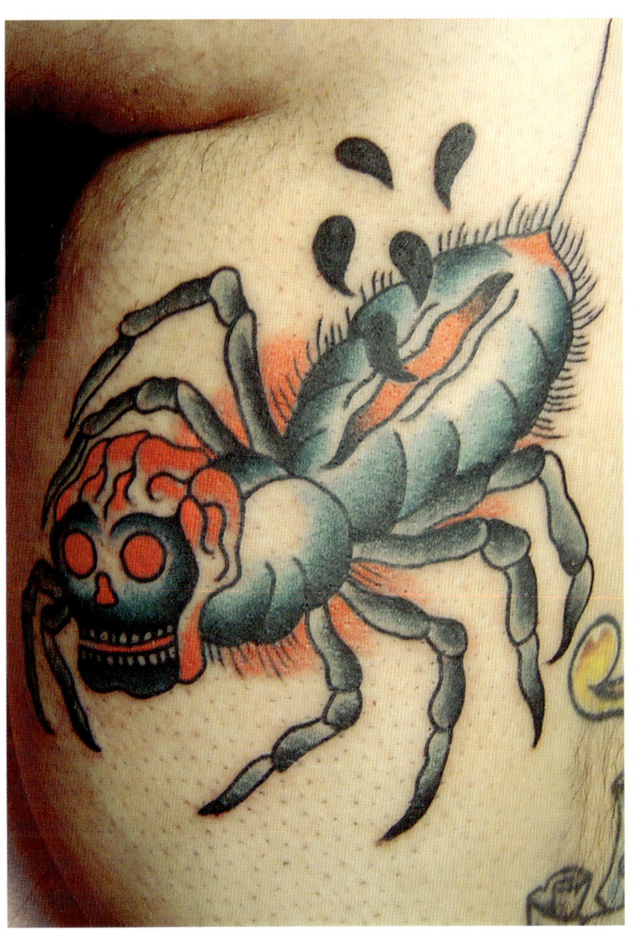

Bleeding spider skull with exposed brains from Mario Desa.

One of the artists who is most well-known for creating these kinds of hybrid images is Mario Desa of Chicago Tattoo in Chicago, IL. His unusual concoctions from Traditional American elements have made his name familiar in the industry. A 10-year tattoo veteran, he is regarded as both a successful traditionalist and an innovative trendsetter in the tattoo community today. We talked with him recently about his bizarre and beautiful tattoo designs, and he shared with us his impressions of the hybrid trend and its roots.

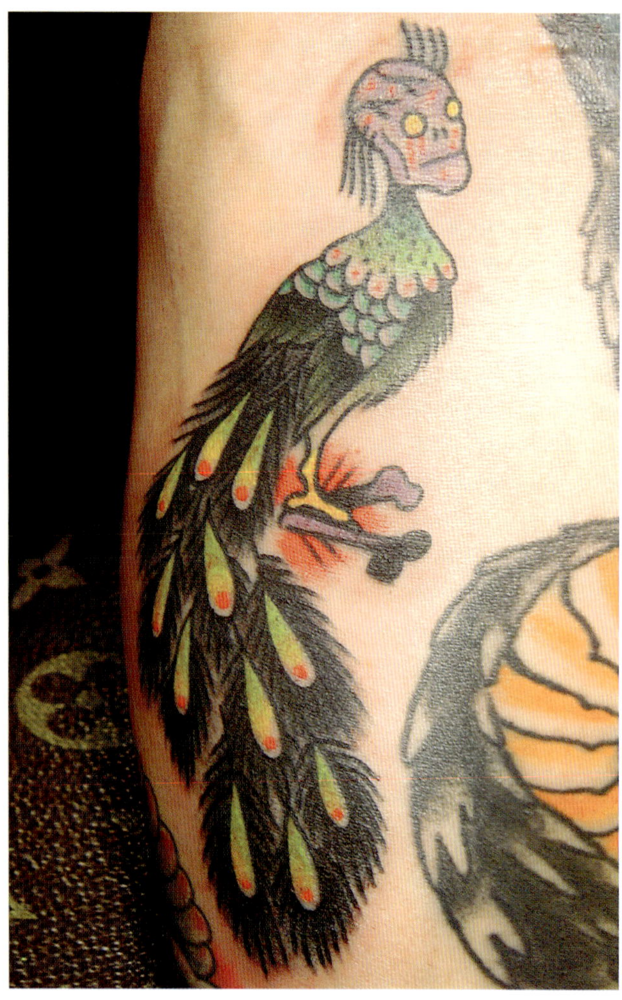

What makes this piece from Mario Desa so disconcerting? Is it the pairing of the lovely peacock feathers with the hideous deathmask? Is it the cross bones the creature is using as its perch? Is it the underlying reference to peacocks and skulls and their various places in myth? Perhaps its all these things…this kind of tension is accomplished through the unusual juxtapositions we find in hybrid pieces, and Mario Desa accomplishes this effect consistently.

Mario Desa Q & A

JS: While I've seen a lot of weird stuff in the tattoo world, you're style might be the weirdest. All of the images you create are pretty unique…how do you describe your style?

Mario: I guess most of my work is based on the American traditional style and technique of tattooing, but I try to introduce different colors and color combinations to keep it fresh.

JS: How did you develop this funky, hybrid style? Did you always work this way, or did your portfolio gradually come to contain the hybrid work?

Mario: When I was in high school, I always used to draw all these weird figures and kind of "hybrid" things in my notebooks, so it is interesting that I ended up drawing tattoos that also look like this. I did not invent the style, but I guess I was drawn to it because I always liked weird art.

And while I do like doing this stuff, I do not think 'cool' custom tattoos are for everyone. Some people just want a tribal armband, and that's great. It is just what they want, and it is my job to do it for them when they come in my shop and ask me for it. They love their kanji tattoos just as much as another customer will love a tattoo from a drawing of a rose/skull/snake morph.

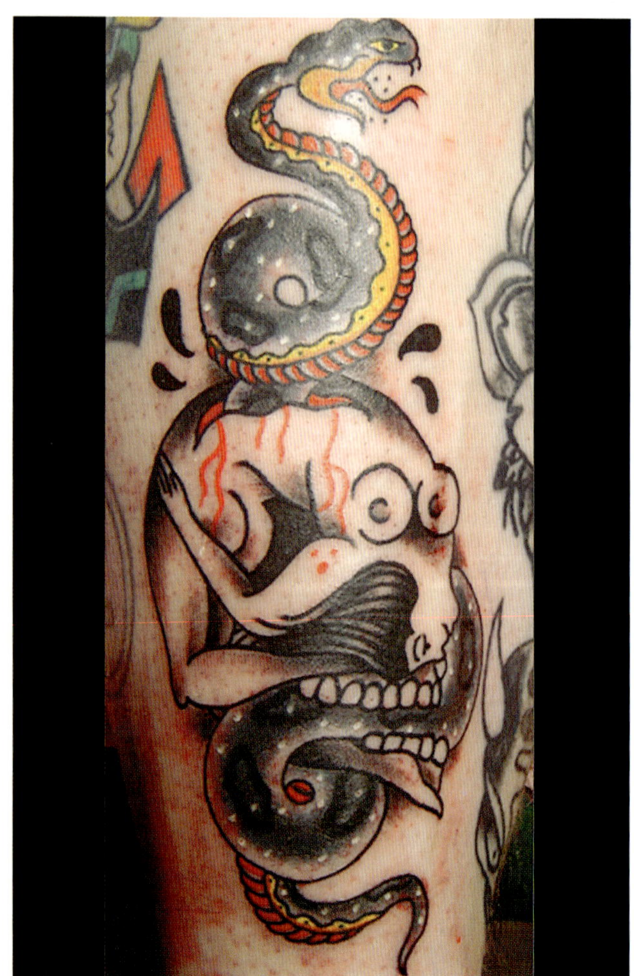

Lady skull snake from Mario Desa.

JS: That is a cool attitude. Many artists who have the reputation that you have aren't as open to doing work outside of their style, which some people might interpret as being kind of snobby.

Mario: Well, money is money! Chicago Tattoo is primarily a street shop, and we do a ton of flash and take tare of tons of walk-in customers, but we have a good balance of custom work, too. It keeps things interesting.

JS: You're right…money is money!

Since so much of your custom work is the weirder stuff, we were curious about whether or not you get weirdos as clients! What kinds of people do you think are most attracted to your work?

Mario: I guess it is usually other tattooists who are into tattoo "culture" (or whatever) who are more interested in getting the weirder pieces. Your average person is already taking a huge step by even considering getting a tattoo in the first place, so they probably don't want to get some weird thing that none of their friends will be able to understand.

JS: While artists have been experimenting with recombinations of traditional elements in hybrid styles of tattoos for a while, they seem to be becoming more and more popular over the last few years. What do you think has made hybrid pieces become more widespread?

Mario: People should know that Ed Hardy was doing work in this style 25 years ago. People tend to bite off of each other a lot or rip each other off, and we forget (or ignore) where a certain image or style comes from. It is important, I think, to remember the roots.

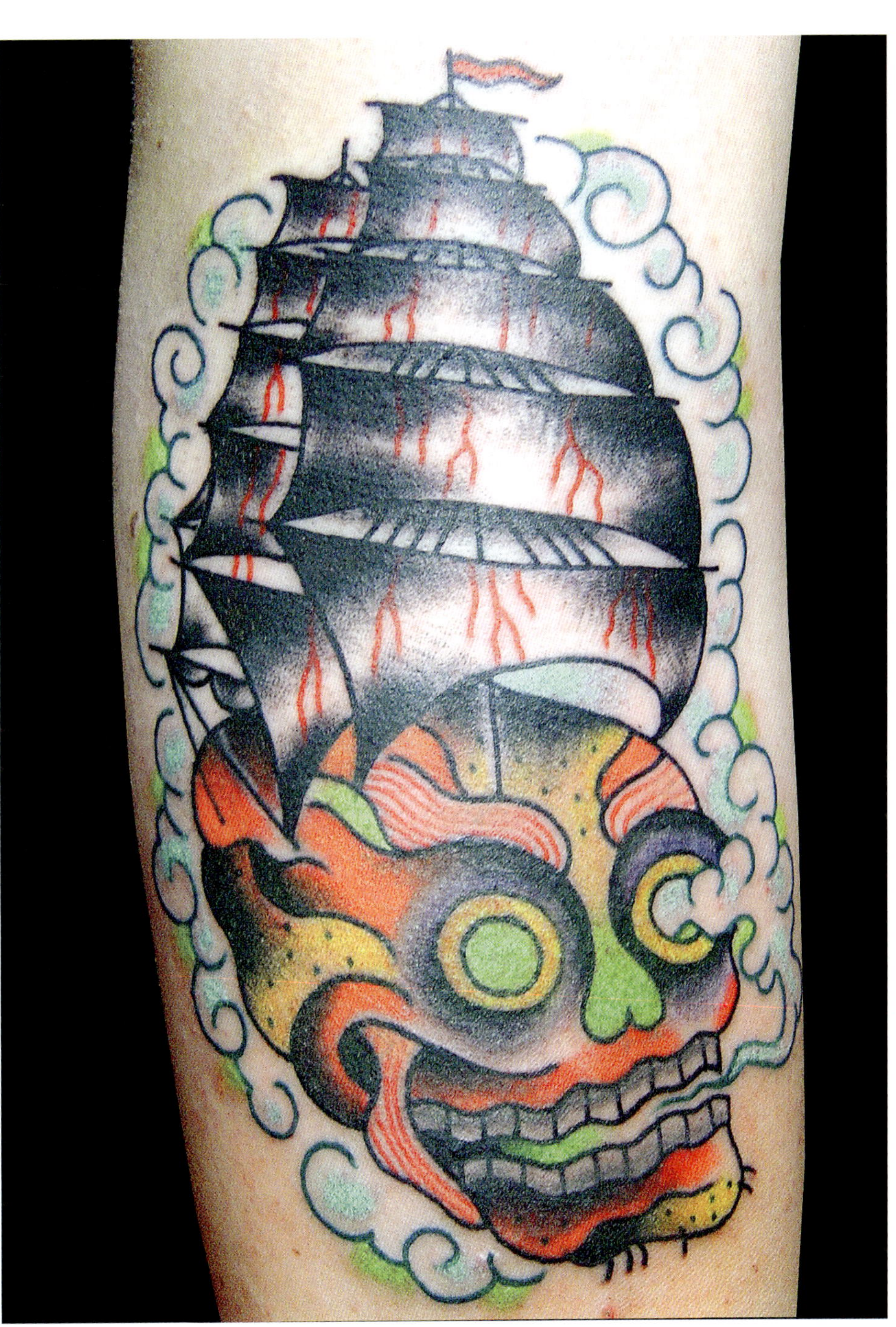

This fun piece hearkens back to traditional tattoos' naval heritage while having fun with several elements. Notice the veins running through the sails. Mario Desa, Chicago Tattoo, Chicago, IL.

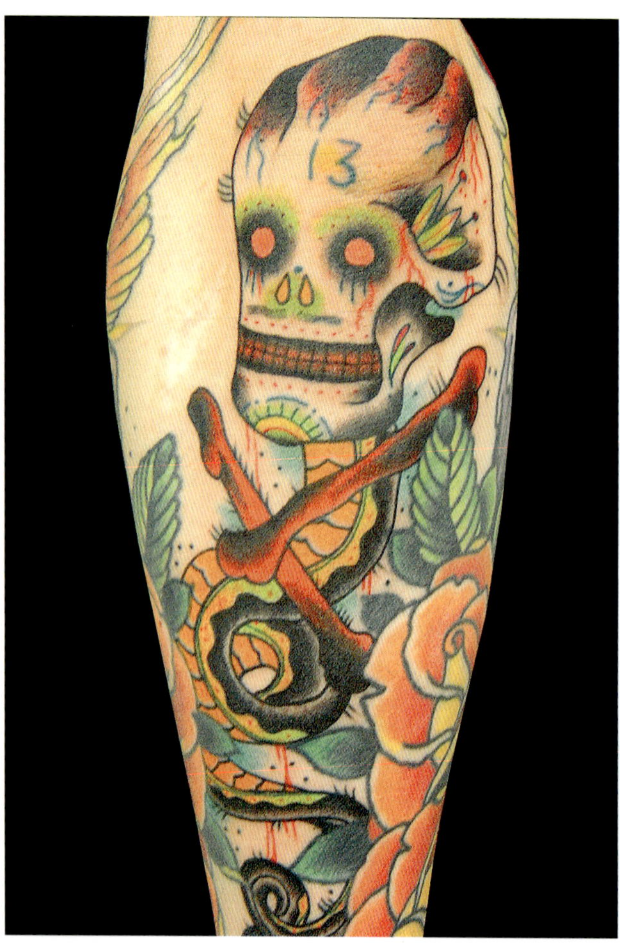

Sugar skull and crossbones with snake body from Mario Desa, Chicago Tattoo, Chicago, IL.

I think for tattooers, it is just kind of fun to draw stuff in this style, and it gives you a little more freedom than when you stick with the same images that everyone is used to. For customers, I think it is similar to getting a tribal armband…the image just looks cool, and it doesn't necessarily have any deep meaning or anything (usually). It's just cool looking and doesn't carry a lot of baggage like some of the heavier styles.

JS: That's interesting. So these tattoos might not be for someone who wants to commemorate a significant event or celebrate some kind of deeper philosophy. They're just neat designs…but they also carry a lot of history on their own.

We are asking all the artists we speak to about their process. Can you tell us about how you design a piece, and how closely you work with clients?

Mario: I am kind of lucky because most people who are coming to me specifically for a custom tattoo are pretty familiar with my work, so they usually just give me an idea and let me draw it up however I want. I rarely have to redraw a design at the appointment. If there is anything specific they want in it, I ask them to bring me the reference. Otherwise, I use various books.

Good reference is really important for me when I'm drawing. I use it every day, still, even for a rose or a skull. I still like to look through books and find a new way to do something, even if I've done it many times before. Too many people use other people's tattoos as reference or just draw a generic (and often wrong)

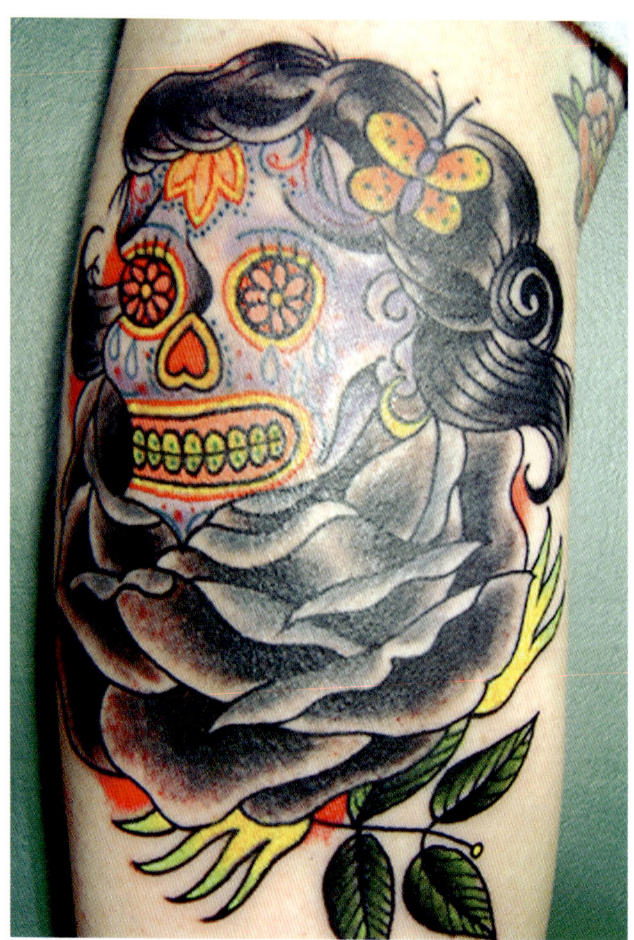

There are many classic pieces of traditional tattoos here: the stylized hair is common in traditional pin-ups or portraiture, and the sugar skull and rose are also common. Here Mario juxtaposes them to achieve interesting effects.

image out of their heads instead of taking time to do the research necessary to get it right. They seem to think they are expressing themselves or being "true," but really, these artists are only cheating themselves and the customer. It's worth it to take the time to do it right.

* * *

Mario brings up some interesting points, especially in his analysis of the clients who seek him out. Since many of his designs, and many hybrid tattoos, are strange images without a lot of mass-appeal, they aren't for everyone. If you are a genuine tattoo collector with many different kinds of pieces, pursuing a few hybrid pieces might be a way to enhance your collection by increasing its diversity and allowing your chosen artists a little more room for creative expression. These pieces are also challenging for your artist, as they require an understanding of several styles and techniques of tattooing and proficiency in melding several approaches together into one piece. As Mario points out, this style is not for everyone. The images aren't often deeply meaningful, as a symbolic traditional piece might be or an Asian design; however, they are fun, funky, and will add interest to any connoisseur's collection.

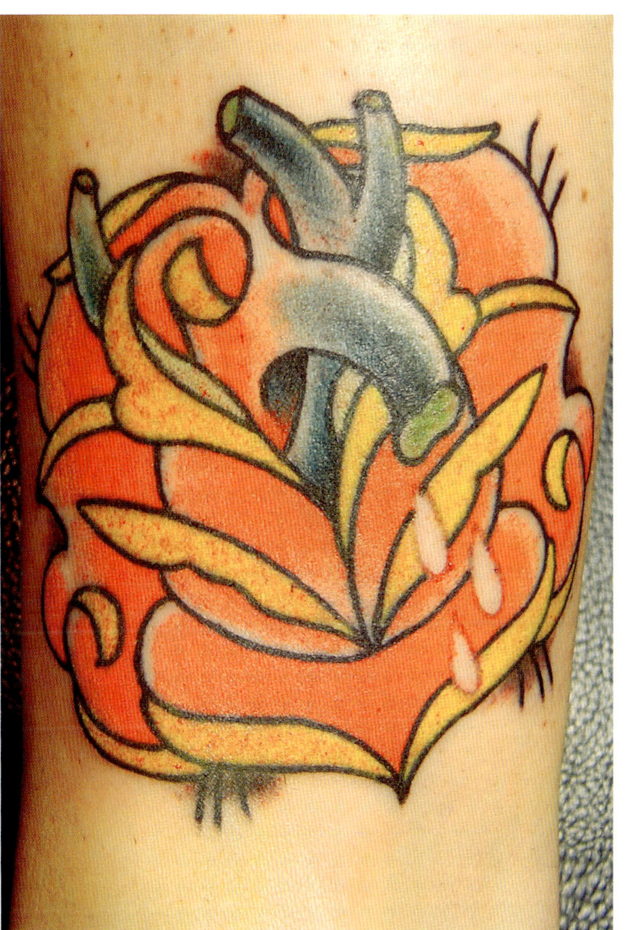

Heart-rose morph from Mario Desa, Chicago Tattoo, Chicago, IL.

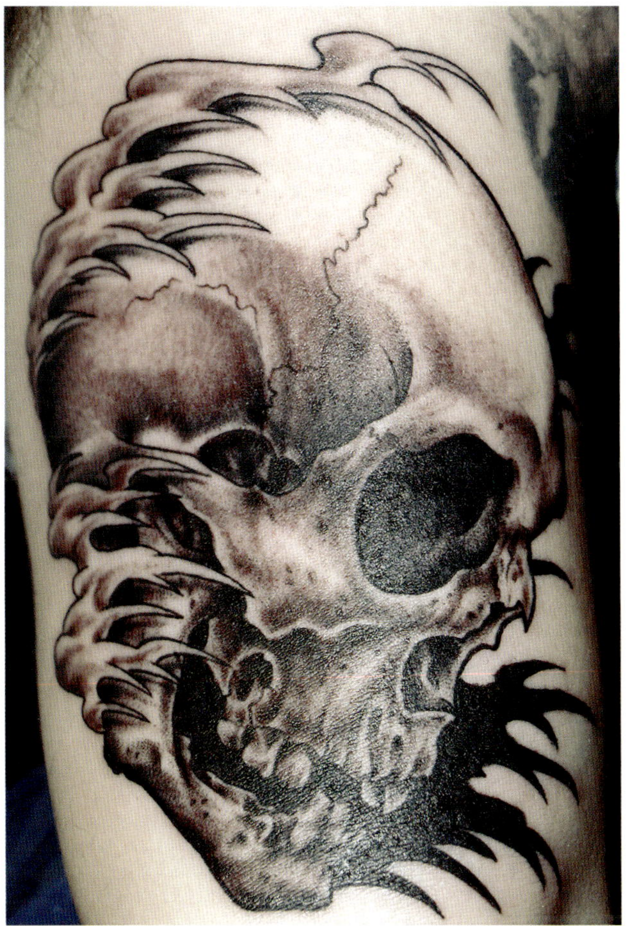

Dave Attonito of Good Clean Fun in Snellville, GA, combines the black and grey classic subject, the human skull, with Asian style finger waves as a framing device.

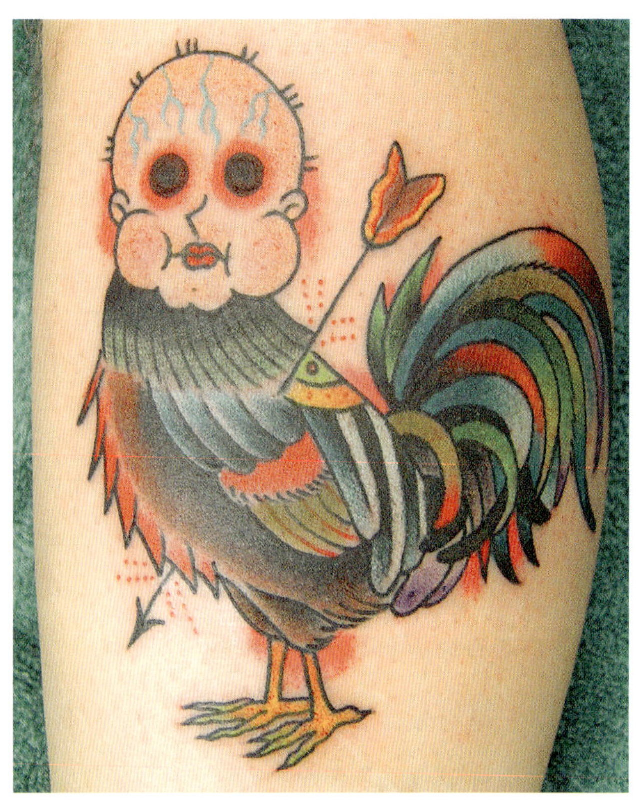

A chicken-baby hybrid from Mario Desa.

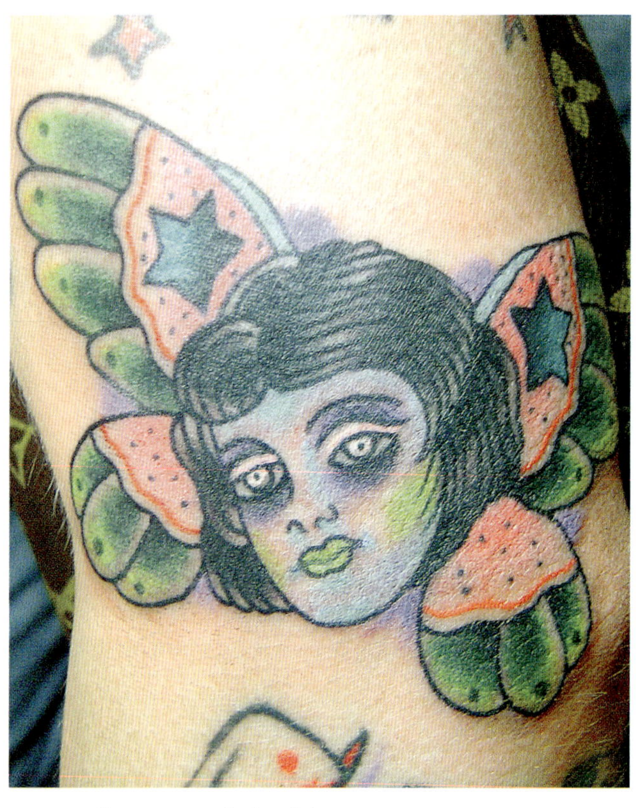

Butterfly portrait hybrid by Mario Desa.

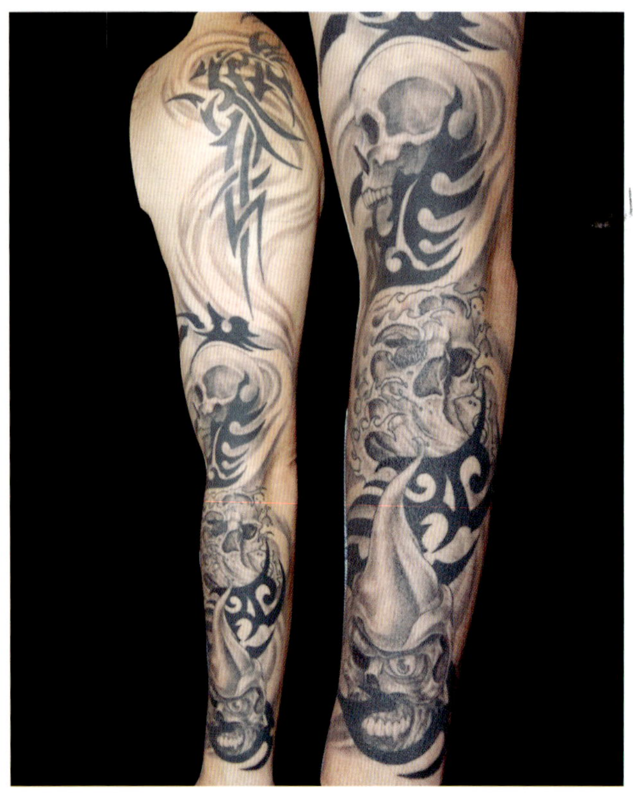

Asian-tribal-black and grey hybrid from John Wayne.

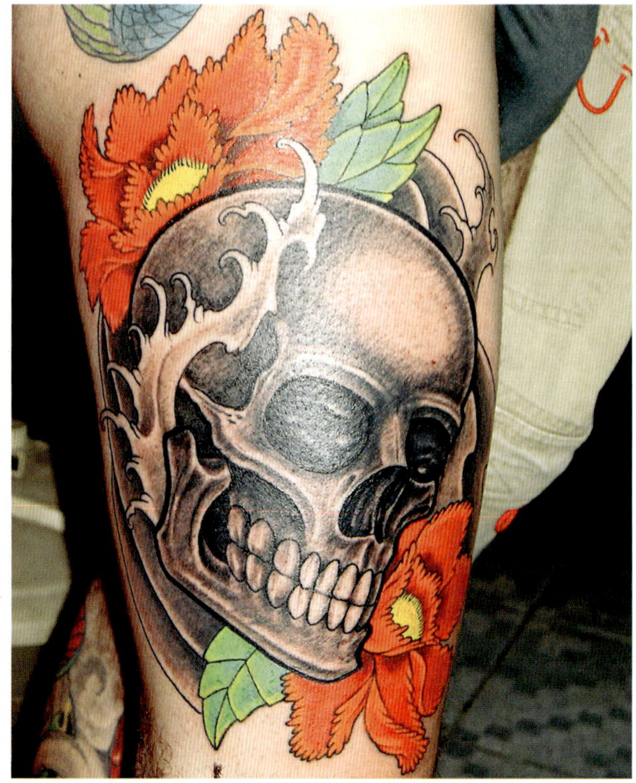

Federico Ferroni juxtaposes black and grey standard subject matter with Asian water and flowers, which creates a bold background to highlight the clean black and grey work.

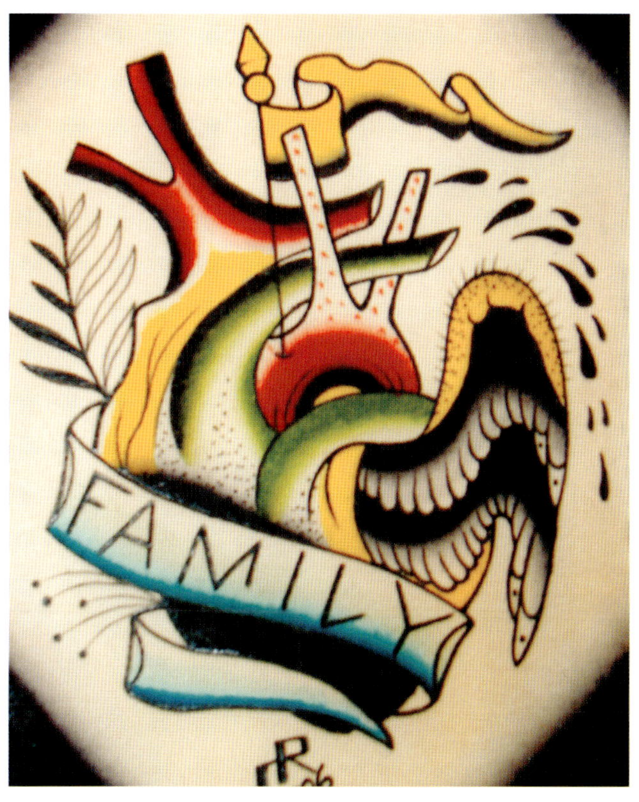

713 Tattoo's Cory Rogers re-creates traditional American classics.

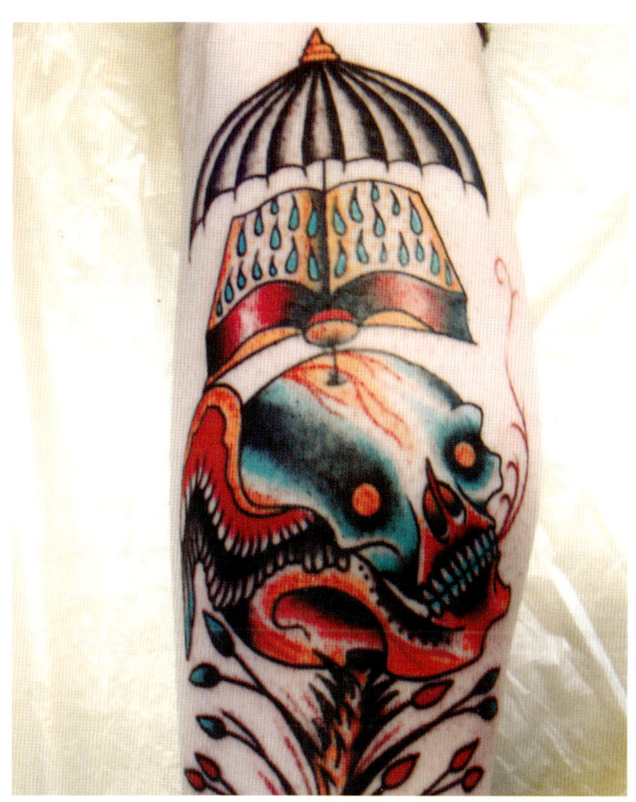

Cory Rogers, 713 Tattoo, Houston, TX.

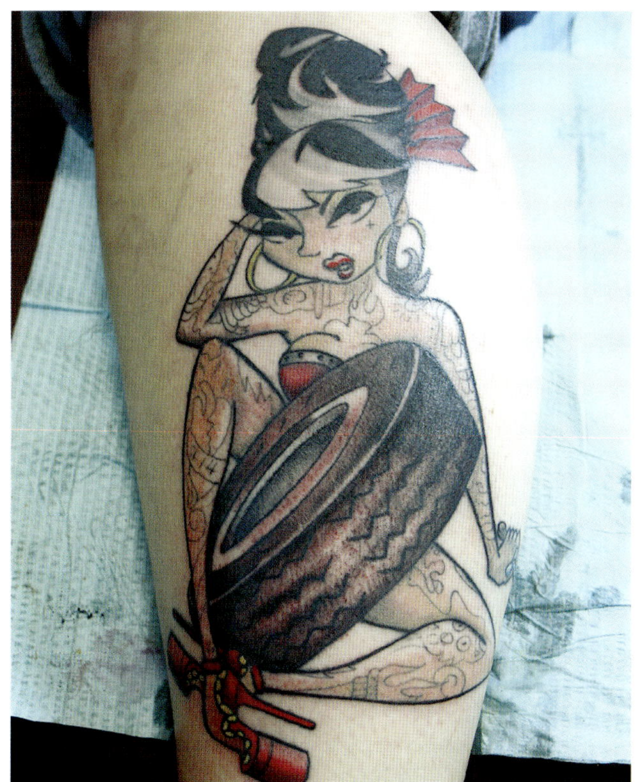

Thom Godfrey of Evil Eye in Bakersfield, CA, offers a pin-up Geisha in New School style, combining elements of three different tattoo traditions.

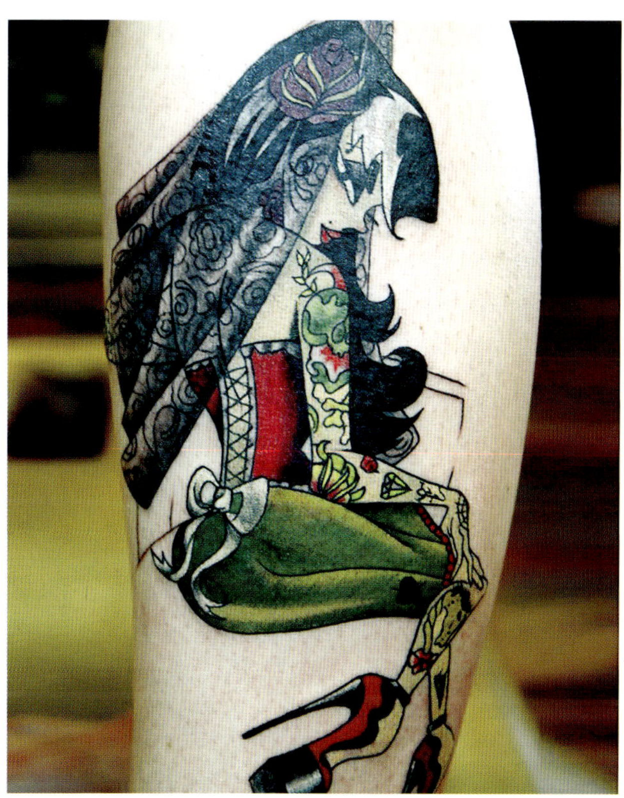

This New School pin-up has a traditional American style rose in her hair, notice that her own tattoos are traditional. Thom Godfrey, Evil Eye, Bakersfield, CA.

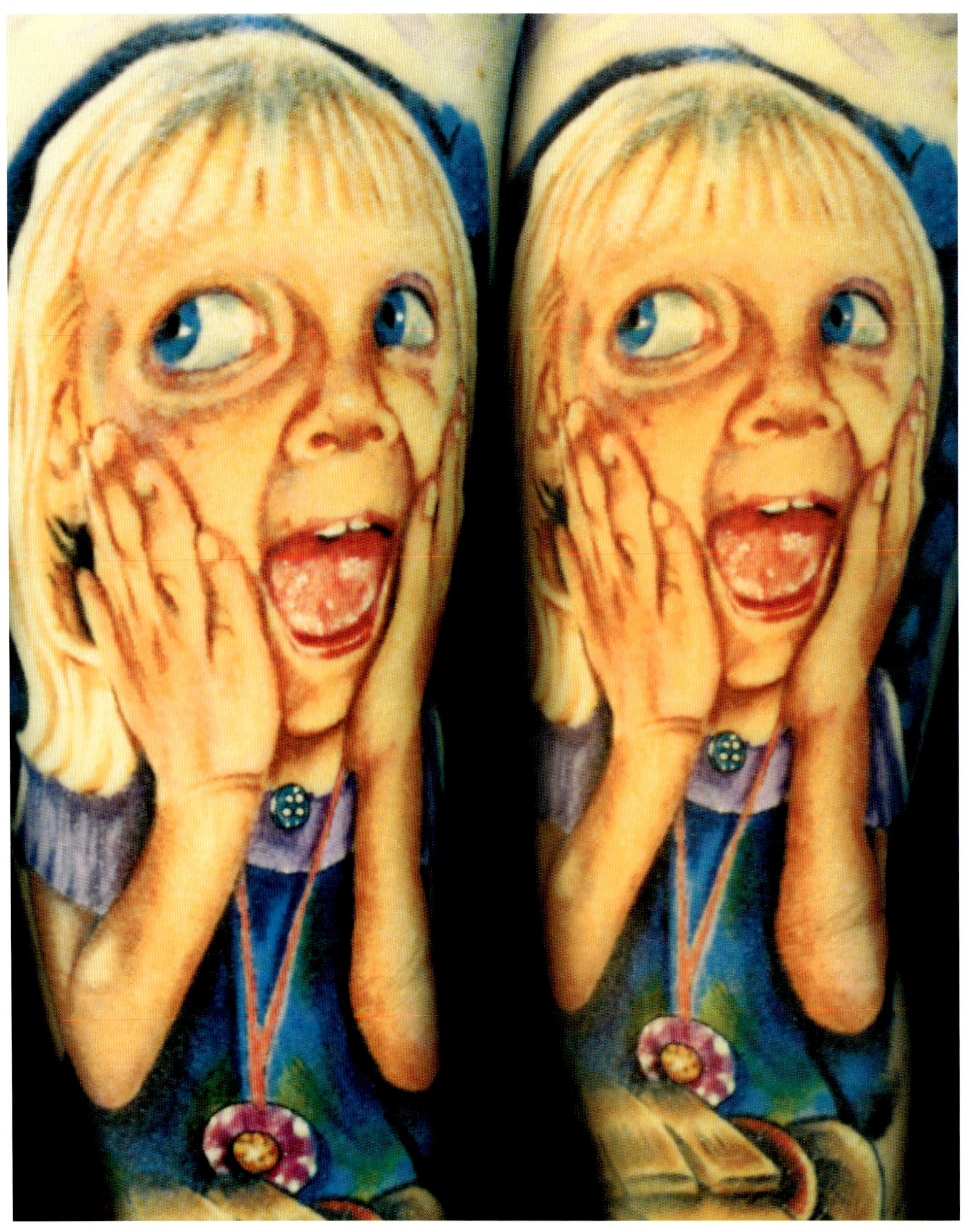

Josh Woods combines elements of the New School style he's known for (the skewed perspective and the child as subject matter) with techniques more common to photorealistic pieces to achieve some pretty trippy effects.

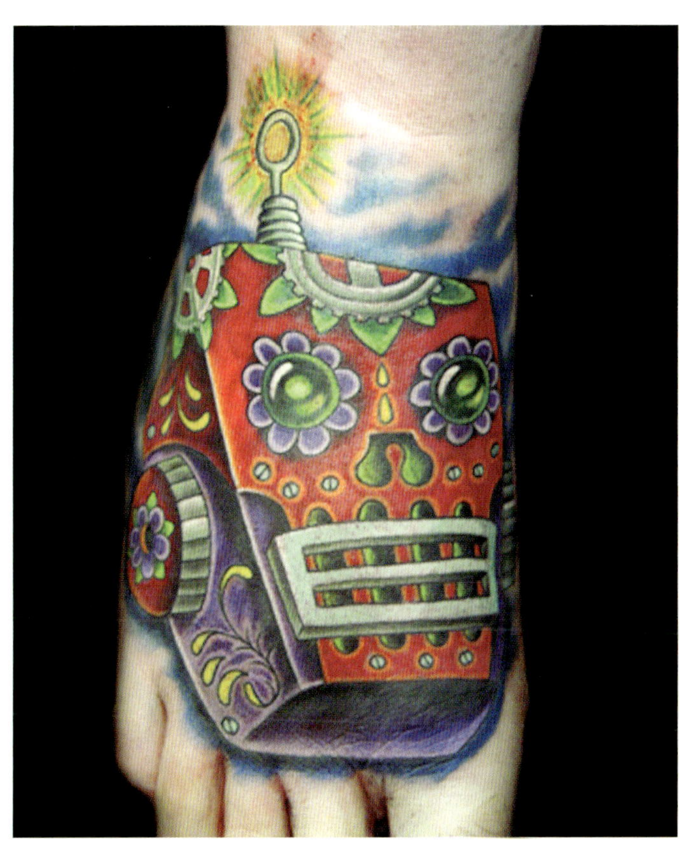

Nate Beavers gives us a New Schoolish robot version of the traditional American sugar skull theme.

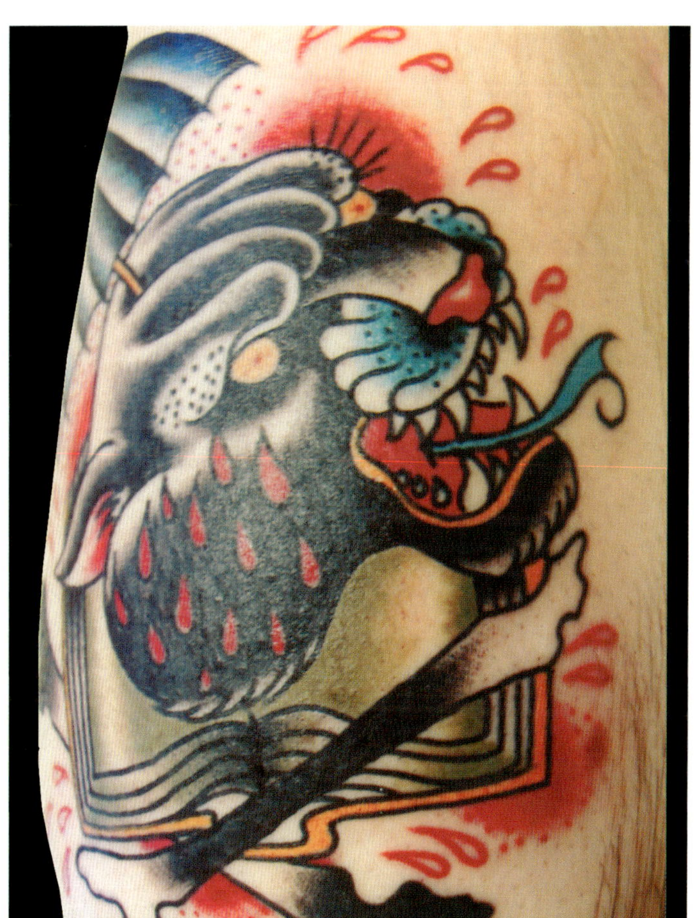

Cory Rogers, 713 Tattoo, Houston, TX.

Chapter Ten

Reference Gallery

At this point, you should have a thorough introduction to many of the styles of tattoo artwork available to you today. From the roots of tattooing to the cutting edge, we have tried to give you an overview of the art and artists working in the most popular styles.

The next step is to find your artist and get your own work! Because we have discussed the importance of finding solid reference, we have included the following gallery as a starting place to help you isolate the kind of image that you would like to have on your skin.

In collecting material for this book, we asked several of our favorite tattooists to share some of their original artwork for this reference gallery. We encourage you to use these materials as springboards for your own unique pieces. There are many different kinds of artists from shops all over the country represented in the following pages (and in our artwork throughout the book), so you might also consider patronizing one of these artists when you get your next piece.

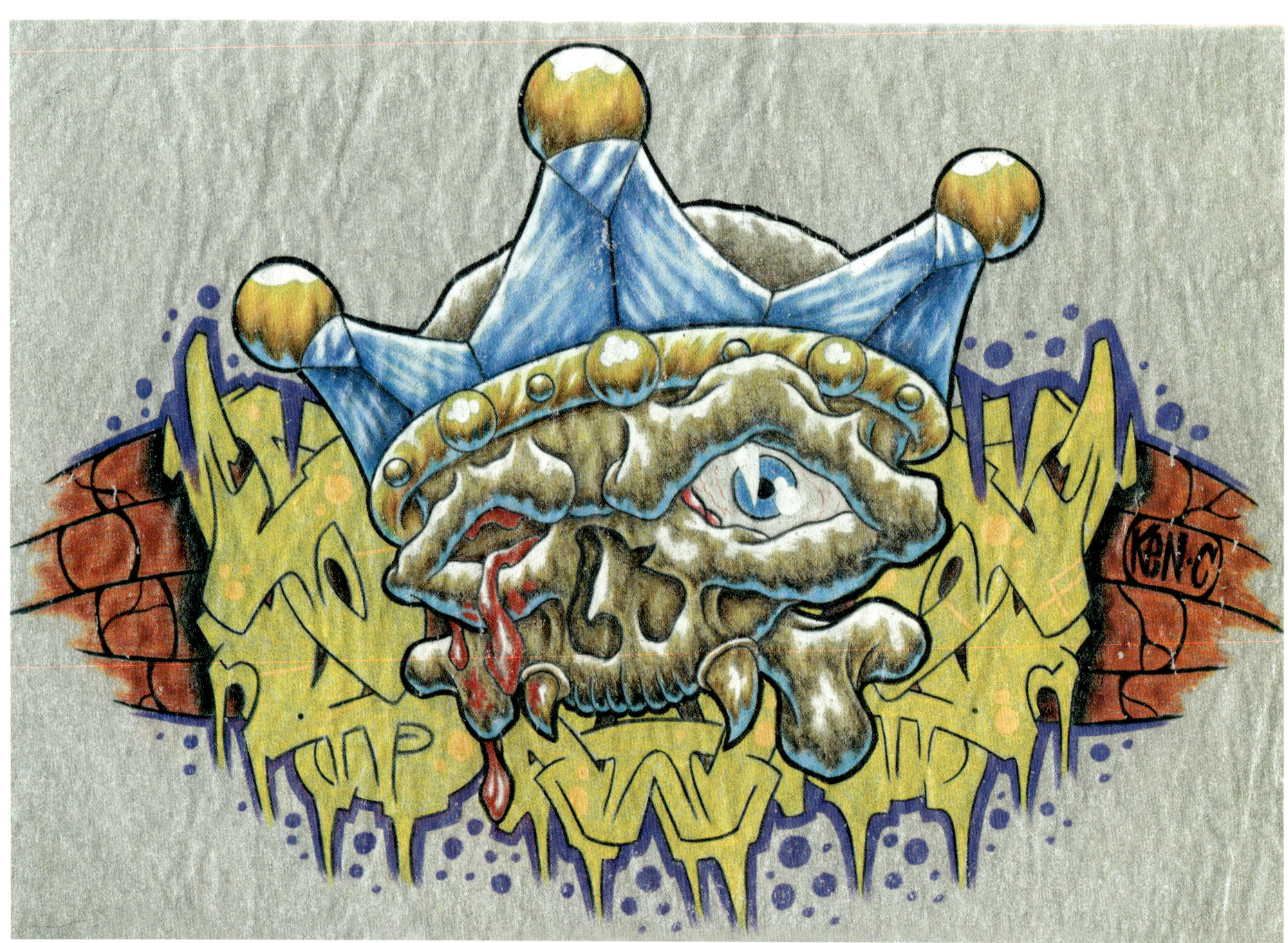

Ken Carrano, www.hollowstitches.com, celebrates New School tattoos' graffiti heritage with this crowned skull.

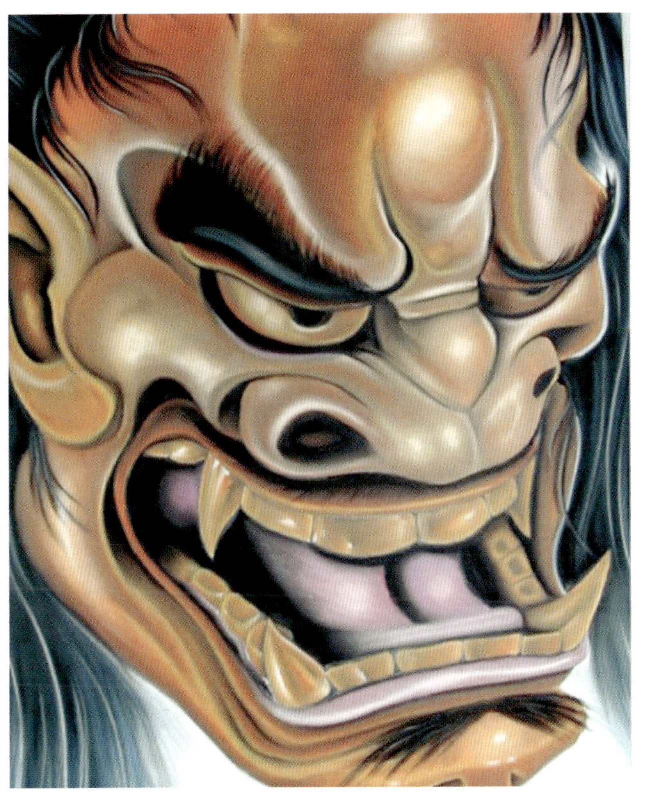

Japanese style Oni mask from Chris Vennekamp of All Or Nothing in Atlanta, GA.

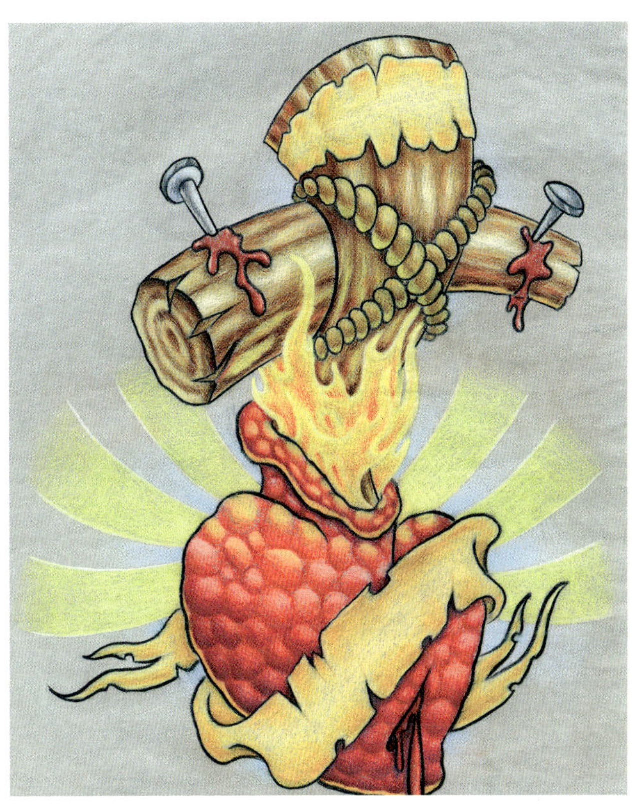

Ken Carrano, www.hollowstitches.com

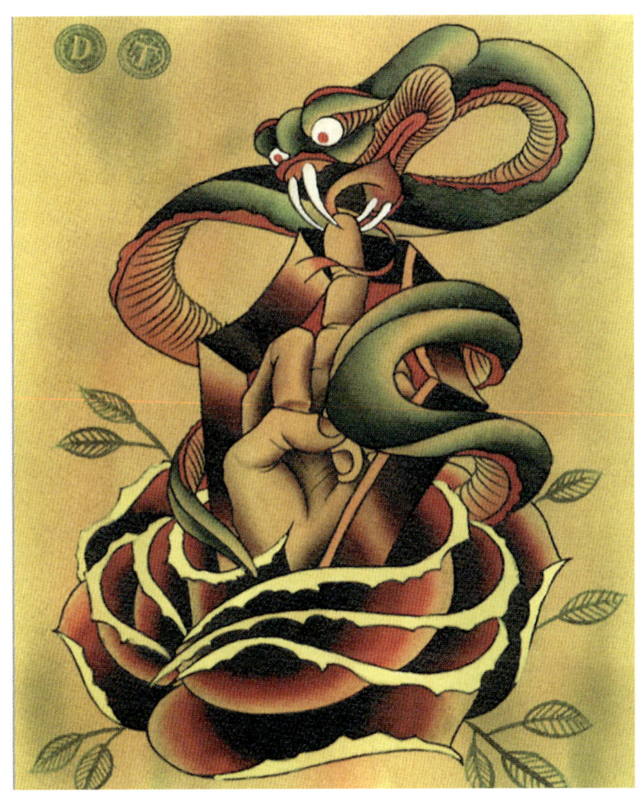

Dave Tedder has combined a few different styles in this zombie middle finger salute.

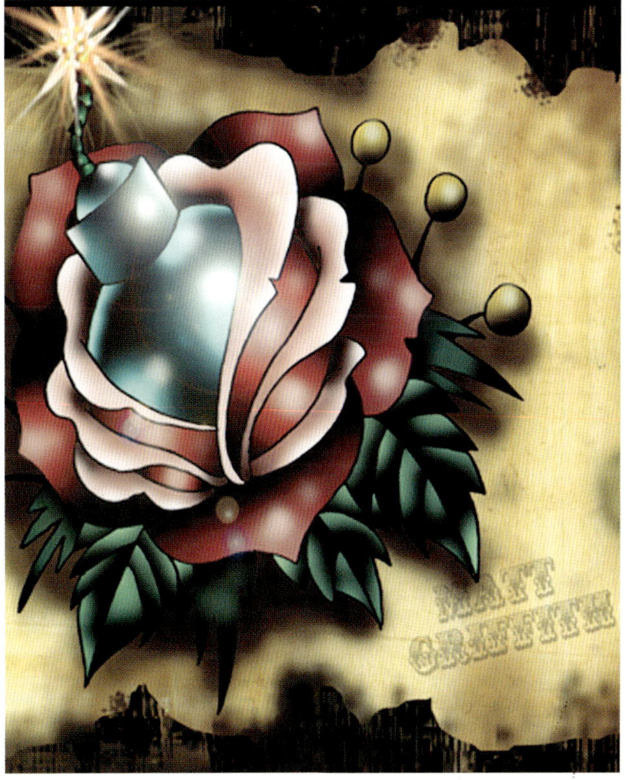

Matt Griffith of Two Dollar Pistol in Chillicothe, Ohio.

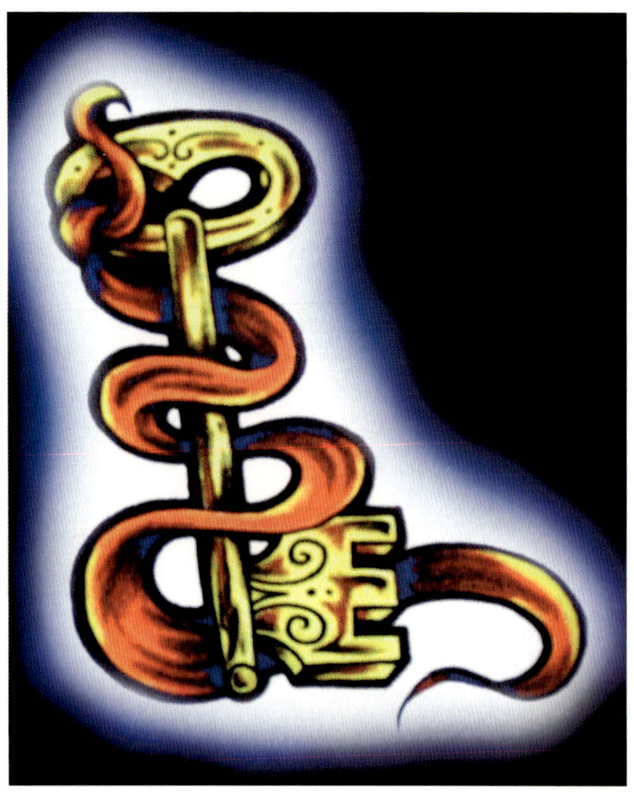

Shannon Schober of Vitality Tattoo in Asheville, NC, offers a New School interpretation of a key.

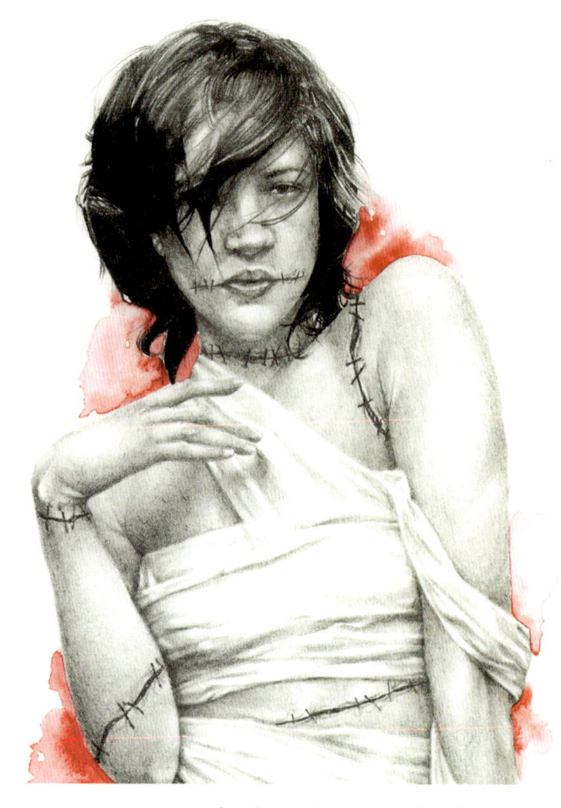

Dave Attonito, Good Clean Fun, Snellville, GA.

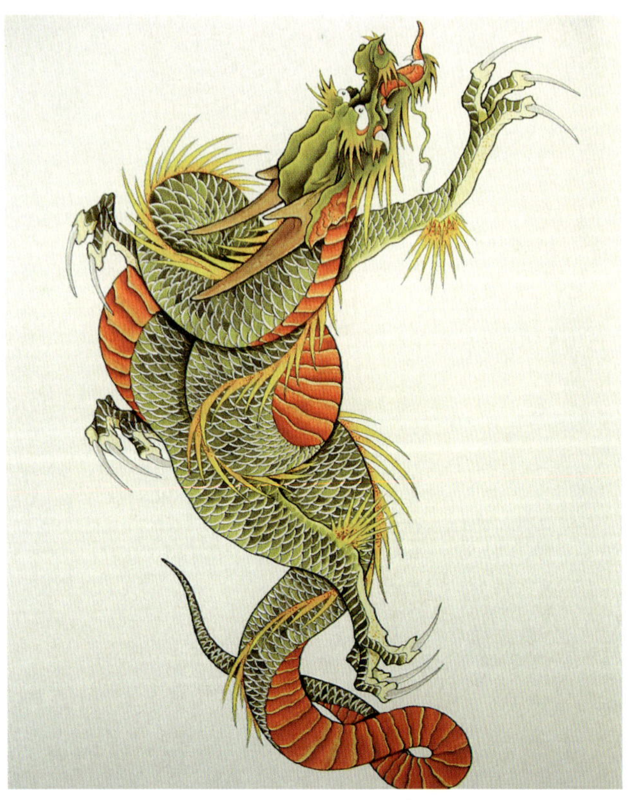

A beautiful Asian dragon from Federico Ferroni, South Beach Tattoos, FL.

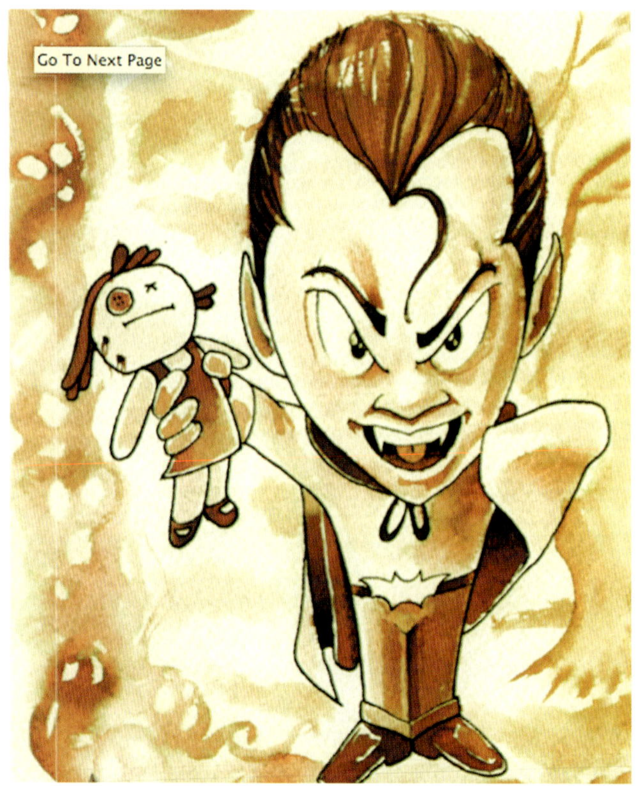

John Lloyd, All Or Nothing, Atlanta, GA.

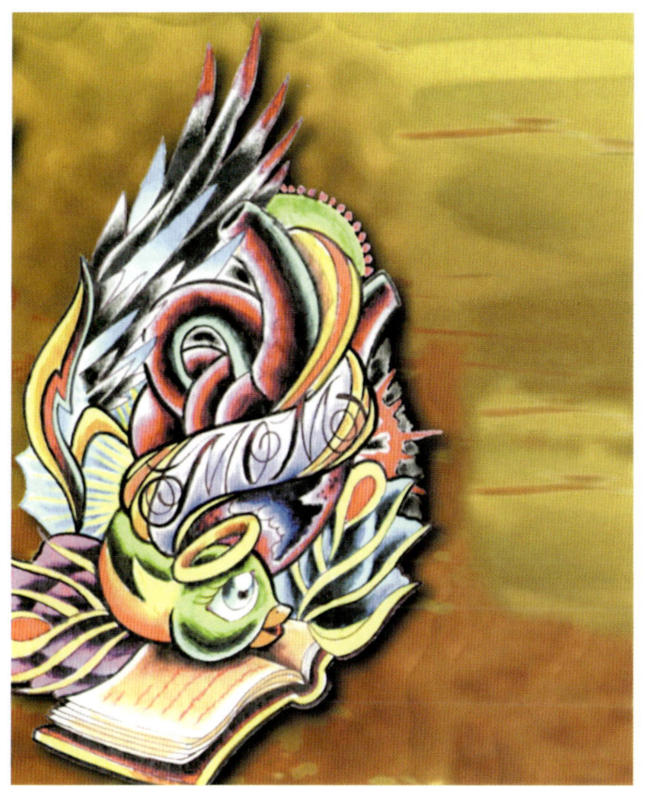

Josh Woods, All Or Nothing, Atlanta, GA.

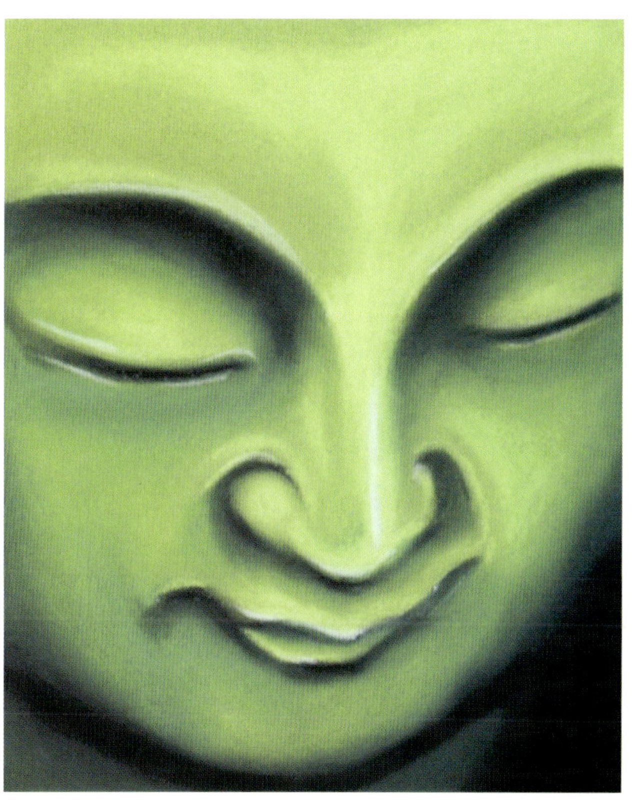

Sean Herman, All Or Nothing, Atlanta, GA.

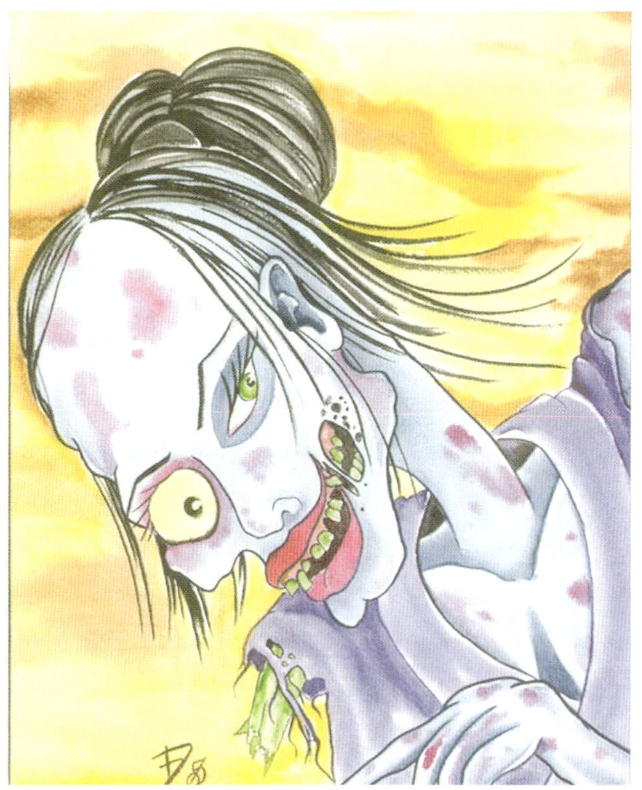

Derek Dufresne's zombie painting has influences that are both New School and Asian.

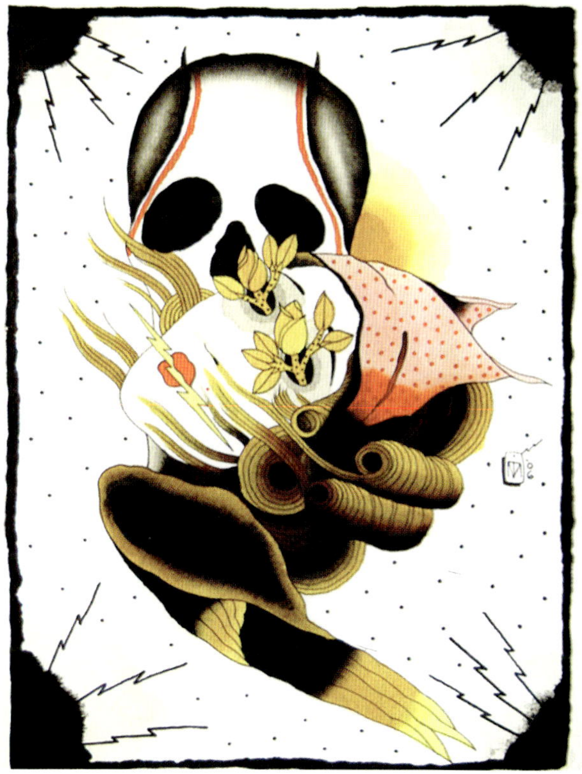

Tim McGrath of 13 Roses in Atlanta, GA, offers a unique take on some traditional American images.

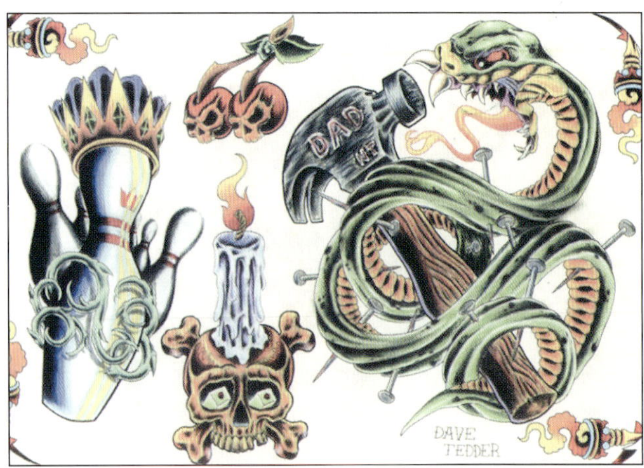

Fun flash designs from Dave Tedder, All Or Nothing, Atlanta, GA.

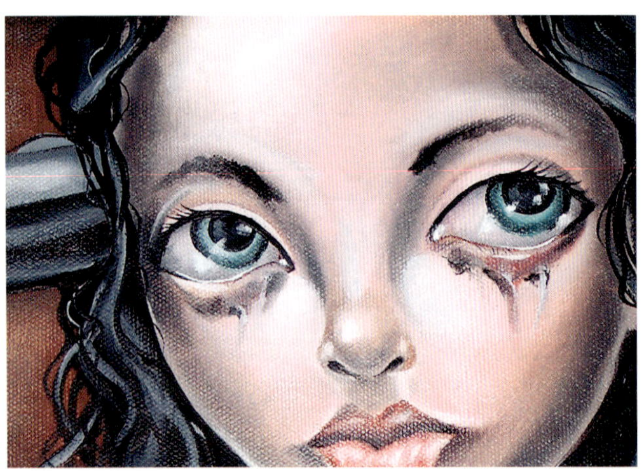

Matt Griffith of Two Dollar Pistol creates beautiful, luminous paintings with characteristic large, wet eyes. An image like this one could make for a strong reference piece for a New School style tattoo.

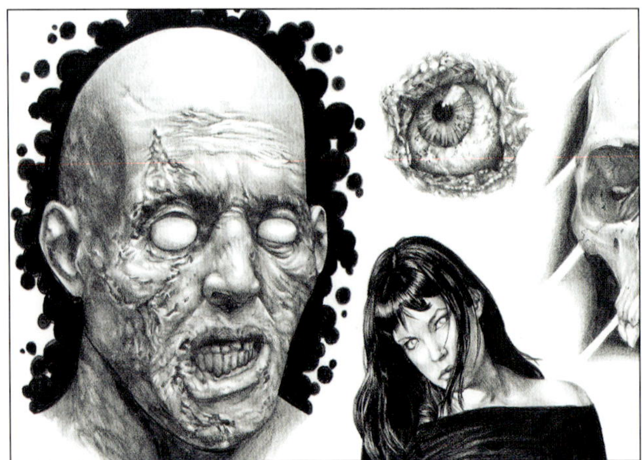

Sexy and scary black and grey designs from the chiaroscuro master, Dave Attonito, Good Clean Fun, Snellville, GA.

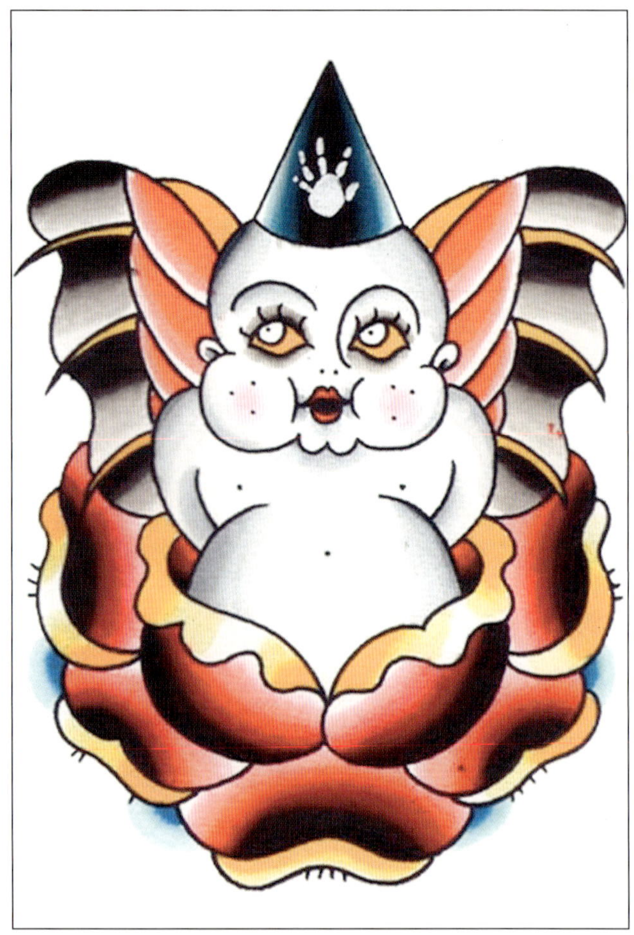

Mario Desa's flash design is an example of his doing what he does best: creating a unique hybrid image from elements typical of a traditional American tattoo. The red, black, and yellow color scheme as well as the straight black shading are also typical of the traditional American style.

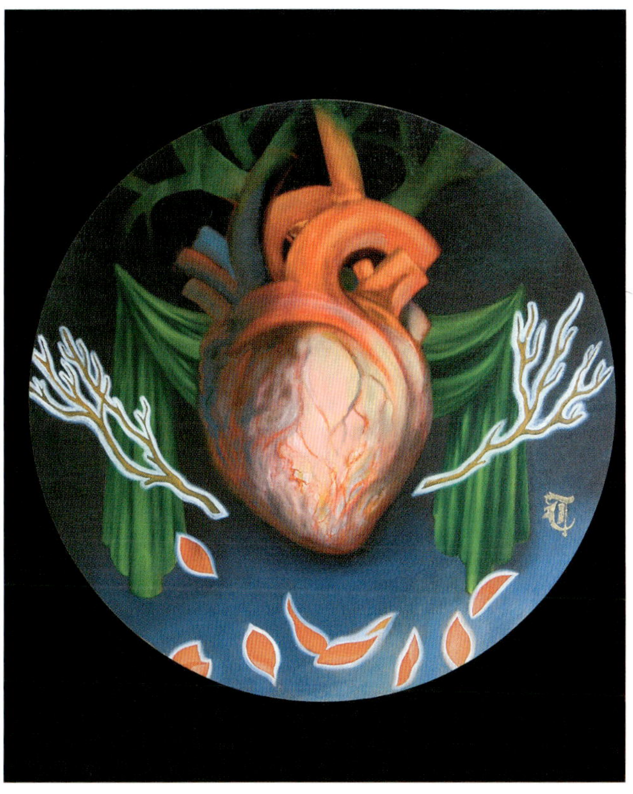

William Thidemann of Th'Ink Tank Tattoo in Denver, CO.

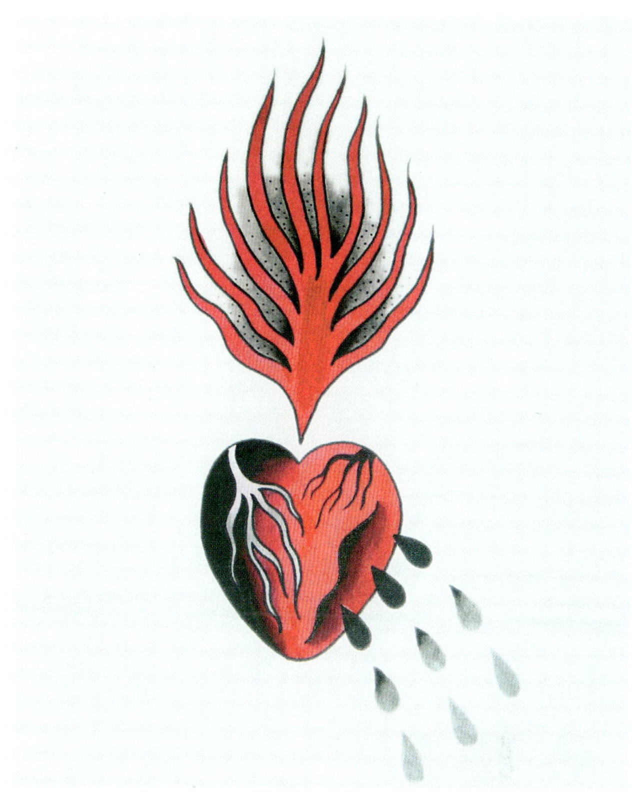

Another take on the sacred heart motif from Mario Desa.

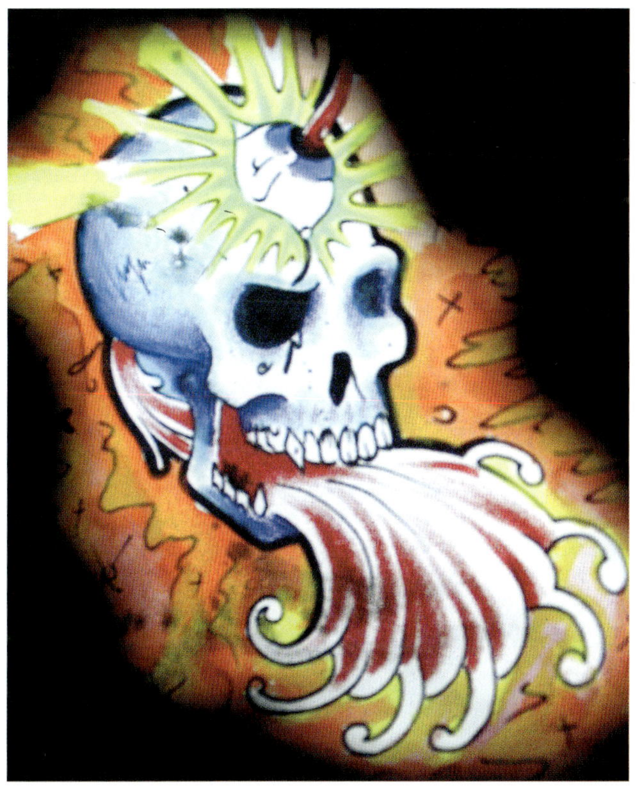

Puking skull from Asheville's Shannon Schober of Vitality Tattoo in Asheville, NC.

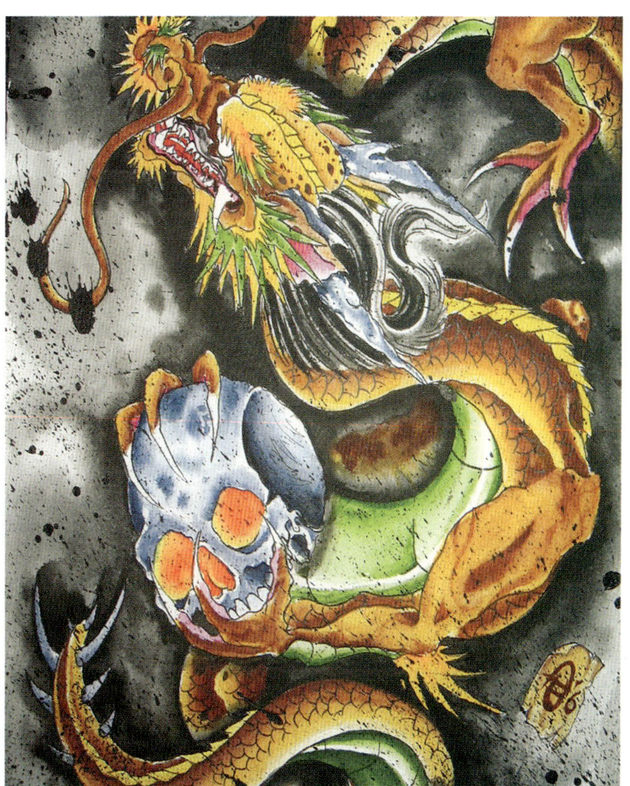

Derek Dufresne, Fleshworks, Victoria, BC.

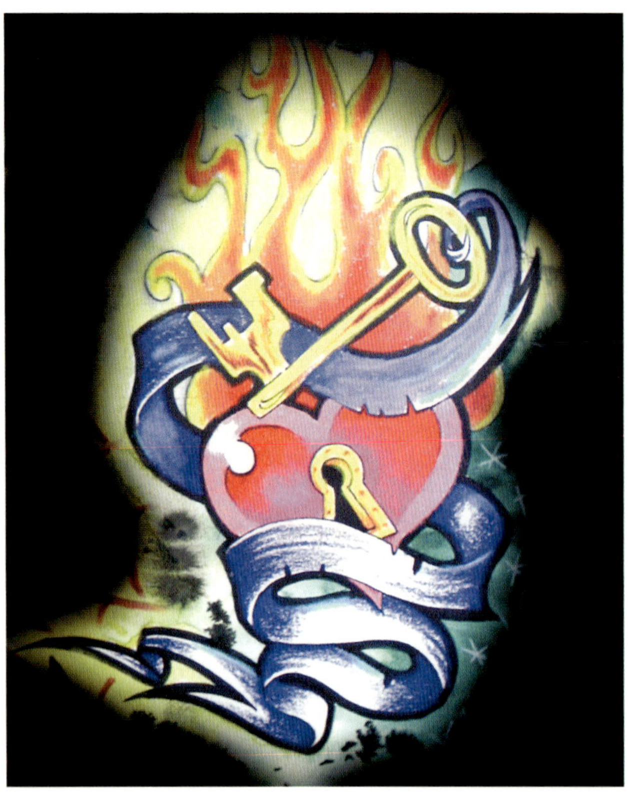

Shannon Schober's heart with a lock and key could be customized with many variations on the banner.

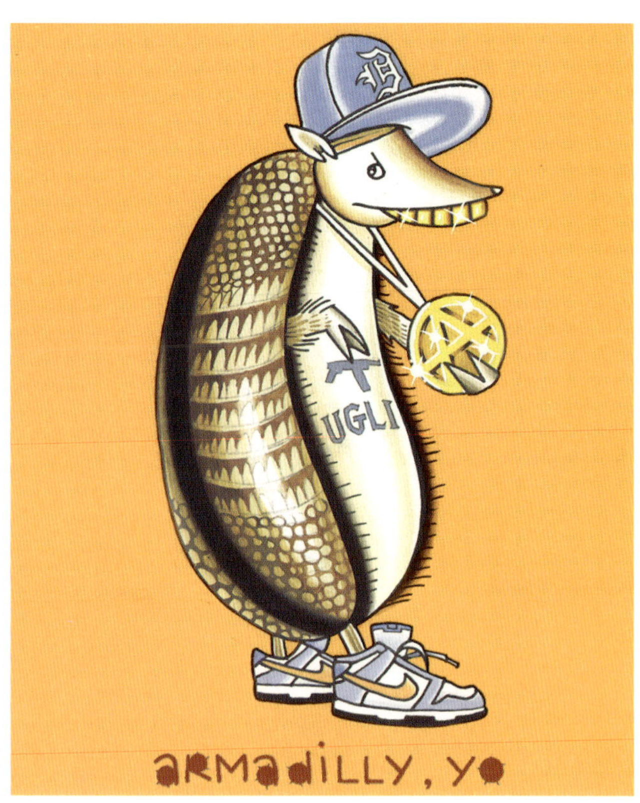

This painting from Mark Heggie would make for a fun New School style tattoo.

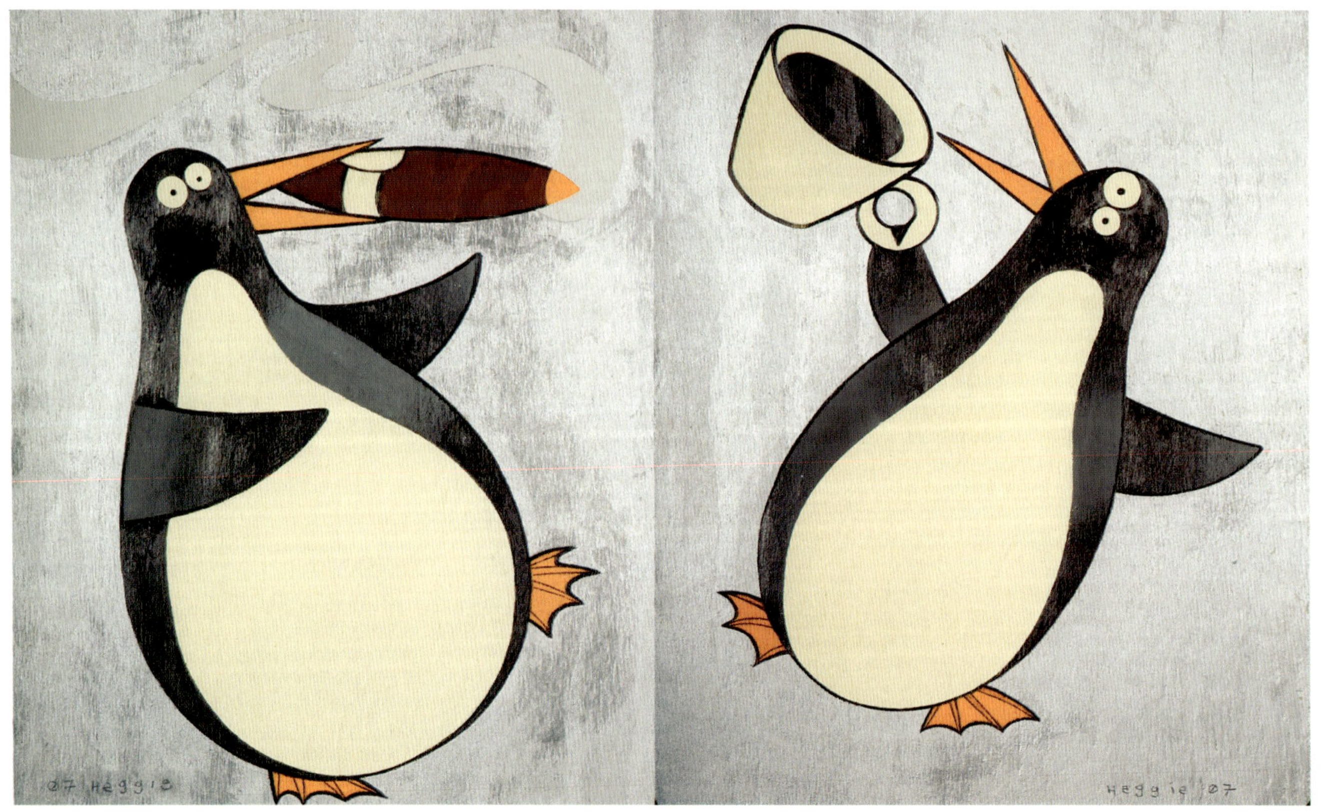

This pair of penguins from Mark Heggie could be interesting reference for a light-hearted tattoo as well. Tattoos in pairs on the backs of thighs, calves, or forearms can be highly visually pleasing.

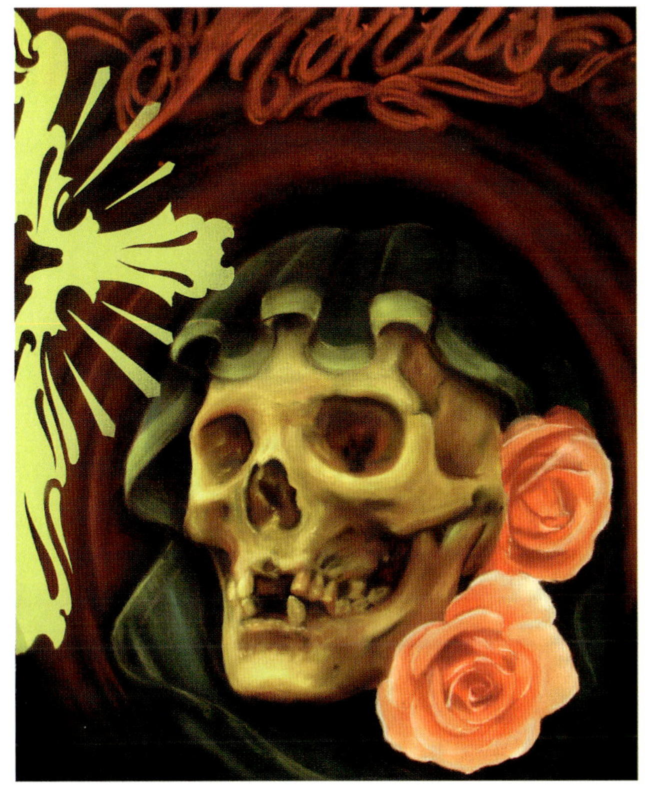

Nate Beavers and Colors One, I45, Houston, TX.

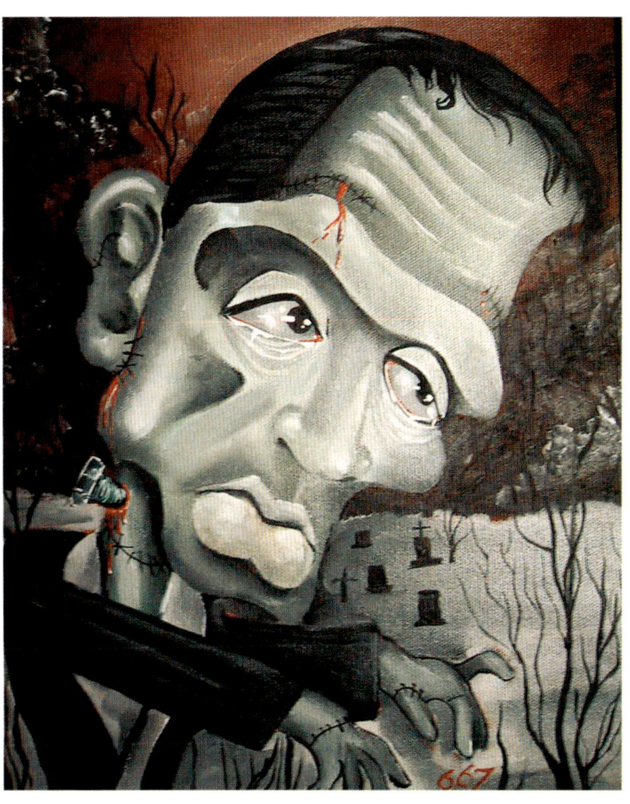

Matt Griffith, Two Dollar Pistol, Chillicothe, OH.

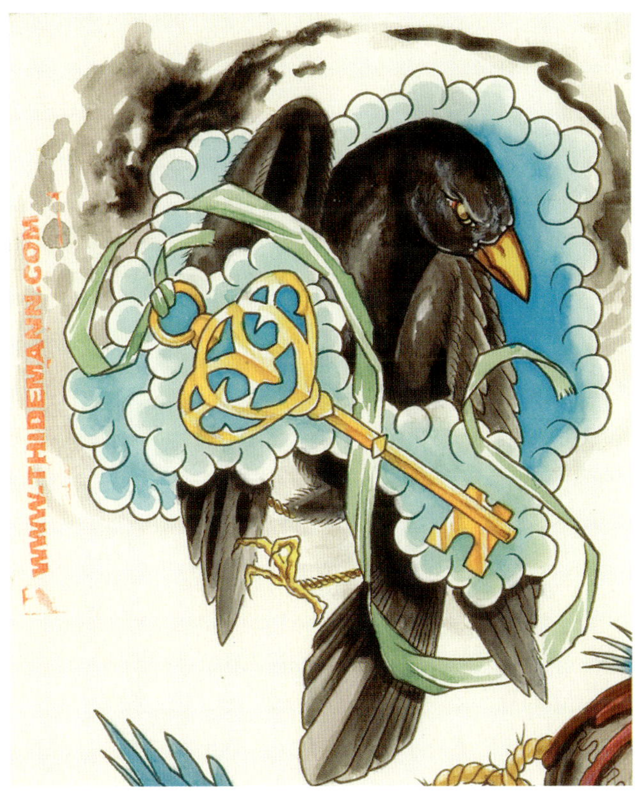

Painterly designs from William Thidemann, Th'Ink Tank, Denver, CO.

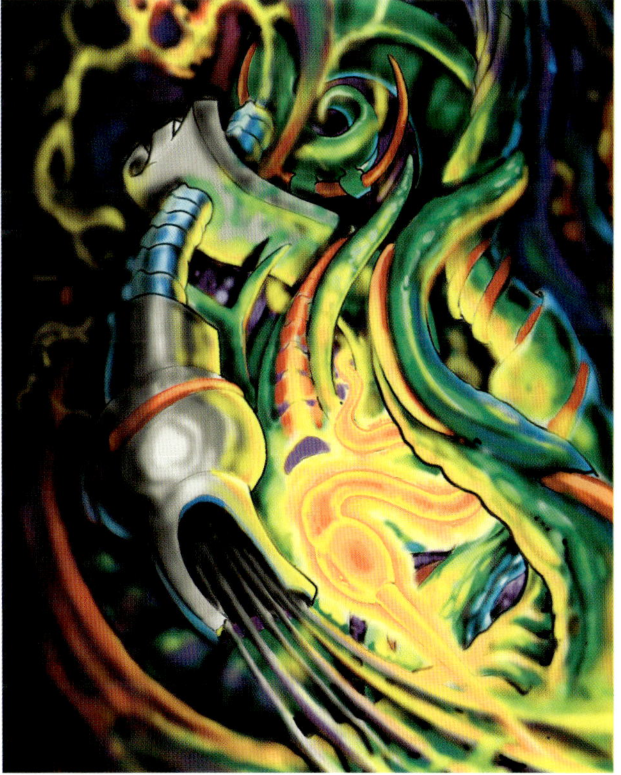

Swirling colors make this intricate biomechanical composition from Zsolt Sarkozi a complex design.

Are Tattoo Inks Safe?

One question you might ask yourself when considering a tattoo is whether or not the inks the artists will be injecting into your skin are safe. For all practical purposes, after all, the procedure is minor surgery. It is wise to consider what you'll be putting into your body before beginning the process, especially as there has been some controversy regarding the composition of tattoo inks in recent years, and a handful of cases of clients having allergic reactions to adulterants in tattoo inks or to the metal pigments themselves.

Most commercially available tattoo inks are comprised of metal salts or plastic compounds suspended in a carrier solution that disinfects and evenly suspends the pigment powders. There is a common misperception that tattoo inks are made of natural pigments. Unfortunately, many of the plant and other vegetable-based dyes available are bio-absorbable, making them useless as tattoo inks because they will promptly be broken down and absorbed by the body. While recent advances in inks have made the use of plant-based inks more feasible, the vast majority of tattoo inks on the market today are metal-based.

The present controversy regarding tattoo pigments has to do with the surprising lack of regulation and requirements for purity in tattoo pigments. The United States Food And Drug Administration considers the inks used in tattoos to be color additives requiring pre-market approval; however, the lack of substantial evidence of a safety concern has resulted in a lack of regulation from the FDA. Additionally, as tattoo sanitation has generally been the province of the various states, the FDA had felt no public mandate to intervene in regulation until the issue of safety emerged after reports of allergic reactions came to light.

In recent years, the organization has been reconsidering its hands-off approach to the regulation of tattoo pigments, and it is possible that they will become more involved in regulation of ink manufacturers and pigment quality in the future. For now, however, the market is wide open, and tattoo artists are choosing inks that they have the most success using and that they consider to be the safest for their clients. The tattoo artist, after all, makes his or her living largely by establishing a reputation for solid work and satisfied clients; he or she would not be likely to continue to use a product that had caused a bad reaction in a client in the past. There is a good chance that the market will regulate itself…that inks that contain dangerous adulterants or metals that cause some people with heightened sensitivities to respond badly will not sell as well as those that artists use with more consistent success.

The danger in some inks is that they might contain pigments that aren't intended for skin use at all…color additives whose original uses include printing ink or car paint. Red inks, as well, have been known to cause allergic reactions more commonly than other colors, as the pigments iron oxide, cinnabar, and cadmium red that are commonly used to make up red ink can be quite toxic. A small movement has emerged both within the tattoo industry and without calling for more regulation of the manufacturers of tattoo inks from the Food And Drug Administration to prevent these materials from being used, and to hold the companies making these products to higher standards of health and safety.

Risks from adulterants in tattoo ink, as reported by the FDA, include:

Removal Problems

Although techniques in laser removal have advanced significantly in recent years, tattoos are still designed to be permanent, and the inks artists used have been engineered to withstand the test of time. Removing a tattoo with the laser process can be painful, expensive, and the result may not be complete, especially for certain colors. Green and yellow pigments seem to stand up to lasers particularly well.

Are Tattoo Inks Safe?

Allergic Reactions

While allergic reactions to tattoo ink are quite rare, when they do occur, they are difficult to manage. Removal of tattoo inks from the skin is tricky and can take a period of treatments that might last for several months, which means that the person suffering from the reaction could have trouble for a long time. The process of using a laser to break down the ink in the skin might further irritate the problem. There have even been a few cases, as reported by the FDA, of people developing allergic reactions to tattoos that they have had for several years.

Granulomas

Granulomas are nodules that form around a substance that the body perceives as foreign, and it is possible for this condition to occur in or around a tattoo in people with heightened sensitivity to a particular chemical, in a tattoo that is misapplied, or in a tattoo with ink that is unsafe. These reactions have been found most often to occur with red pigments; however, they have also been reported in shades of purple, blue, and green.

Keloid Scarring

Keloids are scars that grow beyond their normal boundaries, and they can occur any time that the skin is scarred or otherwise traumatized. Some people are prone to developing keloids, and if you know that you have a tendency to scar in this manner, it might be best to avoid tattoos altogether. Some research has shown, however, that keloids occur more commonly from laser tattoo removal than from the actual initial application of the tattoo. While keloid scarring is not dangerous, it is unattractive and can damage the image of the tattoo. As tattooing is an enhancement in the first place, it is probably a good idea to avoid the process if you are apt to form keloids that will distort your art.

MRI Complications

There have been a few reports of skin in tattooed areas experiencing swelling, burning, or other effects after the wearer has undergone magnetic resonance imaging, otherwise known as an MRI exam. These effects are rare and the condition clears up with no lasting damage, so it is not likely that the mild irritation one might experience from MRI exposure to your tattoo will outweigh the possible negative health effects of not getting a MRI scan that has been ordered by your physician. Notifying your doctor of your tattoo, should the situation arise, will allow him or her to perform the exam with the proper precautions to minimize the potential side effects.

So while there is some risk inherent in inserting any foreign substance into your body, the potential conditions we have covered are extremely rare and are generally unlikely to occur. If you have concerns about the inks your artist will use in your tattoo, talk to him or her. An experienced artist will be familiar with the risks, and he or she will likely be able to explain why the inks you will be receiving are the right inks for you. An experienced artist will understand the process and will have chosen his or her inks from the many available for their quality, safety, and durability.

Another issue preventing successful regulation from the Food And Drug Administration is that many artists mix their own inks, especially older and more experienced artists. Because these "secret recipe" tattoo mixes are a trade secret, you may have less success getting an artist who mixes his or her own inks to tell you about the ingredients. However, a responsible artist will be able to assure you of your safety; and if you have any doubts about your artists' practices, it might be best to find someone with whom you feel more comfortable and who is more comfortable helping you establish a relationship based on trust.

In the end, however, by far the greatest safety concern to consider when you are getting a new tattoo and when you are choosing your artist is sterilization and sanitation. While an allergic reaction could certainly be painful and unpleasant, the effects of a lack of sterilization or poor sanitation practices can be life-threatening. From HIV to hepatitis to skin infections (most commonly those caused by staphylococcus aureus, the "staph" bacteria), these concerns far outweigh any of the negative effects that might spring from ink adulterants or toxic pigments. We cannot overemphasize the importance of making sure that the shop and artist that you choose are properly licensed and practice safe sterilization and sanitation protocols. Unsterilized or used equipment, re-used ink or other disposables, and neglect of gloves and other barriers should be the first things that you look for if you are concerned about the safety practices of your tattoo artist.

Tattoo Removal

While we all want to have the coolest tattoos, we've all been young before, or drunk before, or otherwise foolish and overeager. What can we do when we've gotten ourselves into that worst of all tattoo situations: a poorly executed, unattractive tattoo? The options for tattoo removal have traditionally been very limited; however, developments in laser technology have provided some people who have old, faded, or otherwise displeasing tattoos with alternatives that were not available previously.

Historically, methods of tattoo removal included excision, dermabrasion, and salabrasion. These methods are painful, unlikely to be effective, and require multiple treatments over a long period of time.

Excision is the surgical removal of a tattoo. While it is an effective technique for small tattoos, excision can be complicated for larger pieces. The process includes cutting away the tattoo from the skin and then suturing together the separated edges of the skin. Because the layer of the skin where the tattoo is located is relatively deep, the graft of skin that must be taken can leave a scar that is often more unsightly than the offending tattoo. For larger tattoos, the process of excision generally begins in the middle of the tattoo. Once the sutured area heals, another excision will be made until the tattoo is wholly removed. For larger tattoos, the removal will result in a large area of scars from the sutures, and there is the potential for stretch marks from stretching the skin to fill in the area being removed.

Dermabrasion is the process of freezing the area of skin with the tattoo and then applying an abrasive instrument to the area, causing the skin to peel. Because the tattoo is deep within the layers of the skin, however, dermabrasion is not often successful.

Salabrasion is a centuries-old procedure using a mixture of salt and water and an abrading apparatus to rub the solution into the skin until it is raw and red. The area would then be wrapped in gauze, and the procedure would be repeated until the desired effect is achieved.

These more primitive methods of tattoo removal are less effective, painful, and likely to cause significant scarring. The modern technique of laser tattoo removal, while still far from perfect, is a much more effective method of removing work you no longer want.

In laser removal, pulses of light from a laser beam are passed directly over the area with the tattoo pigment that the wearer would like to have removed. With traditional tattoo inks, this process must be repeated up to 20 times for effective removal. The light beams break down the tattoo pigment, and the body naturally expels the broken down areas through its exfoliation and cleansing processes.

While laser removal is the most common method today, it is quite costly, painful, and still likely to cause scarring. While it might be impossible to remove a tattoo completely, using lasers to lighten an area might make it possible to fade sig-

Are Tattoo Inks Safe?

nificantly an unwanted tattoo that the wearer considers to be of inferior quality, and to free up the skin for a cover-up with better quality work.

Cover-ups are another alternative for eliminating older, unwanted tattoo work. Some artists specialize in cover-ups, and they generally will offer selections of their best cover-up tattoos in their portfolios. If you are interested in having work covered, it would be worth your time to investigate the portfolios of the artists you are considering for their previous cover-up pieces. Cover-up tattooing takes some flexibility on the part of the wearer and creativity on the part of the artist. Finding ways to incorporate elements of the old tattoo into the new design can be difficult, and some tattoos (especially larger ones) are inappropriate for cover-up work. If you are considering a cover-up tattoo, it is important to remember to be flexible and to keep an open mind. It might not be possible to choose exactly what image you want; however, if you find the right artist, you should be able to work together to come up with an image that will disguise the old work while giving you a tattoo you can be proud of and happy with for the rest of your life.

Freedom-2 Tattoo Inks

A brand new development in the science of tattoo ink promises to revolutionize the way we think of the indelible art by re-inventing the indelibility itself. The company Freedom-2 has developed Infinitink, a newly engineered alternative to traditional tattoo inks that are developed from vegetable-based pigments, thereby eliminating many of our fears about the safety of the industrial pigments used in many traditional, commercially available tattoo inks. The Infinitink formulations were developed by biomedical scientists at Brown, Harvard, and Duke Universities, and they were tested following safety guidelines recommended for products intended for human use.

Not only are these inks potentially much safer, they are also more easily removable. While traditional inks take anywhere from 5-20 laser treatments for removal, Freedom-2 inks have been engineered to be removable with just one treatment.

Freedom-2's technology uses biodegradable and bioabsorbable dyes. Prior to the development of Freedom-2's approach to encapsulating these dyes in tiny micro-capsules, the colors would be absorbed and broken down by the body soon after being placed there as a tattoo. Freedom-2 has developed a system using clear, stable polymer beads that can be broken open with a single pass of a laser, allowing the ink to be absorbed and expelled by the body naturally.

The application of the tattoo will remain the same. The tattoo artist will use the current method of delivering the artwork to the skin. The only difference is the ink. Infinitink will be available for national distribution in early 2008. You can learn more and see if there is an artist near you using their products by checking them out at www.freedom2ink.com.

Ultraviolet Inks

Another alternative ink that has been available for a few years is the ultraviolet ink that is only visible under a blacklight. These products' invisibility makes them a popular alternative for people who want tattoos in non-traditional places (such as on the neck, face, fingers or hands), or for people with professions, family, or cultural situations that make tattoos less acceptable. While you won't be able to show off your tattoo in many situations, you can light up the dance floor at night clubs, concerts, and other places where use of blacklighting is common. Like other tattoo inks, these ultraviolet alternatives are not regulated by the Food And Drug Administration; however, their manufacturers stand by their safety, and there have so far not been reports of adverse reactions to these pigments.

Chapter Eleven

Photoshop

Tattoo Art's Untapped Resource

David Allen is a graphic designer-turned-tattoo artist at Blue Bird Tattoo in Portage, Indiana. He also maintains a website, www.allentattoo.com, where he has chronicled his own growth from a tattoo apprentice into a full-fledged tattoo artist and offers his tips and tricks for using Photoshop and other graphic design tools. His innovative suggestions for incorporating Photoshop techniques into the tattoo process were so helpful, both for tattooists

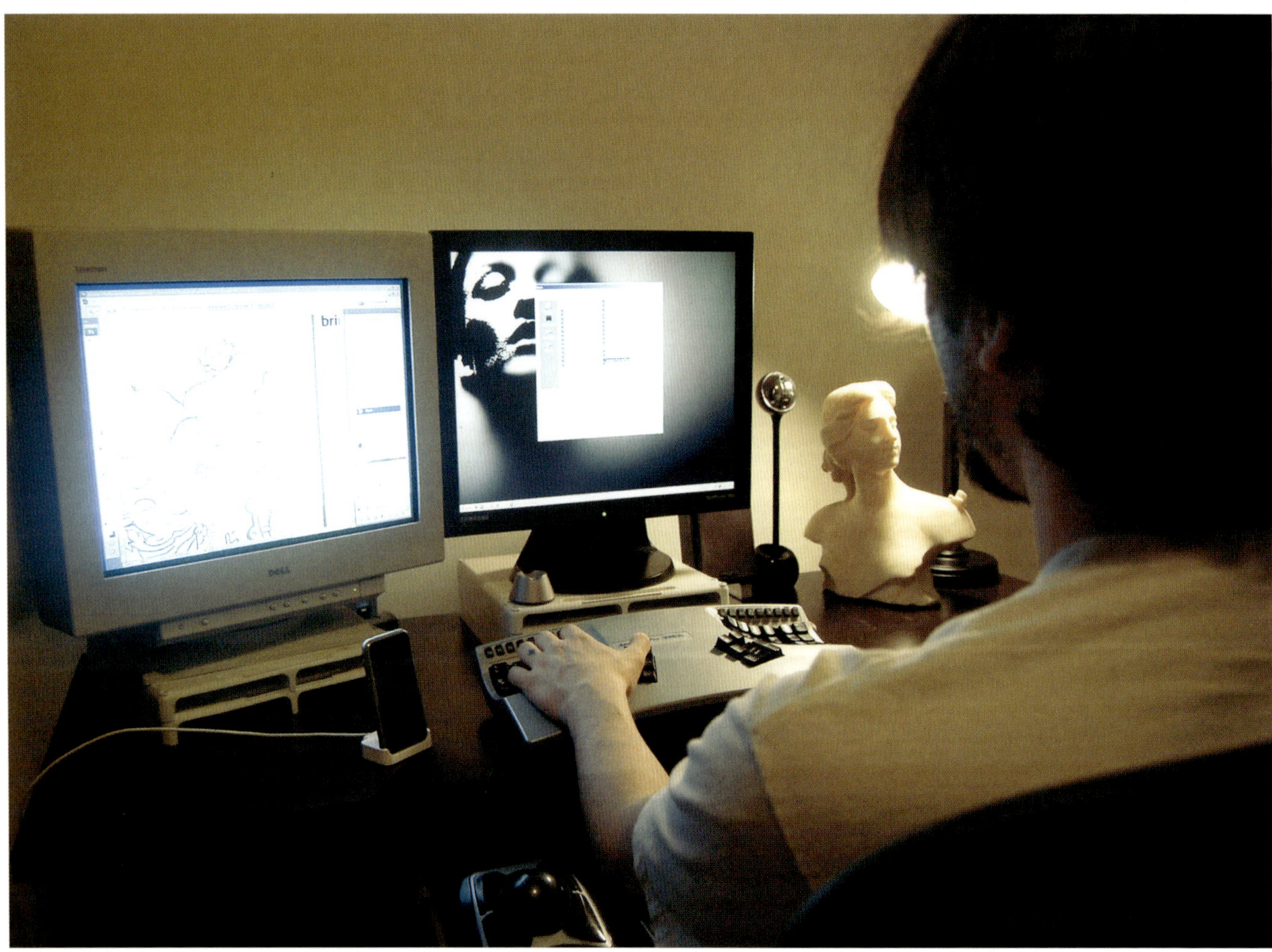

David Allen at the computer.

and astute clients looking for new and interesting ways to manipulate their art, that we asked him to share some ideas for how clients and artists can use Photoshop techniques to enhance their experience of working together. Here's what we found out!

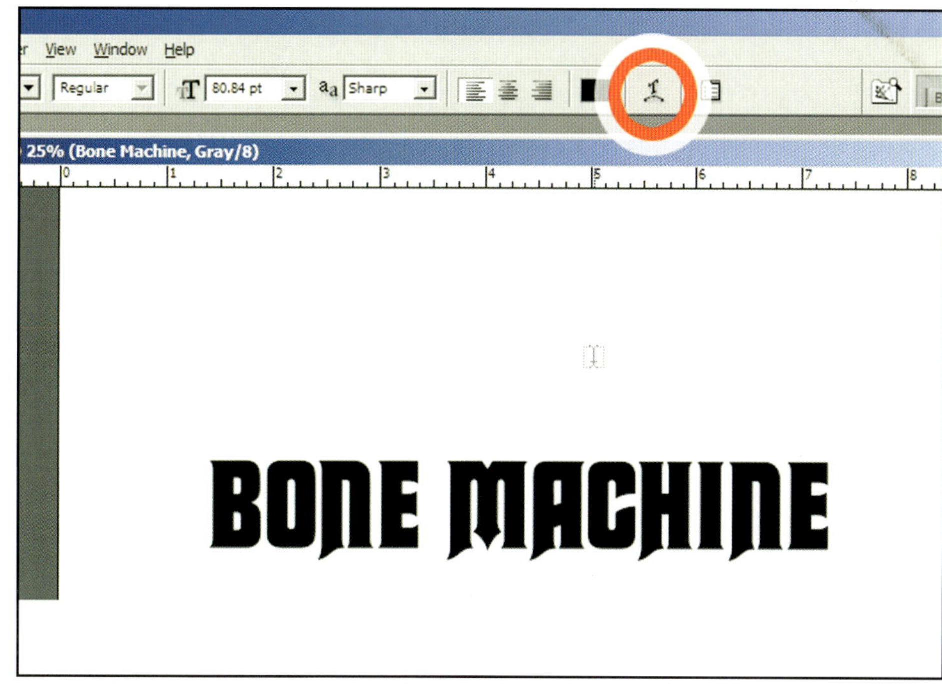

Type it in . . .

Photoshop

It was once a photographic post-production miracle, but now it has become the industry standard for most image production in print, on the internet, and in video. We hear about Photoshop all the time, from complaints about designers editing physical flaws from magazine covers to suggestions that images of celebrities in compromising positions have been enhanced using Photoshop tools. Only recently, however, have these tools come to be regarded as useful for the tattoo world.

Coming from a graphic design background, when I made the switch and decided to enter the tattoo field, I wondered why more tattoo artists were not using the technology available. Scanning drawings and photos into the computer and playing around with them in Photoshop seemed to me to be an untapped resource, and I started exploring my options. With a decent computer and scanner, the process of

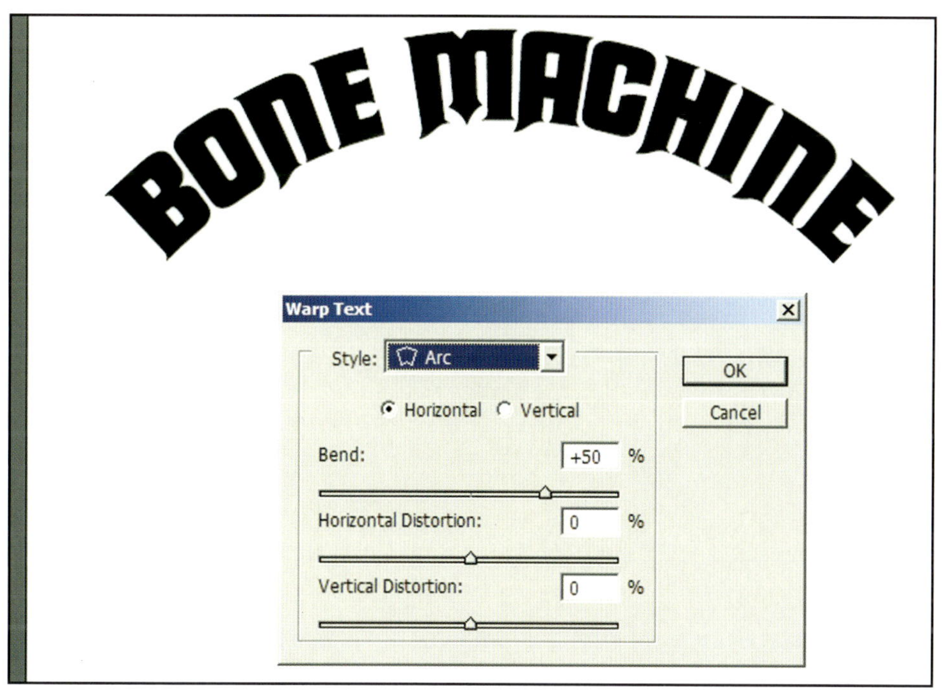

Arc it.

transferring a photograph or a design using Photoshop techniques seemed faster and more accurate than doing it by hand. How could somebody achieve perfect symmetry in a stencil by hand? Why in the world was everybody tracing Edwardian Script letter by letter on an arc template when they could just type it, arc it, and be rewarded with a perfect outline in 5 minutes using Photoshop?

Perhaps because drawing and creating by hand have always been the only possibility available to tattooists, it remains the natural option in the tattoo industry…and so it should be. Tattoo artists are a people of skill and craft, and we have rendered ourselves adept in trades of the hand. From mind to paper, the process calls for us to interpret and then translate visually what the client wants.

With a little bit of knowledge, however, the tools and power of Photoshop can be applied between mind and paper to strengthen the final output, giving us an incredibly precise stencil. Photoshop will never replace the care of an artist working on an original piece, but with so many options to ease our enhancement of an image, it only makes sense to use this technology to make our lives easier and to make the people getting tattoos happier with the increased speed in production and more precise results.

The many options and steps involved within Photoshop can be overwhelming to people who aren't familiar with its many functions, but you don't have to master its complexities before being able to use it effectively. My goal in this chapter is to make my daily Photoshop routine a little more familiar and to give you some step-

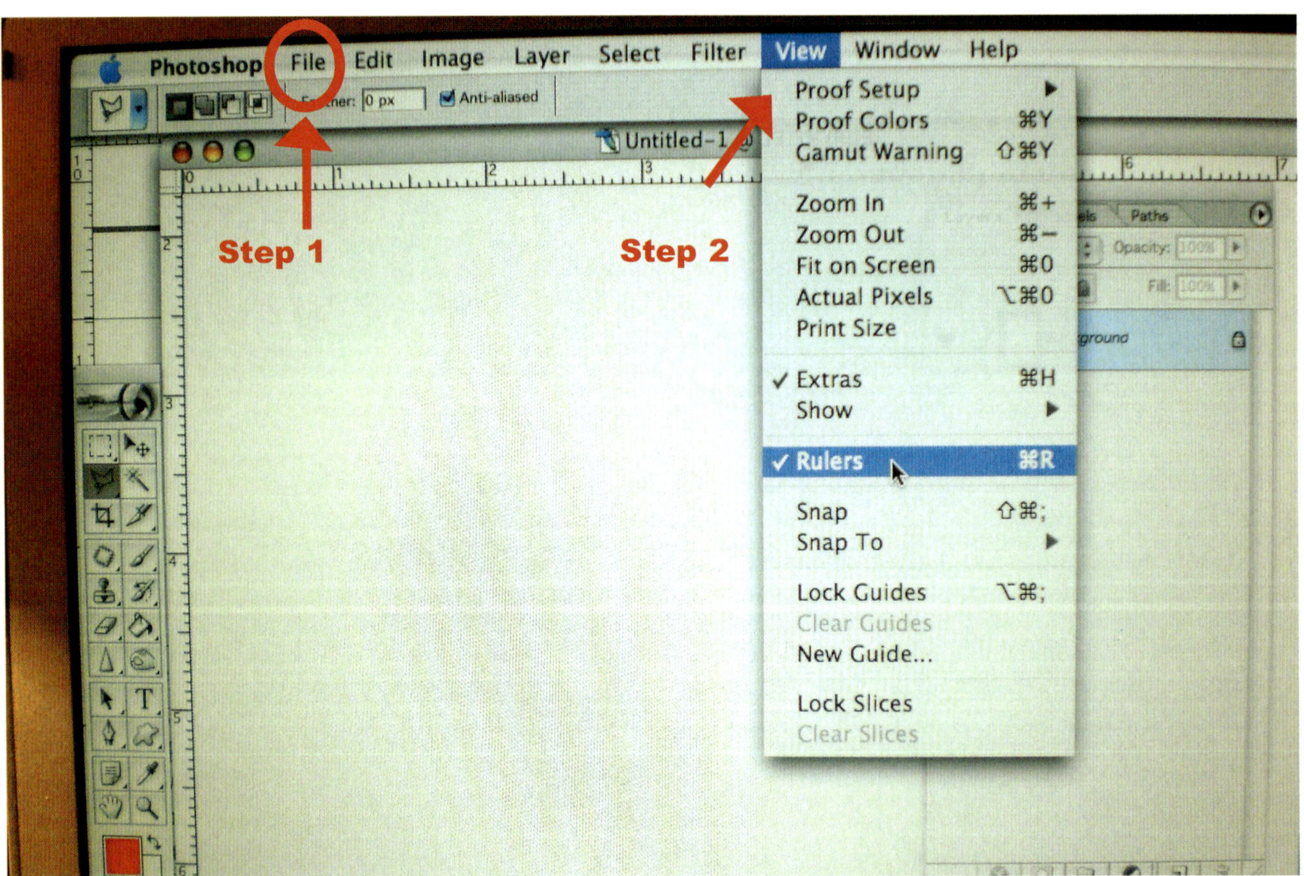

Setting up your document.

by-step instructions for how you can start using basic Photoshop tools to increase your speed and precision. I'll go over one long tutorial and end everything up with some quick tips. The long walkthrough will highlight a handful of different edits that will, hopefully, spur you on to other uses of the technology. Then the quick tips will cover the various quick and dirty ways I have begun to increase my speed in pushing out imagery for clients in my tattoo shop.

While much of this information is basic and might not be useful for someone who already knows how to use Photoshop, it still might be useful for those of you who are more familiar with these options to read it and reconsider how these techniques can be useful in the tattoo shop context. From artists to clients, uncovering the potential to increase your productivity and enhance your accuracy in developing the reference piece for your next tattoo is definitely worth the read!

Let's get started with our step-by-step walk through (at left).

Setting Up Your Document

Let's create a new document.

File > New (CTRL+N) then easily select "Letter" under the Preset drop down box.

This preset is ready with a standard paper size and a resolution of 300 pixels per inch - not 72!

Rulers and Guides

Before I get to work, I always make sure my rulers are showing so I have a good idea of what size my project will be.

View > Rulers (CTRL+R)

If you can right click anywhere on the ruler, you'll have the option to change the measurements. Go ahead and change it to inches (or centimeters).

From the rulers we can pull out some handy guides. I don't often use the word "handy", but dang are these guys handy!

To get a horizontal guide, just click on the top ruler and drag one down. Release your click after dragging it and it'll be placed wherever you are.

A vertical guide will come from the left ruler if you do the same thing.

Quick Tip: If you hold down the Shift key while dragging a guide, it'll automatically snap to the next incremental measurement. Use this to quickly define an exact area.

So if I know my tattoo is going to be about

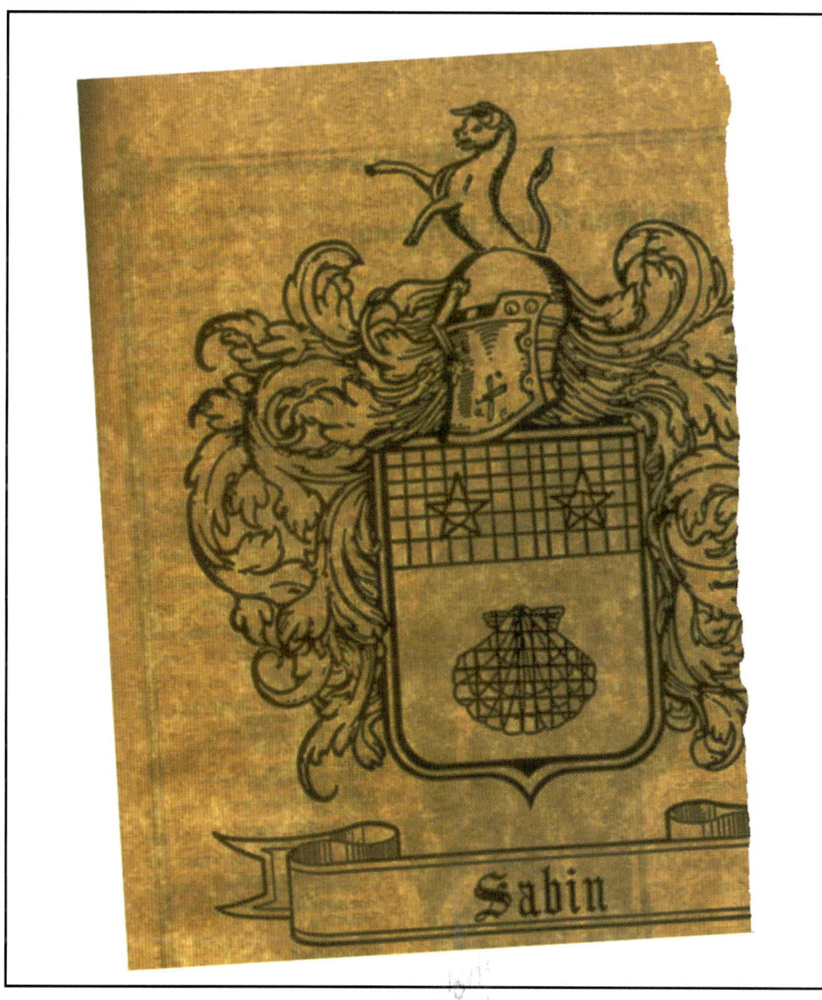

First scan.

5 inches wide and 3 inches tall, I'll pull out four guides and create a visual boundary that'll make life easier. And no, guides don't show up when you print.

About Scanning

When you scan an image, make sure your minimum resolution is 300 dots per inch. If you want the image larger, feel free to scan at 600 dpi (double) or even higher. Then, when you drag and drop that scanned image into the new document we created, it'll be much larger already.

A Walkthrough

Scan, straighten, adjust levels, layers, and flip for symmetry:

A client brings in an old, tiny, and blurry page from a book. On it, he's got a crest he'd like to get tattooed on him. Here's a step-by-step guide on how I'd pull and create a clean outline:

Create a new document (CTRL+N) using the preset "Letter" at 300dpi.

Scan the image. I scanned the image at 600 dpi so it'll already be larger when I drag and drop it into my default 300 dpi document. After scanning, Photoshop will load the freshly grabbed image into a new document separate from our newly created one.

Figure 1: Scanned image (Page 127).

It's crooked, so let's straighten it up. To fix the tilted angle, Photoshop needs for you to tell it what angle should be perfectly straight.

Auto Rotate

1. Select the Measuring Tool. (It's the ruler under the Eyedropper, or cycle to it with Shift+I)

2. Drag a line with the Measuring Tool along a line that should be straight. (The thick line in Figure 2 is a visual indicator, I actually

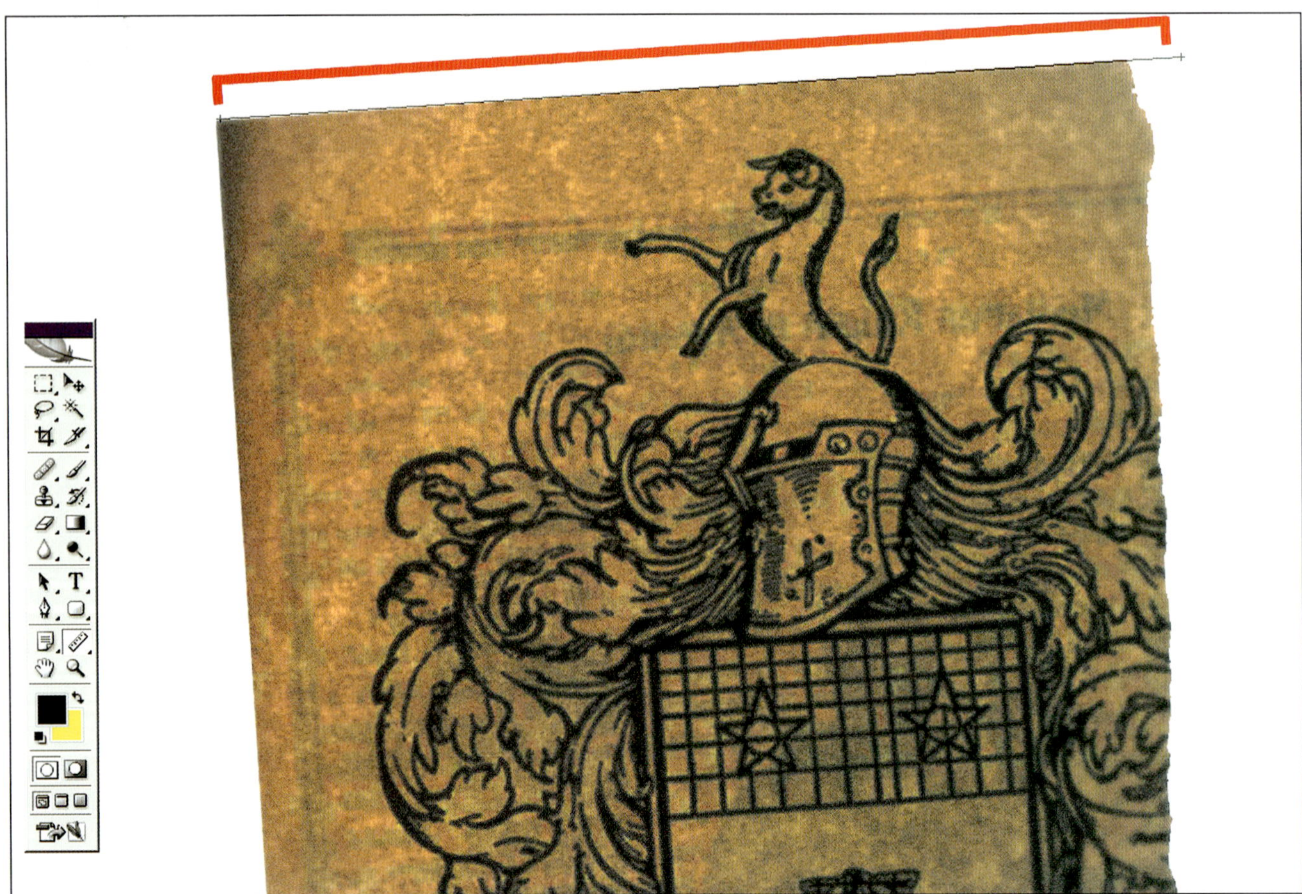

Figure 2

drew it directly on the top of the page.)

3. From the top menu bar select Image > Rotate Canvas > Arbitrary. The correct value and direction of rotation (clockwise or counter clockwise) should be automatically loaded. Hit OK and the image will be rotated automatically back to 90 degrees.

* This is perfect for straightening crosses, lines of text, faces (draw the line from eye to eye), kanji (you can do this vertically also), photos, and just about anything else you can scan.

Figure 2: Measuring Tool (at left)

Figure 3: Rotated automatically (at right).

Now that the image is straight, let's click and drag the scanned image into our default 300 dpi document. Scanning it at 600 dpi helped to increase the size, but we still need it resize it bigger.

Figure 4 & 5

Resize Image

1. From the top menu bar select Edit > Transform > Scale. Or just hit CTRL+T.

2. Drag one of the box handles – the little

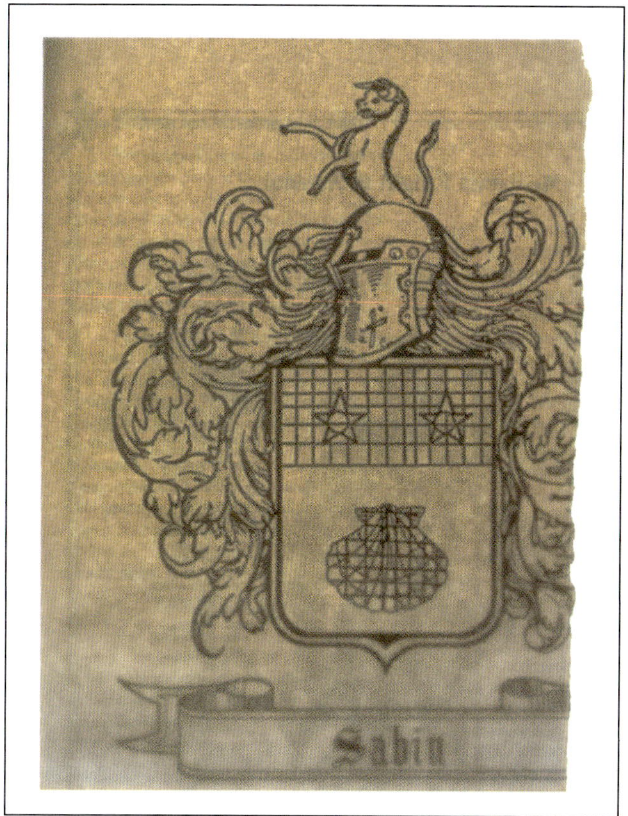

Figure 3.

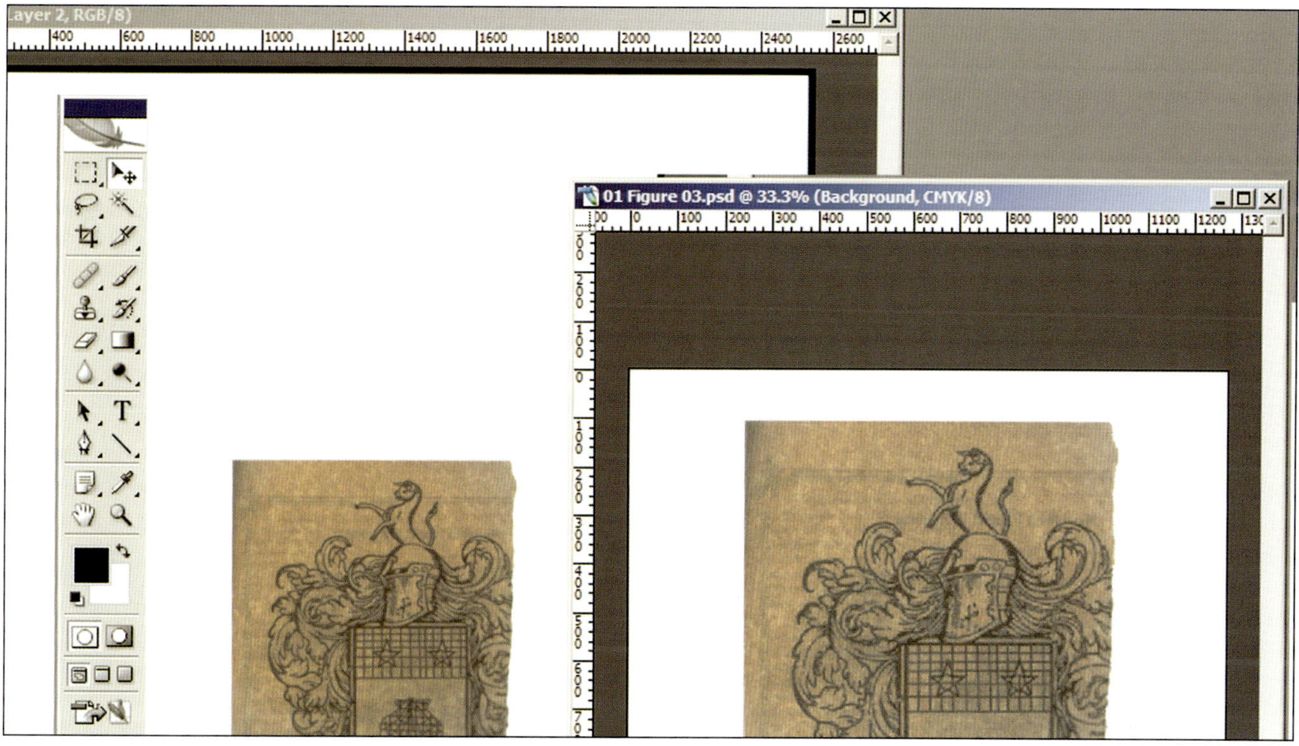

Figure 4: Resizing Image

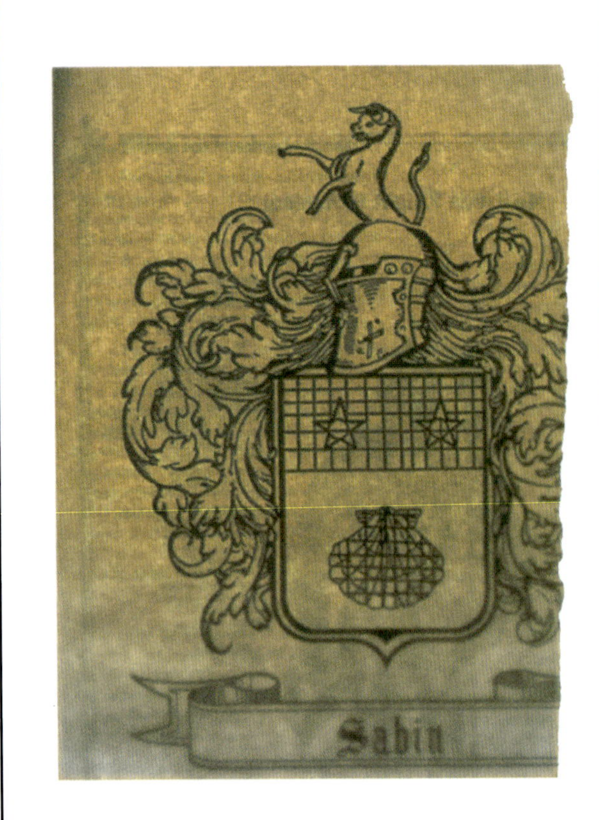

Figure 5: Resize.

squares on the corners and centers of the line – to resize. Make sure you hold down Shift while you drag so it'll resize proportionally. Eyeball the rulers to get it close to the desired size.

3. Hit Enter to accept the changes, or ESC to reject.

The size looks good. Next I have to make the lines darker so I can pull out an outline to trace. It's time to mess with Levels…

A Levels primer

Pull up the Levels window: Image > Adjustments > Levels (or CTRL+L)

Hopefully, the box next to "Preview" will be checked. If not, go ahead and check it so you can temporarily view the results of your editing.

The black, bar graph-looking graphic is your histogram. It shows you the distribution of tones in your image. Dark tones on the left and light tones on the right. You can alter the darkest and lightest points in your image by dragging the black and white triangles beneath the histogram. Any tones that are darker than your new black point will be pure black. Those that are lighter than your new white point will be pure white.

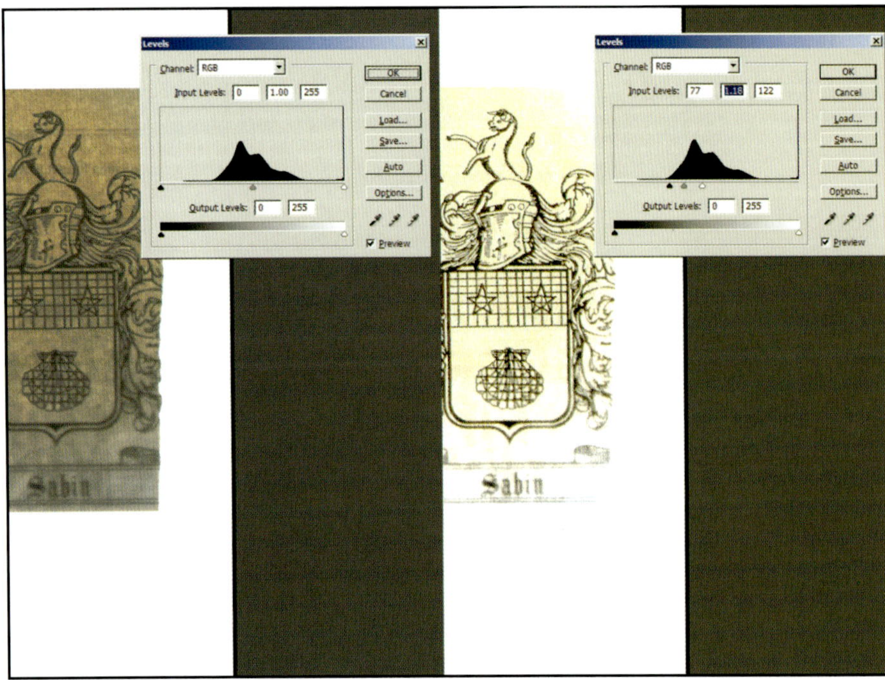

Figure 6: Before and After Level adjustments.

Dragging the grey triangle lets you adjust the middle tones within your image. Go ahead and mess with it. You'll pick it up fast.

Adjusting Levels

1. Make sure the Levels window is open: Image > Adjustments > Levels (or CTRL+L)

2. Adjustments will be different for each image, but for this one I'll slide the black point to the right and bring the white point far to the left.

3. Hit OK. Save your File.

Figure 6: Before and After Level adjustments

Time to print so I can trace an outline. I always print

out a copy about 30% bigger than the actual tattoo size. Remember, we can later reduce the image without losing quality, but increasing the size sucks. Once printed, I like to hand trace the obvious lines and figure out where the line should be over blurry areas. A little compensation here, a little tweak there. If the piece is complicated and I need to visually step back, all I do is turn off the lightbox a couple times to figure everything out.

In this piece, I traced the entire left side as well as the helmet and top bull.

Alright, now for some more intense steps. Scan the freshly drawn outline – 300 dpi will keep it exact with our document. After scanning a pencil outline, I always darken the lines and kill the grey smudges by messing with the Levels again. And, if it scanned crooked, you already know how to have Photoshop Auto Rotate.

Figure 7: Scan and Adjust Levels scan

Click, drag and drop the adjusted scan into our primary document. Now we're messing Layers.

About Layers

Photoshop organizes objects within a document into layers. It stacks images on top of another as if using transparent tracing paper. Each layer can have different images and effects. When the layers are stacked, the images can appear as if they are all a single image. The cool part is that you have tons of options to edit your images without messing anything up.

Make sure your Layers palette is open. (Window > Layers - or F7) You can Create a New Layer by clicking on the button at the bottom of the Layers palette. Or Delete a Layer with a quick click, drag and drop – by dropping the layer to the trash bin at the bottom of the Layers palette.

One last useful tip for the Layers palette: clicking on the little eyeball icon will remove the eye and effectively hide that layer from view. Click on the empty space again and the eye will come back with the view of the layer.

To grab and pull areas from a Layer, we have to Select and Move them.

More on Selecting and Moving

Learning how to select and moves areas in your document is the key to unlocking the power of Photoshop. Objects are selected by using any Marquee Tool and can be moved by using the Move Tool.

Figure 8: Move Tool and Marquee Tools

Selecting options include: rectangular and elliptical Marquee Tools, lasso and magnetic lasso tools, and also the magic wand.

By default the Rectangular Marquee Tool will work fine. It's a matter of clicking on a corner spot, holding down that click and dragging the rectangle over the area you wish to select.

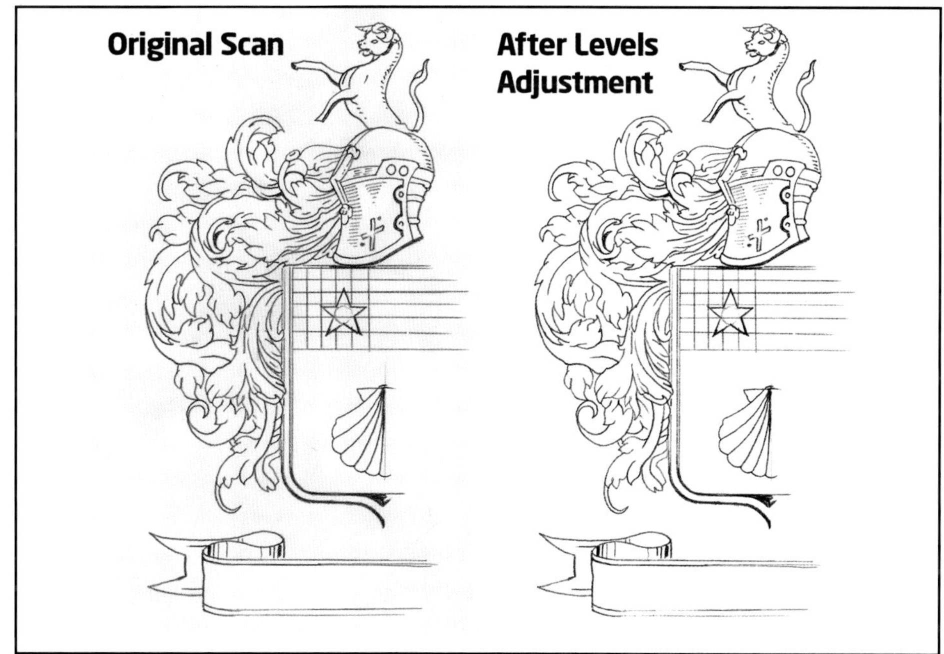

Figure 7: Scan and Adjust Levels scan

Once you release the click, a moving, dotted line (marching ants) will show you the selected area.

Now, the Move Tool moves stuff. It's important. If you are using any tool (well, except the hand tool and magnifying tool) hold down the CTRL key and the tool will automatically change into the Move Tool.

When the Move Tool is selected, click and drag anywhere in the image. If an area is selected (see below) the selection will be moved, otherwise the entire layer will be moved. Also, you can use your arrow keys to move the selection or layer in tiny increments. (Hold down the Shift key to move in larger increments)

We're going to grab the left side of the crest so we can create a copy, flip it and give us a symmetrical right side.

Center, Select, Copy and Paste

1. Let's designate a center line for the crest by dragging and placing a vertical guide from the left ruler.

2. Make sure the Layers palette is open: Window > Layers (or F7) and the right layer (our scanned outline) is selected or highlighted. If not, just click on it. Now, with the Move Tool selected, press your Left or Right arrow keys to center the outline layer with your vertical guide. I used the bottom point of the crest to line up the center. (Figure 9 at right)

3. Select your Rectangular Marquee Tool, click anywhere near the vertical guide and drag. While you're holding down your click, the selection should snap to the guide. (If not go up to View > Snap) Now drag and select the left side of the crest. (Figure 10 at right)

4. Copy your selection Edit > Copy (or CTRL+C)

5. Paste the copy Edit > Paste (or CTRL+V)

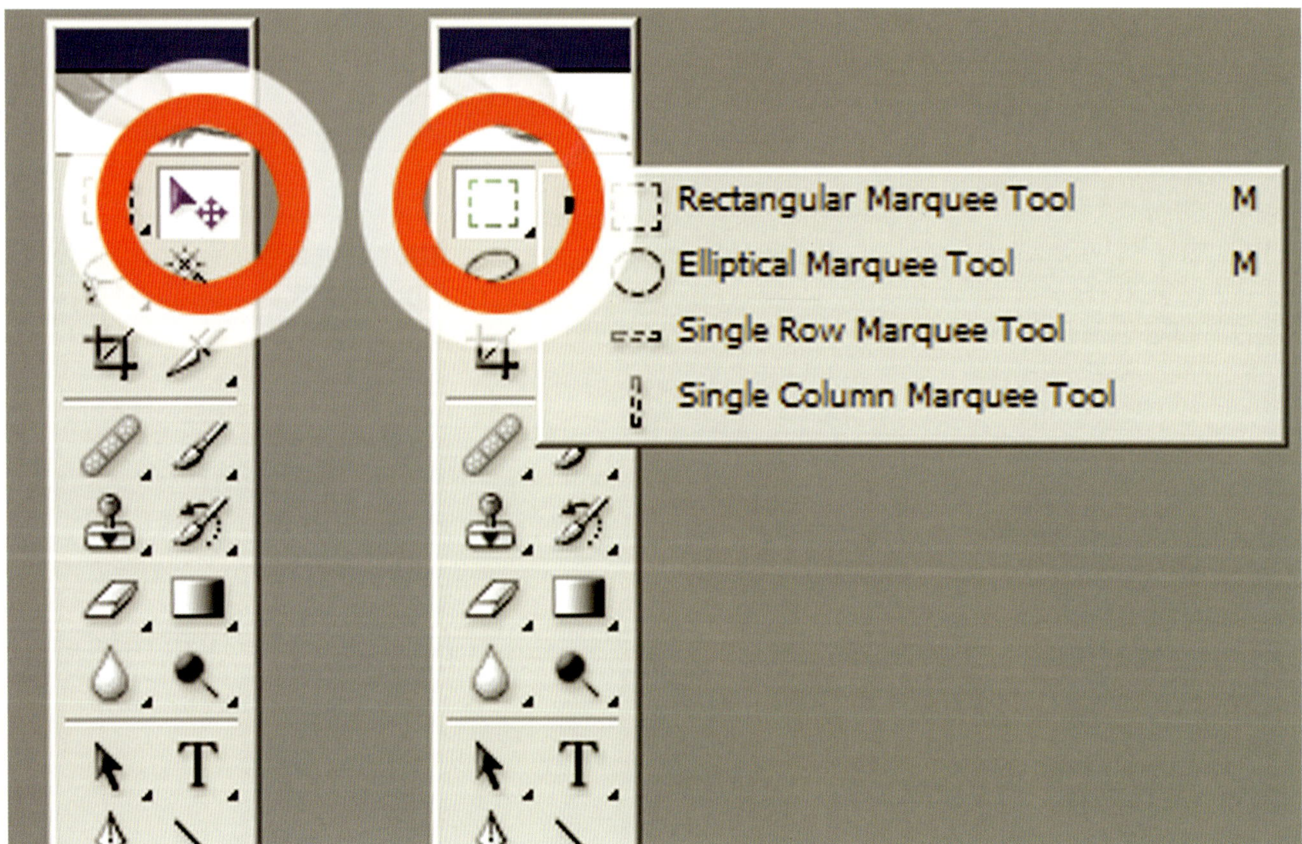

Figure 8: Move tool and Marquee tool.

The copy will now be included in your document as its own Layer. (Figure 10 at right)

So we've duplicated the left side and we're ready to flip it for use.

Flip, Move, and Make other side Transparent

1. Let's Flip the newly Pasted Layer. Edit > Transform > Flip Horizontal

2. Using the Move Tool, click and drag the flipped layer to the right. It should snap into place aligning itself to the left side of the center guide. To get it exact, remember you can use the Arrow Keys for small, exact movement. It should look like Figure 11.

3. We need to erase a couple of obvious features from the right side. In order to see what we're doing, let's Change the Opacity of the flipped layer so we can see through it. Over on the top right of your Layers Palette is an "Opacity" box. You can either click the arrow and drag the slider, or click in the text box and type in a percentage. I changed the layer to 30% Opacity. Figure 12 (Page 136).

All we have to do now is erase stuff and finish up. But in order to see what we're doing, we have to Zoom in. Here's some info on the Zoom Tool:

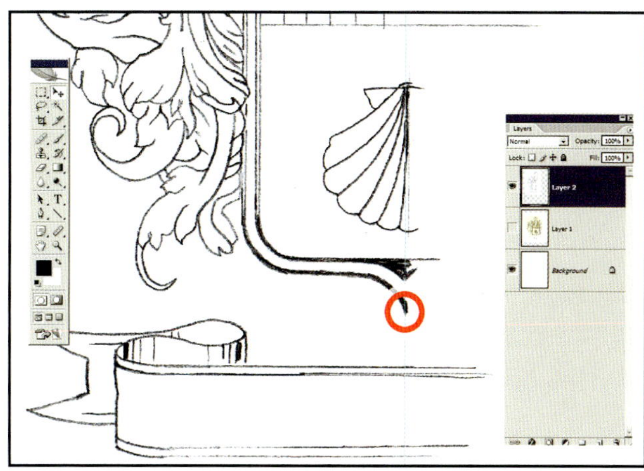

Figure 9

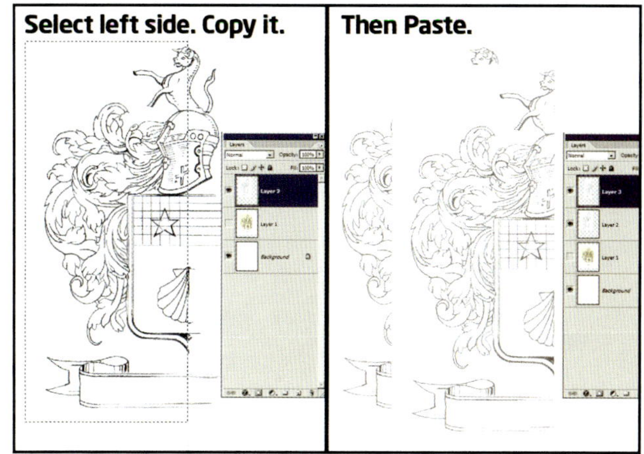

Figure 10

Ah, the Zoom Tool

You'll be using this one a lot. It's the Magnifying Glass icon on your toolbar, or just hit the letter "Z" on your keyboard to switch to it.

When the Zoom Tool is selected, the cursor becomes a magnifying glass with a plus sign. The plus sign zooms you in (obviously). So click to increase magnification. If you want to zoom in on a specific area of the image, click and drag a rectangle around the area you want to magnify. This will

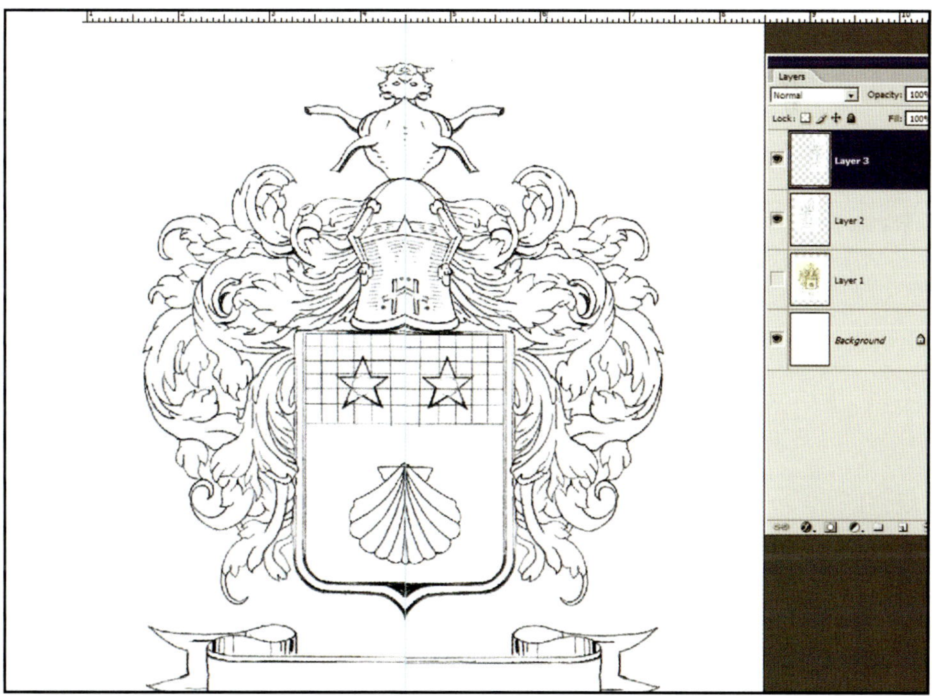

Figure 11

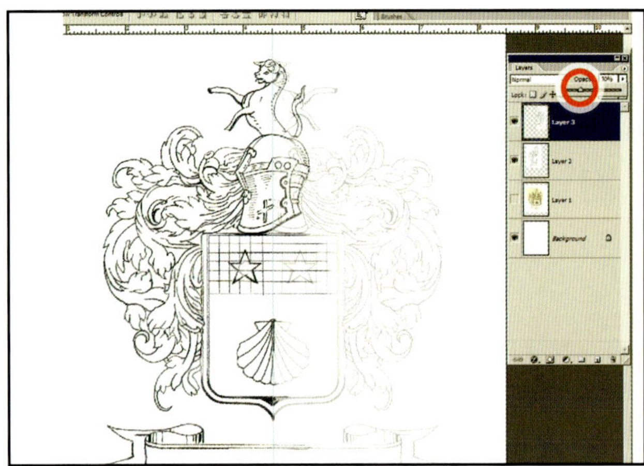

Figure 12

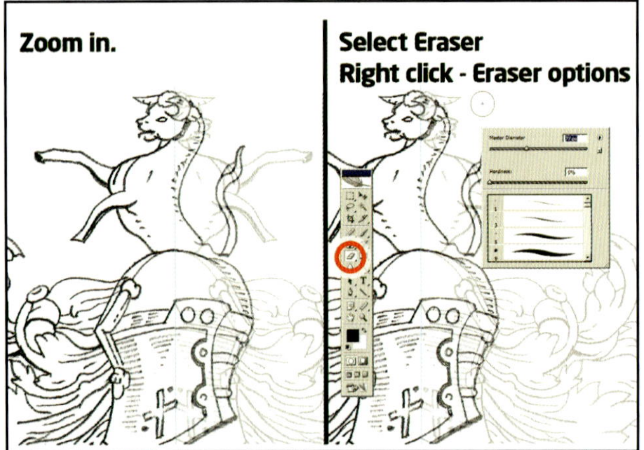

Figure 13

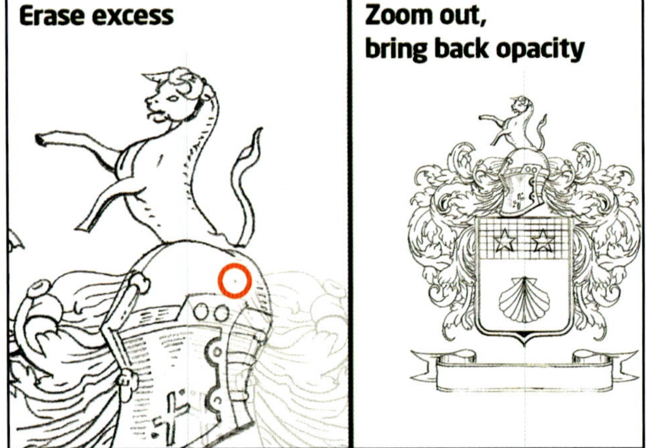

Figure 14

enlarge the selected area to fill the workspace.

How do you Zoom out? To switch to zoom out mode, you can click the zoom out button up top on the options bar. But honestly, it is much easier to use the keyboard shortcut: hold down the Alt key and the zoom cursor will change to a minus sign in the magnifying glass. Click to zoom out.

Last, you've got some extra options to help you out.

- Double clicking the Zoom Tool Button icon (in your toolbar) will automatically resize your document resized to 100%.
- Double clicking the Hand Tool Button icon (to the left of the Zoom button) will automatically resize your document to fit the size of your screen.
- Zoom in, Erase excess, Move view, then bring back Opacity

1. Using your Zoom Tool, let's zoom in on the top of the crest. Figure 13.
2. Select the Eraser Tool (on the toolbar, or hit E key). Right clicking anywhere on the document will pull up Eraser options. If needed, slide the bar to increase or decrease the diameter of the eraser. Figure 13.
3. Clicking will Erase. Some people click and move the cursor around while holding down that click. Others keep clicking all over the place. I prefer the first.
4. Because we're Zoomed in, you'll eventually need to scroll the image down to be able to access more of it. Either slide the scroll bars on the right side and bottom, or simply hold down the Spacebar key – this will turn your cursor into the Hand Tool which lets you click and drag the view of the image around.
5. Once finished Erasing, bring the Opacity of the level back up to 100%.
6. Zoom out (or double click on the Hand Tool) and view your sexy outline. Save your file!
7. Before we print, we can Flatten our Layers into one Layer to make the file size smaller. Just go up to Layer > Flatten Image. You can

not edit Layers when you Flatten your image! So be careful not to save this over your original.

That's it, we've got our outline.

As you can see with the increased clarity and the decreased amount of time required to produce a precise line drawing, using Photoshop is well worth the effort. At first, you might not be as quick with these techniques; however, with knowledge and practice comes speed, and you will see a huge improvement over the images we could produce by just blowing them up on a copy machine and tracing the outline.

The crest outline was pumped out almost 10 minutes faster than copying and tracing. And the seller… well, the seller is the perfect accuracy of the symmetry. When we tattoo over the stencil, our human imperfection comes in. We won't get it perfect, but we can certainly try. So if we can get the stencil as perfect as possible, we've got a greater chance of visual accuracy.

Quick Tips

Creating an Outline for Text

Here's one quick way to pull an outline for text:

Figure: Outline Text Figure

1. Using the standard Letter size for a new Photoshop document (8.5x11 at 300dpi), I'll use my Type Tool and enter some text: "Reagan Youth". In the Character palette, I'll select an Old English style font.

2. Now, simply hold the CTRL button down and click on that text Layer. This selects everything on that Layer, which is perfect.

3. In the Layers palette, click on the eyeball icon next to your Text Layer. This will hide the original text layer.

4. Create a New Layer by either clicking on the icon next to the trash bin at the bottom of the Layers palette or by the keyboard shortcut Shift+CTRL+N.

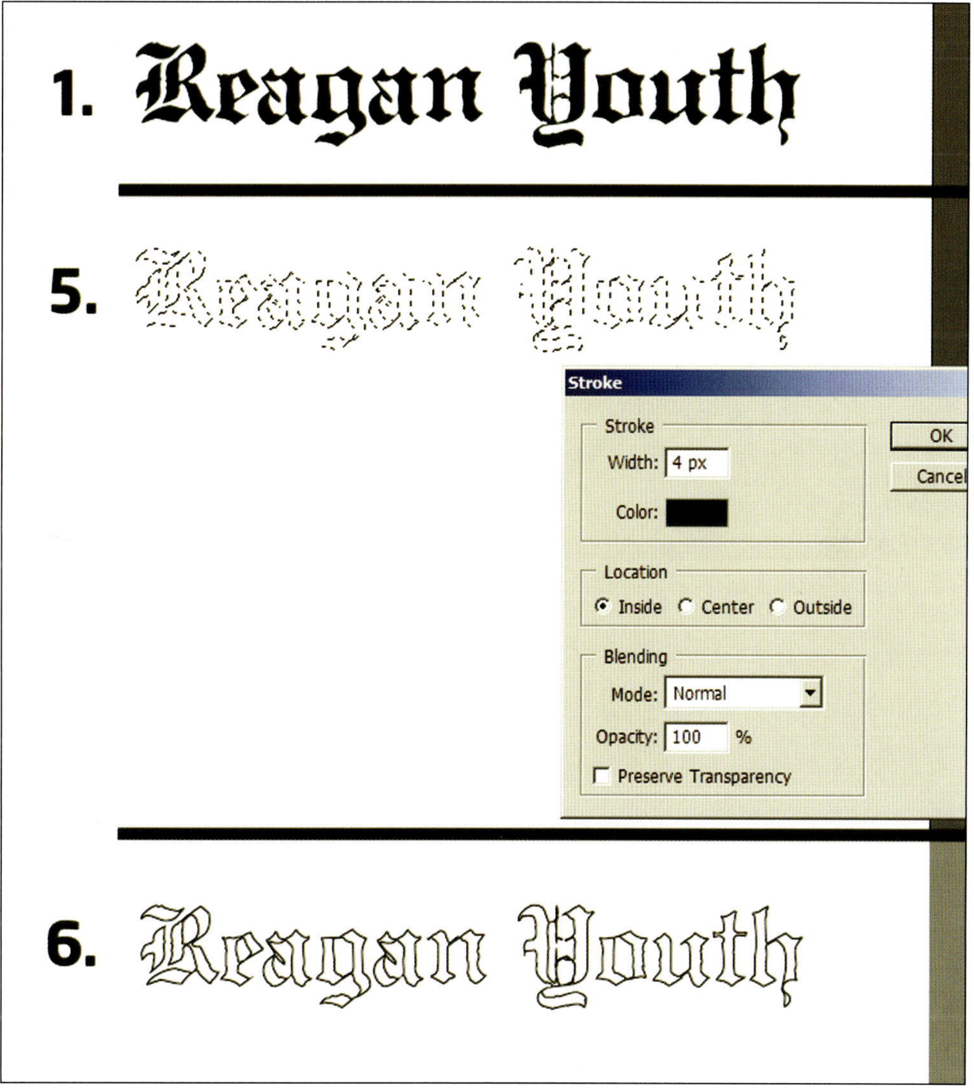

Outline text figure.

5. You should still see the selection (marching ants). To add the outline, go up to the top menu and use Edit > Stroke. The Stroke window will come up. I've found that when using a 300 dpi document, a 4px stroke is perfect for my liking. But feel free to experiment. The Location of the stroke should be "Inside" then click OK.

6. Ctrl+D will deselect the outline. We've effectively created a raster outline from vector text. Now Print it. (CTRL+P)

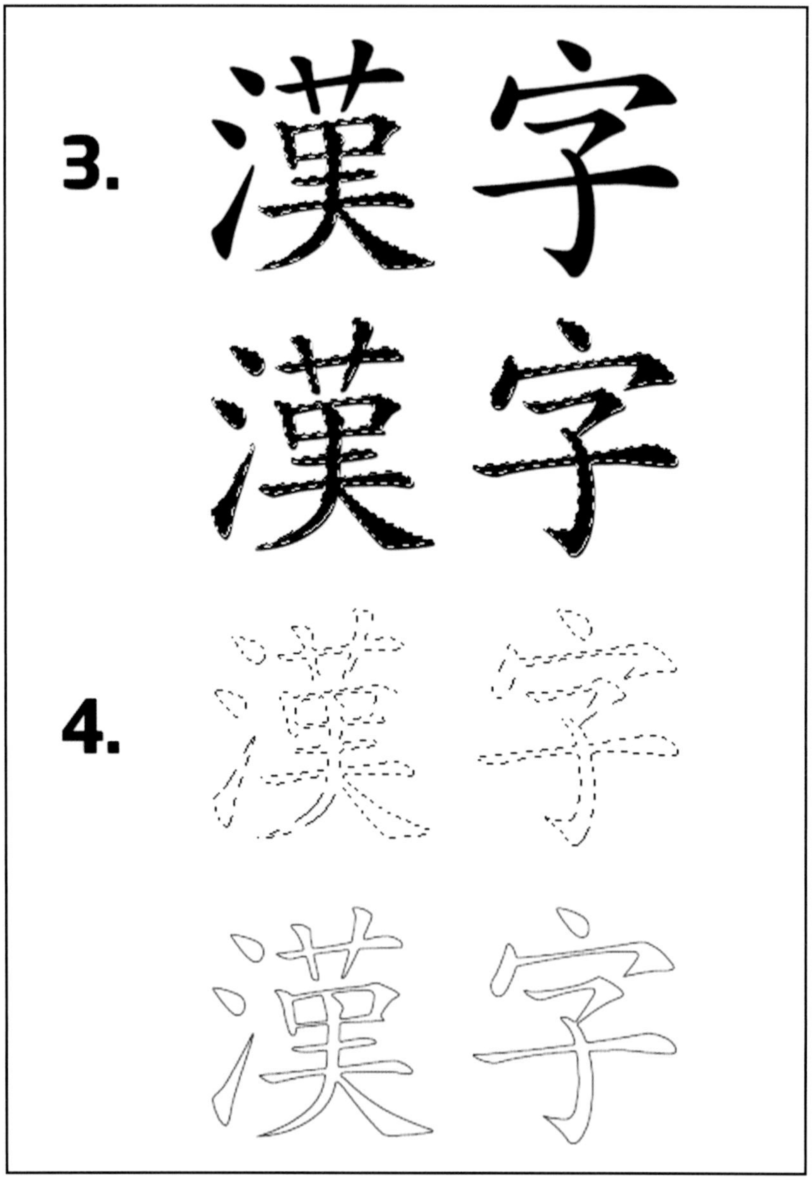

* There is another quick way to create a text stroke by double clicking on the Layer in the Layers palette. The Layer Style window will pop up. Check and click on Stroke – it's at the bottom. You'll have the same options. Choose to your liking then click OK.

Want to pull an outline from, say, a Kanji image?

1. Using the standard Letter size for a new Photoshop document (8.5x11 at 300dpi), open your Kanji image. Drag and drop it into your new document.

2. Resize it to your liking (Edit > Transform > Scale. Or just hit CTRL+T.) Remember to hold down Shift while you drag so it'll resize proportionally.

3. While you're on the Kanji layer, select the Magic Wand. It's right under the Move Tool and works by selecting areas of an image based on color. With the Wand, click on any black area within the character. To add to your selection, just hold down the Shift key and continue clicking in each black area.

4. Once you have it all selected, click on the eyeball icon next to the Kanji Layer to hide it… now continue on to Step #4 up above in the last tutorial (outlining text).

Figure: Kanji Outline

Text Spacing

Kerning is the alteration of spacing between letters. Some letters don't fit well together – see example: When spacing in the standard text is off; here's the two methods I used to change it:

1. Place your cursor between the letters you wish to correct. Hold down your ALT key then use your arrow keys (left and right) to change the distance.

Kanjioutline

2. Or select the entire text. Now, in your Character Palette (Window > Character), pull down the menu in the Kerning box (middle left, below the font size). Instead of Metrical, select Optical. This is Photoshop's fake eye. It mimics how we see and tries to fix spacing automatically. There are times this is a little off; when that happens I always revert to the first step.

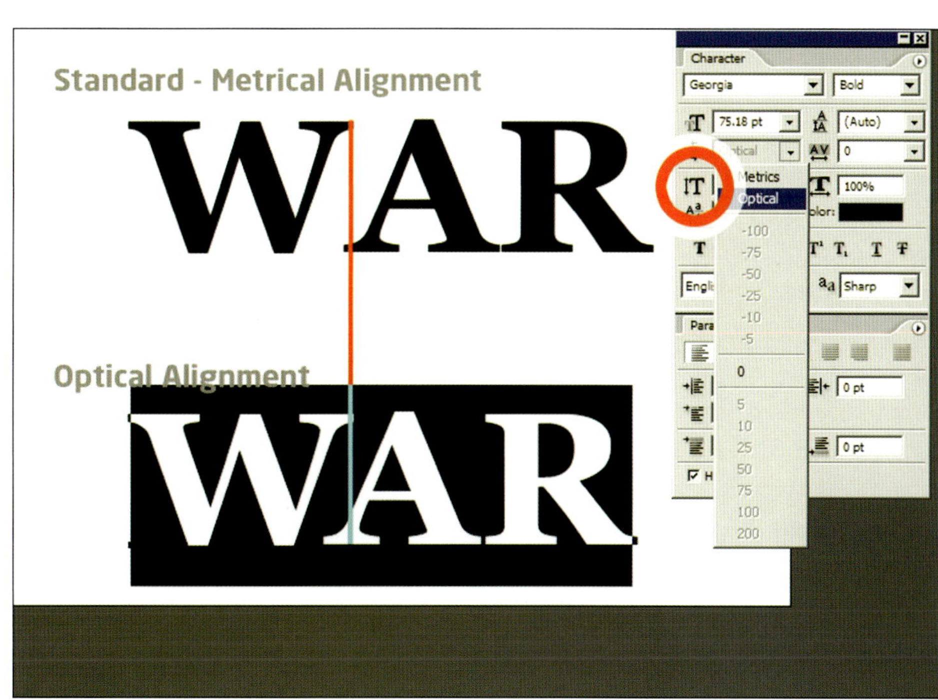

Kerning 01.

Undo and History

Use your Undo options…

- CTRL+Z will Undo your last action (or Edit > Undo)
- Alt + CTRL+Z allows you to sequentially undo more than one action (or Edit > Step Backward)
- You'll use the History Palette often (Window > History).

Every action or change in an image constitutes a new image state. By default, the History Palette records and displays the 20 most recent image states. By selecting a previous image state from the History Palette, you can start working from that point, and it will erase all the states that followed it.

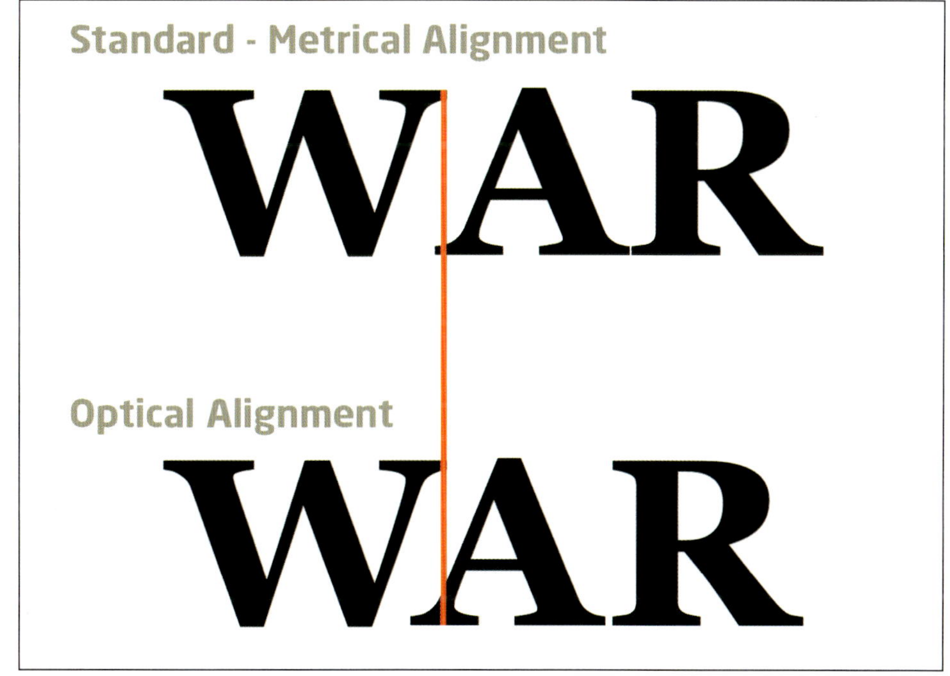

Kerning 02.

Selecting with the Lasso Tool

The Lasso Tool will let you make free-hand selections of irregularly shaped areas, with or without straight edges.

• With the Lasso Tool, click and drag it around like you're using a pen. The point at which you release your click will connect itself with the beginning point, creating an enclosed area.

• Another, more precise way, is to hold down the Alt key and click. This will set a starting point. Keeping holding the Alt key and move the cursor to your next spot. It will drag a line to wherever you click next. Every click will continue to build a selection. Go ahead and mess around with it. Once you release the Alt key, the first and last points will join and you'll have your selection.

Getting an Outline from a Photo

Play around with this and you'll figure out the best look for your liking.

The first is using the Photocopy filter. The second uses halftones multiplied over the Photocopy filter.

1. After scanning in a photo, pull up your Levels and adjust them to the look you desire. I always like stark contrasts... Convert the Image to Grayscale (Image > Mode > Greyscale)
2. Open the Photocopy filter (Filter > Sketch > Photocopy) and slide the settings around. This will produce pure black lines and dots which can be copied easily through your Thermo fax machine.

Figure Portrait Examples

Using halftones to show our shading, we don't want a big mess of dots, so adjusting the levels is important.

1. Create a different document and drag the original photo over to it. Adjust your Levels and pull out a stark contrast. Convert the image to Grayscale (Image > Mode > Grayscale)
2. Now convert the image to Bitmap (Image > Mode > Bitmap). The "Output" should be our standard 300 pixels per inch. The "Method" a Halftone Screen.
3. Hit OK. In the Halftone Screen window, I usually go with a Frequency of 35 lines per inch. A 45 degree Angle is fine and for Shape I like "Line". (The Round Shape will give you the standard circle half tone)
4. Convert the Image back to Grayscale (Image > Mode > Grayscale) with a "Size Ratio" of 1. Hit OK.

Tutorials

There are numerous tutorials and training material available. Look around to find out which one would work best for you.

- ***Total Training – They've an incredible family of Photoshop tutorial DVDs. http:www.totaltraining.com***
- ***Lynda.com – Online training library http:www.lynda.com***
- ***Photoshop User Magazine http:www.photoshopuser.com***
- ***Layers Magazine http:layersmagazine.com***

5. The black areas can overwhelming, so I go ahead and use the Lasso to select and delete the inside black.

6. Drag and drop the halftoned image over to the previous Filtered Photocopy document. At the top of the Layers Palette is a drop down box with the word "Normal" in it. These are Blending Modes. Click the arrow and the box will drop down. Select the "Multiply" option. Now you'll be able to see through the white on that layer. This shows us the Photocopy outlines.

7. Last, move the Layer into place over those outlines with the Move Tool.

We hope you find this to be a solid reference for using Photoshop to manipulate text and images in creating your tattoo. Both for tattoo artists and clients seeking out an original design, employing Photoshop techniques will give you a broader diversity in image options and aid you in the process of making the image unique while increasing your accuracy and improving your final product. It never hurts to add another weapon to your arsenal, and Photoshop is a great one to have.

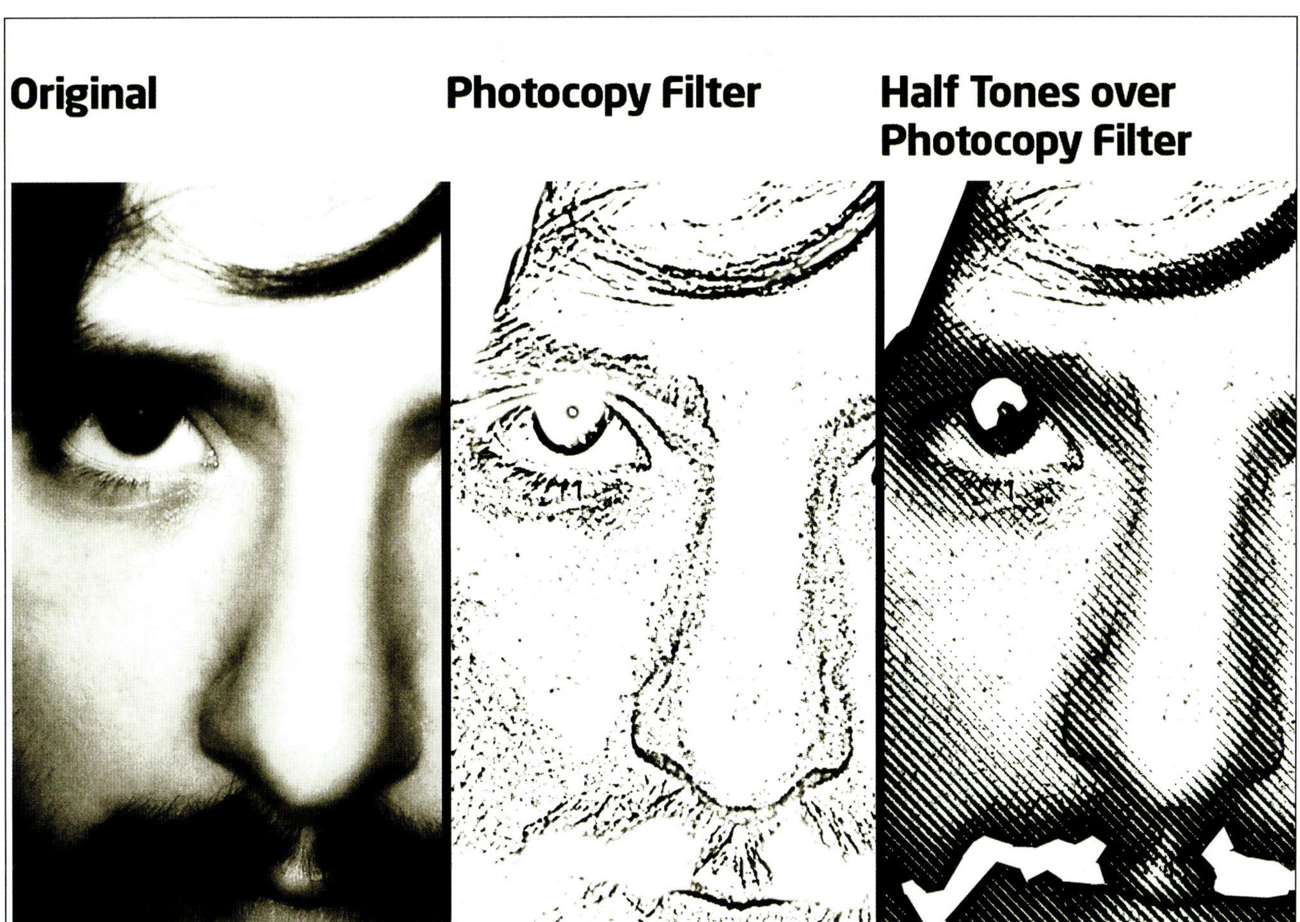

Portrait examples.

Wolfgang Books On The Web
www.wolfpub.com

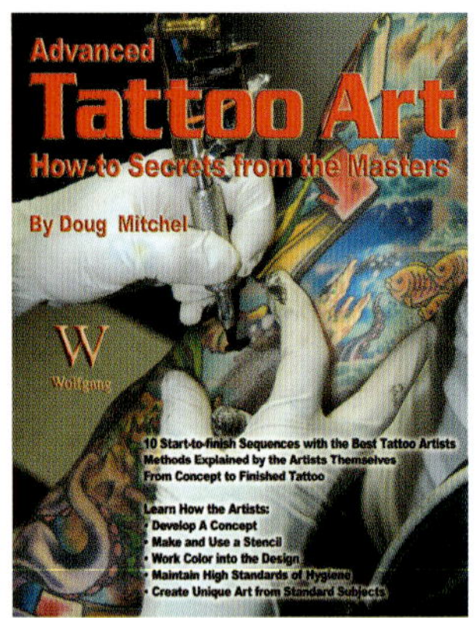

Advanced Tattoo Art

The art of the tattoo has emerged from the garage to the parlor, from the local bar to the board room. With interest in tattoos at a high point, the time is right for a detailed look at the art, and the artists, who create the elaborate designs.

Doug Mitchel takes the reader inside the shops of ten well-known and very experienced artists spread across the country. Both a how-to book and a photo-intense look at the world or tattoos, Advanced Tattoo Art includes interviews with the artists that explain not only how they do what they do, but their personal preference for materials and methods.

Detailed photo sequences follow each artist through a tattoo project, from the customer's concept, through the sketch and outline, to the finished and colorful design. The chapters document not only the techniques, but also the inks and tools used during each step of the process.

Ten Chapters 144 Pages $24.95 Over 400 photos-100% color

Adv Custom Motorcycle Assembly & Fabrication

No longer content to build copies of stock motorcycles, today's builder wants a motorcycle that's longer, lower and sexier than anything approved by a factory design team.

Wolfgang was there at the very beginning of the trend with their Ultimate V-Twin Motorcycle book. Today they're back with their new book, Advanced Custom Motorcycle Assembly & Fabrication. Part catalog, part service manual and part inspiration, this new book offers help with Planning the project, getting the right look and actually assembling that custom bike you've dreamed about for years.

Three start-to-finish sequences show not just how the best bikes are bolted together, but how the unique one-off gas tanks are shaped and then covered with candy brandywine paint.

Nine Chapters 144 Pages $24.95 Over 400 photos-100% color

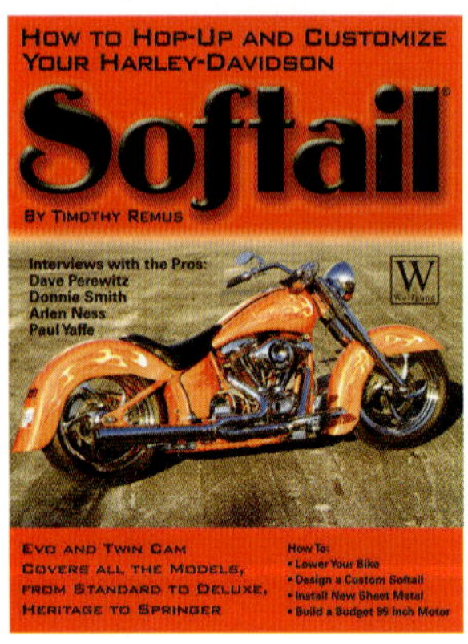

How to Hop-Up and Customize Your Harley-Davidson Softail

Got a Softail? Got a hankering to separate yours from all the other Softails parked outside the bar? Search no farther than this new book, How To Hop-Up and Customize Your Harley-Davidson Softail, from well-known author Timothy Remus. Whether your goal is to personalize that two-wheeled ride or give it more than 60 horsepower, the ideas and answers you need are right here.

Learn how to install a 95 inch kit with over 100 horsepower, add a 250 rear tire, lower the bike, and add extended fuel tanks. Included are customizing ideas, start to finish photo sequences of engine, chassis and paint work, and a list of suppliers for lights, engine hop-up parts, paint and chrome accessories.

The various Softail models are among the most popular bikes ever built in Milwaukee. Make yours faster, sexier and more personal with this all-color book from Tim Remus and Wolfgang Publications.

Nine Chapters 144 Pages $24.95 500 color images - 100% color

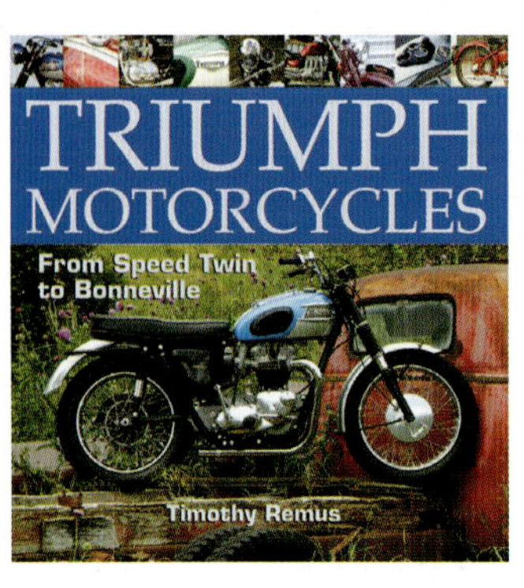

Triumph Motorcycles From Speed Twin To Bonneville

From Timothy Remus comes this photo-intensive, four-color book focused primarily on the classis Triumph twins and triples.

Starting with Edward Turner's best-known design, the Speed Twin, the book moves to the T100, TR5, Thunderbird, TR6, Bonneville, T160 and all the rest. Using deluxe paper for the best possible photo reproduction this anthology of classic Triumphs covers all the significant models produced from 1938 to the early 1980s. Long after the close of the historical Meriden plant the new Triumph Corporation took up the challenge of recreating the classic Triumph models, many of which are included here as well.

Whether your personal favorite is the ever-popular Bonneville from the late 1960s, or a more obscure TR5 with "generator" top end, the Triumphs you remember and lust after are sure to be found between the covers of this book.

Six Chapters 144 Pages $29.95 Hardcover Over 200 color images

More Great Books From Wolfgang Publications!
www.wolfpub.com

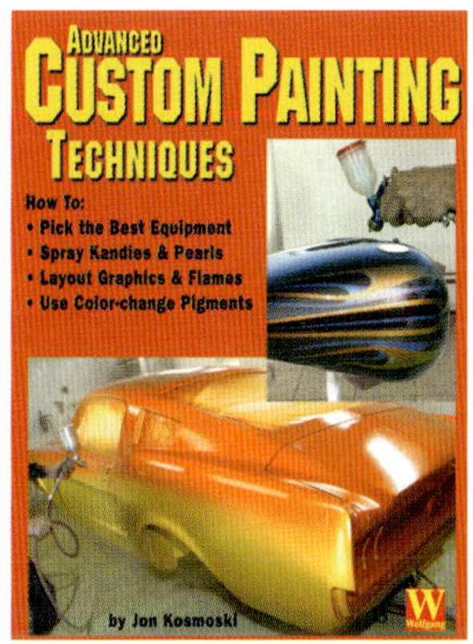

Advanced Custom Painting Techniques

When it comes to custom painting, there is one name better known than all the others, and that name is Jon Kosmoski. Whether the project in your shop rides on two wheels or four, whether you're trying to do a simple kandy job or complex graphics, this how-to book from Jon Kosmoski is sure to answer your questions. Chapters one through three cover Shop Equipment, Gun Control and Paint Materials. Chapters four through seven get to the heart of the matter with complete start-to-finish painting sequences.

- Shop set up
- Gun Control
- Use of new paint materials
- 4 start-to-finish sequences
- Two wheels or four
- Simple or complex
- Kandy & Klear

Seven Chapters 144 Pages $24.95 Over 350 photos, 100% color

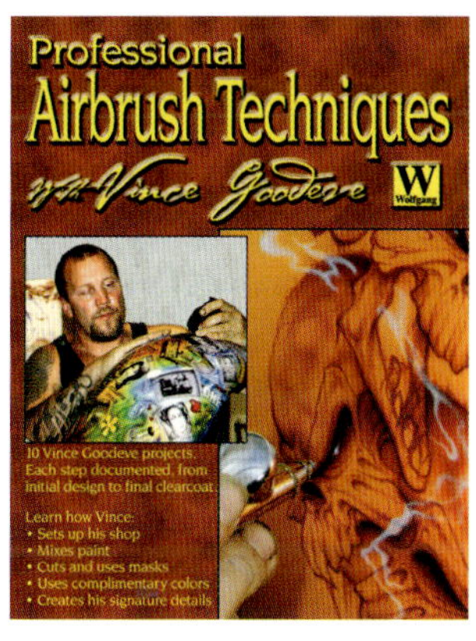

Professional Airbrush Techniques

Written by well-known Airbrush artist Vince Goodeve, this new book uses 144 pages and over 500 color images to explain a lifetime's worth of learning. Follow Vince through multiple photo sequences that explain his choice of color, sense of design, and preference for tools and materials. Early chapters explain shop set up and preparations of the metal canvas. Ten start-to-finish sequences walk the reader through Vince's airbrush work with both motorcycles and cars. Projects include simple graphics as well as complex and intricate designs. Accustomed to teaching, Vince uses a style that is easy to follow and understand. His enthusiasm for the airbrush comes through, making the text easy to follow. Vince Goodeve has something to say to all airbrush artists – whether beginner or advanced.

Ten Chapters 144 Pages $24.95 Over 400 color photos- 100% color

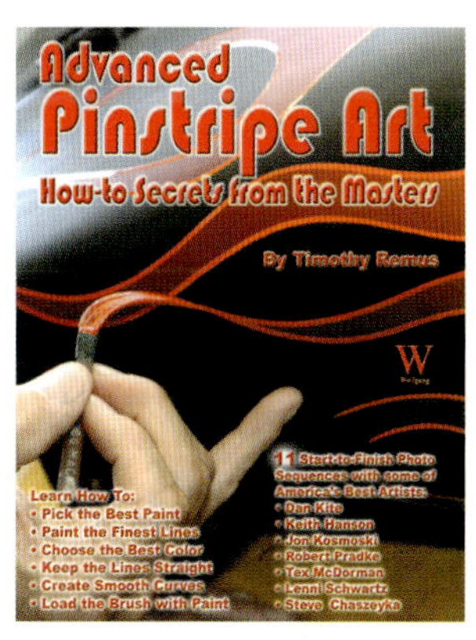

Advanced Pinstripe Art

Since the days of Von Dutch, hot rod and motorcycle enthusiasts have used pinstripes both as stand-alone art, and as a compliment to a flame or graphic paint job.

Timothy Remus uses color images to present the work of 11 well-known pinstripe artists. Each chapter presents one start-to-finish project and an interview with the artist. The photo sequences take the viewer from the initial sketch to the finished design. Text explains each step of the artwork, the interviews explain the artist's choice for paint and brushes. The artwork, often complimented with gold leaf or airbrush colors, is done on panels as well as various vehicles and components.

Look into the shop of some of this country's best pinstripe artists, for an intense and intimate how-to lesson. This is pinstripe school, taught by masters, brought to your own home or shop.

Eleven Chapters 144 Pages $24.95 Over 500 color photos- 100% color

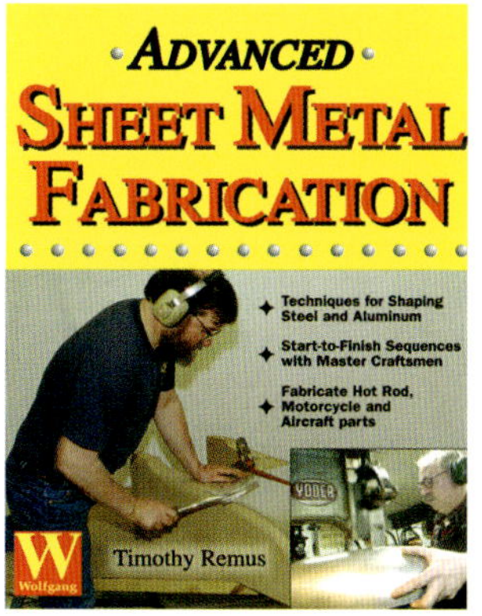

Advanced Sheet Metal Fabrication

Advanced Sheet Metal Fabrication Techniques, is a photo-intensive, how-to book. See Craig Naff build a Rolls Royce fender, Rob Roehl create a motorcycle gas tank, Ron Covell form part of a quarter midget body, and Fay Butler shape an aircraft wheel fairing. Methods and tools include English wheel, power hammer, shrinkers and stretchers, and of course the hammer and dolly.

- Sequences in aluminum and steel
- Multi-piece projects
- Start to finish sequences
- From building the buck to shaping the steel
- Includes interviews with the metal shapers
- Automotive, motorcycle and aircraft

7 Chapters 144 Pages $24.95 144 pages, over 300 photos - 60% color

Resources

We worked hard to make sure that the art and artists who found their way into the pages of this book were some of the best. This list is a great place to begin in looking for your artist for your next piece. If there is an artist whose work you find intriguing from the pages of this book, please check him or her out online or in person. Even if he or she is located far from your hometown, many tattoo artists hit the tattoo convention circuit. You might be able to find one of them at a convention or doing a guest spot near you.

Please patronize the tattoo shops, websites, and other resources that helped to make this book possible.

Adam Patterson, Body And Soul, Jersey City, *www.myspace.com/tocohara*
Part time musician, part time tattooist, Adam Patterson specializes in traditional work.

Amanda Wachob. Blue Moon, Buffalo, NY, *www.amandawachob.com*
Known equally well as a fine artist and a tattooist, Amanda Wachob is a custom tattooist who has been featured in many publications and art galleries nation wide.

Art And Ink Publications, *www.skinart.com*
The Charlotte, NC-based tattoo magazine syndicate publishing Skin Art, Tattoo Revue, Tattoos For Men, Tattoos For Women, and Tabu is the world's premier magazine resource for body art.

Brandon Bond, All Or Nothing, Atlanta, GA, *www.brandonbond.com*
Owner of All Or Nothing and the exclusive ANTI-Art Elite Tattoo Studios in Atlanta, GA, Bond is a dynamo in the tattoo industry. From films to merchandise to some of the most beautiful tattoos being made today, he is building an enviable tattoo empire.

Brandon Heffron, Beloved Studios, St. Paul, MN, *www.belovedstudios.com*
Owner and operator of Beloved Studios, Brandon Heffron is a nine-year industry veteran. From gorgeous color work to beautiful black and grey, Brandon is adept at many different styles.

Bryce Stucke, Body Armor, Clearfield, PA
New School artist and tattooist Bryce Stucke is also the owner of Body Armor Tattoo Studio.

Caroline Hedgepeth, Garry's Skin Grafix, Greenville, NC, *www.carolinehedgepeth.com*
With more than a decade of tattooing under her belt, Carolina Hedgepeth is a small-town artist and painter doing world-class work.

Chris Vennekamp, All Or Nothing, Atlanta, GA, *www.chrisvennekamp.com*
Specializing in bold, painterly Asian work and color photorealism, Chris Vennekamp. Check out some of his art prints, available on his website.

Color, 145 Tattoo, Houston, TX, *www.myspace.com/colorsoner*
Find Color at 145 in Houston, TX, for traditional and graffiti style work.

Cory Ferguson, Enlightened Art, Oakville, ON, *www.corytattoos.com and www.oakvilleink.com*
Cory Ferguson is a diverse artist, but he has become known industry-wide for his unique approach to neo-tribal tattoos. His stippling technique creates interesting, eye-catching effects with geometric designs.

Cory Rogers, 713 Tattoo, Houston, TX, *www.myspace.com/coryrogers*
One of the finest traditional tattooists based out of Houston, TX, Cory Rogers can be found at 713 Tattoo, which boasts world-class piercing and tattooing facilities. Also check out Cory's beautiful traditional-style paintings.

Dave Attonito, Good Clean Fun, Snellville, GA, *www.goodcleanfun.net*
Black and grey tattoos are Dave Attonito's area of expertise. He also builds custom tattoo machines and owns and operates Good Clean Fun.

Dave Tedder, All Or Nothing, Atlanta, GA, *www.davemftedder.com*
Best known for his Japanese and Traditional American work, Dave Tedder is a staple in the Atlanta tattoo scene.

David Allen, Bluebird Tattoo, Portage, IN, *www.allentattoo.com*
Blogger, graphic designer, and tattooist David Allen is an artist to watch. You can trace his progress through his apprenticeship and on into his career as a tattoo artist by visiting his website.

Derek DuFresne, Fleshworks, Victoria, British Columbia, *www.derekdufresne.com*
Specializing in New School and Asian work, Derek Dufresne's Fleshworks Tattoo is the premier studio in Victoria. For a spa-like environment and a state-of-the-art tattoo experience, Fleshworks is a world-class tattoo atelier. Dufresne is also the creator of a collection of Japanese line drawings, Japanese Tattoo Designs Vol. 1 and 2, that could be a wonderful resource for any tattoo artist or serious collector of Japanese style work.

Federico Ferroni, South Beach Tattoo, South Beach, FL *www.southbeachtattoos.com*
This South Beach tattooist is best known for his Asian style work, but he is an experienced artist whose clean work is spectacular in any style.

Food And Drug Administration, *www.cfsan.fda.gov/~dms/cos-204.html*
The Food And Drug Administration lists its policies about tattoo inks with a list of precautions to consider before getting a tattoo on their website. This site also provides links to other resources regarding tattoo safety.

Freedom-2 Tattoo Inks, *www.freedom2ink.com*
Freedom-2 inks are a state-of-the-art, newly engineered product that is meant to increase the flexibility of your tattoo design by providing safer, permanent, but easily-removable alternative to traditional tattoo inks. Available in two models, one that will break down naturally over a period of years and one that can be removed with only one laser treatment, these inks promise to revolutionize the way we think of tattoo art.

Gerald Gaddy, *http://geraldgaddy.blogspot.com*
Charlotte, North Carolina-based tattoo artist specializing in color photorealism and New School designs.

Inked Nation, *www.inkednation.com*
This tattoo community forum is an excellent source for finding tattoo artists and enthusiasts in your area and further afield. You can search for tattooists and piercers by zip code or by name. The bulletin service is a great way to keep up with upcoming events in the tattoo community, from conventions to parties to art gallery openings.

Jason Ackerman, Lucky 7, West Palm Beach, FL, *www.jasonackerman.com*
Jason Ackerman is known for his bright New School color work, especially for his zombie kids and their many, and various, antics.

Jennifer Small is a tattooist at Blood, Sweat, And Tears in Charlotte, North Carolina

Jeff Paetzold, All Or Nothing, Atlanta, GA *www.myspace.com/scorpionnipples*

John Lloyd, All Or Nothing, Atlanta, GA, *www.allornothingtattoo.com*

John Sweeney, Hard Knox, Yonkers, NY, *www.myspace.com/hardknoxtattoos*

John Wayne, Beesting, Belle River, Ontario, *www.beestingtattoo.com*
Working solo in a state-of-the-art tattoo studio in his own home with his wife as his assistant, John Wayne has become known as a master both of color and black and grey. Belle River, Ontario is lucky to have him.

Josh Woods, All Or Nothing, Atlanta, GA, *www.allornothingtattoo.com*
While he is a relative youngster to the industry, Josh Woods is regarded as one of the masters of New School tattooing, and he has been trying his hand at color realism lately with much success.

Ken Carrano, *www.hollowstitches.com*

Kirk Shepherd, Fleshworks, Victoria, British Columbia, *www.fleshworks.ca*

Larry Brogan, Tattoo City Skin Art, Lockport, IL *www.tattoocityskinart.com*
An artist with a portfolio that's strong in almost every style, Larry Brogan is an all-around tattoo master. He has been featured in several magazine articles, and he was also a contributing artist to Advanced Tattoo Art by Doug Mitchel, a previous Wolfgang Publication.

Mario Desa, Chicago Tattoo, Chicago, IL, *www.mariodesa.com*
Graffiti artist, painter, and hybrid tattoo art visionary Mario Desa is a ten year industry veteran with a unique traditional tattoo flavor.

Mark Heggie, Big Top, Utica, MI, *www.markheggie.com*
Art dynamo Mark Heggie has a unique sketchy, loose style that transcends from his paintings into his tattoos. Some of his work reflects a comic influence, others recall traditional tattoo themes, and the rest is pure mad genius. His merchandise is pretty cool, too.

Matt Griffith, 2 Dollar Pistol, Chillicothe, OH, *www.artworkvigilante.com*
Owner of 2 Dollar Pistol, Matt Griffith's New School designs are influenced by comics, graffiti, and often, strangely, the world of Nintendo and other video games. His paintings are also an excellent source of tattoo reference.

Matty Evans, *www.myspace.com/mattyevanstattoo*

Megan Hoogland, Cactus Tattoo, Mankato, MN *www.meganhoogland.com*

Nate Beavers, 145, Houston, TX, *www.myspace.com/nb13*
One of the forerunners of the color realism movement, Nate Beavers is an artist whose portfolio continues to amaze. While he is based out of his shop in Houston, TX, Nate spends a lot of time on the road, so you might be able to catch him doing a guest spot or a convention at an area near you.

Sarah Peacock, Artfuel, Wilmington, NC, *www.sarahpeacockart.com*

Sean Herman, All Or Nothing, Atlanta, GA, *www.seanherman.com*

Shannon Brown, Local Color, West Chester, PA, *www.localcolortattoo.com*

Shannon Schober, Vitality Tattoo, Asheville, NC, *www.vitalitytattoo.com*
With a unique, delicate style utilizing negative space and the body's natural flow and motion to enhance the tattoo design, Shannon Schober is one of Asheville's most-respected artists.

Snakes And Earrings by Kanehara Hitomi
This novel describes one young woman's experience with body modification in modern day Tokyo.

Tao Of Tattoos, *http://www.tao-of-tattoos.com*
This site is an excellent reference for information on various styles of tattoo, artists, designs, and all things tattoo related.

Tattoo Johnny, *www.tattoojohnny.com*
A tattoo design gallery and database of tattoo artists, this is a great free resource for beginning your search for the reference for your next tattoo.

Tattoo Joy, *www.tattoojoy.com*
Cataloging tattoo shops, articles, and images, Tattoo Joy is another great resource for keeping up with the latest tattoo news and doing research to find your next art or artist.

Thom Godfrey, Evil Eye, Bakersfield, CA *www.myspace.com/evil_eye_tattoo*
Visit Thom at Evil Eye for bold color work.

Tim McGrath, 13 Roses, Atlanta, GA, *www.bucktoothtimmy.com*
Check Tim out at 13 Roses, a legendary Atlanta tattoo shop, for funky traditional and other custom work.

William Thidemann, Th'Ink Tank, Denver, CO, *www.thidemann.com*
Writer, painter, and tattooist William Thidemann is a veritable renaissance man.

Zsolt Sarkozi, Dark Arts, Budapest, Hungary, *www.circletattoo.hu*
For some of the world's finest black and grey work, check out Zsolt's breathtaking online portfolio. Getting a tattoo from him would be worth the trip to Hungary.